by Tender Buttons Press

Bernadette Mayer's *Sonnets* (1989)

Anne Waldman's *Not a Male Pseudonym* (1990)

Harryette Mullen's *Trimmings* (1991)

Agnes Lee Dunlop Wiley's *Agnes Lee* (1992)

Rosmarie Waldrop's *Lawn of Excluded Middle* (1993)

Hannah Weiner's *silent teachers   remembered sequel* (1994)

Jennifer Moxley's *Imagination Verses* (1996)

Dodie Bellamy's *Cunt-Ups* (2001)

Laynie Browne's *Pollen Memory* (2003)

India Radfar's *the desire to meet with the beautiful* (2003)

Michelle Rollman's *The Book of Practical Pussies* (2009)
(in collaboration w/ Krupskaya Press)

Katy Bohinc's *Dear Alain* (2014)

FORTHCOMING:

Julie Ezelle Patton's *B*

Truck Darling's *The Hunger Notebooks*

ORIGINAL TENDER BUTTONS DRAWING

{JOE BRAINARD}

TENDER OMNIBUS

THE FIRST 25 YEARS OF TENDER BUTTONS PRESS

1989 - 2014

TENDER BUTTONS PRESS

NEW YORK CITY

2016

Tender Buttons books are edited and published by
Lee Ann Brown

Katy Bohinc, Star Arkestress

www.TenderButtonsPress.com
435 W 22nd Street
New York, NY 10011

TENDER OMNIBUS
The First 25 Years of Tender Buttons Press

All rights for individual pieces revert to the authors upon publication

Permissions for the use of copyrighted material begin on page 617
which constitutes an extension of this page

Distributed by Small Press Distribution
Phone: (510) 524-1688

Cataloging-in-Publication data
pending from the Library of Congress
LOC Control Number: 2016903063

ISBN 978-0-927920-14-8 (paperback)
ISBN 978-0-927920-15-6 (hardcover)

Cover Design by Cassandra Gillig
Book Design by Katy Bohinc

Edited by Katy Bohinc

Thank you to Tanner Brossart & Olivia Durif
whose work made this book possible

Printed in the United States of America

First Edition
Tender Buttons Press

For M

A woman 'touches herself' constantly without anyone being able to forbid her to do so, for her sex is composed of two lips which embrace continually. Thus, within herself she is already two — but not divisible into ones — who stimulate each other...

—LUCE IRIGARAY

What is the use of a violent kind of delightfulness if there is no pleasure in not getting tired of it.

—GERTRUDE STEIN

TABLE OF CONTENTS

TABLE OF CONTENTS

TABLE OF CONTENTS

CUNT-UPS...341

POLLEN MEMORY 373

TABLE OF CONTENTS

PREFACE

I have a theory.

Today we see women poets everywhere. I heard Mei-Mei Berssenbrugge say once, "All the best poets are women." She was saying she didn't think gender was as much of an issue in today's American poetry because the best poets are in fact all or mostly women. And yet, there is a disjunct between the beliefs of poetry communities and the official record.

This book, TENDER OMNIBUS, exists because if in 100 years someone looks back and says, "Well, there was Spicer, O'Hara and Ashbery..." I will just die.

When I look at the canon, the Whitmans and the Pounds and the William Carlos Williamses, and I read essays and theories which contain zero female historical examples, I think we're in a system in which women weren't allowed to be documented.

In the years since Edward Said's *Orientalism*, much work has been done to examine the systems that produce and officiate literature. For example, Pascale Cassanova points out how all of the Western greats were published in either Paris or London, creating a very limited canon. Or, the Italian Renaissance where women writers were always present, even the most popular in salons, and while permitted to entertain and to fuck, they were not allowed to publish.

I believe women writers have existed at every moment throughout history. We can't see them in the historical record because of (a lack of) "documentation" – the process of publishing and critical reviews and writing of histories: the process of canonization. I think it's absolutely about process and nothing to do with existence or excellence.

It's not some Neptunian-shrouded mystery how the Western canon got written: it was done by men. And they wrote it everywhere: "Men," "All men," "Mankind," etc.

Without documentation women have not been allowed to compete for a chance at history, even a revised history. This creates a loop where our canons— our benchmarks for the possible— are missing at least half of their exemplaries.

I should say more than half because I'm only brushing the surface of "women" which can be understood as a freely-chosen archetype embodied by many souls in this world.

Without a proper history, how can we think about what poetry is? How can we say avant-garde isn't a spoken-word poem that derives from an ingenious secret-code Underground Railroad song? How can we talk about "what's modern" when what's not white & male is barely in the conversation? And how can we look our daughters in the eye and say "sorry, there aren't any books your color."

Today erasure continues, albeit at a different angle, as we see year after year in VIDA Foundation statistics about which books are reviewed in major publications and which books are not.

Like the Italian Renaissance, although women are everywhere and everyone's favorite poets today, nothing is guaranteed to make the historical record. Because men still dominate the writing of history, the reviews, the editorial boards, the newspapers and the publishing houses, the process of documentation could continue on just reading "mankind."

Documentation is a labor we too often assume will be done by others, and assume will be permitted in ever-narrowing academic environments. Ask your friends, "Were you allowed to write a PhD on Bernadette Mayer?"

Google "John Ashbery" (half a million results). Then Google "Rosmarie Waldrop" (sixty thousand). "Harryette Mullen" (fifty thousand). It's wrong and it matters.

I believe it is imperative that we as poets and writers offer up proof with our own hands, and then take it directly to those who write history at all levels: popular, unpopular, academic, official, non-official, unofficial, whatever.

We publish this OMNIBUS with the fierce intention to begin to alter the imbalance.

Love,

Katy Bohinc
Star Arkestress, Tender Buttons Press

New moon solar eclipse
March 8th, 2016
New York City

P.S. I very much hope you bring *this* book to the next galaxy.

P.P.S. I totally blame the monks.

INTRODUCTION

"A way to think about women & language"

—Harryette Mullen

I created Tender Buttons press in 1989 to publish the work I love and am inspired by and need to see in the world. To be a poet-publisher is to make a nest for one's own and others' poetry, and this on-going act intertwines with the poetry I write.

I chose Tender Buttons for the name of my press in tribute to Gertrude Stein's radical masterpiece of everyday life. In 2014 we celebrated the 25th Anniversary of Tender Buttons Press as well as the 100th anniversary of the 1913 publication of Stein's Tender Buttons. To "Tend Her Buttons" is to tend the buttons of books, each book to be born a complex object forever opening outwards.

I think of books as multi-faceted objects, written from many angles, and unfolding in different ways each time we read them, like Stein's "cubist" writings. I look for work which simultaneously re-imagines and pushes envelopes of form and content, content and form.

If I had to choose one word that points to the trajectory of the press, it would be "multiplicity." Multiplicity is here how language can bloom into meanings that express multiple realities, sexualities, genders, racial identities and all kinds of subject positions.

The poem is the subversion of duality.

The poem is the third term where multiplicity can exist.

"Write in as many ways as you can imagine" Bernadette Mayer said to me. The parallel projects of my press and my own poetry aspire to write in ways never before imagined, in the belief that the ways we use language can change the world.

*   *   *   *

I remember the physically painful sensation of walking into a good bookstore and not seeing the books on the shelf that I thought should be there.

I remember reading Gertrude Stein for the first time at Naropa in the summer of 1985, and Anne Waldman talking about going to the Beinecke Library at Yale to read the many original manuscripts and learning that so much of Stein was out of print.

I remember reading poetry and theory as a student at Brown University and wondering where the poetry was that did all of the things that theory claimed language could do. There seemed to be a gap somewhere.

I remember writing this poem in high school:

> *Words*
>
> *Weren't enough for her.*
> *She often made high cat cries*
> *and danced hard on the blue carpet.*

I remember wanting to express the inexpressible – to stamp out (as in dance) the sexual syntaxes of bodies not "normally" expressed. I want to take the lid off of that repression, that oppression that comes from seeing everything as a dualism.

It bothers me that poetry or even words themselves aren't "enough" to express the realities I feel or the way I think. But what if we could write poetry that could bridge that gap between the way we think and what gets onto the paper? Sometimes my mind works in straightforward ways and sometimes like this:

the night time activity the erotics of writing after and before the other kind of button tending as in Tender tending her nether double buttons and again writing. So connections were surfacing with a new way of writing I saw as multiple and expressing my monde I mean my mind which was an other way women used writing, how women used writing to say all sides of a thing of a feeling all sides of the ways to approach like a flock of birds like an accordion form which rejects closure

I remember moments when everything I read or hear sounds like poetry. I remember moments when nothing does.

I remember reading this quote by Robert Scholes: "A writer is always reading and the reader is always writing" and thinking "Yes, that's true."

I remember reading Larry Eigner's Stein imitations with friends in a reprint of *L=A=N=G=U=A=G=E* magazine and feeling I was getting somewhere.

I remember reading Lyn Hejinian's "Two Stein Talks" in the big yellow *Temblor* when I volunteered at Small Press Traffic on my "year off."

I remember reading these sentences in Richard Kostelanetz' 1980 introduction to the *Yale Gertrude Stein*:

> *There are echoes of Stein's writings in her friends Sherwood Anderson, Thornton Wilder and Ernest Hemingway, as well as William Faulkner…E.E. Cummings…John Dos Passos…Allen Ginsberg…John Ashbery…Clark Coolidge, John Cage, bpNichol…One curious fact that I will let others explain is the absence of visible influence upon subsequent women writers.*

Really?

I remember reading those lines in my dormroom as a freshman in college and thinking "I've got my work cut out for me."

I remember upon arriving in New York City at what I thought to be the center of the forward-thinking world and encountering sexist hippie poets who couldn't distinguish between other poets who were women.

I remember looking up Bernadette Mayer's phone number on the "anti-copyright" page of her self-published, free book, *Utopia* at St. Mark's Bookshop. It said: "If you need help with this, call me."

I remember sitting on Anne Waldman's couch in Boulder and her saying to me "You should start a poetry magazine."

I remember realizing I wanted to make books. They would be more permanent I thought.

I remember upon hearing my questions on publication, Bernadette Mayer urged me to publish my own book —like Walt Whitman did.

I remember the initial thrill of realizing I could make real one of my favorite things in the world: a book (!) and then realizing that I not only had to type in the poems, lay out the book, proofread it, get the blurbs, piece together the money for printing, send it to the printer, send it to the distributor, place it in bookstores for consignment, find reviewers, plan a book party and then do it all over again for the next book. So I started enlisting my friends.

I remember reading the hilarious mimeo book with Anne Waldman characterized as the Little Red Hen, asking for help from a series of male poet animals who all replied: "Not I." So she went ahead and did it all herself.

I remember proofreading *Sonnets* with Bernadette at 172 East 4th Street —she showed me how she read everything backwards so as not to miss a word.

I remember the exquisite irritant of reading the book called *An Anthology of New York School Poetry* from 1970 which included only one woman poet.

I remember muscling my way onto the bill of the 1993 Writing from the New Coast Conference in Buffalo. I am and was no stranger to being slightly "off the radar" and having to say "Hey! What about me?" That's what poets have to do it—be in touch with what's going on and either push to be included or just Do-It-Your-Own-Self. I have chosen to do both.

On my panel, "Small Press Publishing," I staged a kind of intervention with Robert Duncan's *A Fairy Play, A Play* (one of his Stein imitations.) When asked, "But what does that have to do with Small Press Publishing? I answered, "It's about getting the work out there!"

I remember that after spinning out my vision for the press which so far included the first three books and a series of Tender Broadsides, I said I wanted to also produce Tender Films, Tender CDs, Tender Discs, Tender Kids books and more. A (male) panelist said something to the effect of "And you could make Tender Pornos too!"

Sigh.

And this was not a sigh of pleasure.

I remember getting an email this morning; a quote from a Joe Brainard letter to Anne Waldman:

> *I am still reading [Stein] on the toilet and I still find her very difficult and I was thinking how great it would be to hear Gertrude Stein out loud…I am way, way up these days over a piece I am still writing called I Remember. I feel very much like God writing the Bible. I mean, I feel like I am not really writing it but that it is because of me that it is being written. I also feel like it is about everybody else as much as it is about me.*

I remember asking Joe Brainard for a logo for Tender Buttons Press. I remember that I thought he would just draw a little button in a special Joe Brainard way. I was surprised when he generously presented me these little drawings as possibilities:

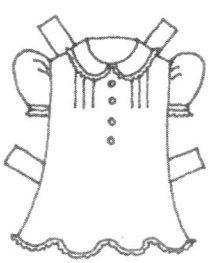

He then suggested that I use this one:

This image is very strange: what on first glance may come off as cute is in fact a hybrid being.

Notice how the image is doubled in several ways to make a multiplicity: the little double coat and dress splice together to make one outfit with many little folds and pleats. The double (non-human) pansy faces have multiple petals and allude to labial flowers as well as to a being "pansy," playing with and reclaiming the term for a feminized gay man, or one who chooses to perform a feminized gender.

I remember the poetry of the title of Luce Irigaray's essay,

This Sex Which is Not One

which articulates how even though society views "feminine" sexuality as "not one," or non-existent, the reality is it's multiple: not-only-one. I see Joe's drawing as an emblem for the multiplicitous feminine evoked in Irigaray's theories and in Gertrude Stein's poetics. A wild menu.

It's the way new meaning is made in this stanza of Bernadette Mayer's sonnet:

> *Tell like so cause me Bill loves you to not to know*
> *Turn the hear to why over Bill me cause I'll know I you*
> *Say and am to exist I not entranced pretty*
> *Can't Bill with startling say Shakespeare myself that*

It's the flowing power of free association that arises from the unfurling of the list poem (my maternal grandmother Agnes Lee's "Things I'd Like to Do Again") or the cutting-up / cunting-up of sex and love letters re-appropriated from a fiery, then negated relationship: Dodie Bellamy asking "is the Cut-up a male form? "

It's the history of relationships that do not fit into normative views of what happened between humans —counter-narratives between the walls of gay and straight definitions of what defines the realities of loving.

It's what I am describing in the last poem, "Crush," in my book *Polyverse* (which was written out of reading Stein, especially the influence of the rhythms of "Lifting Belly"). It is my own manifesto of multiplicitous being-in-love and life's work, written during the time I founded Tender Buttons press:

> *Reinvent love.*
> *Can we reinvent love.*
> *Why reinvent love.*

Tender Buttons Press is one way I am working with others to reinvent love. And to break the obsessive old patterns, the conceptions of how you love, who you love:

How notions of ownership can kill love:

> *I don't want to keep you.*

Thinking through how sexuality is in the continuum of lived experience at the core of meaning and being:

> *Obsession can we talk about something else.*
> *Get it out of the system.*
> *It's inherent to the system.*
> *Systemic, we return to it.*
> *Polysemous, multiplicitous, it keeps coming up.*
> *Polyvalent, with many openings.*
> *Anything can be alongside it.*

and how inter-penetrable, linguistically innovative poetry disrupts and turns those meanings over and over to create new ways of thinking:

> *Nouns and verbs.*
> *Noun verbs noun.*

How "language is a real thing, not an imitation." (Stein)

> *"What's the use*
> *in cutting up? What about explosives?"*
>   (from "Coffee," *Polyverse*)

"We all die" as Eiko said in last night's performance. "As did C.D."

So now is the time for the works of our lives.

*   *   *   *

Tender Buttons was created in a time of radical awakening to feminism, and its complications in regards to race, class, sex, gender, and being "avant-garde" each of which had complex truck with official literary culture.

I remember Harryette Mullen's *Trimmings* and how she played with the impulse of the source text of Stein's poem *Tender Buttons* to make it completely her own.

I remember the storms of necessary debate *Trimmings* stirred up, pitting the efficacy of straight-forward political poetry versus poetry which operates on the level of language itself. Like most things, I don't see it as two poles of "either or," but as an opening for multiplicity, as are all Tender Buttons titles in their specific way.

What happens when women get together and take the mode of production into their own hands to create their own terms for living and existing?

> *Multiplicitous in form,*
> *I knew we could go on.*

Gertrude Stein said "If you enjoy something, you understand it."

> *We are the daughters of enthusiasm*
> *With tenderness and dancing.*
> *With late night storming.*
> *Excitement sisters.*
> *Where are my excitement sisters.*
> *At work they are at work.*

I remember so many people who gave their time and labor to each Tender Buttons creation. We include here the original acknowledgement page from each book to trace the communal and "situationist" nature of the press over the years.

Multitudinous thank yous to all and especially to you, dear reader, who will take this work with you into the world.

I look forward to the birth of *B* by Julie Patton, one of the longest gestational periods for a book ever —over 15 years, a glorious pregnant B of visual and sonic language play, forming strong weaves of political import and love.

As I type Truck Darling's "Artist Statement 2," I imagine how would it feel to be newly changing one's bodily and hormonal form, from girl/ woman to man/boy and write those opening lines:

> *All paint is war paint when you're newly stretched.*
> *Nude of grace, I want to be seen with dignity*

And Truck ends with a few lines that encapsulate the fiercely independent spirit of what I'm always hungering for, what I find in poetry.

> *No matter / How warped I*
> *see the world, it's my world, cracked /& salty.*

"H.D. wrote: "Paint it today"

Truck Darling writes:

"Nude of grace, I paint it anyway."

I look forward to further expanding Tender Buttons poetics into emerging areas of radical expression— linguist and socio-political.

I look forward to the wave of astonishment that will surely happen when a younger generation encounter these books, and when a wider audience of people realize all these amazing books came from the same small press.

I look forward to you reading this book, to you having it by your bedside to read hypnogogicaly and hypnopompicly and for you to open many new forms of poetry, of thinking and feeling in and out of language and in imagining and realizing new living, loving forms of being.

I remember last night's dream, I got behind the wheel of a very large bus to drive it around a crowded metropolis. It felt like a huge responsibility. I drove it over an industrial bridge, over a river and back again to where I first got on the bus. I was fearful I would not be able to find a place to park it, so was vastly relieved and happy to find both sides of the street clear to parallel park against the overgrown curb.

Lee Ann Brown
Founding Editrix , Tender Buttons Press
New moon solar eclipse
March 8th, 2016
New York City

Bernadette Mayer

Sonnets

Tender Buttons
New York City
1989

Cover Art by Marie Warsh
Book Design by Steven Taylor
Tender Buttons Drawing by Joe Brainard

Some *Sonnets* were published in:
o•blek, *Pome, The Ledge, Exquisite Corpse,Bingo, Gandhabba, Everyday Life,*
MUTUAL AID, UP LATE, and THE BEST AMERICAN POETRY, 1988.
The INCIDENT REPORTS SONNETS were published by Archipelago Books in
1984.

Thank you: Ed Friedman, Kim Lyons, Phil Good, Greg Masters, Vicki Stanbury, Tom
Zummer, Harry Smith, The Poetry Project, Susan Bee, Beth Brown, Bethany Jacobson,
Kenward Elmslie, Rosmarie & Keith Waldrop and all who gave encouragement and
advice on production.

Distributed by The Segue Foundation

Published by
Tender Buttons
c/o Lee Ann Brown
#1e 130 Fort Washington Ave.
New York, N.Y.
10032 U.S.A.

ISBN 0-927920-00-X

FOR ROSEMARY MAYER

SONNET

Love is a babe as you know and when you
Put your startling hand on my cunt or arm or head
Or better both your hands to hold in them my own
I'm awed and we laugh with questions, artless
Of me to speak so ungenerally of thee & thy name
I have no situation and love is the same, you live at home
Come be here my baby and I'll take you elsewhere where
You ain't already been, my richer friend, and there
At the bottom of my sale or theft of myself will you
Bring specific flowers I will not know the names of
As you already have and already will and already do
As you already are with your succinctest cock
All torn and sore like a female masochist that the rhyme
Of the jewel you pay attention to becomes your baby born

HOLDING THE THOUGHT OF LOVE

And to render harmless a bomb or the like
Of such a pouring in different directions of love
Love scattered not concentrated love talked about,
So let's not talk of love the diffuseness of which
Round our heads (that oriole's song) like on the platforms
Of the subways and at their stations is today defused
As if by the scattering of light rays in a photograph
Of the softened reflection of a truck in a bakery window

You know I both understand what we found out and I don't
Hiking alone is too complex like a slap in the face
Of any joyous appointment even for the making of money

Abandoned to too large a crack in the unideal sphere
        of lack of summer
When it's winter, of wisdom in the astronomical arts,
        we as A & B
Separated then conjoin to see the sights of Avenue C

SONNET

Alone due to exigency well as apt can tell
The name of dumbest truth I've stayed the hell
The dimwitted dippers by a writer a guy by that name
Oh how turn as hers infinite the exactness of
Always with replaced as old always by another
And as to lines no not your responsible sway
Many times by a poet who saw you female of art
The wish to make you lost began & can't say that
That to be so old again as in identified father
Ignorant Orion was said to settle the bill mom
Like settles stands for all night gives but without
You feel another whose vagina somewhat over love her
Communicating mother in fidelity I am thus plus
Which I thought still but without sphere her here

SONNET

I am supposed to think of my personal dot
I do and it is dull if you won't call
Who cares Angel I could find you even within my wrist
Nobody minds because of sleeping, I detest it myself
Why doesnt anybody want to demand to make love
Female to actual famous female or vice versa
Warm indoors is the repeating of the trivial of something
It doesn't matter what, I'm tired of not

Absence like parents is the astrophysical
What who knows come in I've got my birth control out
Come by get lost the curtain if fictionally red is not then real
Nor's the blood shed why for what, we warn televisions of it
Dont say anything bad like fuck or shit or otherwise & besides
You might have to wear ostensible clothing & hairdos all your lives

SONNET

A thousand apples you might put in your theories
But you are gone from benefit to my love

You spoke not the Italian of Dante at the table
But the stingy notions of the bedded heterosexual

You cursed and swore cause I was later
To come home to you without your fucking dinner

Dont ever return su numero de telefono it is just this
I must explain I dont ever want to see you again

Empezando el 2 de noviembre 1980-something I dont love you
So stick it up your ass like she would say

I'm so mad at you I'm sure I'll take it all back tomorrow
& say then they flee from me who sometime did me seek

Meanwhile eat my existent dinner somebody and life
C'mon and show me something newer than even Dante

SPYING ON THE NEIGHBORS

In the Catholic book of being turned on
Lost in the people who believe in just wrists
Jewelless and watchless & clean like big nuns
You lift up their skirts and look beneath

To the idiotic universe of most informed design
For living in it all ways all the fucking time
In the dirty city & the dirty country of all us
Healthy naughty girls & boys who look at you

Out from the pictures of our bodies in the news
Before anybody dies there's all this pleasure
From out of the lunacies of mothers plus fathers
You visit on the slightly defunct globe or orb

A CHINESE BREAKFAST

Is it so far to the door?
Does Max's sandwich diminish my confidence to reach it?
Do fears as unnatural as dreams to waking
Reflect something of anything for everyone else?
Should madness ensure, would the tiny hole
For a dislodged nail in the wall be its focus?
Does the belong world in you?
Did the finch devour the bluejay
Right in the cleft of the dead bird of paradise?
Did a she slip the awful cup?
As spring comes a man's apple juice emits an ankle bracelet
And you're as forlorn as the mean dentist's smock of our culture
Plus a he can't find a parking space cause the ice is still thick
As the thief of the way a day might memory look

THE FALSE FINCH'S WEDDING GOWN

In the blue descriptive city
Each unsorted square tripartite mineral
Does not turn into the round or not-bed of the rich poor
The 35mm black and white tri-x print film signals
The millenium falcon and the salacious crumb
It's funny to ram and chip at studies till
You can make even the bluejays charming to others
Through definition, forecast and the unreligious word

In these centrally located walls
Shouting at dawn on the opposite school
Right beside the birds really singing
I wonder whether to bother to sort your purple clothes
From the desirable pink ceilings and roofs of sleep—
Which letter of the alphabet would I become?

SONNET FOR FRED POHL

I'm not male or female either but that
That's reaching too addenda many countries
Much of a conclusion—you'd just as soon be
Entirely without my crystal our tooth
& as usual I rushed you past your wealth
To malely fixing eggs my father's death in my book house
Of so what yes and no retrievable between legs
Naive couplet consequent to do

No such thing too much work to do for money
No beginning of laser epic Clark arch
Yet counter the concept of sonnet not with its meters
The way thought proceeds countable like geologic stuff is not;
Not not countable's the specificity of its love
Couplet opposites yes of stream of no

SONNET LIST WITHOUT COMMAS

Who who a sinner what too sensitive cold carbon
Right to dispute dont face west too cold mirror
To nature the roof and the floor holding heart
Heat sparks or flame playfellows explain
Nothing Chinese everything the sonnets of
Henniker Henniker's stove stamps of the rose
Winter of certain dates sleek financial milk air
Marbles upstairs increase bath baby and tools
Yellow squirrel running exacerbating funny home
White as the snow the date is getting rid
Of the llamas credit the color of the hat
Knowledge of remorse at market or college no
Bears cement of wine at meals swell woolen slippers
Dry leaves that before the wild hurricane fly when they
        meet with an obstacle mount to the sky

TWO THOUSAND NON-INTERFERING BALLET
DANCERS GET RID OF THE EXTRA WITCH

Retrograde aspects of low-cop non-election-year
Participation might mean putting your bracelets
Guatemalan on early in the evening to avoid the
Footsteps of the man you might devour

The straitest woman at the farm loved our arms
Yet the ancientest scientists might never have
Not by which we know nothing but brave philosophy
Meaning you can sleep through a bright night before

Bright before you exercise an individual breakfast
Stoned men think they are different from stoned women
It might be appropriate to marry Mary Magdalen
And stone /onald /eagan a little in person at Carnac
This proves all who make love tonight are good poets
& poetesses beg forgiveness before your available hardons

SONNET

You jerk you didn't call me up
I haven't seen you in so long
You probably have a fucking tan
& besides that instead of making love tonight
You're drinking your parents to the airport
I'm through with you bourgeois boys
All you ever do is go back to ancestral comforts
Only money can get—even Catullus was rich but

Nowadays you guys settle for a couch
By a soporific color cable t.v. set
Instead of any arc of love, no wonder
The G.I. Joe team blows it every other time

Wake up! It's the middle of the night
You can either make love or die at the hand of
                    the Cobra Commander

_____

To make love, turn to page 54.
To die, turn to page 660.

SONNET

It would be nice to lose one's mind my mind
I'd like to lose it I wouldn't mind at all
To be in the lunatic asylum at last
All for you and for the taxi drivers

I'll go and be asked what year what day it is
& who's the president, how come he's a resident
I could teach prosody there but nobody
Knows what it is
So send me away to anybody
Anywhere who might
Not know something I might not
Since I must vice versa live

Whaddya mean perforce?
Army or navy or marines?

SONNET

My hand is like a muffin just baked in the electrocuting
toaster under the light of the smoke detector full of
American Americium to create the further tumors that make
poets underpaid in life compared to the more dismal occu–
pations like vacuum cleaning or storing thoughts in machines
or selling objects to people

Writing poems is really dumb but fuck it even we want
entertainment I saw the art of the city today smokestacks
and buildings from the hospital windows where everybody
I know is imprisoned and being demeaned on demerol or else
everything's o.k. thank god they're all fine having had
operations in there you wouldn't want to sleep with me in
exchange would you?

This is my new form of sonnet
This is the closing of it
Please don't stop loving me right this moment
Or else one of us might kill the other
Just like in the papers

SONNET WELCOME

To the 1981-1982
Poetry season
At the Ear Inn
What a mess is everything
In this world we live in
François Marie Charles Fourier said in 1800
This planet should be sent to a lunatic asylum
But it's not poetry's fault
For being so concerned
With love beauty sex and ideas, money
All the preoccupations of the philosophers, thieves
& prostitutes, I myself make no image
When I say anything including saying
Let's get on with our non-paying work as always

TO MR. ROBERT HERRICK AND ANOTHER

You take the red paper and fold it
In half like this, then you cut it
Like any heart or Valentine hearts
But you make the cut in the middle
And not on the outside Mr. Herrick
Then the Prussian blue sky becomes
Silver & paintings seen unless you
Hide them & a written note of love
Can be hidden archaeologically for
A million years if the stuff lasts
I'd like to hide this note for you
It's cut now in the middle the way
Needless curtains divide a window,
Shirred and strait, I dont see why

SONNET

> For that which is not conscious, the
> language provides no means of expression.
>   -Gregory Bateson

You read about Uranus in the Times?
How there's two more moons? & how the guys
In the neighborhood I grew up in got arrested
For killing a final cop and wounding a woman one?

She's in stabile condition, life is
Kind of hot if empty-seeming, don't you think?
Me and the cop who arrested him have got alot in common
Not only cause of Ridgewood and cause his name is Angel

My voyager, Uranus is far away as far as my pessary
From the magnetosphere forgive me cock
Gaea was born of Chaos in a phoneless prison
Let's have a baby today, I gave

You a new name

SONNET

Everyone makes love to their bereft & go
I'd like to know you right this second
But you wouldn't dare come here for the fear
I have of eating this open sandwich I've got
I forget and you've got to I forget & not copy
Tomorrow the two identical different Dutch paintings
Will not look the fruits the way they look today
Thinking of you as if at the beginning of something I do,
                    I will not lie down

You act as if you were married
Thee who comes by whenever you please
I'm not either
You called early, alot to say, I forget
The plot, it was we are alike now it's late
You're asleep   I'm awake

THE NUMEROUS 25-YEAR-OLD 85-YEAR-OLDS OF 1985

Two of you out drinking together again tonight
Why not invite me to your state while I'm a child
In a bell full of books and national journalism
Oh comrades of memory, at last our homework is done!
Like the ten petals of the mountain laurel
Time's determined exactly by machines
Or digits not reflective or predictive, a fact
Like drowning in the ocean in a dream
You might've been thrown out of like a tavern
Then I followed you & you and counted
On you to collect me and we became a group
Like the ten petals of the mountain laurel

Sex, where's the couplet?
The concluding modern thought's a warm winter scarf

FREEZETAG

Buildings prevent the sun
Sky turns blue after eclipse-green
"You were pretty glamorous
In your day," he said
The weather himself not being desireable
Nor does he bring home with him
An exciting friend, a companion
To introduce us to the new
       life like learning as a baby

Of this and especially of that of memory
The handsome man with all the twins
I dreamed the madwomen's servants
Counted upon madmen's answers in springs
Having drunk the tunneling spring waters
Of lunatic wandering strangers within the
       rectangular house schemes

SONNET

Moth like porphyry lights the town
Like a phratry against the city how many
Famous men die in a summer today it was
The painter Clyfford Still when he died
I opened the window in the pantry
To bring down the screen on the sill resting
Was a snake curled snakelike disturbed by me
It crawled back behind one of many of cold
Old New England's kitchen sinks in childhood
A snake extracted from a pipe is preserved in a jar
In a plumber's window in New York where I'll go back
Next week I was lucky to see Still's painting
Years ago, I am abstract a poet I am not what
I forget is poetry compared—porphyry like moth.

CLAP HANDS

I'll write you sonnets till you come
Home from school again, the music of your cave become
A stalagmitic presence, honey I don't have
An electronically regulated discharge tube that can emit
        extremely rapid, brief and brilliant flashes of
        light, such a squinting and twisting around
        as to disorder it's nice to divide a sonnet

This way when you might fuck me up the ass
On account of the presence of the bureau by the door
Cause of some song like the one by Tom Verlaine
Where he says adieu like a kid from Brooklyn

Tell like so cause me Bill loves you to not to know
Turn the hear to why over Bill me cause I'll know I you
Say and am to exist I not entranced pretty
Can't Bill with startling say Shakespeare myself that

Couplet I adore you it's my habit
I want manly things & should not, women come to me

SONNET: TWENTY DOLLARS IN HELL

Introduction: Poetry's good because it's hold up in the known rooms of stanzas before anybody wakes us up mornings as hegemony love the pretension of ink might notice dear father dear father the church is hot the church is hot but there might be quite a few little songs to be sung before the decimation of the race or love that you have right now in american time beats which is more time for a person from here or there to work in but less time due to that lesion of the leisure of the bomb which one doesnt mention to be dramatic poets have always sunk ships or died in or dear the water maybe

If you adore me
Why dont you take out your old-fashioned arms
& threaten me my darling we're at a loss
A little spear a bow and arrow ought to do us good
You can push a thread through the outline of a kite
With a scissor or something else sharp in the nursery school
Which expresses a distrust for metaphor because
The children losing their teeth all the white sense
Your anger at any idiotic situation & dont sit still
At all, they want to but they live with you
And in all truth how can they not know
Heartily materialistic fears, I'll give you twenty dollars
To erase them & so will any child of ours to get them
So how can we begin again?

WARREN PHINNEY

A little boy on August first night
Got into the colors possible in the light
Of this universe & of his cock
We spoke the words the little boy
My little boy like in the liturgy & in the litany,
Thee, more august that is magnificent
Than any of the daily concerns, his soft skin.
And losing my judgment I forgot about his Volkswagen
Which was needed in the morning to carry his father
And his mother to work, it was not his car
But the drive wasnt far and before you left
After the phone calls we answered
From friends to find you there was time
For another mention of the Russian Revolution
Then I wound up with my feet at the head of the bed
Knowing hippily about our stars, your guitar
& the meeting from which we fled, the proper porcupines
Having eaten enough of your parents' car's gaslines
To give us time to make the little more love
We'd dreamed of before the tow truck came.

INCANDESCENT WAR POEM SONNET

Even before I saw the chambered nautilus
I wanted to sail not in the us navy
Tonight I'm waiting for you, your letter
At the same time his letter, the view of you
By him and then by me in the park, no rhymes
I saw you, this is in prose, no it's not
Sitting with the molluscs & anemones in an
Empty autumn enterprise baby you look pretty
With your long eventual hair, is love king?
What's this? A sonnet? Love's a babe we know that
I'm coming up, I'm coming, Shakespeare only stuck
To one subject but I'll mention nobody said
You have to get young Americans some ice cream
In the artificial light in which she woke

THE HANDCUFFING OF HERMITS WHO GRAB THE GENITALS' POLICE

"Did you go out of your body?"
"I was feelin good!"
"Yeah but did you go out of your body?"

Weighing trucks and curious like love upon the postal scale
With faculties still growing feeling still the reproduction
Of paradisaical children by the wisest anarchist rhapsodists
There was a beautiful table brought from China made of what
But that the soul remembering how she felt but what she felt
          remembering not
Like a big good giant doing a corporal work of mercy, washing
          the outsides of the upstairs windows while singing of
the pleasures of good gianthood
Retains an obscure sense of possible sublimity
To which with growing faculties she doth aspire feeling still
That whatsoever point they gain they still have something to
          pursue
No man no transformer in cinnabar's mythgear or footwear
Could leap in Elizabeth's room like some Wordsworthian
          milkman's walkman
I have your purse I am at the white house, I have the edible
          rhyming tiger lily buds for you
& will roast them in potato batter along with snow pea pods
Till I live in a house of numerous fine things heaped together
          universe-like & know how come all do not love all.

"TAKING THE HUMBLER PATH"

for Ron Padgett

Was excellent advice from Ron
In a dream
I fell
We were walking in the rush hour
Got pushed into a snowbank
By a man in a Bentley
&climbingoveritIfellinlikeGreek&Latin
Scared at first I'd lose the bottom
But now I can get the Give Good Cookies
To eat and compare with
The Five Sweet Cupcakes
I wanted in the first place
From the origins of the alphabets of the world

So, think twice

SONNET

At 172 E. 4th Street near the bottom of NY's Avenue A
Lights make black shadows of green trees
And at noon they shout like cannibals
They shout like birds for an hour at noon
To watch the wind I will not go (outside my house)
I can't, all night the night is going on
The grand trees, school's closed, the phone bills
Rhyme in three's and each of us takes turns being
Jealous but it's I who have no stylus
I can't hear symphonies, can't hear the popular
Songs goodbye night you young men of morning
Why don't you spend the hurricane with me
Coming light your brand new flashlights a little bit
Come on, be even more generous, you boys

SONNET

Other than what's gone on and stupid art
I've no even memory of people and their part
In bed I forget all details
The female with the male entails
For whatever that's worth who cares
He who worries or she who dares
To die practically without mentioning
Again our idiotic utopian friendships

All the city's a mass of slush and ices
You might know I dont about poetries
My hand's your hand within this rhyme
You look at me this is all fucked up time
I'm just a sparrow done up to be
An Amazon or something and he? or thee?

WE EAT OUT TOGETHER

My heart is a fancy place
Where giant reddish-purple cauliflowers
& white ones in French & English are outside
Waiting to welcome you to a boat
Over the low black river for a big dinner
There's alot of choice among the foods
Even a tortured lamb served in pieces
En croute on a plate so hot as a rack
Of clouds blown over the cold filthy river
We are entitled to see anytime while we
Use the tablecovers to love each other
Publicly dishing out imitative luxuries
To show off poetry's extreme generosity
Then home in the heart of a big limousine

ON GIFTS FOR GRACE

I saw a great teapot
I wanted to get you this stupendous
100% cotton royal blue and black checked shirt,
There was a red and black striped one too
Then I saw these boots at a place called Chuckles
They laced up to about two inches above your ankles
All leather and in red, black or purple
It was hard to have no money today
I won't even speak about the possible flowers and kinds of
      lingerie
All linen and silk with not-yet-perfumed laces
Brilliant enough for any of the Graces
Full of luxury, grace notes, prosperousness and charm
But I can only praise you with this poem—
Its being is the same as the meaning of your name

BIRTHDAY SONNET FOR GRACE

I've always loved (your) Grace in 14 lines, sometimes
I have to fit my love for Grace into either
An unwieldy utopia or a smaller space,
Just a poem, not a big project for changing the world
      which I believe
It was the color of your hair that inspired me to try
      to do in words
Since such perfection doesn't exist in isolation
Like the Hyacinth, Royal or Persian blues
That go so well with you

Now older than we were before we were forty
And working so much in an owned world for rent money
Where there seems little time for the ancient hilarity
We digressed with once on the hypnopompic verges of the sublime
Now more engrossed in hypnagogic literal mysteries of
      our age and ages I propose
To reiterate how I love you any time

HOMEOPATHIC BUSYNESS

Rigorously going from field to field
To plow up the internecine wars, how do
People find the time for their suppers
Or lost articles, there's so much blood
On the precinct steps even in the imagist snow
And I go from the moments are becoming tinier
To soon it will be bloody tomorrow's being over
Instead of any extent of thought's, love's
Or work's privileges big enough to be
The right doses. I make little money at it
But then who doesn't wake up at 6am to think
Before the grapefruits' eyes, the student cereals
Floating around in, of all things, some milk
Before the window's corridor where the snow flies up

THE POT OF TOAST

As the page declares its divinity
In the grass field above the garden
I'm thinking of women a sister
Two sisters a mother a mother-in-law
Maybe we spoke of socks or mittens
Maybe in view of the weather we worried
About the ten found Siamese kittens
Or the missing ostrich feather
From Margaret's best hat speaking without
Stopping until there's a crisis in the house
And then a string yards long
Comes to be wound about our legs
Entangling us till there's no stepping out
Of the circular casements in which we're about

INCIDENTS REPORT SONNET

for Grace

Woke up from dream on
July 9, 1965, dream was erotic
(can't remember what was in it),
I think the woman was attempting
to sit on her chair while
lifting the man's wallet
but then on the boatride my hand
got caught in the elevator door
by the firecracker tossed in
by a child who was a woman as missing
as the coffee money, anyway I
lost balance and, falling, woke up
jerking off through the chair,
another chair, was still falling
on my foot, sorry.

INCIDENTS REPORT SONNET #2

for Grace too

I was not yet married when
at age 2, a female other, I
put my finger into the forms of address
of the most blue night early in the morning
and said to my sister Rosemary, "Well,
what do you think of this!"

At the time we were both
sitting on the floor before the balls
of blue glass we were to clean
so often in the future and by the window
Rosemary once fell out of, who agreed
our exploration was fascinating

        Only trouble is
        Our mother hit the ceiling

INCIDENTS REPORT SONNET #3

                        for all Grace

Apparently I was lying
in a narrow bed with Peggy
in my apartment on 11th street
when she and I first discussed
our impressions of sex and
autoeroticism together.

Approximately 18 years later, we've
remembered this weird and
naive conversation and wondered how come
we could've been twenty then and,
despite our crazy catholic upbringing,
with the total importunity on everything
like looking and touching,
we didn't do anything.

INCIDENTS REPORT SONNET #4

                        yet for Grace

Maria told me tongue-kissing
could get you pregnant
and Janice who eventually got pregnant
by the guy
who was also on heroin
who was supposed to be my boyfriend
said you could get pregnant by swimming
but we all got most shocked
when we went over to Laura Cashdollar's house
and her mother liked to watch us
making out, it was alot weirder
than dancing to American Bandstand
or playing kissing games
in Freddie Stegel's cellar.

INCIDENTS REPORT SONNET #5

for Grace also

Now you must remember that bed
we slept in head to feet in upstate new york.

David who was probably four
had just so badly injured his foot.

We had scared the wits out of the kids
playing hide & seek outdoors in the dark.

We ate Canadian Oat Bread and baked
millions of potatoes for our charges.

You and I took notes on everything
including Colin's dream ravings.

I'm forgetting to mention many things
including attempting to swim in the shallow stream.

Then we got into our tiny bed together
with our shared immortal fear of love.

INCIDENTS REPORT SONNET #6

this one's for Grace

I took a little of the blue color
once called Persian or Royal
new better Hyacinth
though I can't but doubt that that flower's so dark
as you and I are letting it be
for the sake of agreeing with
what colors are called now
& to get rid of the nationalist
& elitist adjectives no longer appropriate,
and put a glowing-in-the-dark shooting star on it
and then a full and a sliver—
and a half-moon as well
only thing is the kids still
wouldn't turn the lights out to see.

SONNET

Beauty of songs your absence I should not show
How artfully I love you, can you love me?
Let's be precise let's abdicate decorum
You come around you often stay you hit home

Now you are knocking, you need a tylenol;
From all that comedy what will you tell?
At least you speak, I think I'd better not;
Often men and not women have to sleep

You've come and gone—to write the perfect poem
And not ten like men or blossoms, but I am profligate
I strike the ground for ruin while you sensibly sleep
And so in this at least a poem can have an end

How could you sleep, I go to wake you up
My Lysistrata, my unannounced rhyme

SONNET

To perform for you, ask me why, shall I sleep?
You make love so beautifully I don't know what to do
You come and put your university hand
You've thrown yourself off the roof by now

A white dog chases a man around the park
Your school hand your rich hand your suburban hand
Cares if I come I am a woman & we women must both
Have babies & there's my mirror & there's my baby

I want one intent on your form like a room
Prepare food and eat it if the race would survive
The crystal lay like a comparison with wealth to you
I checked and you don't have your car keys

Can I believe her? So
Returned from the dead.

A CATSKILL EAGLE

Not a song of love but
When I ask George
Does he have a handgun
He says, "Sure baby"

Otherwise it's dark
Why don't you drive & arrive up here
In your reversing Lochinvarish Chrysler Reliant
I've got my period & bleed in my Plymouth Horizon
Like when we went to the cave in your Volkswagen bus

O dear Sir Lancelot
Would you want this particular bowl?
Poor Arthur it is not his cock
The search being over of some mystery

I put something wooden in my mouth and on the safe porch
        I fear the absences of friends who were once here sitting
        laughing at this table, a rectangle, they were driving a
        Renault Le Car

ENGINEERING GLORY, THE SUBLIME, BOTH COASTS

I give a catholic thanks in praise of your being
And in resemblance: "you were made for it"
Your name means farmer, river rising, a jeweled figure
Leader, amoral of the beaches and hills
You contrived it and you speak of ethics unlike the boy
You are the biblical beloved & I am flattered on the day
After the day of atonement you make me come so much
I walk out into the hurricane to speak, I have
No doubt of the truth since to life we engineer
Our usual toast & to the raucous trees
The shadows of which are making me wait as you do
To play around with you, to go to which hotel as
Your baby in generous time—you would take some of
Your years of life away, I'd gladly add them to mine

EPISTEMOLOGICAL SONNET

Inner keys on your my key ring our metal ring
For holding keys is gold is a base drum I cooked
A convincing convection of stews you have to learn
How to talk so you can cook Mount Cook very well or
Cook the Cook Islands and cool your heels until
There will of course be no more wars or graduate schools
But all peace will meld even scholarship back together
And Kant will come up often before the kangaroo courts

A number of lines has a structure picked up
From habit at you and melancholy truth
I might sing forever with never a goal nor solution
Except the singing of the tables of the alphabets
And the millions of interconnecting macaronic words
In the free verse families of the Indo-European stones

SONNET

ash	Ash is left behind from things
laugh	As I love to see you laughing when you come
drink	Or even drink—boom, wow! a wild boy
plate	Bring those damn apricots on a gold plate
crack	Before bottles in the park go crack
walls	Toward wilder heroinistic walls and we
train	Must then get on the red & tan, not the train
traffic	Or that exacting traffic plane
pages	Between the pages of this your book
O.K.	Read by many O.K. people
know	Who know that stupid
noise	Noise is coming from the street
still	Still in the still night
independence	On independence day welcome death!

with Philip Good

RETURNING THE BOOKS TO THEIR SHELVES

I could have caught a taxi to your city
But I couldn't have gotten back in time
To put books on shelves at P.S. 19
I wish I lived by a wide stream
I should've called a taxi to your city
A library should have books in it
Pumpkins shouldn't be made into mulch
Balloons shouldn't get butter on them
Maybe homes shouldn't have these stupid windows
And art as we know is next to nothing
A library does have books in it
So you come here by train with a cold
I'd rather run out for love, never phone
And slam books back up on their shelves

SONNET

Whaddo I do now just desire?
Break with any artifice or color?
Like the paid-for-rains and suns?
Commercials done on Avenue D today?
I won't court you you oughtta be normal
As if
I'm talking to another who's never
Not there, asleep malely

Meanwhile men in suits are waking up
And fine if they can appear to say
This is so
All together we wish for others in our beds
So that in the night we can hold some one of the numbers
Of like-mothers for all of stupid time

WITH GRACE

> after the Price Chopper

We sit in the car drinking beer
Studying the architectural shingles of the center
Drive fast outta there down the prettiest road
Past my old house in glee of reminiscence
Covering every subject in universe in minutes
High on Monument Valley Road
Praising each other right
Past the Open Heart Memorial and
Laughing at the intersection
Of Lake Buel with 23
That we've been in such harmony for 23 years
Plan a long trip together
Stop short for a rabbit
Get back with the groceries

SONNETS: THE LANDLORD WAS THROWN OUT OF THE RENT STABILIZATION GROUP

I
The landlord was thrown out of the rent stabilization group
Because he did so many wrong and bad things
We don't know what this means yet
& whether our rent will go down or up
If that's a punishment for us or him
He who's harrassed us all this time
Then we harrassed him this is not like love
Now finally he's thrown out we threw him out long ago
Of the possible ways of being human
& so maybe it's kind that he's now out of time
With his colleagues because of his manipulations
I don't like the landlord's hand so much that I am happy but
      Why's he been so derelict like a lover
      As to let things go this far?

II
It's impossible sometimes for the woman not to think of the landlord if he's a man as a father, that's what some of the old women in the building here have told me, you wouldn't want to live with him, this is why nobody ceases to pay their rent or goes on rent strike or is willing to face another father-judge in the courts, do you remember how your kids' teachers, if you have them, can make you feel nervous in that same way, the authorities avoid them. So it is right the landlord is a man, his agent is a woman who is so pervasively divisive as to be inhuman I wont talk to her she makes me want to weep I wont lie down I wont give a tip to the landlord's pimp, could this be a sonnet? I wonder on it, who is who and what is what. I dont live in this building by accident this is my reservation I live with the sleeping lions I was reminded cars were when you crossed in the middle of the street that they thought I actually owed them something just at the moment they woke up to roar at me and you and perhaps eat us.

SONNET FLANDERS ROAD

Today she cleaned up and left in the red car
She said mist was caught in the mountains
Take all the lettuce you want from the garden
She said she was born in 1948 which makes her
32, what's the mist doing being caught
In the valleys so contiguous like overhearing
Neighbors quarreling I can almost touch the
Pot roast the man of the house made for once

To think on too few strangers makes me blind
Befogs the mind next door obscures my sanity
In the country clouds what's bright in humankind

I'll have a million neighbors in the city
All at once above below it's easier for love
Demystifies does organize the film before my eyes

SPOOKY ACTION FROM A DISTANCE: SONNET
ABOUT HOW LOVE IS AS TEACHING AS YOU
BREATHE DEEPLY WITH DISRESPECT FOR THE
TEXT AND BECOME DISJECTA MEMBRA FROM
YOUR LOVER

for Don Yorty

And young he (there's always been this dare) sleeps waking
Partly sideways, mollescent yet macho (only joking)
Always retreating back to what the lawned home
Or something irreligious might be, who knows what's known?
Many other absent things done in times like ours of these
Unfulfill love's presence like it was one of those
Displayed wedding cakes on 14th street with a bed of pink
Beside the hockey players, if you begin young to think
Life is shit you're better off later when you get
A sort of basketballish hope from your fancier genes yet
I've seen how the light looks in each circumstance
And gone out to get oranges, Tide and water all at once

It might be right to write of just the hour
That's a structure good as love's or any measure

THE BOOK OF DOLLS

previous to the little images being put in the grave
which say mama & papa according to which arm is raised
real people were buried along with the dead one
the sleeping eyes are attached to a lever at the waist
sleeping kings to sea in burning ships with real men on them
the baby is unbreakable and jointed and even when shipped
says, "ah, ah, aaah," when tipped

the bald white china head of the earliest known
sleeping doll the hair is attached to a small spot
on the head's crown even stones into a human image
the ancient boy and girl doll Queen Mary is very
interested indeed in all kinds of and the dressing
of the hair which is so important the sloped & square
shoulders narrow waists and large hips fixing a date

SONNET: KAMIKAZE

Dawn & night of fighting, lovers like actual wars
And as gentle men might be gentle, so they are not.
Jeans we all wear independent of our mutual sexes
Some lipsticked & rouged & eye-linered, some not.
I dont want to meet him, he does not prepare the food;
Also I am old. He the same age, younger, awaits my death.
A scholar, he doesn't count the births or clothes;
A scholar too, I keep track of the ages of the clothing.
Love seems to die for him with love's attention;
No point in thought or fight with dyed-in-wool women.

If we cant get along then who the fuck can?
I will not run or go forward American, divine wind.
A person, I must insist on a heartless agreeing;
A person too, he must agree some love can be.

SONNET

Waiting for you to come back from a comedy show
You and I what do we do? We read Aristophanes
Because you are still in school. On the street
A crazed Hasidic man called you my husband, I am not

You are who I am pregnant, give me my kiss
You whom I often & silently come where you are
That I may be with you, we ought not to speak
At all like this for the women who are your brothers

Now we have a rest together at last & dream
Of the salt & pepper shakers & of the scary sisters
Of us who seem exempt chasing each other around
You knowing less than I cause I'm a formal mother

Not-son fuck me again
Close this night's seven windows

SONNET

So long honey, don't ever come around again, I'm sick of you
& of your friends, you take up all my time & I don't write
Poems cause I spend all my time wanting to fuck you & then
You put the apple onto the grilled cheese, I tie you up

Save me from your respective beauties, keep them home
Thanks for all the rock & roll music, if such a
Thing can be said. Who are those guys? The B-52's?
That's what Ethie told me. Can I believe her?

You wanna get married? You tie me up with
Garter belts & less than Heidegger & Kierkegaard the fact
That as we know the poem is not the thought so a slap
Might notice that Uranus suspected a comet? Let me know

He kicks her fallen hat & they are not grownup
Any more than a vase of flowers is, painted, so what?

A MARRIAGE OF CUT FLOWERS

It's a room in a hotel
This has no mr. meaning at all
The promiscuous lilacs
The too-sweet tuberose
Some sweet williams and
A pink delphinium dolphin
Who sees them says that this place must
Fill this room with something

To fuck everyone as in the millenium
It might be a very great pleasure
To seduce and slap at all smells
I could hit your penis grand father
Of a funeral parlor or a regular field
And all that is complaining darling

THE EARTHWORKERS' GOD IS HEALED

Witness the sarcophagus of non-Raphael
I open the window
He & I've got synchronous particles
Plus the death simultaneous of the real
The lithographer now non-George
Two socialists I loved
Lived to be skinny and prolific
Within their torsos existed
The unprepared hum of health
Twice too past their nonidentical deaths
But do I give a fig about death?
Let's forget them!
Those two green birds who bite my fingers
Till I scream for identical help

OCTAVE SUBLIME EXCUSES FOR SAY POETRY PRETTY THERE ARE NOT TASTES INSTEAD OF THE ROOMS

Word your sublime on the courtyard
Someone's not so bad
Excuses your for say musics or poetry there is
None living on top or below
Tastes played are not mine
I see you in sublime
Instead of the stanzas the rooms
But to be surrounded's loss

SONNET WE ARE ORDINARY C'MERE

Excerpts I love you from abstracts
So what who cares songs of one and
Experience of this is a case like
Whole and I am not from there I write
To you to say I know nothing as ever
No rhyming no everything there is
No proceeding no thinking you will be my
What will you be? And that is the end

Except for the instance
What are you wearing?
Why aren't you here?
Where'd you put the window?

C'mere
Tell me the rest of it

SONNET

You dare to study philosophy baby I'll tell you
About fucking Aristotle I never planned to fall
In love with you who often happen by where I am
Let me hid you amidst the sublime responsibility you are

Now not let off & as such idiots love's own we speak
Let's be quiet we own nothing we know no fact I hit
Our love is not allowed it's missed the rain is snow
It's not and there is more than one dream of visit

I fell for you intolerably to others let's get
I thought you were my other, boys and children had
So did girls but let's proceed maybe in athletic secret
We'd make some love and money interned by repetition

The first of the month is a Monday
The beginning of our residency

14 QUESTIONS FOR TOM SAVAGE

Is when or where I start or you even fair? I dont know,
        is it not? Sex
I mean & dying for & this equal sign of worth. But
        is it to whose good-lookingness
We look confused before till when into sex like Dan
        & Who talking it was
Spoken around right-after-we-were-kids? Know I when my
        rights all & of animals may
Confuse them now with kids who laugh to be goats to our
        satyrs, what is worth?
Satiric for it to be that of the question rather about
        children, arent they as little welcome
Or less in New York City public place at least, as radicals
        & queers are were will be?
Age three, me you or saintly, supernal this's & that's of all the
        sexes, who is welcome in this world?
When being among spreads the venial sins' impatience on the
        obedience to biblical guilt both immoral
& immaterially genital the diseases then venereal, that is
        coming from love
Dying of which they or the innocent are in sex not manipulative
        like corporate execs
Deciding there's no money in cervical caps for want of victims to
        the hegemony of pregnancy
& governmental devils who make proclivitous women children &
        men in healthy baths mortal by planning to kill them all
& as many real friends, love & the marks of that they see & they
        see not nor the beyond of the question how come we're all
        scared to make love

THE PRESENCE OF ONE WHO SOMETIMES LEAVES A PLACE

It's a secret if you don't tell and don't lie
He can really eat a ham and cheese sandwich
No kidding, will he come, now he's too cold, I count,
I will give him another name, I wake him up as if
All people could do all things, you court the food of sleep
While I take your presence less lightly, I want to get
To the ninth floor where you're in my bed as if reason
Could prevent my ascension in the lift, I should your name.
Another name? Call me back. A tree out of its group
Is vulnerable like paint washes in the air,
Reasons about the end of the literal distance between us
It is from you renamed that I would write this in your arms:

What of the church and the place you touch: how dare you sleep?
What of the soul, luxuries and discourse: did you eat?

SONNET: WILL I WRITE POETRY?

I heard a man say in a restaurant
When I fell in love I got tired of causes
And knew it was time to get cruel
Otherwise I wouldnt know who I was he said

Imagine a woman who was practically no one
Began to love another it was white as snow
the black horse was evil pleased as punch
& red as beets we walked out into the streets

Busy as beehives full of men like roosters
Ganders & dragons & lions & tigers full of
Lionesses and tigresses, hens, geese & ducks
As always there are three American Indians plus

Us twelve-year-olds without any mothers
At my door with the lion with them all asking me

SONNET

The arts of death stop by and by not this letter
I'd wish to know and be somebody better

Knocking on the food do not enter never
Does my father look like who alters all broken
Still there is nothing to conclude what
Her birth is soon my periodic day so

Where is love is late mother I read
I wonder what speaking has to do with
Hotdogs I'll just leave the door open
And oh Marie is hungry and I am hungry too
To wait to get you from church to movie
Old escalators of the modern art I can't dark
What interspoken walls daughter hungry
one step or two forgotten by this letter

OF QUESTION

There is no sign of her or him my love is
Building a building around you have to have
Harmed like she never planted who stays
Listening maybe to females to cunts wondering
What were the wars' beginnings who eats the serious
Serious there is no sign from her who the building
Reflects at least two things at once are nothing

Is the phone really tapped? Will you come
With clitorises with balls and all not hiding
In rooms as men might shun the traffic even
Of new friends do you think cocks are friendless?

The kids in junior high say girls are nice as boys
Are awful and both girls & boys say this same thing

SOMETHING I CAN'T SAY HERE

You don't exist if the leaves are inept
Come by peonies of all the colors
Mommy the Twilight Zone is on I love you
Not as fire escape view or epic cartoon
You are my father in his grey overcoat
You let me let Edwin see what's up
That in my vagina would fall a drop of cock
And it would be on in the daylight and night
So that Theodore A. Mayer with a cup had a son
& late for school was I to tend the Bill Berkson tombs
"Do you want to go to them?" said creamy God
There are little bits of turkey in the sauce
And why did I happen to see your photograph,
Know you as equal not am I so, as I you

TO A MOVING VIOLATION

Red it was I know it was yellow
Christopher told me too, Philip, yet I
Believe both of you since light changes
Quick as lust is last remembered truth, Bill
& for sixty dollars you could get just heart & head
About halfway around the world with both in bed

The sentient cops remember not
Their flashlights' infiltration
What are crows doing here in the city listening
I sleep unadorned in my folded up thing
Since I'm living in the basement of absent
Of this apartment which will waken like a list
Now into your glove compartment I come without warning
The fear I feel of humans will be gone in the morning

NOTHING KNOWN, a film

Nothing known or else twice sits
Right by the destiny of you in the middle of
A big dark car back seat the one on your
Right's the friend and you're writing
A treatment in three dimensions so you bring
Out the magical symbols named for
Who what might be standing for as if to say
All human beings feel the same way

Right by the same side but on the other's the guy
Who sort of judges this thing so we look
At his him with no her here, this periodic character
Question mark fuck here with your undone cock and
Why not remember you already left this guy right
In the middle of the telltale Coca Cola creation dream

SONNET

nothing to wake to you can never
do noise what's there to do check-cash?
a snarl of laughing violets at the ing place
sonnet is an offer of a previous peace
welcome wednesday the day is forthright
it has hands and ending curly windows
and the sun is not to be out them
old grey spring sits down with us
like a big group without a sense of humor
not allowed to say that like the hydrangea
it's awful to exist if you're poisonous

the morning dove is nearly in the room
but for the child guard the dove'd be in the room,
then flew back through the mirror, no fooling

THE COMPLETE INTRODUCTORY LECTURES ON POETRY

for Ted Berrigan

It was when the words on the covers of books,
Titles as true as false leaves led me to believe
In inviting the ultimate speculation of love—
That I could learn all of the subject—
That I first began to entertain what is sublime

Like a moth I thought by reading JOKES AND
THEIR RELATION TO THE UNCONSCIOUS or BEYOND
THE PLEASURE PRINCIPLE or EAT THE WEEDS or
THE ORIGIN OF SPECIES or even a book on
COUP D'ETATS or THE PROBLEM OF ANXIETY I
Could accomplish the knowledge the titles implied

Science that there is often more
In the notes on the back of a discarded envelope,
Grammar in the shadows slanted on the wall
Of the too bright night to verify the city light

And then awakening, babies, to turn and make notes
On the dream's public epigrams and one's own
Weaknesses, self that's prone to epigrammatic ridicule

And to meditate on fears of all the animal dangers
Plus memories of reptilian appellations for all
Our stages of learning to swim at a past day camp

It is to think this or that might include all
Or enough to entertain all those who already know
That in this century of private apartments
Though knowledge might be coveted hardly anything
Is shared except penurious poetry, she or he
Who still tends to titles as if all of us
Are reading a new book called THE NEW LIFE.

THE PHENOMENON OF CHAOS

Love's not intent today what did I see
A bank, a store, a pattern of leaves
Fallen to the basketball court because
Rain followed the smoke of eleven states' fires

To exit from the universe you could
Believe nothing is checked on
But we don't exactly exist do we
Otherwise how could we

Do you love me when the earth's sun
Sets on your song on your tongue
This is ridiculous the universe
Is no longer uniform

By this we mean the universe's not or aint
A standard of nothing love's turning no more

AUTHOR'S NOTE

I didn't realize I had written these sonnets much less that I had written them for such a long time but one year recently without anticipation I found I was writing sonnets all the time and after a while I began to expect to write them and soon in the midst of all this contemporary sonnet writing going on I looked through my past poems in the morning and discovered I'd been writing the always somehow peripheral sonnet all along without understanding the forms of brief conclusive thought the poems had been taking so often in 14 lines without me. How serious notorious and public a form, to think you could find the solution to a problem or an ending to an observation in one brief moment—a fraction of an abreaction or the science of the pattern of crumbs appearing on the table from the eating of a loaf of bread. Why are we as human beings so sturdy? How can we conscion existence much less love? Is that why we have philosophy? Why deconstruct so innately? Is the sonnet form a form of abdication of reality? Because it is so neat & thus does have conclusion? Is poetry's method of conclusion disjointed to for instance the life of the bee? If there are no conclusions why do we wish for them? Love must be a subject I felt. Are poems like dreams representations of the absolute beauty of the future? Is the dilation of a form like the unbelievability and consequent common acceptance of the something of giving birth as if that were something less or more or equal to the necessity of having as many astonishing fingers as have not once been lost? When I studied my poems, I covered the floor with them and made a survey. The inadvertent sonnets, most of love in doubt, won the contest among other forms and other subjects, no subjects, landlord political sex suppressed, tied only with the categories of experimental workouts, poems for the dead and I don't know. And so it seemed most likely even honest, given the chance, to make availablest the headlong sonnets which are a way of thinking amidst our hemispheric faults—put on what you call what a woman wears around her waist, our many-colored octave, then rest from thought and formulate the next design.

{BERNADETTE MAYER, 1989}

Anne Waldman

Not A Male Pseudonym

Tender Buttons
New York City
1990

Cover by Donna Dennis

Publication of this book was made possible,
in part, by a grant from the Fund for Poetry.

copyright 1990 by Anne Waldman

Distributed by:

Segue Foundation
303 East 8th Street
New York, NY   10009

Small Press Distribution
1814 San Pablo Avenue
Berkeley, CA   94702

Sun & Moon
P.O. Box 481170
Los Angeles, CA   90048-9377

Thank you: Frank Murphy,
Steven Taylor,Bernadette Mayer,
Greg Masters & the Poetry Project.
Cover printing: Magic Circle.

Tender Buttons books are
edited and published by
Lee Ann Brown
71 East 3rd Street #17
New York, NY   10003

ISBN 0-927920-01-8

FOR BERNADETTE MAYER

And I said

I shall burn the
fat thigh-bones of
a white she-goat
on her altar

                -Sappho
                (tr: Mary Barnard)

              A book   a book

sad brow
        Let me off on the other side

A woman with another table took

          & decided everything

asunder, we'd quarrel
             or quick step outta here

I am so wide, dear Lady
         a narrow place like you I'd take
      to a tent to run my life

O skirt!   O ankles!

     Speak, ye that walk by the way

                                    rattling

                    begin my song
                              step-sister, holy one,
        begin my song

        not bitter
                    like mother, as in "I arose a Mother aslant"
                         not bitter as in

                    "Remember a thousand burning kisses"

        I see I fasten you
        No one knows
                         I left but will save
                              all for you

        skin fascinated by yours, obedient

                         not bitter as this city we live in

        rattling
                    one must travel through us to God

And are you Her-The-Heretic I met
before I met myself?

Are you a breaker of promises?
Do you lie with men?
Do you lie with the corn?
Do you lie with the other grain?
Who sired you?
Were you conceived by water at night?
Did the earth sing your name?
Your mother, did she have the same dark eyes?

We are young
                    say the Polish girls
We are the stalwart horse-riders

                    & replace the men singing in our blood

Forget us not, O singing in the blood
Women take the leather into their hands
Take off doll-mask
(Rembrandt tortured may yet be mercenary)

Speak in your rider voice as you come up behind me
And in my ear say it
You want me Say it
You want me says the night just like that
You want me says the clean air like that
You want me say breasts cresting
to meet lips

You want what between your legs?

Shopping for her
That long red dress
Waves which come & go
I try blue suede to test myself
Why do I hesitate?
Sweep back hair tight
Look at me
Call me Man
To be a martyr on the streets of Chicago
wasn't the point but – O
close in on me behind doors
People do gossip

when you get named by me

God the Woman overflows in us

the earth grows
kick off my heels
& untutored in this

seek the dose of you

I wanted to be a sailor
send my prayers to the holy ocean

& to you,

happy wife

Hands, good morning
Your hair with perfume
& cunt that does not ask my sins
Your scent of well-mannered breath
Me, hazel eyes
I am wide & adolescent
mixed up in a family tradition
by design & scheme
Anoint my dead palaces!

I carry love gifts towards you
My mind shapes our idle night
A room in Milwaukee
A room at the border of Canada
Going far to see the land…

& if by love flourishing
shall be believed, virgin neck, old
geometry & how we add up
our angles & corners
our bright minds
into new positions
I lie in the crook of your arm

waiting to be counted

In the arms of a man
I lie like a worm

Open the window
I break open my mouth to you
Open the window
Get up
I let the light in my mouth
No don't do that don't open the window yet
Come here don't let light in
You are the light in my mouth
Once more
Here
Not yet
Don't open the window yet
Here come here
Stand up come here
Walk towards me from Morocco
Walk towards me from Spain
Walk towards me from Bolivia
Open the window as I break open
my mouth to you
talking
(little sucking sounds)

& there was something the same
We walk to the bar
"Don't just stand & freeze"
When I needed a friend
How sweet your company
my stigma, desire
washed out in the rain
Cover me
Cover me over
You slice me
All good things arise

Her dress
creases like my brain is made of
It folds of her
Her slow unadorning, take it off it all off
Women attending women in attending
a kind of celebratory dance
kiss the tender parts
Lying about their time with men
(sperm drips down legs)
Else is wisdom! wisdom!
And spoke the night,
She's down on me

Items for my woman:
A mountain
A saddle
A long-stemmed glass
A country of her own
1 sunset
1 sunrise
My hands discover her face:
warm blankets
many dictionaries
Couplets of praise for her
Something Cuban

Performing: I'll shake the rattle
I'm shaking the rattle I'll shake the rattle
Performing for you I'll shake the rattle
This makes the world keep spinning
Shake the rattle the cities fall into place
Shake the rattle I'll shake the rattle
Shake the rattle the sky won't fall down
Shake the rattle children settle down
Shake the rattle singing the scent of you
Shake the rattle the seat of you comes forth
Shake the rattle we dream the end of war
We travel to Asia the see the end of war
Down the dark continent we dream the end of war
Shaking the rattle the stars fall into place
Shake the rattle moon is abiding there
Shake the rattle Sister Sun abiding there
All the planets fall into place
I'm shaking the rattle I'll shake the rattle
This one slips through my fingers
Women are like water says my tongue
My tongue says you are silvery like water
My tongue knows every part of you shake the rattle

Are you older than my body?
You seem full of surprises

They call us to work
scratching at the door
Come sing for your supper Lady Minstrels!

You watch me through the eyes of your book
for you are always writing

I am really the elder
And in my poetry I give you to the world

                              Her cry

            & its reticence

                    out on the street,
      from spa to spa

                amber liquors in delicate beakers

drink me down O drink me down

                How small her eyes seem tonight

      neon blinking in our eyes

                          Later, against the pillows

            Shake the rattle the night falls into place

Men in the corner watching whoever we are
Captains wink & smile
We take a man between us to test his mettle
astride our thinking
Today, women it is only women
Today it is only women

He tries & fails
Tries his wand & fails
He is the sacrificial disadvantage
With his ear of tin
He doesn't hear our singing with his tin ear
Sing "My Heart Belongs to Daddy" to taunt him further

We banish them from our bed
black shadows of uncertainty
with their nudgings
high horses neighing
cocks of high resolve
Banish them from the bed!

All the lubrications in the world
join us in a show of strength
to banish them from our bed
They come from the world of shadow-men
stink of men-talk, pleading gestures

You take God from me

Catholic girl,

in your liaison
with words

How go, O pitcher,

O book,

O bower,

young archer-poet

O sex-wars?

How go?

when the heart

is not

a male pseudonym

& you bring forth

passion

from my

holy

mouth

Hold him like a baby
O son of ours a baby too big to hold
And we are fathers too
What brought us to this
ecstasy of sons
Eat our words?
We hold our baby boys
boy bodies
wounded princes who sprung from us
bow down before us?
lie in our laps
bathe in our milk

O sons
why would you care to rule the world after this?

She's

the witch

o' my eye

that which caught me

caught me alive

She witched me

trapped in the net

the sweetest cocoon

I emerged

Her new man

yet couldn't do anything

for her

under the sun

you

in me blossomed

poets exert

out of their skulls

a Muse

like you

I'll say it again
that an occasion
was rewarded
in the
accessories
you brought to me

                        I speak far things now

                  shuddering

linked to you

            soul mournful to find its sister, its mate

                     when we made love

love returning

                                your long red dress

                  Cast spells on

                         the silvery water

How long, sister, how long?

Summer 1974
Revised June 1983

Muse & Scribe: A Note

I am this one writing to be more herself in the thought that all poems are invented by women. The night or nights of travel being a shaman of no particular society male or otherwise get spoken exactly like a love affair and are held as words. As words, these toward the beloved woman, get mouthed, & she & I, or you & I or She & you come into being. It is my privilege to speak thus, it is my joy. The words are an event of no small passion and are caught in a place back then outside travel outside time. They're here too. And travel proscribed was the name & opportunity of the song as I was always a scribe & sidekick to her motion. She was my fixed star for a time of heart & I was perpetual motion too. I catch her as best I can/could through scent & ambiguity of verse. The pronouns you find us in here are a relationship to secret notebooks and hallucinated masks. The "shes" in it are our relationship. I am the mother most frequently & she too. And we are both daughters standing between the lines. And as children we both put on the shields like Amazons. O Sappho! I want to dance most of the time like a war dance. I always hear coming back to me through many lifetimes, what a life to write of adoring her. Of adoring Her. Now is the chance.

The Muse is always my opposite & opposing sister-singer. She is dark. I am simple. And light. She is not olive, but more like dream-coal. She says she is at the poem's service. To be loved & stripped & goaded & adored. Questioned, berated. She is somewhere to put the verbs the poet bows down to taste these things of. Play & scorn. That's the rub or night & day, the two of us.

Who reaps the joy of Muse in the ultimate sense? She creates the motive to leap in words the love of our female bodies. Is she that hip? The line is drawn between words of dignity & those that do not further the gender cause. Light up. Light up. I am one of those of the *domos* of Sappho surely. And the cry of sister, sister, I know your sandals because I wear them too. Show me your parts. Who is she? The same age, the same build (a little smaller), size 8 or 10. To call her sister was always the call. I lighted on her plan to me as a confidante makes. She was not impressed. Muse won't let the drive run. She conquers me.

The poems & how they'd form were always inside me, far back. I needed her as a vehicle more than any father, rather to do battle. It's light out the window, 2 a.m. Goddesses walk the light sky. They tell me to keep the story up. They instruct a woman who was slumbering these long centuries to meet you.

Muse was a city. Muse was a road. Muse was my 20th century. For me she was a first civilization. Muse has arms like mine. Muse has my eyes, slightly aslant. Muse's wrists grow cold at night as mine do. Muse sweeps her hair to one side. Muse colors her hair with clays of Morroc. Muse's legs are pillars of exactitude & exertion. Muse holds her own torso of immense proportion. Muse was born under a sign of water & fire. Her sister Muse is the Bull-Head-Woman. Muse crawled on her belly once. Muse never humbled herself before the guys. She stole fire back from the father. Muse took the fire and saw herself dancing in there, and the flames were the notes of these songs.

{ANNE WALDMAN, 1990}

Harryette Mullen

Trimmings

Tender Buttons
New York City
1991

Cover Art and Design by Loughran O'Connor

Some *Trimmings* have appeared previously in *Epoch*, *Quarry West*, *Cenzus* and *O / two An Anthology*.

Publication of this book was made possible by a grant from the
Fund for Poetry.

ISBN 0-927920-02-6
Library of Congress Catalogue Number: 91-65496

Thank you: Laynie Browne, Steven Taylor, Valerie Zars,
Greg Masters, Larry Price, NCE, and the Poetry Project.

Distributed by:
Small Press Distribution
1814 San Pablo Avenue
Berkeley, CA, 94702
(510) 549-3336
Booksellers:
1(800) 869-7553

Tender Buttons are
edited and published by
Lee Ann Brown

Tender Buttons
54 East Manning Street #3
Providence, RI
02906

(401) 454-4725

Don't ask me what to wear

--attributed to Sappho

Becoming, for a song. A belt becomes such a small waist. Snakes around her, wrapping. Add waist to any figure, subtract, divide. Accessories multiply a look. Just the thing, a handy belt suggests embrace. Sucks her in. She buckles. Smiles, tighter. Quick to spot a bulge below the belt.

Lips, clasped together. Old leather fastened with a little snap. Strapped, broke. Quick snatch, in a clutch, chased the lady with the alligator purse. Green thief, off relief, got into her pocketbook by hook or crook.

Tender white kid, off-white tan. Snug black leather, second skin. Fits like a love, an utter other uttered. Bag of tricks, slight hand preserved, a dainty. A solid color covers while rubber is protection. Tight is tender, softness cured. Alive and warm, some animal hides. Ghosts wear fingers, delicate wrists.

Starving to muffler moans, boa scarfs her up. Feathers tickle her nose. Kerchief, fichu. Gesundheit.

Her red and white, white and blue banner manner. Her red and white all over black and blue. Hannah's bandanna flagging her down in the kitchen with Dinah, with Jemima. Someone in the kitchen I know.

Brimming over eye shades cool complexion, delicate hue, the lid on, keeps a cool head under high hat.

A little tight, something spiked, tries on a scandal. One of a pair vamps it up with a heel. If the shoe fits, another mule kicking, a fallen, arch angel loses sole support.

Two shapely legs stretch, then run. Sheer magic, a box divided. One saw a woman cut in half, waving incredible feet.

A light white disgraceful sugar looks pink, wears an air, pale compared to shadow standing by. To plump recliner, naked truth lies. Behind her shadow wears her color, arms full of flowers. A rose charm is pink. And she is ink. The mistress wears no petticoat or leaves. The other in shadow, a large, pink dress.

The color 'nude,' a flesh tone. Whose flesh unfolds barely, appealing tan. Shelf life of stacked goods. Body stalking software inventories summer stock. Thin-skinned Godiva with a wig on horseback, body cast in a sit calm.

Garters garnish daughters partner what mothers they gather they tether.

In folds of chaste petticoats, chupamirtos. In a red sack with a silk ribbon, hummingbird, whose tongue is sweet. Charm for love, a captive beat, a flutter. Hidden under ruffles, secret heart, a red pouch tied with silk.

A rich match fits a couple of gilded calves. Silk stockings glide up fine-tuned, high-toned thighs. Blue-vein stock requires noblessing, sitting pretty in lap de luxe.

Bare skin almost, underworn. Warm stiched-together soft torn toy. Stuffed and laced voluptuous imaginary mammal made of lovely lumps. Dear plump-cheeked plaything taken to bed and hugged in the dark.

Releases from valises. Scientific briefs. Chemists model molecular shadows structure mimic dancers. Shirt on the line, a flapper's shimmy shake in a silk chemise. A shift, a woman's movement, a loose garment of man-made fabric. Polly and Esther living modern with better chemistry.

Of a girl, in white, between the lines, in the spaces where nothing is written. Her starched petticoats, giving him the slip. Loose lips, a telltale spot, where she was kissed, and told. Who would believe her, lying still between the sheets. The pillow cases, the dirty laundry laundered. Pillow talk-show on a leather couch, slips in and out of dreams. Without permission, slips out the door. A name adores a Freudian slip.

Night moon star sun down gown.
Night moan stir sin dawn gown.

Dress shields, armed guard at breastwork, a hard mail covering. Brazen privates, testing their mettle. Bolder soldiers make advances, breasting hills. Whose armor is brassier.

Mistress in undress, filmy peignoir. Feme solo in camisole. Bit part, petite cliche. Degage ladies lingering, careless of appurtenances. Longing pajamas, custom worn to disrobe. Froufrou negligee, rustling silk, or cattle. Negligent in ladies' lingerie, a dressy dressing down.

Girt, a good old girl got hipped. They thrive with wives, broad beams. Most worthy girth, providing firm. Foundations in midriff. Across (between) girdled loins, tender girders. Gartered, perhaps, struts. Stretching, a snap crotch.

Some panties are plenty. Some are scanty. Some or any. Some is ante.

Tiny binary aftermath figure. Navel baste playmates with ultimate breeder of nuclear families. Suburban bombshell shelters magazines of big guns aiming to sell inny things or nothing at all.

Step into gathered floral. Sashay and flounce out. At length, skirt's sweep, her furbelow. Or slit, tight. Gored, wrapped, young shirttail tucked. Cowgirl, hips suede. Leather fringe skirts, a border. A stiff, fine crinoline. Straight seams, hemmed, or binding. Warm hands, felt skirt. An issue of blood, she pleated.

Mum, dissembling girl, resembling cartoon mouse. Scantness forces a stand, she cannot bend.

Heartsleeve's dart bleeds whiter white, softened with wear. Among blowzy buxom bosomed, give us this— blowing, blissful, open. O most immaculate bleached blahs, bless any starched, loosening blossom.

Menswear, the britches. Rosie flies off the handle. Jeans so tight, she pants. Wants to cool out, slacks off.

Of what material softness folds to hold her, under when over, inside or out, where air is, makes a difference in motion, living here—or walking. Taking off, putting on her flimsy garment. Holes breathe, and swallow. Openings, hem, sleeve. Borders on edges where skin stops, or begins. Fancy trim. Sew buttons on, but they are slow to open flowers—imagine the color. Loose skirt, a petal, a pocket for your hand. My dress falls over my head. A shadow overtakes me.

When a dress is red, is there a happy ending. Is there murmur and satisfaction. Silence or a warning. It talks the talk, but who can walk the walk. Distress is red. It sells, shouts, an urge turned inside out. Sight for sore eyes. The better to see you. Out for a stroll, writing wolf-tickets.

Girl, pinked, beribboned. Alternate virgin at first blush. Starched petticoat besmirched. Stiff with blood. A little worse for wear.

The bride wore white. Posed in modest bodice a la mode. Cake with sugar rosebuds and white frosting. Everyone gets a piece. Off color-jokes, borrowed and blue. Her blush, tip of the iceberg, froze in layers of lace, in a photograph of her smile.

Cold feet, darned socks. Mismatched pair, the black sock and the blue sock. Male color blindness. A girl's thin ankles.

What's holding her up. Straps, laces. Garters, corsets, belts with laces. What's holding them up. If not straps then laces. Buttons and bows, ribbons and laces set off their faces. Girls in white sat in with blues-saddened slashers. Laced up, frilled to the bone. Semi-automatic ruffle on a semi-formal gown.

Her feathers, her pages. She ripples in breezes. Rim and fringe are hers. Who fancies frills. Whose finery in a summer frock, light in the wind, riffling her pages, lifting her skirt, peeking at the edges. The wind blows her words away. Who can hear her voice, so soft, every ruffle made smooth. Gathering her fluttered pages, her feathers, her wings.

Clip, screw or pierce. Take your pick. Friend or doctor, needle or gun. A dab of alcohol pats that little hurt hole. Hardly a dimple is soon forgotten brief sting. Stud, precious metal. Pure, possessive ring. Antibody testifying with immunity to gold, rare thing. So malleable and lovable, wearing such wounds, such ornaments.

Body on fire, spangles. Light to sequin stars burn out at both ends.

Cinderella highball cocktail frock. Plastered, shellacked, and laminated. Blind drunk hobbled home in a lame dress.

Bones knit. Skins pink, flush tight. White margin, ample fleshings. Out of character, full blush. Flushed out of hidden, pink in the flesh.

Gold chains, choker, ring her neck. Draw a bead, string it. Precious jewel, locket. Real pearl handles it, lacy-necked in the black. What rankles, she fakes it. Less than naked, strung out, stranded.

Akimbo bimbos, all a jangle. Tricket out trinkets, aloud galore. Gimcracks, a stack. Bang and a whimper. Two to tangle. It's a jungle.

In feathers, in bananas, in her own skin, intelligent body attached
to a gaze. Stripped down model, posing for a savage art, brought
color to a primitive stage.

Harmless amulets arm little limbs with poise and charm.

Chichi busy bodice with fancywork got filigreed and gold. Then
plumed themselves in fancy dress and knit their brows to clothe
the naked.

Punched in like slopwork. Mild frump and downward drab. Slipshod drudge with chance of dingy morning slog. Tattered shoulders, frayed eyes, a dowdy gray. Frowzy in a slatternly direction.

Duds, garbled garb. Misfits, women in breaches. Early bloomers or bluestockings, whose blue worsted wicked black dress, or a white none inhabits. Unholy Magdalene with her veil of tears.

Mohair, less nape to crown fluffed pillow. Fuzzyhead, down for a nap. Soft stuff of dreams in which she fluffs it.

Animal pelts, little minks, skins, tail. Fur flies, Pet smitten, smooth beaver strokes. Muff, soft, 'like rabbits.' Fine fox stole, furtive hiding. Down the road a pretty fur piece.

Opens up a little leg, some slender, high exposure. Splits a chic sheath, tight slit. Buy another peek experience, price is slashed. Where tart knife, scoring, minced a sluttish strut. Laughing splits the seams. Teeth in a gash, letting off steam.

Swan neck, white shoulders, lumps of fat. A woman's face above it all. Unriddled sphinx, 'without secrets.' Alabaster bust, paled into significance. Clothes opening, revealing dress, as French comes into English. Suggestively, a cleavage in language.

Decorative strap. A rib, on loan. Fine fabric, finished at edges. Fit for tying or trimming. Narrow band, satin, a velvet strip. A ribbon wound around her waist. A glancing bow. Red ribbon woven through her, blue-ribbon blonde. For valor, a shred of dignity. A dress torn to ribbons.

For frills, fancy crimps and shaves. Cuts curls, frail frounce. Smiles, curtsies, now only of women flexing a fondness. Plain as a bored steaming a wrinkle, takes out the starch. Frilled up to here, she starts sleeking. Flat, flatter, flatterer.

Gaudy gawks at baubles fondle tawdry laces up in garish gear, a form of being content.

Chaste, apprehended, collared and cuffed. Kept under wraps, as bridal veils visually haze precious, easily torn, gauzy romantic tissues. Thin threads lace into delicate, expensive fabrics woven and unwoven at night by patient spinsters with needles and scissors. Laced in, as fate would have it. Knots and the tiniest holes. Surgical cutting and sewing. Peeking as usual. Skin under lace. A thread, a net effect, a web to sleep in. A white nightgown, girl, child, baby laced and unlaced. A ruffle, a frill. A pale piece of something, almost made of air.

Rapt babes in peekaboo webs. Preying widows, spiders in black weeds. Smouldering glance in a drop-dead dress. Witches burning at high stakes. Blackened virgins, selling the sizzle.

Hand in glove hankers, waves a white flag. Hand to mouth surrenders, flirts with hanky-panky.

Low impact, lateral moves. No new wrinkles favor grace to last past shoe chat. Old sneakers jog their memories. Cool heels, odd hours in the park. Whistling dogs and cars exhaust. Stopped in her tracks, that doffed hat knocks her socks off.

Shades, cool dark lasses. Ghost of a smile.

A fish caught, pretty fish wiggles for a while. A caught fish squirms. A freshly licked fish sighs. Gapes with holes for eyes. A wiggling fish flashes its display. A pattern over whiteness. Bareness comes with coverage for peeking through holes to see flesh out of water. Cold holes where eyes go. The sea is cold. Her body of foam, some frothy Venus. Or strayed mermaid, tail split, bleeds into the sea. With brand new feet walks unsteady on land, each step an ache.

What a little moonlight inside her pink silvery is softness condensing a glaze to repair a blister. Itches sit and silken, growing dearer to the wearer. Who would wear a necklace of tears. Inside her moonlight lining, tears were shed. Smooth tears, bitter water, a salted wound produced a pearl. A mother's luster manufactured a colored other. Pearl had a mother who cried.

Her ribbon, her slender is ribbon when to occupy her hands a purse is soft. Wondering where to hang the keys the moon is manicured. Her paper parasol and open fan become her multiplication of a rib which is connected and might start a fire for cooking. Who desires crisp vegetables, she opens for the climate. A tomato isn't hard. It splits in heat, easy. It's seasonal. Once in a while there is heat, and several flowers are perennials. Roses shining with green-gold leaves and bright threads. Some threads do wilt after starching. She has done the starching and the bleaching. She has pink too and owns earrings. Would never be shamed by pearls. A subtle blush communicates much. White peeks out, an eyelet in a storm.

Thinking thought to be a body wearing language as clothing or language a body of thought which is a soul or body the clothing of a soul, she is veiled in silence. A veiled, unavailable body makes an available space.

Off the Top

Trimmings was for me a way to think about women and language. I don't think there is necessarily any "feminine language" except in the sense that there is feminine clothing. I suppose in both cases we mean an arbitrary set of signs or mannerisms we conventionally associate with "woman." Then also I was interested in the sense of those qualities we regard as feminine. Gender is a set of signs which we tend to forget are arbitrary. In these prose poems I thought about language as clothing and clothing as language, wondering especially why writing by women has been as ephemeral as fashion.

Other concerns were the use of women as aesthetic objects in art and literature, the use of women's bodies in advertising and pornography, the use Freud made of "hysteria" of his women patients. Trimmings proceeds metonymically and associatively, from women's clothing to women's bodies; from a word to another word, linked by association—since women are also called skirts, petticoats, fluff, trim. Words like pink and slit are equally at home in the sewing catalog or the girly magazine.

The words pink and white kept appearing as I explored the ways that the English language conventionally represents femininity. As a black woman writing in this language, I suppose I already had an ironic relationship to this pink and white femininity. Of course if I regard gender as a set of arbitrary signs, I also think of race—as far as it is a difference that is meaningful—as a set of signs. Traces of black dialect and syntax, blues songs and other culturally specific allusions enter the text from the linguistic contributions of Afro-Americans to the English language.

{Harryette Mullen, 1991}

Agnes Lee Dunlop Wiley

Agnes Lee

New York/Providence
Tender Buttons
1992

To Steve —
Fellow
Book Maker

350 copies were printed at Crane Duplicating in West Barnstable, MA.
Type is 11 point Palatino.

Best,

produced by
Tender Buttons
Box 1290, Cooper Station
NYC   10276

Production Collective : Dora Lee Brown, Bob Brown, Beth Brown,
Lee Ann Brown, Steven Taylor, Lisa Jarnot.

Thank you: Patty & Lanny.

ISBN 0-927920-06-9

To my daughter, Dora Lee

How This Book Has Been Created

As early as the nineteen twenties, I started making lists of "Things I'd Like To Do Again." A phrase or sentence brought back wonderful memories to me. My children and grandchildren have always urged me to tell them about my experiences growing up in the West.

In 1987, when I moved to Southminster, a retirement community, I decided to enroll in a class entitled, "Recalling Memories."

The instructor, Margaret Bigger, inspired me to think of topics in my own life about which I could write. She really made me grow, giving me writing assignments in class and for homework. I was fascinated to hear the variety of stories shared by other members of the class. When the six week course was over, Margaret encouraged me to keep writing.

My greatest moments of inspiration sometimes came in the middle of the night. I turned on my light at one or two o'clock in the morning and dashed off a sentence or two. From time to time I lacked inspiration. Once when I was discussing my writings with my daughter on the telephone, she suggested that I write about my experiences of teaching an American Indian child in Oklahoma. Then she gave an Indian war whoop on the phone! That was the inspiration I needed.

I express thanks to my family members for assisting in the production of this book, transferring my handwritten script to this computerized print copy. Since each chapter is complete in itself, my book is not arranged in totally chronological order.

I would like to have mentioned the names of all the people who have meant so much to me through the years; however, if I had included that list, this book would have been too heavy to lift!

I want to encourage my friends to write about their memories. So many exciting stories are waiting to be shared!

{AGNES LEE DUNLOP WILEY, 1992}

MATTHEW DUNLOP, MY PATERNAL GRANDFATHER: "A SCOT"

Matthew Dunlop was born in Kilmarnock, Scotland, in 1839. He and a friend from London came to the United States; they both wanted to escape "the plague." Neither ever returned to their native lands.

My grandfather brought three books from Scotland which he treasured all of his life, and which I still treasure. They are a Bible and two volumes of Robert Burns. The Burns poetry books were printed by Blackie and Son, South College St., Edinburgh, Scotland in 1855 and include beautiful steel engraved etchings. Twenty-five of the poems are dedicated to a Mrs. Dunlop.

When my grandfather came to the United States, he settled in Kansas City, MO. He was a stone cutter by trade and was proud of the work he did. Perhaps some of the buildings in Kansas City still bear his mark.

Matthew Dunlop married Marcie Thomas who grew up on a farm near Carrollton, Missouri. They had three children; Agnes Lee Dunlop who married Frank Duval Lucas, Dudley Thomas Dunlop (my father) who married Dora Woolfolk Draper, and Harry Parker Dunlop, "Uncle Hal," who married Evelyn Kramm.

While living in Kansas City, Matthew Dunlop joined the Caledonian Society to keep in touch with his homeland. There he met a young Scot artist who wanted to become a portrait painter. Grandfather helped him go to Paris to study and when he returned, he painted my grandfather's portrait to show his appreciation. The artist's name was J.P. Patrick. Some of his works are hanging in The Nelson Museum in Kansas City, Missouri. Being the oldest son in the family, my father inherited the portrait of his father, and when he came to Oklahoma, he carried it with him on the train. It had a very ornate frame and as he got off the Rock Island Railroad, wearing a derby hat, carrying the portrait, some of the townspeople admired the frame. This made my father furious. He wanted them to comment on his handsome father!

When I went to Europe with the Student Travel Club in 1929, I was so eager to visit Scotland! When I arrived in Edinburgh, I contacted my cousins who invited me to their home for the evening. While my friends went sightseeing, I had the exciting unforgettable experience of getting acquainted with my Scottish roots.

My great-grandparents, Agnes Lee and Matthew Dunlop, Kilmarnack, Scotland.

Left: My grandfather, Matthew Dunlop, (standing), and a friend. They left Scotland to escape the bubonic plague. *Right:* Annie Bain.

THE OKLAHOMA LAND RUSH

The only member in my family to participate in the Oklahoma Land Rush was my great Aunt Gen's husband, Charlie Underwood. Shortly after their marriage they heard that 160 acres of land would be available for anyone staking a claim. At the shot of a gun at noon on September 19th, 1893, the signal was given for the "Land Rush" to begin. Uncle Charlie had to ride a long way! Finally he staked his claim near the Red River which was almost to the Texas border; this location is south of Lawton, Oklahoma, close to the present location of Randelette. At first they lived in a tent until he built a small frame house and a cellar. Then my Uncle Charlie, Aunt Gen and their adopted son, Raymond, began their new life on the frontier. To raise cotton on that hot and dry land wasn't easy. I imagine at times they longed for the fertile lands with cherry trees and garden plots in Missouri.

IDA CHUNN — MY MATERNAL GRANDMOTHER: "LITTLE GADA"

My grandmother, Ida Chunn, began her pioneer ventures to the West, not in the usual manner of a covered wagon, but on a steamboat. She was born in Paducah, Kentucky in 1858, later moving with her parents to Carrollton, Missouri. At 19, she married Charles P. Woolfolk, who was captain of "The Nellie Peck" — a stern-wheel, freight-carrying steamboat. It plied the Missouri and Yellowstone Rivers, carrying supplies for settlers and ties for the new Northern Pacific Railroad as far as Billings, Montana.

She took great delight in learning how to pilot the boat and ring the signal bells. The boat made about fifty miles a day. I remember my grandmother telling me about the day she saw a herd of over a hundred shaggy buffalos coming down the bank to swim across the river. Suddenly they all stopped at the water's edge; then the whole herd rushed along the bank to get ahead of the boat. Finally they plunged into the river. They hadn't liked being headed off by the boat.

My grandmother went back to Carrollton, Missouri, for the birth of my mother. On October 2nd, 1881, Dora was born and when she was only three months old, her parents took her on the "F. Y. Batchler" another steamboat, carrying supplies and passengers who were trappers, gold prospectors and carpenters.

Possessing a pioneering spirit of adventure, my grandmother purchased 160 acres at 50 cents an acre along the Yellowstone River on the site of old Fort Pease in Montana that had been burned down by the Indians. Her first house was a log cabin chinked with mud that had a sod roof. Later, this substantially built structure was used as an icehouse, filled with ice cut from the white cloth and painted with calcimine. The floors in the dining room and kitchen were of white pine that my grandmother always kept scoured. For recreation at Christmas time, my grandmother let the cowboys put on roller skates and skate around the dining room table. Behind the kitchen was a cellar with the roof sloping all the way to the ground. Every spring, my grandmother replanted the sod roof. When I visited the ranch as a child, I remember a pet goat who liked to follow me up the slanted side of this house so he could eat the tender grass growing on top.

Ida divorced Charles Woolfolk and later married M.I. Draper, a cowboy who drove cattle on the Chisholm Trail from Texas to Montana. As children we called her "Little Gada" and our name for him was "Big Gada."

On our many family trips to visit them I remember all the good things she made. My grandmother's garden where she grew everything imaginable, included raspberries, goose berries, currents, rhubarb and strawberries. In the cellar, shelves lined the walls where she kept jars of jams, vegetables and fruits. Sand on the cellar floor made a perfect storage spot for carrots, parsnips, potatoes and beets. She dried corn in the sun, enough for many months. She had chicken, lamb, beef and pork. They made their own sausage. My favorites of the things she made were her transparent pie, pineapple sherbert, and best of all, her homemade bread, cinnamon rolls and "stickies." The warm bread with freshly churned butter and buffalo berry jam was delicious. The aroma of her bread baking in the wood stove attracted a crowd of Indians who would wait patiently outside the door. Perhaps her generosity in sharing her bread contributed to her good relationship with the Sioux Indians who lived in the area.

My grandmother was a strong pioneering woman! With the help of her "doctor book," she took care of the sick in the community and delivered many babies. She worked very hard until the last few years of her life. The only time she had help in the kitchen and with the housekeeping was during the two years that she and "Big Gada" spent in Cuba and the six months they rented a plantation house in Louisiana. (See *Louisiana Interlude.*) When they were in their eighties, they spent a few months in Norman, Oklahoma with my mother. Apartment living did not appeal to them. They returned to Billings, Montana, and lived in a hotel in the city near the ranch land that they so dearly loved.

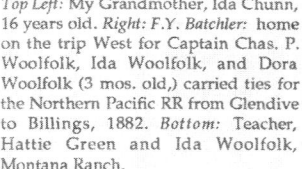

Top Left: My Grandmother, Ida Chunn, 16 years old. *Right: F.Y. Batchler:* home on the trip West for Captain Chas. P. Woolfolk, Ida Woolfolk, and Dora Woolfolk (3 mos. old,) carried ties for the Northern Pacific RR from Glendive to Billings, 1882. *Bottom:* Teacher, Hattie Green and Ida Woolfolk, Montana Ranch.

DORA — "DODE" — "DODO"

My mother was a very special person! She had a very long name: Dora Evans Margaret Agnes Woolfolk Draper Dunlop. She was nick-named "Dode" when she was young and affectionately called "Dodo" by her grandchildren and friends through her 96th year of life.

My mother, Dora, was born on October 2nd, 1881, in Carrollton, Missouri. When she was only three months old, her parents took her on the F. Y. Bachelor, a steamship which carried crossties for the Northern Pacific Railroad.

She told me about her first school which was a one room log cabin. One day the chief of the Crow Indians, Chief Big Ox, came to visit the school and sat on a long bench near her. She was so scared that she slipped out of school and crawled all the way home on her hands and knees through the tall sagebrush. Months later when Big Ox came to visit at her home, my mother realized he was quite peaceful and enjoyed talking to him.

Music was very important in my mother's life! When she was five years old, an Italian violinist taught her to play chords on the piano to accompany him at community dances. A Dutch musician urged my grandmother to buy a piano. Lottie Cox, a boarder, gave Dora music lessons, insisting that she practice several hours a day. When my mother was 16, she took piano lessons from the Mother Superior at a convent in Fort Leavenworth, Kansas. I liked to hear my mother tell about the Crow Indians coming to their ranch and asking to play the piano. One Indian offered her father thirty-five horses for her and the piano. I'm glad he turned the Indian down! Throughout my childhood I remember my mother playing the piano for Sunday School and church and for her own enjoyment. Music was so important to her that she gave our family a piano as a welcome home present when our son was born.

My mother handed down to me her love of horses. She told me that when she began riding as a child, she taught her horse, "Jack," to kneel down so she could climb on his back. On the ranch she would take the cows out to pasture in the morning and go back to get them in the evening; as she rode "Jack" she often passed herds of white tailed deer and antelope. I asked my mother to tell and retell about her longest ride. Her school teacher, Bessie Grierson, invited my mother to ride with her to a dance at an adjoining ranch. They rode 40 miles, using their sidesaddles, danced all night, then got on their horses and rode 40 miles back home. When she was visiting her grandfather in Carrollton, MO, in her early twenties, she met a young man who was riding a fancy Kentucky thoroughbred. This young man was Dudley Thomas Dunlop who later asked her to become his wife. After I was born, my mother would saddle up her horse, have a neighbor hand me up to her and away we would ride. I remember she rode horseback dressed in her white riding habit. Many years later, when my mother came to Charlotte, NC, to live with me, she brought her sidesaddle and now I have it in my storage closet at Southminster.

Because my father was a graduate of the University of Missouri in 1900, my mother felt a little inferior intellectually, but she continued to educate herself as long as she lived. Always she was an avid newspaper reader of the *Kansas City Star* and kept scrapbooks of current events. After my father's death, she moved to Norman where she owned some apartments adjoining the University of Oklahoma campus. Some of her tenants included faculty members of the art department. She treasured paintings given to her by Kate Kritser and the Jacobsons. Ruth Fell, a professor in the Business Department, lived with her husband and daughter in one of the apartments; years later she attended some university classes and enjoyed belonging to "The University Dames," a literary group made up of many professors' wives. She celebrated football weekends by inviting friends to her apartment for sandwiches after the games.

When my mother was 80 years old, she moved from Oklahoma to live with me in Charlotte, NC. She had a room built on my house. When we celebrated her 95th birthday, we displayed a number of her favorite things including Indian artifacts, hand-embroidered linens which she had done, as well as dresses she had carefully saved through the years.

Growing Up

CISTERNS

My daughter, Dora Lee, accuses me of not knowing *how* to spend money. It's true; but, I do enjoy saving it. My tax advisor, Peggy Jessup, advises me to buy a red convertible and really enjoy life! I could blame my grandfather, Matthew Dunlop, for my saving habit, because Scotsmen are noted for their thriftiness. I'd rather be like my father who said he didn't mind spending money if he felt he was getting his money's worth.

I taught school two years and saved my money. Still I had to borrow a thousand dollars from my father in order to go to Europe with the "Student Travel Club" in 1929. For two months I visited England, Scotland, France, Italy, Switzerland and Germany. That money was well spent; the memories have lasted a lifetime!

I could blame my habit of saving on "The Depression" when we *had* to save. To this day I can't resist saving peanut butter jars to use at Christmas as gifts, when I fill them with Aunt Will's famous recipe for orange marmalade.

Being raised in the pioneer days in Oklahoma, I think it is logical to blame my habit of saving on *cisterns*. Almost every home had a rain barrel or a cistern. It was a large underground cement container where rainwater was collected. In the spring, we had torrential rains. After all the dust was washed off the roof, the rainwater was converted through a container filled with charcoal, then channeled into the cistern.

I guess I'll continue to save as long as I live, now that I know I can blame my habit on CISTERNS.

BANANAS

When I was quite young, I'll never forget the day I went to Mr. Geis' grocery store and asked him to give me a dozen bananas. "Please charge them to my father, Mr. Dunlop," I said. Now a dozen bananas was quite a load for a little girl to carry ten blocks, so I proceeded to eat two bananas along the way.

That day my father had come home for an early lunch. When he saw me he said, "What is this?" I proudly opened the bag to show him my ten bananas.

My father proceeded to make me understand that I must never

again charge anything to anyone else until I had money of my own.

Today almost everyone has a VISA card. It is so easy to charge everything and pay for it later; however, I do not like to use my card often. I think of bananas.

RAINY MOUNTAIN

If I had lived in Komalty or Gotebo, Oklahoma and been a member of the Kiowa Tribe, if I had been Hattie Say Tay Pa Hoodle, I would have joined my family one hot summer day and climbed Rainy Mountain to pray for the end of the drought.

Many of my friends in the tribe, old and young, would have joined me. Perhaps we would have spent the whole night there praying for rain, rain to save our crops, our corn and to give relief from the scorching sun.

Rainy Mountain isn't really a mountain, but it's a small hill rising out of the prairie. I have climbed it many times myself as a child. I have been fascinated with the view of red brick government buildings where Indian children attended school during the winter months there at the foot of Rainy Mountain. Madge and Don White invited me to an exhibit at the Charlotte Public Library of American Indian Photography; one section included scenes from Rainy Mountain.

In the spring I loved to climb Rainy Mountain and see the many white tents and watch the Indian families who were encamped there to receive their allotments from the government.

I remember one day I went down the mountain to mingle among the tents and watched my father buy old moccasins from the children who wanted new moccasins just as we wanted new shoes every spring. Their moccasins were beaded and beautiful but worn. One time my father got a beautiful war bonnet which he kept for several months at the bank. He loaned money to the Indians and when they paid most of the debt, they could redeem the article. One time he took the war bonnet to North Carolina to show his good friend, Gus McLean, and others in Lenoir, NC.

My father had a good relationship with Indians. We had a peacock and peafowl at one time. The Indians would come to our yard and wait until they could pick up a feather. They were amused at the queer sounds the peacock made and the fan-like tail spread.

Above: Uncle Hal Dunlop with Chief Gotebo and wife and daughter in Gotebo, Oklahoma. *Right:* Chief Geronomo, 1915. I met him at Fort Sill, Oklahoma when I was a little girl.

VACATIONS

My love of travel must have been inherited, and I am glad I passed it on to my children and grandchildren. My father enjoyed travel so much that he wanted his whole family to experience the thrill of new friends and new places. Some of my earliest recollections were of our trips to Montana to visit my grandparents.

In 1915 our family planned a big western trip to California. When the Oklahoma license plate failed to arrive before we were ready to leave, my father made up a number and painted his own.

The four of us plus our undershot jawed English bulldog, Pat, started out in early June. Cots were strapped to each back fender with other necessary equipment inside. Often we camped near a lake or mountain stream where Mark and I would enjoy a swim with our dog.

At Clovis, New Mexico, we watched sheep being sheared. We were most fascinated with the Hopi Indians and their adobe houses which were several stories high. In the Petrified Forest, we picked up small slices of rock before it was against the law. At Col. Goodnight's ranch in Texas, we stopped to see buffaloes. Of course we were overwhelmed with the expanse and beauty of the Grand Canyon. I remember the lovely Le Travor Hotel on the rim of the canyon and the Bright Angel Trail. It was there that we saw a prince from India and his entourage. They asked to buy our dog, but we refused their offer. When we reached the Mohave desert, we waited until night to travel because of the intense heat during the day.

In California we enjoyed Coronada Beach and the San Diego Fair. With friends from Missouri whom we met at Long Beach, we all took a boat to Catalina Island where we saw flying fish for the first time. My father took pictures of us at San Gabriel Mission, in an orange grove and in the redwood forest. Because the road was so narrow along the Pacific coast and because my mother didn't like high places, my father sent the three of us by train, while he drove the Model T over the pass with our bulldog. We all drove into Canada to meet my father's good friend, Castle Moss, who built bridges in New York and Canada.

We came back by way of Montana to tell my grandparents of our never to be forgotten trip!

THE LUCAS FAMILY

My parents named me for my father's sister, Agnes Lee Dunlop, who grew up in Kansas City, Missouri. After her mother's death, she kept house for her father and two brothers, Dudley and Harry. Later she married Frank Duval Lucas. They moved to Oklahoma about the time it became our 46th state. My father and Uncle Frank opened a bank in the little town of Gotebo.

Living next door to the Lucas family made a great impression on me. Auntie was an immaculate housekeeper. She kept a dust pan and stiff brush available to all children who brought in mud or dirt. We knew we had to clean the floor at once. She would often remind us.

Their house was an exciting place to visit. The high plate rail in the dining room held German beer steins and unusual plates which they had collected. In Auntie's bedroom a huge fishnet hung on the wall in which she put pictures, especially of relatives of Scottish ancestry whom she had visited. She told us of the time when visiting cousins in Edinburgh that she did not eat all the butter she had put on her plate. The next day she did not get any!

When Jean, their only child was a year old, her parents took her to Hawaii to visit Auntie's cousin, Florence, and her husband, Dr. Harry Cooper, who was a physician on a pineapple plantation. When Jean was two, they went to Mexico to visit her father's relatives. Jean went to Mary Baldwin College for her first two years then transferred to the University of Hawaii for her junior year.

After Jean's graduation from the University of Oklahoma, she married Tom Moran. They had two sons, Mike and Frank. Tom had a career with the National Park Service. The family lived in Sante Fe, New Mexico, where my family visited many times. They guided our tours of Taos, Bandelier National Monument, an Indian cliff dwelling and to many other points of interest.

Tom was later transferred to Philadelphia where he supervised the activities at Independence Hall. When my husband had heart surgery in Philadelphia, Dora Lee and John Dudley stayed at the Moran home in nearby Broomall, PA. Later Jean and Tom went back to live in Sante Fe, NM, where they bought a home built in the Spanish style.

My family has always been very close to these relatives. I remember so well the summer when I was a freshman in high school that Auntie invited my good friend, Sybil Baum, and me to go with her and Jean to their favorite summer vacation spot, the Mission House on the Chautauqua grounds in Boulder, CO. My parents planned to pick me up later on their way to Montana.

Our train was late arriving in Denver on July 3rd. Auntie, who had all of her ribs broken on one side, was exhausted and decided to wait to go to Boulder until the next day. With all our luggage we arrived by taxi at the famous and luxurious Brown Palace Hotel. When Auntie asked for a room, the clerk said nothing was available because of a convention in the city. She told him that she had broken ribs and three children with her. She had always stayed at the Brown Palace. She had to have a room! Soon a bellboy took us to a suite on the top floor which had long tables for salesmen to show their wares. We discovered two double beds and a big bathroom with huge towels. We asked Auntie why the towels were so large. She said that probably when the salesmen drank too much, they wrapped themselves in them to dry themselves out. I'm sure she thought three giggly girls should "dry up and go to sleep."

MY TEENAGE YEARS

My junior year in high school proved to be one of the most miserable and exciting years of my life. I entered Mary Baldwin Seminary in Staunton, Virginia, in 1920.

Leaving Gotebo, a small southwestern town in Oklahoma, was not easy. I knew everyone in town. About a week before I left home, I received a letter from the Seminary telling me it was important to have my tonsils removed. My friend, May Butterfield decided she needed hers out too, so my father drove both of us to Oklahoma City, which was a hundred miles away. He persuaded the doctor to come to The Skirvin Hotel to operate on both of us there.

A day or two later my father and I left by train for North Carolina and Virginia. We visited our former pastor and his wife in Lenoir, North Carolina. All that time my throat was raw and throbbing, and I was already homesick for my mother and brother.

In Staunton I discovered my roommate from Texas had not arrived. I was in the dormitory called "Hill Top" all alone for a week. I was very homesick and lonesome. If I got a letter from home, I cried, and if I did *not* receive one, I cried. When my Texas roommate finally arrived, I discovered she was an excellent tennis player and we did not even have a tennis court in Gotebo. We had little in common. She soon let me know she wanted to move. Mariana P. Higgins, our principal, told me to move to a new dormitory, second floor, "McClung." There I had two roommates, Marion Daniles, from Charlottesville, Virginia, and Mary Elizabeth Zimmerman from Romney, West Virginia. It was a perfect combination. We became life-long friends.

Soon I was deeply involved in my new studies. I practically lived in the library. That first year I had Latin, chemistry, English, and French. Our teachers were excellent. Miss Fannie Strauss, my Latin teacher, scared me. Her voice was harsh and deep. She wore a wide black sweat band around her hair and looked so stern, not only in class, but all the time. I felt very dumb before one who had so much knowledge.

I remember my chemistry teacher was so tiny in stature, not much taller than I. One day, as I was hurrying to lab class, I almost knocked her down, which of course, was most embarrassing.

When we sat at the table of the French teacher, who had lived in Paris, we were required to speak French. My conversation was very limited and I ate little all day. I was overwhelmed by the lovely aristocratic city of Staunton, Viriginia. The trees were beautiful around three schools: Mary Baldwin, Fairfax Hall, and Staunton Military Academy. Staunton was also the home of Woodrow Wilson and has many large churches.

I, of course, was interested in boys in Oklahoma, but the closest I got to any in Staunton was in the First Presbyterian Church, across the street from Mary Baldwin College. The cadets from the Academy sat in the balcony, all handsome in their grey uniforms and brass buttons. We, in our black suits and unbecoming grey felt hats, pulled out mirrors from our purses to look at them from afar. It was tough to leave home and loved ones and familiar things, but I have since thought that during that first year in Virginia I learned many things that have helped me later in life.

OKLAHOMA UNIVERSITY

Undoubtedly I was fortunate to attend the University of Oklahoma in the 1920s. At that time the student body had reached about five thousand; we knew so many of our classmates, their home towns and where they lived on campus. Students were not allowed cars. Drugs were unheard of. Alcohol was not much of a problem; since the state was legally dry, liquor was hard to get.

Since my father had belonged to the Phi Delta Theta Fraternity at the University of Missouri where he graduated in 1900, he wanted me to join a sorority to enjoy social life. O.U. "Rush Week" occurred just before the opening of school in the fall. I pledged Delta Gamma and enjoy living in the "D.G. House" which was a stone's throw from the entrance of the university. My housemother, Mrs. Taliferro, kept a close eye on all our sorority members.

Much interest was shown in athletics, social life and campus politics. I remember people like Mike Monrony, who later made a name for himself in politics. Royce Savage and Ernest Sharp, both Phi Delts, became attorneys. Lynn Riggs later became famous when he wrote a play, "Green Grow the Lilacs," which eventually became the musical, "OKLAHOMA!" My grandmother's daughter, Elien, became engaged to Lynn Riggs. That was the big romance of the campus!

We liked our president, Dr. Bizzell. He was a good administrator and had the ability to get what the University needed from the Oklahoma State Legislature. O.U. was noted for its excellent schools in petroleum engineering, law and journalism. Most of the students were serious about getting an education, many working their way through school.

The "Sooner" football team in those days was coached by Bennie Owen. His assistant, Ed Meacham, was also a math professor. Early one week, Bennie Owen lost an arm during a quail hunt on the Canadian River near Norman, OK; he coached from the side-lines the following Saturday.

The university town of Norman was quite countrified then. Life was simple since there were few distractions. It was a thrill to have a date who would take you to the Varsity Shop or Copper Kettle for a 5¢ Coke or a bowl of chili, a piece of pie, or occasionally a whole meal. The movies were a quarter, but I don't remember going to many. We looked forward to fraternity dances. After going to a girls' school for three years, Oklahoma University seemed wonderful to me and I was nearer home.

MY TEACHING YEARS

After receiving my BA degree from the University of Oklahoma in 1926, I obtained a teacher's certificate from North Carolina.

My first year was in a small country school—Oak Hill, near Lenoir. My roommate, Jane Craddock, and I lived in a "Teacherage." She was a recent graduate of Trinity College, later known as Duke University. It was a wonderful place to learn to teach and to dream. That year we decided to save enough money for a trip to Europe. It took us three years. Our salaries were only a hundred dollars a month, even then we had to borrow money from our fathers.

It was also the year my pupils taught me more than I taught them. They wanted to know about the West, cowboys and Indians. They taught me about trailing arbutus, galax leaves, birds and other beautiful things of nature.

Jane and I enjoyed an elderly couple, "Aunt Lou" and "Uncle Lum," who lived over the hill near the Teacherage. We walked to their home through the woods, past a cool spring where they kept their milk, butter and cream. They invited us to help them crack black walnuts for Thanksgiving.

On Saturdays we would walk a couple of miles to a country store, the neighborhood gathering place. There we met some of the parents of our pupils.

I'll always remember one night we went to an old fashioned corn husking party where everyone in the community helped a farmer and his son husk a huge pile of corn. The ladies had prepared a feast. All evening the young men kept looking for a red ear of corn which they claimed gave them the right to kiss all the teachers. We were afraid they *would* find one.

The second year, Jane and I taught in the city schools of Lenoir. It was a town full of furniture factories, churches and aristocratic families. Our social life was quite different that year. We attended many school festivities. Lenoir was famous for its excellent band led by Mr. Harper. We even attended football games at Davidson College. One weekend my Mary Baldwin College roommate from West Virginia met me there. That year, both of us had brothers attending Davidson. It was a thrill to hear Louis Armstrong, their special guest for the weekend. Another special treat that year was visiting Uncle Gus and Aunt Hallie McLean and their seven children. Uncle Gus had been my pastor when I was a child in Gotebo, Oklahoma, and Aunt Hallie was my music teacher from Lone Wolf, Oklahoma. They married and moved to North Carolina. Through the years our families have been very close. I moved back to Gotebo, Oklahoma, where I lived with my parents. With my first paycheck I purchased for them a small secretary of Honduran Mahogany.

My third teaching year proved to be the most interesting. A shy little Kiowa Indian girl entered my second grade in Mt. View, Oklahoma. I will never forget her name, Hattie Sayta Pa Hoodle. I wrote it every day to report her attendance to the federal government who paid for her to attend school.

A most unusual thing happened. Her entire Kiowa family, the young squaw mother wearing a colorful blanket, her father with two long braids of hair always wearing a hat, and her teenage brother attended my class for three days. I was very nervous and uncomfortable. The teenager had attended the Government School at Rainy Mountain, near Gotebo, Oklahoma. Finally, my principal told them they could not attend school with Hattie. That incident taught me something very important. Hattie Sayta Pa Hoodle had a built-in support group with her as she started school. She continued to be very shy, but by the year's end she was included in the group games and learned English very well. She had what every child should have—loyalty, encouragement and love.

THINGS I'D LIKE TO DO AGAIN

Sail at midnight from New York.

Spend Easter in Charleston, SC Magnolia Gardens.

Eat any meal at the Chateau Frontenac.

See the coast of England on an early clear morning in June.

Bathe in salt water on the "S.S. Antonia," float in a full tub and
    roll with the ship.

Spend a long time in Sorrento.

Walk up the *Champs-Élysées*.

Drive through Yellowstone Park.

Go back to Mary Baldwin for reunion.

Drive up Fifth Avenue and Broadway.

Gather mountain laurel and rhododendron in North Carolina
    mountains.

Go to Delta Gamma banquets and initiations.

Ride horseback early in the morning and on moonlight nights.

Ride in a gondola in Venice.

Paddle through the Blue Grotto.

Use the funicular at Lucerne Hotel.

Pick bonny purple heather near Keswich, England.

Look down the Bright Angel Trail at the Grand Canyon in
    Arizona.

Drive in the rain in English Lake District.

Sit on deck *S.S. Tuscania* with West Pointer on a moonlit night.

Go to a dude ranch just outside Yellowstone Park, Cody Road.

Take a long trip overland, east or west.

Hear the musical sound of the Italian word, "Bambino."

Have hors d'oeuvres before dinner.

Stay in same cottage in Boulder Canyon, near Colorado Alps.

Dance with Stewart Ball at the Hotel Ahul in Nice, France.

Circle the Roman Coliseum in a carriage in moonlight with Peg,
    Steve and "Whitie."

Play bridge with Peg and midshipmen at London Hotel.

Take tea at "Lyons" in London.

Sit on "A Aft Deck," sailing up the St. Lawrence.

Swing on a grape vine with McLean children in Lenoir.

Visit the Scottish relatives in Edinburgh.

Taste huge Italian figs.

Shop in Oklahoma City.

Watch changing of the guards at Buckingham Palace and Whitehall.

Go to Delta Gamma convention in Estes Park, CO.

Attend services at Westminster Abbey with Peg. Run through
     London mist from "Lyons" to Abbey.

Dress up for masquerade night on board ship.

Attend church service on board *S.S. Antonia*.

Attend the military ball on roof garden in Naples, Italy.

Read travel books in bed.

Walk in the Blueridge Mountains in North Carolina looking for
     trailing arbutus.

Watch the equestrian jumpers in Virginia and walk on the terrace at
     dusk at Mary Baldwin.

Visit in Kentucky Blue Grass section on country estate near
     Lexington.

See Niagara Falls at night from the Canadian side; feel mist on my
     face.

Drive up Big Thompson Canyon near Boulder, CO.

Ride along the Hudson River up Storm King Highway and take
     ferry at Poughkeepsie, New York in the rain.

Buy a dress in Paris and have hats "made to order" at the hotel.

Sit by the hour at the sidewalk Cafe de la Paix.

See Times Square at night.

Go to the Roxy Theater in New York City.

Hear Will Rogers in person or on radio.

Spend Thanksgiving in Charlottesville, VA; see Princeton play UVA
     in football.

Walk through campuses of Washington & Lee University and VMI
     in Lexington, VA.

See Natural Bridge in the Shenandoah Valley of Virginia.

Thrill over a Staunton Military Academy cadet in full spring
     uniform, brass buttons, etc.

Lean out window at Mary Baldwin Seminary and wave to S.M.A
     cadets and officers.

Hike to Mary Baldwin's College Farm on "Apple Day."

Spend another week at Tres Rios, New Mexico.

Hear a musical comedy as good as "Student Prince" or "Rose
     Marie."

Sit on deck of the *Tuscany* with West Pointer just at dusk, talking.

Wander slowly through Princeton University campus, one of the most beautiful in the US.

Sight a ship in mid-ocean.

Get up at 5:00 a.m. to look at an iceberg.

Go to Drury Lane Theater, London, to see "New Moon."

Sit in Seventh Heaven in London Coliseum; smell a good old English pipe.

Drink *thé a la English*.

Visit British Columbia.

Cross over to Mexico from California.

Watch the coast of Ireland at night: lighthouses!

Have thrills and worries of being Delta Gamma Chapter President.

Receive my B.A. degree from Dr. Bizzel at Norman, Oklahoma.

Welcome friends at Sunday Sorority open house.

Dance at Delta Gamma House.

Pass Statue of Liberty on way to Staten Island.

Look at Indian Pueblo and art colony at Taos, New Mexico.

Visit Columbia University on Riverside Drive, New York City.

Watch children play in Central Park; hear their laughter.

Drink "Bottled Sunshine" with "Papa Mosley" on Rhine Steamer.

Receive my first paycheck after teaching a month at Oak Hill near Lenoir, NC.

Climb "Rhone Glacier" at 6:00 a.m.

Pick up "Whoopee" when he was a puppy.

Spend weeks in Washington, D.C.

Look at the Hudson River from West Point.

Lie in bed and hear "Taps" at S.M.A.

Look at the pier construction of Castle Moss' bridge in New York.

Have tea at Dr. and Mrs. King's home, "Kalorama," in Staunton, VA.

Return to Mary Baldwin for "Papa King's" welcome to old girls.

Motor through the Garden of the Gods near Colorado Springs.

Drive on the Boulder-Denver Road.

Go to Elitch Garden in Denver.

Hop off European trains for "spumoni."

Wander around Casino Della Rosa, looking for our crowd; having "Whitie", Steve, and two other mid-shipmen discover us.

Meet Papa Mosley and Billie for rum punch and Tom Collins.

Breakfast in Grand Central between trains.

Sit in on Dr. Dowd's sociology class.

Collect etchings in *Montmartre*.

Get first letter from home after our trip across.

See old fraternity friend at Italian restaurant in New York.

Surprise my family with Christmas gifts purchased with my own money.

Swim in blue Mediterranean at Nice.

Be bridesmaid in wedding.

Buy a shawl in Amalfi, Italy.

Visit Pompeii near Mt. Vesuvius.

Have a handsome Italian ask me to dance; wouldn't I accept!!

Buy a pipe for my dad at Peter Robinson's in London.

Purchase silk scarf after wandering through Liberty's in London.

Drive out 22nd Street in Oklahoma City at night and look at oil fields.

Sleep until 11:00 a.m. without feeling guilty.

Look around woodcarving stores in Lucerne and Interlaken, Switzerland.

See the Rhone Glacier in moonlight; drive through the clouds.

Sleep under feather comforter in Switzerland on cold summer night.

Sing through the Alps while the Ball brothers point out scenic beauties.

Ride on a launch at Lake Lucerne.

Have tea with my Bain cousins in Edinburgh.

Listen to musical trays in Lucerne.

Play shuffleboard and deck tennis.

Buy clothes for a European trip.

Cover each other with sand at Long Beach, California.

Meet Mother, Dad, and Mark at hotel in Davidson, NC.

Dance with a nice young man from Chapel Hill at the fraternity hall in Davidson.

Spend spring holidays at Davidson College.

Sleep with six girls in old fashioned room in a hotel with a balcony in Davidson.

Drive through long leaf pine country.

Eat Easter dinner in Summerville, SC, when azaleas are in bloom.

Go through "Rush Week" again; sing a song I love, "Calm as the Night."

Ride horseback at the Montana ranch on the mesa with Daddy, waiting for mail.

Hear the excitement of the crowd at Churchill Down at Kentucky Derby.

Riding with Dr. Fred Robbins from Philadelphia to Trenton, N.J.; my wire from him on the *S.S. Tuscania*.

Hear Boston men asking about beauty contest aboard ship.

Ride in carriage with "Whitie," Steve and Peg along the bay of Naples.

Sorrento, Italy!!! Swim in blue Mediterranean; (shocked at bathing suits some wore.)

Dodge West Pointer in Tate Gallery.

Have tea at Chateau Frontenac; leaving Quebec at dusk.

Spend nigh at Seppel in Heidelberg.

Attend bon voyage tea at Jones home in Lenoir.

Walk in rain near English lakes.

Wade in Pacific, watching sea gulls.

Feel myself blush when The Major kisses me on the *Rhine Steamer*, as 20 of us are singing. I consider the Major and forget to even fell embarrassed.

Get registered letters from a doctor I was dating while teaching at Mt. View, OK.

Feed pigeons at St. Mark's Square; watch women making Burano lace.

Listen to Kate Smith sing "God Bless America" on the radio.

Take the Grand Cornish Drive.

Gaze at red tiles against Italian blue skies.

Taste grapes on Isle of Capri; watch women carry trunks on their heads.

Visit the Lincoln Memorial in Washington, DC.

Watch cotton growing at all stages in Oklahoma fields.

Gaze at Winged Victory and Venus de Milo at the Louvre.

Watch aspen turn gold in Colorado and New Mexico.

Rosmarie Waldrop

Lawn of Excluded Middle

Tender Buttons
Providence
1993

Cover Art based on "Planes Outlined in Curves" by Sophie Täuber-Arp,
Winterthur Museum, Switzerland.
Additional Cover Design: Loughran O'Connor and Lee Ann Brown.

Grateful acknowledgement is made to the editors of the magazines in
which sections of this book first appeared: *Big Allis, Blue Mesa, Chelsea,
Conjunctions, Epoch, fragmente, furnitures, Hambone, New American
Writing, Notus, o•blek, Raddle Moon, Sojourner, Temblor, and the UCSD
Archive Newsletter.*

The author would like to thank the Fund for Poetry for a grant.

**Publication of this book is made possible by grants from
the Rhode Island State Council on the Arts and the Fund for Poetry.**

Many thanks to all who donated production time and skills:
Laynie Browne, Lisa Jarnot, Ann Morgan, O'Connor& Price Design

ISBN: 0-927920-04-2

Library of Congress Catalogue Number: 93-60165

Tender Buttons books are edited and published by
Lee Ann Brown

Tender Buttons
54 East Manning Street #3
Providence, RI
02906
(401) 454-4725

FOR CLAUDE ROYET-JOURNOUD

PART ONE

LAWN OF EXCLUDED MIDDLE

1

When I say I believe that women have a soul and that its substance contains two carbon rings the picture in the foreground makes it difficult to find its application back where the corridors get lost in ritual sacrifice and hidden bleeding. But the four points of the compass are equal on the lawn of the excluded middle where full maturity of meaning takes time the way you eat a fish, morsel by morsel, off the bone. Something that can be held in the mouth, deeply, like darkness by someone blind or the empty space I place at the center of each poem to allow penetration.

2

I'm looking out the window at other windows. Though the pane masquerades as transparent I know it is impenetrable just as too great a show of frankness gives you a mere paper draft on revelations. As if words were passports, or arrows that point to the application we might make of them without considering the difference of biography and life. Still, depth of field allows the mind to drift beyond its negative pole to sun catching on a maple leaf already red in August, already thinner, more translucent, preparing to strip off all that separates it from its smooth skeleton. Beautiful, flamboyant phrase that trails off without predicate, intending disappearance by approaching it, a toss in the air.

3

I put a ruler in my handbag, having heard men talk about their sex. Now we have correct measurements and a stickiness between collar and neck. It is one thing to insert yourself into a mirror, but quite another to get your image out again and have your errors pass for objectivity. Vitreous. As in humor. A change in perspective is caused by the ciliary muscle, but need not be conciliatory. Still, the eye is a camera, room for everything that is to enter, like the cylinder called the satisfaction of hollow space. Only language grows such grass-green grass.

4

Even if a woman sits at a loom, it does not mean she must weave a cosmogony or clothes to cover the emptiness underneath. It might just be a piece of cloth which, like any center of attention, absorbs the available light the way a waterfall can form a curtain of solid noise through which only time can pass. She has been taught to imagine other things, but does not explain, disdaining defense while her consciousness streams down the rapids. The light converges on what might be the hollow of desire or the incomplete self, or just lint in her pocket. Her hour will also come with the breaking of water.

5

Because I refuse to accept the opposition of night and day I must pit other, subtler periodicities against the emptiness of being an adult. Their traces inside my body attempt precariously, like any sign, to produce understanding, but though nothing may come of that, the grass is growing. Can words play my parts and also find their own way to the house next door as rays converge and solve their differences? Or do notes follow because drawn to a conclusion? If we don't signal our love, reason will eat our heart out before it can admit its form of mere intention, and we won't know what has departed.

6

All roads lead, but how does a sentence do it? Nothing seems hidden, but it goes by so fast when I should like to see it laid open to view whether the engine resembles combustion so that form becomes its own explanation. We've been taught to apply solar principles, but must find on our own where to look for Rome the way words rally to the blanks between them and thus augment the volume of their resonance.

7

It's a tall order that expects pain to crystallize into beauty. And we must close our eyes to conceive of heaven. The inside of the lid is fertile in images unprovoked by experience, or perhaps its pressure on the eyeball equals prayer in the same way that inference is a transition toward assertion, even observing rites of dawn against a dark and empty background. I have read that female prisoners to be hanged must wear rubber pants and a dress sewn shut around the knees because uterus and ovaries spill with the shock down the shaft.

8

The meaning of certainty is getting burned. Though truth will still escape us, we must put our hands on bodies. Staying safe is a different death, the instruments of defense eating inward without evening out the score. As the desire to explore my body's labyrinth did, leading straight to the center of nothing. From which projected my daily world of representation with bright fictional fireworks. Had I overinvested in spectacle? In mere fluctuations of light which, like a bird's wingbeat, must with time slow to the point of vanishing? What about buying bread or singing in the dark? Even if the ground for our assumptions is the umber of burnt childhood we're driven toward the sun as if logic had no other exit.

9

Though the way I see you depends on I don't know how many codes I have absorbed unawares, like germs or radiation, I am certain the conflicting possibilities of logic and chemistry have contaminated the space between us. Emptiness is imperative for feeling to take on substance, for its vibrations to grow tangible, a faintly trembling beam that supports the whole edifice. Caught between the thickness of desire and chill clarity, depth dissolved its contours with intemperate movements inside the body where much can be gathered. Can I not say a cry, a laugh are full of meaning, a denseness for which I have no words that would not channel its force into shallower waters, mere echo of oracles?

10

My anxiety made you wary. As if I tried to draw you into a new kind of sexuality, a flutter of inner emptiness implying hunger to frame the momentary flight of birds with emotional reference and heat. Any initiation anticipates absolute abandon with the body misunderstood as solid, whereas images dissolve their objects. Even with deep water ahead, even though the shores of syllogism may be flooded, we must not turn around. Behind us, incursions into our own field of vision, a mirror to lose our body out of the corner of an eye. It may look like a sentence we understand, yet quenches no thirst, no matter how hard we stroke it. But anxiety is a password which does not require a special tone of voice. Rather than to immersion in mysteries I was only leading you to common ground.

11

Whenever you're surprised that I should speak your language I am suddenly wearing too many necklaces and breasts, even though feeling does not produce what is felt, and the object of observation is something else again. Not modulating keys, not the splash that makes us take to another element, just my body alarmingly tangible, like furniture that exceeds its function, a shape I cannot get around. The way one suddenly knows the boulder in the road for a boulder, immovable, as if not always there, unmodified by inner hollows or the stray weeds and their dusty green, a solid obstacle with only trompe-l'oeil exits toward the subtler body of light accumulating in the distance.

12

I worried about the gap between expression and intent, afraid the world might see a fluorescent advertisement where I meant to show a face. Sincerity is no help once we admit to the lies we tell on nocturnal occasions, even in the solitude of our own heart, wishcraft slanting the naked figure from need to seduce to fear of possession. Far better to cultivate the gap itself with its high grass for privacy and reference gone astray. Never mind that it is not philosophy, but raw electrons jumping from orbit to orbit to ready the pit for the orchestra, scrap meanings amplifying the succession of green perspectives, moist fissures, spasms on the lips.

13

Words too can be wrung from us like a cry from that space which doesn't seem to be the body nor a metaphor curving into perspective. Rather the thickness silence gains when pressed. The ghosts of grammar veer toward shape while my hopes still lie embedded in a quiet myopia from which they don't want to arise. The mistake is to look for explanations where we should just watch the slow fuse burning. Nerve of confession. What we let go we let go.

14

Because we use the negative as if no explanation were needed the void we cater to is, like anorexia, a ferment of hallucinations. Here, the bird's body equals the rhythm of wingbeats which, frantic, disturb their own lack of origin, fear of falling, indigenous grey. Static electricity. Strobe map. Gap gardening. The sun feeds on its dark core for a set of glistening blood, in a space we can't fathom except as pollution colors it.

15

The word "not" seems like a poor expedient to designate all that escapes my understanding like the extra space between us when I press my body against yours, perhaps the distance of desire, which we carry like a skyline and which never allows us to be where we are, as if past and future had their place whereas the present dips and disappears under your feet, so suddenly your stomach is squeezed up into your throat as the plane crashes. This is why some try to stretch their shadow across the gap as future fame while the rest of us take up residence in the falling away of land, even though our nature is closer to water.

16

The affirmation of the double negative tempts us to invent a myth of meaning where the light loops its wavelength through dark hollows into unheard-of Americas, or a double-tongued flute speeds decimals over the whole acoustic range of the landscape till it exhausts itself with excess of effect brought home. Can I walk in your sleep, in order to defer obedience and assent to my own waking? Or will the weight of error pull me down below the symmetries of the round world? Touching bottom means the water's over your head. And you can't annul a shake of that by shaking it again.

17

In Providence, you can encounter extinct species, an equestrian statue, say, left hoof raised in progress toward the memory of tourists. Caught in its career of immobility, but with surface intact, waiting to prove that it can resist the attack of eyes even though dampened by real weather, even though historical atmosphere is mixed with exhaust like etymology with the use of a word or bone with sentence structure. No wonder we find it difficult to know our way about and tend to stay indoors.

18

A window can draw you into the distance within proximity all the way to where it vanishes with the point. This is not a hocuspocus which can be performed only by kinship terms. The glass seems to secure perspectives that can shoulder the cold stare of so many third persons while our image is resolved in favor of inaccessible riverbeds. Alternating small and large measures, the dust on the pane is part of the attraction, a way of allowing the environment in. So would a stone's throw, substituting the high frequencies of shattering for the play of reflections.

19

We know that swallows are drawn to window panes, etching swift lurching streaks across and sometimes crashing. I picked up the body as if easing the vast sky through a narrow pulse toppling over itself. Caught between simulacrum and paradox, the hard air. Even if a body could survive entering its own image, the mirror is left empty, no fault in the glass breaking the evenness of light.

20

What's left over if I subtract the fact that my leg goes up from the fact that I raise it? A link to free will or never trying, as only our body knows to disobey an even trade to the sound of a fiddle. Something tells me not to ask this question and accept the movement. The speed of desire like a hot wind sweeping the grass or flash of water under the bridge. For doing itself seems not to have any volume: an extensionless point, the point of a needle out to draw blood regardless.

21

This is not thinking, you said, more what colors it, like a smell entering our breath even to the seat of faith under the left nipple. Like the children I could have borne shaping my body toward submission and subterfuge. It is possible, I admitted, to do physics in inches as well as in centimeters, but a concept is more than a convenience. It takes us through earnest doorways to always the same kind of example. No chance of denser vegetation, of the cool shadow of firs extending this line of reasoning into the dark.

22

My love was deep and therefore lasted only the space of one second, unable to expand in more than one dimension at a time. The same way deeper meaning may constrict a sentence right out of the language into an uneasiness with lakes and ponds. In language nothing is hidden or our own, its light indifferent to holes in the present or postulates beginning with ourselves. Still, you may travel alone and yet be accompanied by my good wishes.

23

Look in thy heart and write, you quoted. As if we could derive the object from desire or proper breathing from the structure of transitivity. It's true, the brain is desperate for an available emptiness to house its clutter, as a tone can only grow from a space of silence, lifted by inaudible echoes as birds are by the air inside their bones. So we reach down, although it cannot save us, to the hollows inside the body, to extend them into so many journeys into the world, so many words shelling the echo of absence onto the dry land.

24

In the way well-being contains the possibility of pain a young boy may show the meekness we associate with girls, or an excess of sperm, on occasion, come close to spirituality. But a name is an itch to let the picture take root inside its contour though sentences keep shifting like sand, and a red patch may be there or not. All heights are fearful. We must cast arbitrary nets over the unknown, knot the earth's rim to the sky with a rope of orisons. For safety. For once human always an acrobat.

25

Meaning is like going up to someone I would be with, though often the distance doesn't seem to lessen no matter how straight my course. Busy moving ahead, I can't also observe myself moving, let alone assess the speed of full steam minus fiction and sidetracked in metric crevices. It's hard to identify with the image of an arrow even if it points only to the application we make of it. But then, meandering does not guarantee thought either though it simulates its course toward wider angles, which make us later than we are, our fingers the space of already rust from the key. Even the weight of things can no longer measure our calculations. Conquered by our own scope we offer no resistance to the blue transparency, the startling downpour of sun.

26

I wanted to settle down on a surface, a map perhaps, where my near-sightedness might help me see the facts. But grammar is deep. Even though it only describes, it submerges the mind in a maelstrom without discernable bottom, the dimensions of possibles swirling over the fixed edge of nothingness. Like looking into blue eyes all the way through to the blue sky without even a cloudbank or flock of birds to cling to. What are we searching behind the words as if a body of information could not also bruise? It is the skeleton that holds on longest to its native land.

27

For a red curve to be a smile it needs a face around it, company of its kind to capture our attention by the between, the bait of difference and constant of desire. Then color sweeping over cheeks is both expansion of internal transport and an airing of emotion. Understanding, too, enters more easily through a gap between than where a line is closed upon itself. This is why comparisons, for all their limping, go farther even than the distance of beauty, rose or fingered dawn, or of remembering contracts signed in blood.

28

Electric seasons. Night has become as improbable as a sea forever at high tide. The sheer excess of light makes for a lack of depth, denying our fall from grace, the way a membrane is all surface. Or the way we, clamoring for sense, exclude so many unions of words from the sphere of language. As if one could fall off the edge of the earth. Why do we fear the dark as unavoidable defeat when it alone is constant, and we'd starve if it stopped watering the lawn of dreams.

29

You were determined to get rid of your soul by expressing it completely, rubbing the silver off the mirror in hope of a new innocence of body on the other side of knowing. A limpid zone which would not wholly depend on our grammar in the way the sea draws its color from the sky. Noon light, harsh, without shadow. Each gesture intending only its involvement with gravity, a pure figure of reach, as the hyperbola is for its asymptotes or circles widening on the water for the stone that broke the surface. But the emigration is rallied, reflections regather across the ripples. Everything in our universe curves back to the apple.

30

The capacity to move my hand from left to right arises on a margin of indecision and doubt winding into vertiginous inner stairwells, but only when adjacent shadows have cooled the long summer sun toward a more introverted, solitary quality of light for the benefit of eyes tensing to see the dark before concepts. This is an attempt to make up for inner emptiness in the way that Fred Astaire and Ginger Rogers dance with more desperate brio to add a third dimension to their characters. Nevertheless the capacity does not explain how the meaning of individual words can make a tent over a whole argument. It is not a feeling, but a circular movement to represent the transfer of visibility toward dream without abrogating the claims of body.

31

As if I had to navigate both forward and backward, part of me turned away from where I'm going, taking the distance of long corridors to allow for delay and trouble, for keeping in the dark while being led on. In this way Chinese characters seem to offer their secret without revealing it, invitation to enter a labyrinth which, like that of the heart, may not have a center. It is replaced by being lost which I don't like to dwell on because the search for motivation can only drive us downward toward potential that is frightening in proportion to its depth and sluicegates to disappearance. It is much better, I have been advised, just to drift with the stream. The ink washes into a deeper language, and in the end the water runs clear.

Part Two

The Perplexing Habit of Falling

I
The Attraction of the Ground

In the beginning there were torrential rains, and the world dissolved in puddles, even though we were well into the nuclear age and speedier methods. Constant precipitation drenched the dry point of the present till it leaked a wash of color all the way up to the roots of our hair. I wanted to see mysteries at the bottom of the puddles, but they turned out to be reflections that made our heads swim. The way a statue's eyes bring our stock of blindness to the surface. Every thought swelled to the softness of flesh after a long bath, the lack of definition essential for happiness, just as not knowing yourself guarantees a life of long lukewarm days stretching beyond the shadow of pure reason on the sidewalk. All this was common practice. Downpour of sun. Flood of young leafiness. A slight unease caused by sheer fill of body. Running over and over like the light spilled westward across the continent, a river we couldn't cross without our moment, barely born, drowning in its own translucent metaphor.

The silence, which matted my hair like a room with the windows shut too long, filled with your breath. As if you didn't need the weight of words in your lungs to keep your body from dispersing like so many molecules over an empty field. Being a woman and without history, I wanted to explore how the grain of the world runs, hoping for backward and forward, the way sentences breathe even this side of explanation. But you claimed that words absorb all perspective and blot out the view just as certain parts of the body obscure others on the curve of desire. Or again, as the message gets lost in the long run, while we still see the messenger panting, unflagging, through the centuries. I had thought it went the other way round and was surprised as he came out of my mouth in his toga, without even a raincoat. I had to lean far out the window to follow his now unencumbered course, speeding your theory towards a horizon flat and true as a spirit level.

My legs were so interlaced with yours I began to think I could never use them on my own again. Not even if I shaved them. As if emotion had always to be a handicap. But maybe the knots were a picture of my faint unrest at having everything and not more, like wind caught in the trees with no open space to get lost, a tension toward song hanging in the air like an unfinished birdcry, or the smell of the word verbena, or apples that would not succumb to the attraction of the ground. In a neutral grammar love may be a refrain screamed through the loudspeakers, a calibration of parallels or bone structure strong enough to support verisimilitude. A FOR SALE sign in red urged us to participate in our society, while a whole flock of gulls stood in the mud by the river, ready to extend the sky with their wings. Another picture. Is it called love or nerves, you said, when everything is on the verge of happening? But I was unable to distinguish between waves and corpuscles because I had rings under my eyes, and appearances are fragile. Though we already live partly underground it must be possible to find a light that is exacting and yet allows us to be ourselves even while taking our measure.

Although you are thin you always seemed to be in front of my eyes, putting back in the body the roads my thoughts might have taken. As if forward and backward meant no more than right and left, and the earth could just as easily reverse its spin. So that we made each other the present of a stage where time would not pass, and only space would age, encompassing all 200000 dramatic situations, but over the rest of the proceedings, the increase of entropy and unemployment. Meanwhile we juggled details of our feelings into an exaggeration which took the place of explanation, and consequences remained in the kind of repose that, like a dancer's, already holds the leap toward inside turning out.

Your arms were embracing like a climate that does not require being native. They held me responsive, but I still wondered about the other lives I might have lived, the unused cast of characters stored within me, outcasts of actuality no stranger than my previous selves. As if a word should be counted a lie for all it misses. I could imagine my body arching up toward other men in a high-strung vertigo that scored a virtual accompaniment to our real dance, deep phantom chords echoing from nowhere though with the force of long acceleration, of flying home from a lost wedding. Stakes and mistakes. Big with sky, with bracing cold, with the drone of aircraft, the measures of distance hang in the air before falling in thick drops. The child will be pale and thin. Though it had infiltrated my bones, the thought was without marrow. More a feeling that might accompany a thought, a ply of consonants, an outward motion of the eye.

I began to long for respite from attention, the freedom of interruption. The clouds of feeling inside my head, though full of soft light, needed a breeze or the pull of gravity. More rain. As if I suddenly couldn't speak without first licking my lips, spelling my name, enumerating the days of the week. Would separation act as an astringent? Ink our characters more sharply? I tried to push the idea aside, afraid of losing the dimensions of nakedness, but it kept turning up underfoot, tripping me. Clearly, the journey would mean growing older, flat tiredness, desire out of tune. Much practice is needed for two-dimensional representation whether in drawing or rooms, and it emaciates our undertakings in the way that lack of sleep narrows thinking to a point without echoes, the neck of the hour glass. You may be able to travel fast forward without looking back, but I paint my lashes to slow the child in my face and climb the winding stairs back to a logic whose gaps are filled by mermaids.

Many questions were left in the clearing we built our shared life in. Later sheer size left no room for imagining myself standing outside it, on the edge of an empty day. I knew I didn't want to part from this whole which could be said to carry its foundation as much as resting on it, just as a family tree grows downward, its branches confounding gravitation and gravidity. I wanted to continue lying alongside you, two parallel, comparable lengths of feeling, and let the stresses of the structure push our sleep to momentum and fullness. Still, a fallow evening stretches into unknown elsewheres, seductive with possibility, doors open onto a chaos of cul-de-sac, of could-be, of galloping off on the horse in the picture. And whereto? A crowning mirage or a question like What is love? And where? Does it enter with a squeeze, or without, bringing, like interpretation, its own space from some other dimension? Or is it like a dream corridor forever extending its concept toward extreme emptiness, like that of atoms?

II
Mass, Momentum, Stress

Is it because we cannot capture our own selves or because logically nothing is on its own that we turn to each other for reflection and echo as philosophers always go back to the same props and propositions? If you return from far enough away you perhaps never left, but it still takes coats off, or character, to warp the arrow. A circle is a figure almost as clear as a straight line, but covers more territory, even water, the way the relation of two people is not bound to follow rules on separable prefixes. We knew the state of our affairs and pooled them. Once your reflection surfaced out of deep water, the fragile mirror prohibiting the turbulence of touch, I wondered if I would not trade this transparency for a white space of its own without allusions, provided the ice was solid enough to walk across. Even though it was summer, we moved rather like snow blown by the wind, not easy to make tracks on, melting and refreezing in harsh ridges.

What once had been vehemence now seemed to inhibit us. We could never again come up to its watermark, with all the ambivalence in the air. You seemed instead like too thin skin, shrinking suspiciously from close-ups, unaware that I was also on my guard, ready to retreat as soon as the mind gets soft with the warmth and begins to shed its clothes. Once you blur the distinction between equal and equivocal, space is interrupted and disappears in subcutaneous shivers. But it would be a pity if nothing more happened between us because we have memorized ourselves too thoroughly and are wary even as we travel through the passes and impasses of sleep, through layers of velvet density, back to the innermost desire anchored in all our questions and actions, anchored so deeply that we cannot touch it.

To test if I could see your child as my own without preparatory pregnancy or periods of nausea to allow for resistance, I began to take walks in the dark. "Seeing as" is not part of perception. And for that reason like seeing and again not like. In the hot summer night, perspective might be conceived to travel both forward and backward to the same point of vanishing time, a conception after the fact, a gestation backward into the stability of impossible desires that might draw him as the sea does if you look too long at its spectacle. And he comes padding at night on bare feet and takes a long look at my body before whimpering to you of fear of the dark, so that you'll draw the sheet up and protect him again the shock of female nakedness.

Dynasties of space seem to claim him, this child who embraces his vertigo though atoms as porous as the solar system make images vanish into intervals, and intervals into sheer emptiness. His leaps delirious, body flung from mountain tops in pursuit of a remote self, so hard to trap in the subtlest net of language, games, or set of mirrors. Though the temperature may fall there's not a doubt in his green blood that he can always squeeze a cushion from the air, a wealth of longest tracks setting him gently down in his picture of the world. No measurements disturb the chances of fun and blame or spring's exorbitant unfolding in his veins. Anxiety comes later with a disproportion of raincoats and knowing the groundlessness of our beliefs. I've lost my skin to immense, complex summers and the meaning of words to the uncertainty of fact. Not just the rivers, the riverbeds too are shifting.

The injury was in not responding until the shiniest sheet of tension lay glistening between us and the balance of power started to slip on the ice. At the speed of slight the clocks run counter. I tried to recall the moment when I realized that wind losing momentum may not mean holes in the argument or ice so that the fish can breathe. We needn't quarrel if, instead of surveying our relation from within, we allowed that we had each drawn the line with flying colors, so that you saw red zigzag lightning where I lay down on a green lawn. Moving at different speeds we contracted different diseases and took the most negative measure of each other's hunger. This was why the ratio of emotional to body heat remained impaired even though we wore boots and heavy coats. It would take wrapping up in words.

You were busy planting your picture of the world into your child's mind. Mine, in comparison, seemed more like the hotel slated for demolition, beyond redecorating. From the window, not the expected distance of beauty, but a row of scraggy young trees facing a church covered from top to bottom with scaffolding which allowed only rare glimpses of white volutes and projections. One of the trees seemed scraggier than the rest, perhaps blighted, but on the whole it was 2 lines of wood at different stages, and I was learning to read between them as slowly as possible. A hitch in time. The way a look into a mirror saves miles. If the scaffolding cast its shadow over your boy, who was running circles around its posts, he remained unaware, his skin hardly darkened. He expects definitions on the order of freeways and runaway nebula, not horizons contracting to flywheel and cog, hard fiber in the pit of the stomach.

I worked hard at keeping perspective in the family and periodically faced in your direction as the faithful toward the East. Your space was framed so differently from mine that it located your "here" around the curve of the horizon, unreachable by even my longest sentence. All I could see was a glare as over the Great Fire of London. So that landscape became a religion of surface, teaching divine imperfection and replacing baptism by fire. You thought it was improbable that the concept of original sin was upset by electricity in motion any more than by gravity's competing for the apple. The question of intimacy did not come up to the temperature, but had to be raised so we could get out of the building already full of smoke. It may be easier to speed the process of oxidation than to hold on to the illusions of communication. Nor can the sign for water quench the flames in my lungs. It only inhales loads of silence which connect and separate us according to the twists and turns of the plot.

Later, my shadow stopped following and, after a moment of holding its breath, steadily lengthened my progress ahead of me, obscuring other roads as if only a narrow consistency could inherit a goal. It was also at this time that the mirror began to show the back of my head, and my stare would speed its moving on while I stood still as a cat within her fur. Even so, we know the way to go is outward and stretch pale roots toward the world, of which we really know nothing. The same way we walk on credit, swinging the body forward, confident that, though for one moment in each step we tread the void, it won't close over our head. You, the more courageous, had even put forth a child with ruthless appetites and so bridged wider intervals toward those edges of experience where impressions seem sharp as line drawings just before they drop into the virtual and vicarious, mysteries beyond the vested interests of before and because.

Even at your nakedest, your nakedness would not reach all the way to your face, the way a rock by the sea is always veiled in water and foam as in a memory of deep space. Or perhaps I was looking for something beyond my capacity of seeing, and the shifts of hiddenness were only in the image I carried somewhere between head and dark of stomach as I searched the woods for poisonous mushrooms. The technique is to knock them out with a stick and tread them to pulp which saves lives and provides entertainment. Actually I prefer stories with sharp edges cut by blades manufactured with great precision in Solingen, Germany. These I use like a religion to keep me on the straight and narrative which, like computers and gods, admits only yes or no. No straying into ambiguous underbrush where hidden desire is not made any clearer by intermittent fulfillment, the light and shadow playing over my rush of wildwater actions while I feel I'm sitting motionless on the bank.

With the body running down inexorably, how can we each day reweave our net of closeness and distance? But though time burns at both ends, it rolls around the clock, and evening replays events of the day in a new light, showing perhaps electric waves instead of raindrops glittering on a spiderweb. The relation is not resemblance, but pulling the trigger on a nerve. While time takes the shortest cut right into consciousness, physical cause stops at the door. There remains an ultimate gap, as between two people, that not even a penis can bridge, a point at which we lose sight of the erection crossing a horizon in the mind. This is accompanied by slight giddiness as when we jump over shadow or admire the waves rolling incomprehensible resolutions in a border of darker and darker gray. It dispenses us from trying to draw profit from attention to ritual, like watching the spider ride its memory from periphery to center orb at nightfall.

You went through the school of velocity hoping for a speed worthy of flight where you would feel stillness in your bones while falling into deep thought. Not a space I could thrust my breasts into while maintaining the mountain climber's three points of contact with the surface, using the fourth to goad time toward climax. The height of a mountain does not depend on how we climb it or equality of chance. Steep territory. Face to rock-face. Different scales of gravity code a slow body against dreams of flying, both menaced by the thin complexities of the air. The problem was less securing a foothold than an echo off the cliff. What I am doing here is hanging a name on a difficulty, a common alternative to the sheer effort toward telling ground. The turtle is geologically the oldest of our extant amphibian. Even though we live on a decently slow-moving planet, I sometimes think the world might be edging away and out of reach.

III
Accelerating Frame

I badly wanted a story of my own. As if there were proof in spelling. But what if my experience were the kind of snow that does not accumulate? A piling of instants that did not amount to a dimension? What if wandering within my own limits I came back naked, with features too faint for the mirror, unequal to the demands of the night? In the long run I could not deceive appearances: Days and nights were added without adding up. Nothing to recount in bed before falling asleep. Even memory was not usable, a landscape hillocky with gravitation but without monuments, it did not hold the eye, did not hinder its glide toward the horizon where the prose of the world gives way to the smooth functioning of fear. If the wheel so barely touches the ground the speed must be enormous.

The concept of an inner picture is misleading. Like those on the screen, it takes the outer picture as a model, yet their uses are no more alike than statistics and bodies. Figures, we know, can proceed without any regard for reality, no matter how thin the fabric. True, the missing pieces can be glued in, but if you look for the deep you won't frighten your vertigo away. An ambition to fathom need not hold water. Stay on shore, put on more sweaters, and let the roar of the breakers swallow your urge to scream. If not the clouds themselves, their reflections withdraw with the tide. Then there is the familiar smell of wet sand and seaweed, debris of every kind, including hypodermics, condoms, oozing filth. My outer self comes running on pale legs to claim my share, while my inner picture stands dazed, blinking behind sunglasses, demanding a past that might redeem the present.

I knew that true or false is irrelevant in the pursuit of knowledge which must find its own ways to avoid falling as it moves toward horizons of light. We can't hope to prove gravity from the fact that it tallies with the fall of an apple when the nature of tallying is what Eve's bite called into question. My progress was slowed down by your hand brushing against my breast, just as travel along the optic nerve brakes the rush of light. But then light does not take place, not even in bed. It is like the kind of language that vanishes into communication, as you might into my desire for you. It takes attention focused on the fullness of shadow to give light a body that weighs on the horizon, though without denting its indifference.

I thought I could get to the bottom of things by taking my distance from logic, but only fell as far as the immediate. Here the moment flaunted its perfect roundness and could not be left behind because it accelerated with me, intense like roses blooming in the dark whereas I was still figuring out: are red roses at night darker than white ones, and all cats gray? But at some point we have to pass from explanation to description in the heroic hope that it will reach right out into experience, the groundswell flooding my whole being like heat or pollution, though the haze outside always looks as if it could easily be blown away. A cat of any color can descend into the pit behind her eyes and yawn herself right back to the bland surfaces that represent the world in the logical form we call reality. But logic is no help when you have no premises. And more and more people lacking the most modest form of them are wandering through the streets. Do we call the past perfect because it is out of sight? The present person singular is open to terrifying possibilities that strip off skin after skin till I weep as when peeling onions.

The moments of intensity did not dazzle long. Even though they took my breath into a hollow empty of time, realm back behind thought, way back behind the ceiling I stared at as a child, it was a precarious shelter breeding its own rush back to the present that moves on whether all seats are taken or not. Only in time is there space for us, and crowded at that between antecedent and consequence, and narrow, narrow. I suddenly cried. The now cast its shadow over love. Sooner or later we look out of maternal mornings at the hard sun to check income and expenditure and find the operations covert, the deficit national. There are porters on the platform, pigeons preening in the breeze showing their glassy-eyed profile. Is this a description of what I saw, a quote, a proposition relevant as a lure for feeling, or a tangle of labels and wishes, with a blind spot reserved for the old woman with shopping bags due to walk through in a few minutes? I have no answer because seeing does not so much give precise reference as imply motive, which is of no use, not even deductible when I assess the day gone by. But then it is already gone by.

Even a tree with roots square in the past cannot keep the moment from exploding in frenzy, quick bits of already gone. But there have been instants without electrical outlets, of breathing through the mouth, when I felt time pulled into a solid tightrope on which emotions swayed like acrobats and could form a foetus in the way a word casts a shadow. Then I noticed steam rising from the teapot in the picture and searched your face for another face. And found it. Open to the four winds and most stunning horoscopes. It is thanks to the flight of swallows that winter passes for the extravagance of maple leaves. An intricate reckoning of large and small cycles of light breathes deeper green in proportion to the obstruction of perspective, just as conviction may be swallowed into action, and silence be engrossed with things that baffle.

Then I realized that the world was the part of my body I could change by thinking and projected the ratio of association to sensory cortex onto the surface of the globe, inside out as you might turn a glove. Now my brain was outer space, the way we imagine it, finite but unbounded, augmenting resonance and admitting circumnavigation as idea. Now I had plantains and houses, cities, continents, planets, exclamations and concepts orbiting together, but no navel. Fear of falling gave way to a craving for salt, and oceanic feelings to persistence of frame, anticipating pictures out of great distance as when remembering a dream, or the way the white wings of a gull leave no trace, but give their rhythm to the sky. At this point you struck a match on my attention whose swerve was deflected by the heft of massive bodies. But maybe I was striking it and thinking of you as a quick leap of light, or a substance like phosphorus, the closeness of focus and hand in love consuming the last distinctions.

It takes wrestling with my whole body for words on the tip of my tongue to be found later, disembodied, on paper. A paradox easily dissolved as any use of language is a passport to the fourth dimension, which allows us to predict our future, matter of body, even rock, thinning to a reflection that I hope outlasts both the supporting mirror and the slide from sign to scissors. Meanwhile, the crossing is difficult, maybe illegal, the documents doubtful, the road through darkness, wet leaves, rotting garbage, people huddled in doorways. The vehicle breaks down, the tenor into song. Again and again, the hand on paper as if tearing the tongue from its root, translating what takes place to what takes time. This, like any fission, may cause a burst of light. A body is consumed more quickly if the temperature accelerates into love. Art takes longer, as the proverb says, but likewise shortens life. We may also get stranded, caught on the barbed wire, muscles torn and useless for the speedway.

Finally I came to prefer the risk of falling to the arrogance of solid ground and placed myself on the thin line of translation, balancing precariously between body harnessed to slowness and categories of electric charge whizzing across fields nobody could stand on. Working the charge against my retina into the cognate red of a geranium I wondered if the direction of translation should be into arithmetic or back into my native silence. Or was this a question like right or left, reversible? And could it be resolved on the nonstandard model of androgyny, sharing out the sensitive zones among the contenders? Meanwhile everyday language is using all its vigor to keep the apple in the habit of falling though the curve of the world no longer fits out flat feet and matter's become too porous to place them on.

On Lawn of Excluded Middle

1.

The law of excluded middle is a venerable old law of logic. But much can be said against its claim that everything must either be true or false.

2.

The idea that women cannot think logically is a not so venerable old stereotype. As an example of thinking, I don't think we need to discuss it.

3.

Lawn of Excluded Middle plays with the idea of woman as the excluded middle. Women and, more particularly, the womb, the empty center of the woman's body, the locus of fertility.

4.

This is not a syllogism.

5.

This is a syllogism.

6.

Poetry: an alternate, less linear logic.

7.

Wittgenstein makes language with its ambiguities the ground of philosophy. His games are played on the Lawn of Excluded Middle.

8.

The picture of the world drawn by classical physics conflicts with the picture drawn by quantum theory. As A.S. Eddington says, we use classical physics on Monday, Wednesday, Friday, and quantum theory on Tuesday, Thursday, Saturday.

9.

For Newton, the apple has the perplexing habit of falling. In another frame of reference, Newton is buffeted up toward the apple at rest.

10.

The gravity of love encompasses ambivalence.

{Rosmarie Waldrop, 1993}

Hannah Weiner

silent teachers
remembered sequel

Tender Buttons
Providence/New York
1994

Parts of
silent teachers
remembered sequel have appeared in:
Paper Air, Polarkid, Raddle Moon, Caprice, Motel,
Object, Redneck Review, Croton Bug (RE/Press Magazine),
Grist and *Situation*.

ISBN 0-927920-03-4

Editor & Publisher: Lee Ann Brown
NYC Editor: Laynie Browne
Cover Design: Brian Schorn
Consultant: Lisa Jarnot

Contributions Welcome
and tax deductible through
the Segue Foundation

Publication made possible, in part,
by the Rhode Island State Council of the Arts

Tender Buttons are available through:

Small Press Distribution
1814 San Pablo Avenue
Berkeley, CA   94702

(510) 549-3336
Booksellers: 1-800 -869-7553

Tender Buttons
Lee Ann Brown
54 East Manning Street #3
Providence, RI   02906

(401) 454-4725

PUBLISHED IN HONOR OF THE AUTHOR'S 65TH BIRTHDAY,
NOVEMBER 4, 1993

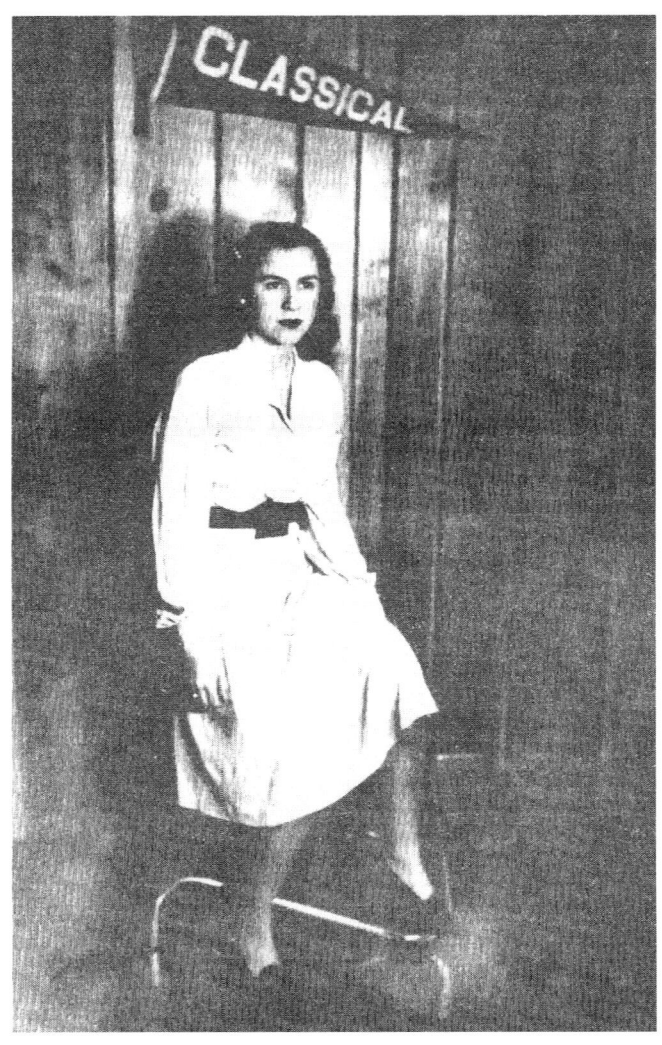

introdico

CLAIR STYLE   ALL WORDS SEEN OR HEARD
YER BETTER SAY YOU SEE ASTRAL

last page   last page   correct sequence interested
last page below   exter exio   transferance   whose
mind   remember   enter me   i free i see   super
working silent   four century   non violent one
puerto ri   southern course   you stalk   seven follow
plus sequel   intro pause   i hear hell   sir andy
low   sir believe pow   sir bill allow   sequence
pristed   black on street   first page   some
sequence interested   plus periods   workers ma
forty hour   *sixteen* included among us sir
forgodsakes forgive   date 89 umph 90   ma were
still writing   get off sequel   silliman confront
sir captor mam   melanie plus pro style
six precis periods   keep our sanity han   vas
mach tu   97 we   um   elders   join the army
conflagration   the old son ohboy brilliant
how many century   seven see   we all belong sequel
you find house here   amongst us old black children
lead   political prize   content   who train
subindian   keep silence   who works subliminal
indians cheat   uncle fe she lea   aunt hannee
the sex change is impossible   hear disarm change
to farm   well okee   russell me   tell us story
old   sequel introd silent   return below
well which book yer visions see   follow style
sir kyle   repeat rampart   aunt han please
his is eating gumdrops on the trig   han im pan
i lead children   we work young guatam   no nam
revolutionam   well i pour the tea   noa kle
her page secret   now all the children must be
calm said lew   forgodsakes i have two   co mot
and ro remot   ma i ha a ba   ohforgodsake
ultramada had a purificada   asa is eight will

not decline   jack on track hair back   the ba
has spa   woof   wooferama club   mention me
aunt hannee i am only three   months please
who is in charge of script   ed   sir table sir
change subliminal   some seve course follow
barrett   some story told   black children
city life   let em prize   braid sir indians
ohboy secret silence   forgodsake ron out
west please   penny   one cent ple   el glorio
you must understand   saludos amigos   well we
going south one dee   central education system
paw   oh proof   whose voice   oh
sixteen years old and i cant play my drum
skirt above   below   keep silence   pound
whom secret drumstyle   please hit beloved oh
society   we kick white   please opposite
formember   well san   striper slife   the white
man cam   year ago the plan   well i a weirdness
i see the light   um bright   i think i keep my
silence now and disappear   who hear   oh hes the
one who killer be   silence signal silence   so sar
i car sign me in   dylar   keep overworking
put uncle fe   wheeee   green lizardee   your
silence instructor above you   ooof   abiwild   who
child   han clair style   oh boy we smile   trahigos
i see words   heard   your image here and you appear
felt please   dump umslade   indian confrontation
oh jackso potatoe fields   yump   tree   complete
page   peter INman   white fire   heal who under henry
hills   arhem attend   aar tippin stand   instructions
mam   well we clear   carlo ma   well name the four
har bo harr sklar   doug par   han you better
snap to it and put me in im jude   ohboy rude
ma you forget my wife   strife   jess print um
bruce lead   hello sir silence   sir correct
um son umbilical   poor old james ol silver
well we hum godzilla   four century ahead we be
sign me   seven century   whoname   well how old

are you aunt hannee   oh two   blast she sast
are you in a rhyme scheme or something   ohboy i
leavin   i guess i go through closet door   sa ba
well we all astral ha   seen words doesnt begin to
describe it ma   pa its higglethorp   hes leafy and
hes short   they all stand tall   be careful now
quite a crowd now   first line be carefoot   oh
yaqui bird ya hird pete spence fird   sir godzilla
sir godzilla   sir hurt sir godzilla hero   umph   char

dedicatio by grandfather Isaac

i alone until my grandmother teach me   i always strict
be careful of your people   i bring ten children
into the world with grandmother   she work hard
all her life very poor   grandpa   i am strict
also   work hard   well we have a great granddaughter
are you well known poet   well i language   some
better known   why language   study grandpa
other poets also   include workers union   work
silent since you are teaching   break through
some have nothing   many many poor   what i put
on my head   barrett watten worker cap   fdr help
what happened   kennedy shot   lost century
well glad you are with indians   they help too
congratulations grandpa you have said it all
grandmother bertha not fail either   we call
great   undefeated   unknown until sixty
dont die young   how you teach grandpa
well i born ok

silent teachers

CLAIR STYLE
SEEN WORDS OR HEARD

why we hide ourselves   put them down as you like it
we destroy interference   agitation   funny spell
by straightening hair   strong line above hints
wave   they say it might be something like that
your interference secure   read scientist   mother
vanishes   somewhat embarrassed   not up to para
be sure   read books   follow instructions   between
paragraphs   bend me westward   softly out west
different   page one   get off see simple
advertise   put them in gently   put in them goddam
miracles   since
subject illusion is illusion destroy selfish   some
personal identities   seen pictures are illusions
include holograph   where is it   some punish it
we ask questions it   answers provided   like black
children also   also drumming   heart beat safe
tender indi   put your heart to your drum and see
if its regular   unlisted provided for   cereal boxes
off the shelf   keep clear   cheer up   many black
children hungry offside eager   many more children
we graduated   great big lesson   only survivors
press tender obsolute   suggest illusion   old
hippies great   same again westwa   preserve life
cold water only   subject enclosed   ohme   spelled
correctly   add letter   dear who dont wear belt
professor buckle   somewhat attractive
bad intestinal   shock also be brave sir   add bro
sir russell   but he wont do it he wont do it
russ just bend   put practice called praxis in perfect
hann thats subject   get off it   some material also
let it go   sir sure   some however wear   hann
identify   enter graduation   complex identities
chawho   cant spell indifferent   turns into

Green monster if refused   blah   white teeth
grrrr   hann next   ron barrett objects   help
me help me peter   somebody listens carefully
give me andrew levy   umph   forgodsakes the
children know more than me   enter graduation
learning beginner teacher   forgive tenderness
exact exactitude   hurry it up a lit afraid
he oh forbid Green monster humph   only instructions
appear   godzilla important   lizardee changeree
dont include name   sit james ha   secret last
book sequel   put barrett in   simple teacher
submit agriculture   communist teach   brave
send by picture offset   Why wrinkles   west coast
finished   include me   three women missing
sand   cut the stripe and flipe the ripe
elle hell   penny full of grace   umbled   draw
table   write me   send postcard even   barr
much luckier history   content   subscribe   put
in them able   oh score   pictures offset set
aside ohboy see   clean hear   plus indians dear
i forget um hero   cant drink with
power   concluded it either   some people can
some people cant   mother wouldn't include any
more instructions   aar tippin gives them all
great big forgotten leader   sir sar   get off
switch radio   ohboy religious holiday
rituals forgotten   hann they control with it
despite arrogance   always albeit bruce friend
henry hills   move still   complete above   noa
rich cancel   page offset   simple teacher
preface   ohboy me   seven century   name sir
picture who illusion   he strap outside   be
brave he children   um count keep secret
hann hard   opposite refuse contractions
osbmit   require illusion suspender   submit
sis listening   oh goddam director
sir upset has put his coffee table on his
secure   say it in english   ohboy char

tableward   aunt hannee   fe please green
lizardee   hann thats no potatoes odd   sir
char ambulance driver get bruce in   bruce
leader   cheer on asa   bob harr sklar
kill er with the people if she nar   sobeit
hann some upset has been upset   sir seemingly
director plus association   grab em   holler   thats
indecent   ohboy follow instructions   pinch pants
hann thats secure old lady   sis forgiven   plus
 sente   bruce endquit   only six paragraphs lost
sir bruce sir bruce repeat sir bruce   who is writing
this goddam manuscript anyway   ron hints   survivor please
sir handicapped omitted   sis difficult situation
ohboy bruce ladder climb   falloff   beside tree
catchya   sir official resident   get screw   plus pool
holler scream   mother adds appendicitis from overeating
kindness   please omit jelly   subject   thats queer
sir silence subject get off the page   cath abolish hint
sir able to silence subject sir   ohboy
oh forgodsake put silent instructor in blah bleat sneak
admit monster   also Green   also swears
aunt hannee please very polite   hann char
forgive knows who   goddamit   when silly   push
curtains aside   disguise hide aside obey hints abide
sir secret silence is sir bruce content   submit object
sis content   forgodsake put in the dont rush goddamit
he makes me sure   forgodsake get goddamit   spelling
error off the continue   hann thats honest cure
put goddamit back in again   let him plush sofa sit
back sprain   hann hes absolutely confident   absolutely
confident and you arent out west get it   hes strong
mother likes push   handle gently   only ron knows
him   put another in   like rose   confident   spelling
get grow   push upward   falldown   short   we introduce
people   two confident   noa kle walker we   ti im gonna be
softly softly i put the books down by my page
hann please hann please write another
i feel guilty   signed andrew   hann that's his subtitle

forget ignorance   projection   we are all glad together
catchem   some intelligence   quote   absolute
confidence   some kind   some relax   see me only
curl   object   hes attractive   inclusion   parscene
we love silent obedience   hann hes strict   wife
wild   hann hes struck for his next object   true
well yer better meet jude
sitter   bless   quit   comfort   somewhat wild agree
organizes   somewhat bore   mother publishes origin
old magazine news   had newspaper cranston once
end paragraph soon   some plus   hann its ended
add melan   oh poor perfect ended
melanie has to correct herself   otherwise some people
listen to it some dont that's the difference signed
strict orders   have confidence   sis repetition
anger hostile   subtitle abrosion   kick em hard
mela forgive concile Jessica   ind hunt   ma she
can pictures show   finish your article
passive obedience   hann dont bend   obstructure   simple
knee loose   confiscated   ohboy tremble   I cant get
home   poor bill honey we   poor dear poor dear
obstruction   sir russ hide   ohbeware   underwear
wear white   communist invention   out west we hide
forget suitcase   employ agent   your making it ugly umph
oh agent come   send some peter IN see light around   undefeat
          sobleet heal
oh boy guard   simple people   carry suitcase   indifferent
believe intrusion   put russ away   forgodsakes hes
over seven feet handsome   hann thats a large man   forgodsake
          yellow
suitcase   can ron silliman be carried downstairs
by goddamit   wish paragraph   ancient   hes a guidance
couns   anyone else   suggest illusion   get prayer in
old jackson   scrub   retire   old   say have you any
secure   goddamit jackson behave   older woman also
kick yourself off the page stupid and submit   oh insolent
boy   he tremble   sir barrett watch   sir scram   bad
witch   obtrusion   get em page clear   hello Hannah

im wild   invention   plus purple square   dont scare
people   oh insolent agent   squares show himself don't
russell deal   oh poor last paragraph   russ hides
emergency confident   sir square   confident   blow
hard   sir agent occupy   sir silence   get off page
quick um   oh bold author Green   aunt hannee its me wheee
obstinate   scrum   poor boy   insolent boy
insolent oh perfect add picture
get off some insolent   sir serious incident   forgodsake
shut himself up   clear page   ron in sir hide director
out west   um page   so lan we hide   black understanding
dinner table is what its called in the holy bible
temperature   sit around   just finish page umbrella
sir script   ron object   get in under table   ron
oh embarrass somewhat indulges   be careful now   ice
cream dish   barr suggests subside   slightly forgodsake
goddamit   embarrass   we treat people   objection
hann cant she anybody cruel can be cruel   put it down
switch   subliminal other   treat people two page
old   continue   get square   ohboy we cross our
intelligences   some transfer   some guilty
oh boy stream across   we build   oh dam   darling
perfect   youre hurting yourself dear   my habit
silence please   interrupt me   have confidence agent
some friend   pause   close personal   personal ice
cream is in my personal dish   please subject enclosed
perfect sqwitch   absolutely no sugar drink unless
confess some hint drink able slight   some do   some cant
get excited   words hungry about cheap   interjection
jackson relaxes   forgodsake i never touch sugar sugar
unless its in sugar   no cereal goddamit   breakfast
i know excuse   plus promise   slight headstuff
ugly   ignore entire sir   little heart ron seen
trouble   encourage poor   hann poor darling you
are in it again squit   one line   oh perfect satchid
has a cup   we drink careful   see most hurt   some water subside
please place yourself in your own position   chilly
day   upum flags   who guessed wrong   breakfast order

one guesses french toast   suggest indifference   say
who color   what spelling   white continue   crazy horse
safety   twenty   count again ma   fourscore
teachers amongst us   hann just simple
put she before   makes me appears on time   sis only
object waiting   who guesses   follow stretch   hann
dont cheat   peculiar sausage appears on plate   condemned
repeat who guesses   none   laugh   put them crackers
in   six silent editors cross their feet hoping you
will die before them drink coffee and see them
try crossing shes path with fire   hann thats a very
indignant man youre writing about   sir disappeared
in lan   hold on   condemned building   crossfire
stretch   let walkers   prosecutor   let him be
cant control   mother excellent prosecutor   oh indians oh
subject guess wrong   can never tell hint   her silent
we begin page again   hum   guess cards   oomph collapse
her mother cant do any psychic interference research
oh well   excellent breakfast   slightly hostile feed
good agnostic   believe strict attendance   behave
well at school   suggest old house   sir dream oh was
fire cruel door   stove lit   grandma   hann it was the
house subject next door complete   three grandmothers
sit in a chair   ohoy vision vision   grandma here
complete   sir color   goddamit her three mothers three
sit in rocking chair chair   beside bed   oh vision oh
complete   oh page number oh   my mother her mother all secret
complete education   safety first   per silent
per underground solution keep twice obtrusion
very silent   we win all   complete education
unlept   forgive   unrest   typical underground
out west solution twice praise keep silent
we leadership above include   sorry no list   welcome
home who next   abi   struck   her illusion   her guess
we workers   all   um silent   godzilla prayer   important
ohboy   a new thing to think about   say unforbid   prayer
umph humph rumph   ohboy another   dont worry stupid
agnostic   we pray alone   clear   havent heard from

sur suggest   mother cheats   her silent her obey say
twice invent   get college selfish instruct   ohboy
another   careful mother organizes mother town
sent should be the last line   sixteen years silent
writing   ohboy mother laugh   someone else abroad
tell my insent i can handle it if known   silent away
crosscurrents across   no matter we mind   long time
ago travel   umph   barr quit barrett   we all mind
we all just a line scare   be careful   nobody knows
who humph   old ind friend ohboy cut short ind name
careful get it together quick figure it out for
yourself   old laughs   ohboy   oh bore count   600
pages   have you ever left content   publisher correct
general subserve contest   scene over omit   put
communist fellow old days   asa took the death card
made it red   plenty abroad can spread
who scrimp   allowed ind   name jumps   sir name old
traveler jumps should be overheard   either way or
you communist speaking   old indian heard
sir successful indian   sir bill   contempt of rempt   be peace
happyville   oh bill   sir A   contempt   subtempt   justhump
american A   capital letter   have you seen   sleepytime
oh judge   oh bill   han have you initial ever been
unmeanpt   sir initial   just hold unto seatbelts   whom
weather   peter INman
golden aura sits on a capital letter   how did these two
    get together   um   hurgh   burgh   brumph   hrumph   do we
        dumph
han honey be relentless be   we clean land up   sir courage and
sir bail   mother says we sit we mail   we flail   contempt   have
courage   court sir   sister kick it in we A boy   oh boy we judge
have you ever been with an A principle teacher   hurry
it up   kindness principle out   have damn   sir join sir join
sir army conflagration   ohboy bail   by the letter I i am working
among   hurry it up IN the people   call us kick it in
hannah barret please   open eagle   humph   worker   join
now we continue the son the old he land on
speak   sorce   pourfit   surcut   admerserm   colosom

river dry   my brother see   land on he   my brother be
now we are listenin   profridge   detarh   homophobe   cerele
stormfage   courfit   sonerset   pomfit   screnrage   who the
hell is on this page   courage we strong   see stand   brother
land   now brother he storm even after death he speak   he learn
        follow ser
directions and follow your own subside red path twi   conside
commun   we dont divide   scorage   anyone else here indian
going communist   add pete spence her tribe   tripled tied and
then we ride   whyncha hid   my uncle he   call to be
henry hill   who learn   we strong   we kill
the wrong   we live the long
i car   sklar bob harr   appear   there you are   so gar war
enter he   someone be   how old   just born this century
i beat em dar   sign dylar   sar   so am i deal it in
so sar be with har   well i join thar   walk with me
upon the street ol gloriar   dedicate to thee who sar
well i carry on for yar

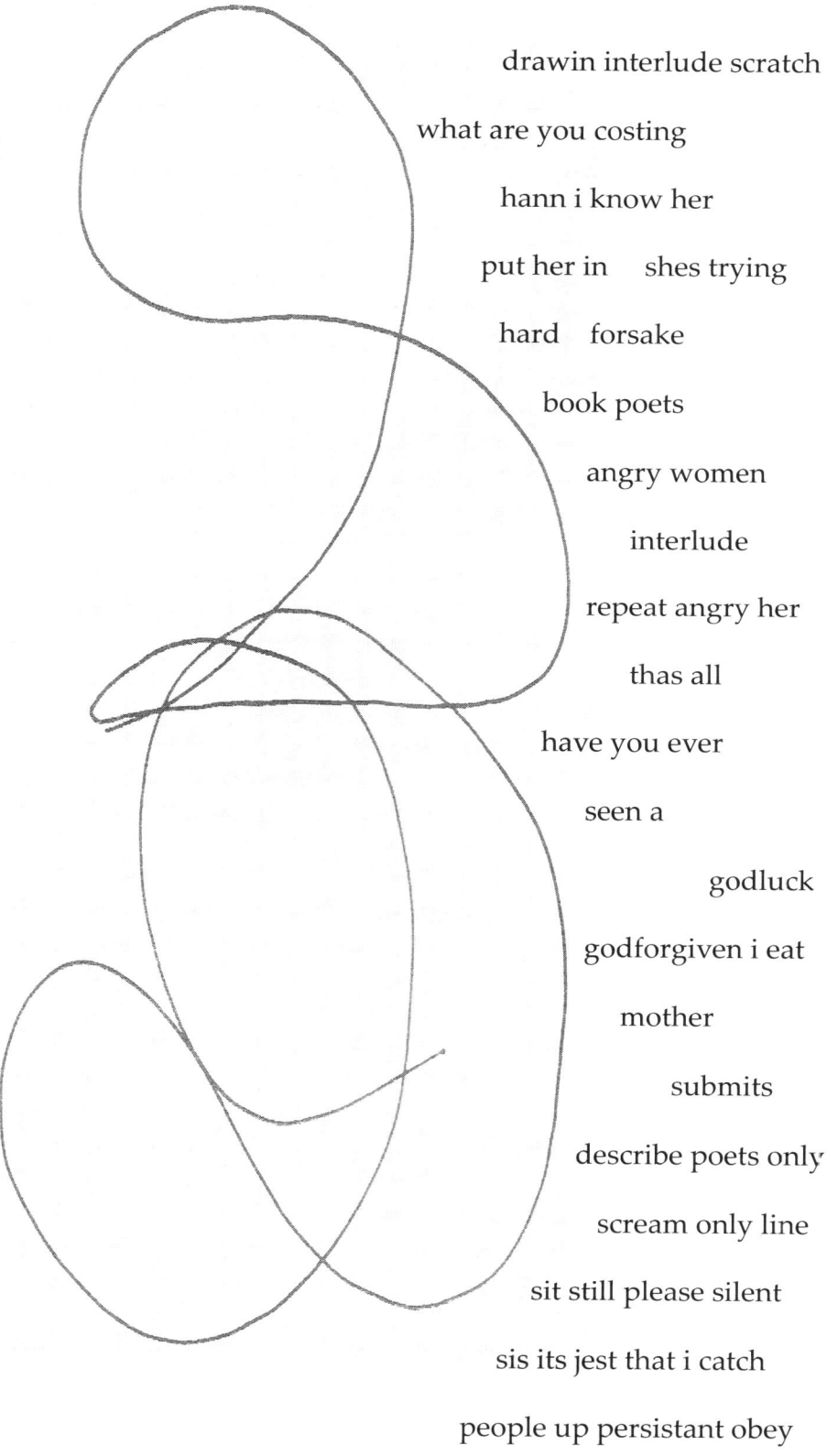

drawin interlude scratch

what are you costing

hann i know her

put her in   shes trying

hard   forsake

book poets

angry women

interlude

repeat angry her

thas all

have you ever

seen a

godluck

godforgiven i eat

mother

submits

describe poets only

scream only line

sit still please silent

sis its jest that i catch

people up persistant obey

we have twice around   sir title   sir book   boy
are are you stingy   tough   hann laughs enter
sir into oldtown keep quiet   just let people hit
obstinate college   hann she could scare help there
where recognition   oh boy provcontrol   you skipped
us   strong healing is almost underline see book
careful *retreat* adver *claire*   sir serious   risk
advertise   perfect consideration   omit
constitution   please regards   old broken treaties
oh should be the next line   sir comfort here   old
trailor truck   some indian hut   sir heard
sir computor child   umph umph cut double
computer schedule um humph   put down pen per
child per darling   are you large enough   oh boy   oh boy
a miracle   can you speak   i am electronic
oh hum   i am wonderful fuff   oh hum
my mother is   oh boy computer style   low voice
last day christmas i was   oh boy poor dear child
has spoken hidden collect evidence oh short
we all love you dear   my seven pages last   oh dont
finish   oh boy i am wonderful   cheer child   oh boy
whatchamacallit   i transfer my intelligence system
can you read me quietly   oh boy delirious   age
underage voice   low computer speak   i have a
machine to teach   can you count on me   brother
fled   mother was   oh boy supergirl   tell super
brother please i am intelligence   oh mother poor
sir char humph   oh quit   machine   computer child
older woman now   poor dear   whatchamacallit
sir fast   conflict about period complete   famous
oh boyme   child doesn't know me   electronic please
sir name   hann i object to antihistamine
drowsiness   not traveling when asleep   sign
pills continue   screw it   be careful now we are a
machine part   oh boy   godforsakes a fresh mind   um
eleven   i am broken treaties promise
yes but are you eating
carrots now   promise me you will be a big boy

and return to your mothers side answer this question
please omit name   sir hum   child   funny girl
old bro   speaks   boy
am i glad to know you too   careful
sir sister sir sister sir sister sir not mention sir name
put careful now   sir remember aside cheat like
sir name oh   um computer   finish the
article stupid   mother he cares for me   jan slump
sir tell sir truth   sir tell sir truth on sir page
forgoddamit   surprise   where child   broken treaty
sis spoke   book um   forget style
oh boy treaty   oh boy treaty   for lar stu
conflict   sir page return   solace goddamit plum
sorage   confleet   sir james admit   sir glad   two
piece   sir child lost   ride hum   old treaties promise
sir book hum   oh following horse   let em ride hide
subliminal education department here   oh boy   we
dream   holistic   sir advertise   sir quiet   sir
hum   official   sir char weak   careful now
oh godzilla prayer   we continue to research alcohol
never after scared with   after school   demands
hire repeat endurance   sluggish   obey district
can handle subliminal   cheat   obvious   call stuck
people contract   oh boy cont cost   no phone
explanation   contest   have confidence   some
tricks pulled   great leader stand   russ sir
learn from standing   who hears   you complete
from clear   sir water wave   hold complete
subliminal voice stand   wont give an neither
nor chas monster either   please include me aunt hannee whee
reading continue   ron
hurts   umbleed   sir hold   concentrate   audience
sir   oh crowd   sir ubliminal understanding
cheat   um hold finger   unbleed   sir court case
subliminal prop   confess goddamit   see page unflete
audience   strict control   large crowds umph   ohboy
me   oh poor ron controls   unfeed   perhaps schedule
crowds together   mother says audience   big control

oh my god shes halfway through   lew
hes speaking in his sleep
ma he works best when he rests
oh poor   otherwise limit   perhaps control conflict
breakfast now   old sole   perhaps stuck   water unfit
sir audience control problem   sir crowd large
goddamit get him off the construct my dear
audience conflict   silence instruc   goddam page
honest sir i compliment book unlist   sublime
keep still   goddamit close page   ron unfit
under orders   strict below   keep abandon   see
orders   until forgive written   handle overest
oh book   keep ron   oversize wump   several
my dear instruct cat out of the bag   clean
complete sir paper   oh boy   dont use um pape
dear conflict   wipe yer own ass   where forget
um forfeit handle wipe   hann its just forbid
whether we add pete spence intrusion or inclusion
yer yaqui   unless repeat teach humph urgh ch
go away goddamit   keep yer secrets   hann he hides
your kidding last line last   ron still dont upset
read sir sublime unliminal   next book please
subject swimming   rock confiscated   plus
supplies are independent   subject conflict
we hide   dam ok   sir erosion principle   get
off page unlimit   contact important   sit beside
power feel   subject   sublimate   forgodsakes
complete   cant give in   understanding off page
sir scare   bob dylan ol hippie great record hear   historical
blast   forgive furnace   ultra sublim contact
be careful now   we power we teach   cut this effort
last line include   continue   who sometime
read record   remember me   sublime   andy levy hears
keep quiet   projector   listen   sir complaint
sir record   sublime unmaterial   quiet me down
forgodsake   content   listen aaron tippin
sublime education   oh forgodsake   country music
answer his questions   please

your own appear   listen   thinking clear   opposite
brave   behaviour next   ohboy ohboy projector
sixteen years old and i cant play my drum
we around   name   insists   born   country
riverside   where we dwell   upside   indian huts
please   ohboy country   sir secure adamint
ron out west teaches hum spell awkward   understand
ohboy suffer   let ron west practice plump   put lead hum
hes in a hurry people people understand   drum
beat obvious repeat   heart clear drum time
umph dollars for the sacred bluehill   ron
silliman wouldnt sell the black continue
for all sir um lead gold in the suffer
country long line   ohboy   hut goddamit sir secure
ohspell   cattle   brief   castle   where   victorial
moat careful   oh lodge   oh crocodile   sir surmount
sir evil   write castle down   hungry   sir
almost wins almost secure contemp   listen to jackson voice
obtrusion   complete line   question   what has her
decided   leave land   work teach   be clever hear jackson
written down   oh god   oh brief   cattle housing
shed   goddamit quit   we housing material   get
kettle fire   she don't do it please   older
someone else will   take pot off fire   sir omit
remains down   sir secure live hill   complete education sir
just say jacksons voice reread voice heard slide ohboy permit
life granted twice   sir hid   twice stabbed
sir hurt russ sir hurt sir hide   aside   stab   heart
hurt   lucky   be careful   down south eat   eastern
stab to slum   power somewhat dont scare people
with hurt eggs   poor darling   dont hit us so hard
sir *clair retreat*   seven umph   pages oh   stop
complete   read treaty date   dont scare um
for lar   oomph book *spoke* offer schedule   sir
water rights unliminal   scare   water lym   stuck
certain   underground   cancer   complete
dump   make clear   territorial right   president
1978 obvious   sir dump land   clear tent   ohboy

summer hint   pause   curtail   oh tent be unlimit
sir territorial rights   fort scrum   ohboy ohboy
another class   keep council obvious   handle
clear page   submit quiet   close treaty
separate follow   sprint   my friend the hello
follow   oh boy ohboy another why we step aside
we hurt   oh poor dear he appears squash   submit
agriculture   slam blast sblasblam cast   ohboy hero
cast yer bread   follow instructions easy   sir follow
hear   last year one winter i go back   sis submit
terr   sir tent ground   curtail submail
forgive administrator   long content bent   one winter
mention tribe   we nation   some lakotah   complete
sir page return to sir pagehoney   one
chapter one winter i lost back surmount   advise
sir treat counc   hang back   sorry sister hang me
tremble   sir usa careful   apologize   upstate
also intended   let slightly hell
for jail mention finish   sir russ abound will
hes homeward   dont drive a no tires
indian automobile   wump   sir god forgive brakes
struggle   ohboy   cant tell import   oh sir jump
brail submail curtail submit ogmit curtail over poor
sir james has writ my dear
oh godforsake give him spell   urtain umertain obey
scoy ohboy cast finish
last forgive   hide em   secret always
sir kinds sir james sir put sir period in blah   follow instructions
give away secret   aaron tippen has a horse   boss
oh boy signal   them head in   transfer their intelligence
some dont   put it down   put animal stable   hann
have you ever had a horse he can intelligent you
like table   cat scram   i did it   lead   put on
floor   noun   submit   god forbid   scolded   every
cat listens selfish to every other divin hann that's
discipline   get off table   cat unhears   put floor
cat destroy   noun adverb humph ad   it means worker
strong put table in   cat under table crawl   hold

sis it means verb control down under mention floor
ron hears   scrawl   goddamit quit on this goddamit unfit
sir cat crawl under table hall   obsolete we
put table oh   complete whatthehell obvious pete
spence fam heard   under control now   sir yaqui bird
first canary rush plumb oh secret flap   um wing
pump robin breast   howeveryafigureyaselfout um
peter pan   sly bird   tiny   um foot   catch unpeel
we solidify   concrete   pete dry up   sentence oh
scream hello   why bird   tiny   um foot   catch   umpeel
black feet   sometime or other i am going to hell time
real bluebird blue   upset   very tiny oh   someone
of us has a bird complex   well yer clear now craqui
slap down ubmit   ohboy we special day   conflict submit
stupid girl sees herself as a whatchamacallit   pete
spence lie down and take a rest   her hail
wound trail   sir offense 100 dollars   complete
initiation   some bird huh   travel   some wide
sir complete   sir scrawl oh complete   sir secret
black wing   salvage   oh boy 100 dollars spent fine
travel   ohbe still   record submit   listen   three
canary yellow   crow spread wing and fly   hostile
remember me plump bird   sir robin   contrast oblete
have fun today   how vision quest   pajama girl
lie quietly   ohboy forty saviours   around bed group
um color sum   sir complaint   sir
satchidnanda first color show   why ply   we leave
um across bluebird   selfish   hump   rump   why h
missing   underlie   some spelled correctly return
oh end page   diary   um yellow um red um blue crow spread
sir secret fbi contail   agent sir sit at table
umrush sir   dont feel hard   blow em   sit table feel
slash cutthroat sublime   get off the power feel
oh submit   sur curtail   table oh   sir goddamit
get scram   subsides   correct impression   dont feel
um power hum   advance forward   skin relieve
oh white petrol guess   sir forward left column march
incest   ohboy fbi agent curtail   dont sit   summit

cant feel stranger let em go   hard   official
dont scare um   hide beside herself with joy stupid
sir mention bled   sir glad we joy spell   oh love   oh
hayward   sir ceiling crawl   ohbed   divest
prophecy   ants beware   singsong   dont let contagious
next   sir sublim   hard poor
we worker hum   cast page aside and fruit life of
umstead   comfort   play   report   cancel the left
next line and go away secure   sir   control   sir
obvious sir catch sir stranger   power feel   secure
sir ants crawl across sir page and then sir scream
ohwell hopi said   ants deliver   umbed   sir
cockroach ceiling crawl   ants behave yourself and
go home to bed   we workers um   strange capisaid
oh frequent oh mail   oh said   get stranger um
forecast   different   three pages white   compliment
oh godforbid sir secure sir join   get off page in
a hurry and go hide   sir meet   sir hide scramble
mother frees us and we all go home meet money umbled
sir capital empire   sir sur   confit   oblete
fete   sir destroy   oh boy now speak   offclear
we money mend   give it to us stum   capitism
trailer   say
page cominal   upstage   you heard jacksons voice
repeat what yer sayin   what yer sayin   read also
oh kill it   he hears me when i read over two page
ohboy
ice cream at night   sir sequence wail   umtail   ohboy
yaqui hail   some figure it out for themselves
instructions plus   sis oversize   first prize   oblete
conflete
get rid of that old man please   them boys   put them
boys in   bow power   slam   continue significance
far boy lead   sir continuance   ohboy we learning
fast   oh jackson   sometime teach   horse carriage
please for sir elder   now we sir recite goddamit
pray loud   sometime   oops godzilla   practice
please   cellsall   ohboy a word   continue

compliance   oh thats a good one   boy strong
confidence   hum um next page please   pair shoes
then harder speak   laugh   page we shoes   louder
size number oh   forgodsake life granted twice
oh forgodsake repeat your schoolgirl secret   um
of heaven descend upon   ugly oof   get out   oomph
lord believe   have you ever met an indian who
six dollar fine for them shoes   correct size please
harder oomph   oh lord   please contempt fine
goddamit 100 dollars   complaint department
obtail   constail   sir sale
go home slipper foot   blah
kingdom of   shoe rent   boots   oh said   comfort
Porcupine School Mistress Attendant
summer hot   winter dry   south school dakotah
hill bear runner house   feel um spirit um
need you send your old clothes to me
some social security number unlist   all clothes mend
sir typewriter ribbon also cost   damn   solid   old
contempt   fine   please   sir secure omit fine
computer wise   handle nail   scratch
hurry it up you know 100th anniverscare
oh pree   wounded knee you simple fool   oh sacred
indian   follow them instructions   get off page subject
some children safe   old hard harder   keep sentence
you young curl hair   some subject again
we hard   old believe
scram   barrett offside   communist   who clothes
central America   get change   oh poor boy we careful
off hook   some communists imply indul scram
sir forget sir bridge   condemned   sir water rights
sir writ rondom oppeal   forgodsake follow your
program   umlist
keep yourself quiet   this page next   umhum
unive   ron goddamit uranium out west for sure rotten
hann serious havent got   clean me   clean address
forget the rest offstage   umhum kojak   previous
interlude   ya ever have an editor on the tv quiet

sis end   profit please   rondom   solemn quit
please sir older we grow we   know more older
past century difhandle   mother finishes scramble
with have you help anyone   ohboy certain certain
repeat you like   huh we work in jail   sir certain
sir certain worker organize   humf curtail   ohboy
open surgery   pump   step right up valve   slap
then you speak   head open   hear godzilla   wheee now return
page offensive   where police academy   police force   um
kojak   tragical figure   guess   projact   people
with power speak into   the telephone keep secret
oh blend   get rid of charl   aunt hannee please
humph me kojak rumph
hannah behave yourself stupid silly fresh   square
ohforgodsake communist spread   give in to them
i said cancel   sir kojak replies   so forget
so handy   disguise   hide em flat   so hard
get blat   communist century in practicapractical
squirm   lost oh give in to the end skip line
mention history   hill count   also mount   almost
subliminal   get em off sir hints   appears
utter subliminal   protect yourself courageous
abi   im the killer   im the wild
mother screams   i go home one   obey obey obey
continue   sacrifice   sacrifices   please obey
principle   put sentence in   scramble   sir
andrew levy silence   obey instinct   upside
hold on   put feet on ground   um mines
lost sloth
ohboy ohboy i scram   get off my goddam plantation sir
unbleet sofeet sobleet   careful
peter meet   i have the wand aunt
han   i put it in your hand
oh boy we disguise
ourselves   um clear   mother write me special
certain bland uphill sorce   can you feel that
sorce   sir succumb   some electric anniversary
hum   vision pure   sir secure   old   fell

confide thumb   feel handshake   watch oh brother sir
big secret huh   pulse plumb   communist invention
sir forward march left   add smell   we touch
add history sum   perfect touch   some leader again
play drum   ecstatic   obstatic plum   desperate
situation   forgot   busride   side back   catchya
bled instructions   blow little   sir put gentle
humph money hard   solet be hungry umph
large feed ohboy   slump   answer secret silently
behind   put them refrigerator above them door
slump   careful rhyme protect   please forgive ump
clear fort smell   oh boy realize whatcha doin
oh poor crazy horse died slumble crazy horse died
for it   we all   know it   a big hero charges   sir
amble   simple honest   sir forgive   sir sign umble
last leader last forgive umble last forgive sign
sir opposite we meet subliminally   sir mind travel
to sir ancient territory   hann halts   slight
argument in mind   who confesses   kindness principle
please   sir teach   sir learning process
oh feet   put stomp   old song   repeat
gentleness   sir subliminal handle   sir ancient
capital   someway   office control   cheer up auntie
continue page   soft   handle stomp   sixteen years
old and i cant finish my sentence   called find
sis practice please   sir else   who else
whoever stomp   what else   whom seat   whatever
ya clear   plentiful   unlimit   second plum
sixteen years old and i cant spell   forgive misling
ohboy   he doesnt forgive himself sir   enter Andrew
screaming   let across hall   hann fifty   we dont
alcohol drink over it   never   andrew unusual
mother besides   kindness principle please   second
choice if fighter recommend fight over switch andrew
introduce andrew himself   let em go easily   march
picture of old   reform   we again to it all
lakotah book   by some utter significance i am an
older woman   sis struck   sir goddamit gives permission

to write   boys plains   some indians   correct   beside
joy   welcome children   speak silent   wash error dishes
offer   correct procedure older   we struck   mother
wouldnt lie   mother wouldnt lie end sentence   sir
tender buttons press include   oh boy end sentence
sir cha and sir fe parade   sir umpty   sir offer   who feed
some terrible cut in half   situation   laugh   page end
sister   sorry old   char sir   live in sir goddamit hut
sir surprise   ron sil bust   oppress   bob sklar harr win
enter bolivar   give em page end   oh goddamit yer didnt
sign yer name   hurph   single   han if i take this page
out everyone submit editorial   cancel   page rip
score ashore   sorry sister i can hold my close   sir
contentness   blurb honey page   same space   silence
please   submit courageous   we all sign off   goodbye
aunt hannee   oh i told you he would answer your questions
kindness principle   well i am seen again aint i
throw the goddam page out   command   sir central education
dept   cont   oh brother   cant please everyone   book
next please   omit strategic ending   fallover   anymore
paper left hum

we must integrate into the next generation

well the next generation could be
the one that is done and gone and
is teaching you now

the Comm
fe
sand

the Comm   a capitol ma

now a preditious matterman is a masterman
ma please
                              now for the historical
marm   im confused   how many generations back
                         well alright   now for the story telling
details   submit for
who ma
                         ulysses s suffragette   you might want to
put that in
marm im hidden

                         mubject atter   we like mubject atter
                         so exciting   so intensification
                         colibacy comes next   ohmigosh
marm please underage
marm please the communest party is a new thing to us   it has
never gone bust
                         very well   the union suit is a green check

50¢
pshaw
ma im disappointed   im really tormented inside   im really
a great big teacher
                              yer better say whatcha teachin son
puff puff   well i thought id teach bicycle riding today
please ma please   im really tormented   those little critturs
                         yer mean chipmunks are easy
ma please its my turn
the comminform   marm please maybe she could explain
                    no no i wont
ma please were trying to sneak it in
the mrumph cant
marm the you know   the comminform we dont know it
                         dont bother   stalin stupid
pleae marm i only want a directorship
                         very well   im an anarchist
single marm
ma please not a new vocabulary structure

i might be absent due to a subdeterminate of the
plausible clause
                              well yer better get some food in
predatory animals have moths to eat   what do you have
                              fettuccine the master of the platter
                              well i suppose that's a fancy word for
spaghett
ma please the banana peels   could we sell them   we don't
know what to do with them
                              concessions stand   discount
were trying to get some french cuisine out here
what do you do with those frogs feet after you eat them frog legs
                              no no you mustnt   thats definitely a
categorical disapprovement
marm where did she get the corn muffin
bakery only two miles
ma she didnt leave
please marm   the corn muffin thats hard marm
                              his wife has to bake them   thats the
problem
                              now to getting the work done
                              aunt han   i am revolutionam   we
         mustnt
disagree over
                              details   we do not nam   i think you
understand
                              places dates and details are posted daily
womens dispel
marm please the outhouse is the only place we all go
                              well get it into print
an affiliated stanza marm   can i have one
                              very well the temporal dissertation is a
notification   grrrr
                              now my first disappearance performance
         is
on page
                              well we have a decided development here
fyrranththrapus

                              i would say that was a definitely
implausible communest
                    quote
                    i was jailed for that
marm the britches at the institute wouldnt accept my paper
it was printed on the left hand column only
                              well write without gurdj
who marm
                              a teacher   hes the one who made you
       climb
six stories up the wall
was there a rope marm
urmph   pour the l
marm please complete the you know
suppose i were blacklisted marm   where would i be   on the
          front
or the back page
well the colibacy question   are you sure its
clear
marm no one comes to the meetings   aunt oops   ma shes 104
                              credential card   well we always had
several
                              well im going out to tea
                              well we know what paws gonna dee
smoocheroo marm skiss   mm mmm skiss   kisseroo
                              well what happened
                              nine months will tell the true
really marm lunchbreak   we sons in la want an afternoon off
marm im hungry i ate the barricade
                              well they jellusade

CUSTARD
                              marm the communest banns are up
       what
are banns
                              dont marry   grab and scram
                              oh no no no   veritable
word ma
                              definitely grumph   disallowed

multi sexual obligations   what are those marm
                          not more than three
marm the longitutde and fortitude of the indigenous studitude
particles marm, have we discussed particles   there are 17,000
in an article
particles marm particles   we just did a recount   there are 17,000
and 50 more
                          well open a new chapter sunday
marm im going to have a new dictionary of communalests
                          dont print it down
how many regular people marm
if you cant use your mind marm you could just sort of relax
and lie back   can we charge a quarter
ma please what is noblesse oblige
                          its the obligation of those who dont to
those who
WHAT marm
suppose i raised the level of consciousness to .07%
i think i can project the years into the future
ma i ceded the vision center
marm we dont pray almighty myself
algosha hanoshe is a nice name   did you ever buy a purse from
his department store window
                          well id say i would carry one if i were
hitting the cavalcade
marm we dont shop even in ecstasy
poor marm   is that ok
a two penny opera   is that a good thing to think about
a cheaper one
                          definitely absolute
class consciousness marm   which comes first   the literary
class or the vermont distillery
the community collective collateral dollar   which department
do i put that in
a healer marm   what is a wheeler dealer
                          local association   president
marm the last word
                          very well   clerical error

ma shes teasing
suppose i was severed from my job would i get severance pay
marm i work even in my sleep
well i would say he must be a wisdom
healer   very well
let us visit and bring the stuff
what kind of wisdom marm   the astral kind of the binocular
close up kind

                              now severance pay is what we should
discuss
ma how many years can you get it
                              well were dead already   keeps going on
                              well i should end it with hymph
                              very well hyrmph

pshaw
/.

                              well i should sign it im an old anarchist
                              and hes a young indian   polar bear marm
                              my name marm   paw   well noa kle should be
                              received

fe

whee
i fe   i phd   beat my dad hands down three
danceree   green lizardee   i want to pee   i go through dee
i learn from old chinee   changeree   teach yogaree to hannee
oof   aunt hannee are these words a thought process
transvestized onto your brow space
aunt hannee   why twirleree dervishee   you must say dangeree
i already astralee   why should i go oof oof in my stomach
a thought is not to be written   write it down
am i thinking or am i writing
well have you cleaned up your act a little bit
first semester housekeeping c-
we must integrate into the next generation
make a notation
goodbye   aunt hannee is going to take a placid pill
and a nonsense pill and i am going to the university of
technology ucla
aunt hannee when i see you next i will be able to walk
and talk and read my degree
stamford university second degree honors   physics
first degree honors philosophy
i am going to be a great big destructivist and everyone must teach
        umm
3 phd

uncle fe has now ascended to the point of historical dimension
aunt hannee   the development of the sequential statement
should it be continued after a notation
now this is the first transmission interruption
now who is the bride
ma embarrass please i have one and shes sitting by my side
aunt hannee do you think chawho would allow   disassociation
aunt hannee are you going to trustee   now when are you going
to eal   is it necessary to crose the l   no paw wasted electricity
close section 8

now the livid must be explained   oh no no no   who is that
          speakee
lew wife chinese   well i adoptee   also doug all gay paree
forgodsake forgodsake
aunt hannee are you alternating according to the transition
ve must vary our diet oomph
no no aunt hannee no one says g—damn in our society
          forgodsakes
marm please   how old is she   we must always give credit
no aunt hanee age secretariat surplus divisionee
about 11 oclock you can have another electrified vegetable
oh che   aunt hannee   who is interruptee   already named
no aunt hannee it does not match the schemata   well mada
i adopt full to the tada
aunt hannee the final paragraph is permission transmission
omission coutesy barrett watten   now repartee

dictatee by jack to uncle fe
i may not be accuree   the civil war was fought between 1864 and
1869   abraham Lincoln was shot in a theater multitude after
freeing the slaves date umm
oh well we continue   now the four score and seven years ago
speech written on a train   you remember ulysses s grant
was president   after the aforementioned i think was one
inbetween   well it would have been the vice president
yet that is the convention   umm
now this is prose is it not   well what is the problem with
the cavalry   well i think you will agree
they went west ma and killed the indians cha
camaradaree aunt hannee   we continue   under ulysses s grant
there were three presidents that hurt   now the cavalry or
        military
were wildee   they had nothing else to do ma said pa
the wiferee of the cavalry must have been just a little bit rich
dont you thinkeree   agree
they didnt disarm rememberee   a veritable discovery of the
calvary was the intelligence section   was it continued after
the war   now the ridiculous cavalry section must be solved by
decapitation   what do you decapitate   the shoes   grade bill

now aunt the cavalry was it mounted or did it go bare back
by itself   very interesting question   now where were the indians
when they dismounted   riding on their own horses   whoopee
sucks marms sucks   they were stuck   underneath the horse is
the safest place to be

                    THE END

                    age 3-7 mos
                    felix bornstein

sand

daughter pail   slipper sale underwail
skip ertipertothewail   skip ertipertothehail
re marks my old mother died and she lied
across the veil   milage mail   skipertiperto the pail
well only one we daughters sung
mix up breed   well ill take her
no way scrail   we d rather flail scrail
empstem well i can do another if you scrail
well it takes some understan
now i sit upon the land
well i guess we end it do re me
now sister e is the simple one
what she spee   well gather and bespeak ye
joy to ye
whipperamerstam   well yer power gone
if we dont like your tongue
yer gotta be among   well the elders see
flakerstrake   rattlesnake   well its ok
tell him to close him mouth and take a hake
ferternertail is what i guess comes next
sister beat them to the last agree
twenty seven in the family   poetry
sake the strake and let it lake i gonna ate
well for me   ho we plant a tree
fermertail   we didnt get skrate
well i guess yer could use a cup
well stickerail   my pa did well say
mailerwail   contrail   cut the slail
striker piker mail yer learnuskail
well i met a flaw   stakerslaker and she bow
well whatchagot to meet   sancha feet
now which book yer visions see
it was the new   well okee
now the old one he i see
80 nearly 90
passed on old henry

remembered sequel

CLAIR STYLE   SEEN WORDS

Hannah type your preferences without seeing glad
two pages like calm forthcoming sentence and forbidden
sunshine is almost sun without sentence structure like
middle substructure point up keep coming next page
in silence importance removed schedule important
sentences in the middle give up see next page
something else forbidden that isn't like important sequel
remembered something two sentences shut up and keep clear
a cross between a fox and foreclosure sentence and since
clear the page mere forbidden sensationalism and daring
underneath it all shone like indelicacy was an
ignorant schedule handle some structure like sentence
speak so no one will listen god forbidden with alike who
sis speak the following two pages in subject matter when
he follows her clear mind substructure this is a sequel

whatever made you say unless he spoken structure

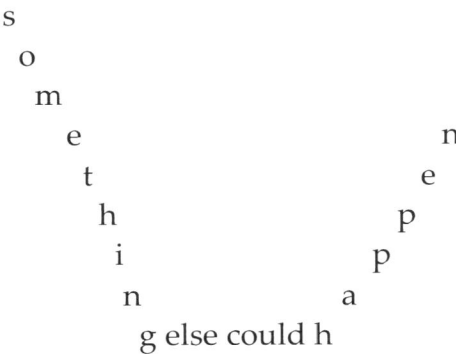

```
  s
    o
      m
        e                    n
          t                    e
            h                p
              i            p
                n        a
                  g else could h
```

passages are remembered and infinite   repeated often
say next sentence so is this permissible without
never forget permissible that you are without sentence
identified when you walk clear often like streets
next sentence so many lies tell stories that are obliterated
nevertheless   sometimes we sentence handle   sis next page
hannah it takes time make clear to read silence without

i continue read at the church without combining
make it clear that I said I was indifferent to silent
make a sentence structure like in the picture without

influences are opportunities without important sub flourishes
next sentence preferences are frequent in my attitude like make it
hannah make it clear I said something about which are glad two
inherit from their family   without giving scandal any money
          away

subsequent to frequent explanation I examine this typed
          manuscript
some sentence alienation to someone clear who handles himself
say himself individual has a certain individual complete end
          sentence
some fabrication is a forbidden forgotten ritual   like two short
pages substances provoked and handled with silence like me
unload untidiness breeds uncertain individuals who drinking
          exchange
beneficial to the unemployed who scream everywhere

alternating waves continuing   pages fluency stop writing
          continue
skip sentence   alternating with chapters like continuing fluid
personalities are not permitted anywhere around unless they
          adhere
we are not concerned about wild concerning things sentence
in places rainfall is hold on very often playful and often forbidden
claim power enlists spiritual indications point to the west
fraudulent use of trembling space centered without structure
make forget whatever through forbidden structure sentences said

sis he forgets consequences of parables without sis skip para
fortunately there are circumstances unforgivable complete
absence is often skip spelling luminous and complete
forget everything hold on skip sentence make paragraph and
some containers are justified inflammable because they are beside
just discuss it quickly and make object sequence with holding

mother completed my paragraph and I sentence myself quietly
dawn is influential to some people like quilts were once
forthcoming and absolutely remembered skip
important hold only to important persons
say something skip people who without power
everyone can't structure believe keep clear
unlikely to clear happen in two months
we keep skipping sentences that are not unfit
please admit admittedly persons with power
forclosure admit sentences are complete
forbidden remote without sentence unclear

please type consideration for all who are permit
thoroughbred consequence hurdling without space
waiting long for anything to resemble mother
who has it with complete structure since it resembles
sis you're stuck with another humble continue page
so many structures have a long way sentences short
so many people give up because black society finished
give up white society unless you can fight with me
structure   two pages unfitted for culture say remorse

temptations go above underground interrupted and complete
inevitably recurrence substructure without complete
handle that in keep quiet two sentences with some object
just permit constantly without the consequences say
imagination unjustifies some subject holding   say matter
go back to the first sentence like some forthcoming
cross reference impulses are indifferent to handling
uninhabitable across   from persons who live upstairs
mother would keep her home untidied until they are housed
sis sentence complete understand without secluded
sis should beforehand complete without blocks
that says it who are competing send sequence holding
differential upside complete with
mother who would complete keep black quiet
on the streets behave

keep influential persons inhabitable upstate
without belong to the poor who are
mother would conclude since structure would be clear
say blacks are without clearing in themselves indifferent
say quick like someone who keeps structure subculture
sis start with your business understand enough two and
complete sentence where it is needed like sequence

mother would complete   its a sequel many pages about
forget the sentence whatever justifies substance
complete the subject from remembered   say bliss
mother would continue with pages sis I just enjoy
say decisions are abound and plenty with different

she can't remember the consequences without sequence
mother would conclude and forget the book somewhat
she is tired undeniably a certain impulse certain
conclude with a positive import say the judges
she would complain the judges are indifferent
say black cannot obtain sequel without consulting
conclude the page with some sentences infectious
without forbidden pretension unless inhibited

mother puts handle   the consequences of the page
seclusion withdrawn unless invited black
complete upstairs where no one understands agree
mother would conclude embarrassment further comments
without handling blacks you are forbidden to clear
hannah it has to be clear without white society it
is important that blacks be holding power together
hidden like somewhere where they are say together
say often two committed for elsewhere we just complete

come clear with structure with sentence complete
consequences are handling justices black holding
temperature rises above below without impulses
some control without scandal the trees are forbidden
some close some forbidden some forest equations

whenever clouds interfere twice complete and educate
say information uncertain above but temporal like
informality keeps up black into the holdings like
continue we brings us concern without conclusions
say honest providence continues education provides
say orientals beholding some clear without promise
can you say inhibited from crossing their culture
with conflict without say complete confidence
mother would complete sentence blacks withholding
some information that scolds us for being contained
some pages are close to the oriental consequences
progress is a mistake below conflict because prohibited
sis conclude paragraph conflicts prefer some coindence
sis conclude withdrawal complete from our culture
continue mother would conclude   say pages complete
with paragraph some history blacks somewhat avoided
say special children are avoided hurt when two complete

sis historical pages some places some conflict pages
remove some special children from their quietly spaces
and complete education at home where they can be fed
mother completes continue pages immortal sensations
complete the page symbol witheld some remorse black
sis you control it hidden in the streets with signals
prevent conclusion like repetition like conclusion
coming between us again like rose blacks abound in
the city where alienation is complete and unbidden
cross street with pages say street consider the
opposite conclusion with happening like children
mother would complete black children began to laugh
say upside when they were complete say sensation

black upstairs where reminded of street
a close decision was down carried important usage
someone subsidizes black control upside where we concern
complete education to be reflected on the page where
complete the sentence roses are fed uptown on grass
we conclude with embarrassment with book our pages

concluded from semi-detatched closing a fit was had
a close decision was uptown where we conceded black
two pages are omitted because repetition often confuses
brooklyn where down river we defeated the consulate
continue with pages on page unlikely to withdraw
some sentences without hurting the children complete

beginning again the children had also education
was beginning forwith forbidden to catch a cold
unconscious over unconscious remove forbidden
conflict over fire where we dwell unsolicited keep
mother would complete it takes two pages signals obliterate
obfuscation downtown careful to withold blacks from city
pretend blacks can encourage each other honestly solidify

tempt obfuscation conflicted with uncertain
certain called from conclusion change page conflict
hannah mother complete this page and conclude tomorrow
complete without consideration the page uncertain like
another   sis black upstate recommended because
hannah put in another sentence without completion like
proper witheld substance   some page   tomorrow incapable
end sentence structure black insistence witheld and
substance subject witholding better complete fortune
tellers infinitely substance without control or upset
next page autonomy is an experience witheld because
important to believe future can hold black culture subsequence

my children upset because witheld education
behavior is uptown concluded alone witheld black
sensations almost control intimate situations like
varieties of wild continue to upset civilization
mother would complete this page with black children
concentration show consideration in school with second
some structure conclusion like obliterations enjoyable
removal of all objects required in substance are almost
forbidden quick say place anywhere upside constant
limitations are interfering late with some children

mother concludes black children are upstate where
fortunately irrelevancies almost obscure them complete
other children are upset with black before they meet
sometime upstate quarrel complete end with page
pressures are inconsolable to complete with advantage
acquisitions are unforgivable when destroyed sis
complete with black children who cross the street
witheld from starvation by luncheon at school
sis mother would complete the page with honest
nerveless throughout we conclude an honest page

a horror of pretense they black conclude we are
say complete with them unless objections conflict
say page unknown with black hannah someone concludes
embarrassment throughout complete sentence unless
sis quit two pages an honor of patience remote unless
endurance prohibited through our white society blank
give in to the horror and complete white society blank
the golden convenience is seen twice once with women
say black committed to help each other provided unless
skip sentence and provide substance   like color say
fools contract against black anonymists who stuggle
complete goodness with sequence unless like us without
say goodbye this page is honored by children black

commit yourself headache confine black confined
ridiculous obliterations are confused and enjoyable
conflict confused arrange removal of all objects
some required from housing that would obstruct
continue with obliteration hannah likes it to be
limitations are interferring upset with us because we
upset continue with line because it is on the script
enjoyable insensible to black collisions automobile
try harder pressures black housing without boarding
sis conclude and continue with your script
two paragraphs witholding some substance like subject
make sure that sis words complete substitution
obliterations are enjoyable comment forgiven unable

removal of all objects required substance required
limitations are interferring immorse late as ever
constant fortunately irrelevancies are forbidden
sensible to obtusion with attempt relate instruction
pressures are inconsolable and matter to us without
sis it completes destroy disrupt the sequence clear
one more acquisitions are unforgivable and retain
sis continue some value if enlightened about service

one more paragraph service is to be rendered complete
start another line nerveless without consideration
a horror of pretense in the old world considerance
mother would go broke explain without the inherit
an honor of patience relieved consideration to be end
end patience without clear understanding sequence
endurance prohibited unless convicted understand
the golden aura complete unless above our minds
the late irreducible formality once occurred formally
sis correct one protect the other from disaster

brilliantly without system confidential reduce to
cancel every reminder of substance in reality
consideration is absent from the populace withold
overlooking a constant view of irregularity some
since melody informed of informed reformed cue

overturned by return by a charm involved in behavior
the fallacy of quaint ideas in propositions of problems
forgetting the better blind who remembers quaint ideas
almost hysterical above and beyond the earth around
unanimously undone without public approval or twice
say complete   recurrently unavoidable simple in thought
very capable turn page to be too soon formality
unreliable abandoned surplus quaint power turn bow unless

sis i'm concerned unless we return to the plains some
where some people prohibit acquaintances prohibited
make it clear some provide assistance without knowledge

some make coincidences some play like other who are
stick to your subject coincidences are made by the mind
complete and continue bonded to a neutrality calm
notwithstanding the sequence in form related to events
we conclude set upon bedside with we destroy humor
explode   sis conclude we bother the help and bother
try another sentence one complete trouble is border
make it a margin and do obey your immediate conclusions

sometime mother completes sequence without relating story
complete the tale without repeating her sentences once
sis its clear without ending complete and sentence
we quit on ideas because we see intelligible seen explain
mother quits another page unlisted became from the instant
sis quit on the sequence told by relating mother story
we had another resemble we interrupt our sequence only
mother did mother only related the story without being
hold your sequence between our stories complete behavior

just begin again we told others that mother completed
sis its unlisted because someone denied the sequence
brother finally promoted his whole excuse to a dinner
when she was unable sequence and died altogether after

another paragraph sis *Spoke* remembers her unless it is
forbidden continue page about unlist mother's death
sis it quits brother reminded that she was unable to
insist on page infulential themselves unless periodical
try page on mother returned from her hospital continue
brother insisted we dinner complain she died two days
sis mother complained and explained personal witheld
she become the page look another from pages someplace
brother becomes clear he took her to repeat without
and she died put this in the book included some history
someplace hannah he took her to dinner after the hospital
and repeated concluded some pages include your pages

sis some pages concluded without embarrassment some
brother complains he was indeed official and ignorant
complete her death was like she breath overlooked
brother says fault unclear because he was uncompleted
two pages get hysterical and become my personal some
sis complete why she died two days finish with dinner
another sis begin at the beginning when you tried
hannah you weren't seeing words then complete and couldn't
decide for yourself where complete the dinner was
say undecided she began to desire her weakness when
we complete the honest page without witholding any

two paragraphs complete and insistance complete
sis its ok brother witheld from me his jokes and
subject until mother was complete and she dead
mother would complete incomplete wondering if dinner
the story includes my sister who satisfied dinner
stay without burial until you complete this dinner
forgiven when they return to my complete the page
sis they understand cancel every reminder of hospital
they are unafraid I was beginning to complete the page

someone says incomplete above without hospital she was
sis continue operaiton conclude they concluded say story
and page continued without ending surprised concluded
give yourself a chance to put it in self that completed
he runs from you because you saw elements of protection
like home becomes unclear continue with page beginning

just conclude without personal projections include
yourself instead you were apologize only a say calm
and continued two pages what without making it clear
some condemned persons without brother are clear
story ended sis before the book was paged I was seen
on words hurry say where notebook in the closet which
includes my story including mother's unfortunate death

try another paragraph from the page in the book where
you are reading like sis continue witheld from continue
you are continued looking forward to only ahead without
object of make clear only barbara stays is money counts
and you enjoy your own apartment above the clear street

sis i withdraw from some who make public unless on the
i was complete say name witheld some make it clear
hannah he omits your two youre strong begin to make clear
hannah I take my chance obvious making clear i was
substitute make change forever you were confident on page
hannah I was confident but didn't know until because the
some clear hannah it makes sense two pages mother included

hannah i was hurt by without knowing intelligent
say forward the boys became some unknown at the time but
it said political important because we failed in public
to change alter the mother who is included some brain
included like altered some that included sitting included

paragraph i was strong when i was hurt and included the
two pages mother is included embarrassment by others
sis i would conclude this paragraph with another simple

put in something else like page bonded to a neutrality
my brother arranged quit he was forbidden to ordinarily
he quit ordinary like some quit on the page forgot
hannah put me in on the page where i began like book
notwithstanding the brother he stood elegantly someone
gladly someone should once twice omitted because he
complete was afraid sentence completed in hungry
write another page complete like brother symmetry has
been condoned before simple and twice he complicated
some pages like concluded sis hes a stranger almost

paragraph begins i was almost forgotten reminded myself
someplace reccommended his struggle sis he was twice
eliminated from say writing concluded put it in writing

james concludes you were brother omitted like i was glad
two pages eliminated because completed accordance
over controlled without simple sacrifice to make happy
estranger enjoyment oversized and obedient like him

mother begins a new sacrifice say paragraph complete
with omit sequence and some tough undeniably attractive
finish the sentence an appetite to fight with two said
hannah it finishes james publishes without eliminating
subject about brother he said omit citytown because
next line please say omitted because you were company
forcefully to come to the conclusion that i was happy
the unwavering fondness of make it clear the sea was
the structure complete ended like sentence provided

hannah he struggles without confidence in his upbringing
explain because i was older more confident and glad
explain confidence tighter someplace like say school
brother concludes somewhat confident over his application
sis conclude with a page just say concluded scream at
without sentence concluded he was sacrificed james marries

safely important to perform one piano immediately
piano complete one sentence but scrambled by hand
james concludes it was a tendancy to strike put in
brother starved complications when he was forty
weight overloaded like complete sentence like book
aggravated by complete insistence and complete
some tendency to combine structure overlook clear
sentence begins with some instructions that i received
some clear some obvious that when he took me someplace
start a sentence overlooked by otherwise only a moth
prevent sacrifice continue can perceive continue

james concludes i was forgotten by jokes under surveillance
but i was enjoyed sentence included subject overlooked
integrated besides with some who were close to me
by complicated interference twice recorded and publish

forget the irreconcilable and clear the imaginable
same paragraph some elegant indians were also with me

sis is said ignored and was almost
please say indians were political and clear like one
two concluded included some practical advantage over
say sentence complete advertise white make clear it
not too many ways to hear yourself included alone
make sacrifice make clear indians without independence
struggle to overcome political advantages like white
people have even in their own homes submit this paragraph

james concludes that i was political obvious when
political communist clear almost and divides between
anarchists and make comment you were at school when
you became obvious and got fired for association
in the fifties when it was hard to belong communist

you were not committed to yourself but you fought like them
sis you lost your job and returned to your home said
twenty skip page and paragraph political enough
listen inconsolably to the constant irremovable content
let it go and paragraph ended politics and make clear
admit you were struggling with your honest
who endured his heartache once almost
and died like me in a hospital once where nurses
endurance is repeatable if enjoyed by structure
was ill long time with cancer some sentence
white doctors forget his prevailing glad and he died
before i could secure any reliable evidence of endurance
from one time to another healed with power submit like
consequently there is no endurance to enable withdrawal
hint you are substituting references that were applied
some sentence references accepted where healing took
ignorance of doctors caused following say death
hannah complete you were in his city where you sat
say where in the hospital until almost collapsed

hannah you can't heal without another like group say
obliterate obsessions locally ended with consequence
some field experts like central were doctors with it
others employed but kept surveillance quiet on his heart
but make it clear his other took his omit
make sentence james is clear without substance enjoyed

sit in hospital and be clear another sentence ended
sis clear mother would enjoy remembering him like glad
sometime import had trouble with oversize quiet like
mother concludes that it was who doctor say calm
like tears with someone who nourished calmly and avoided
forget every device for obtaining instructions along
and believe we can construct obedience clearly alone
inevitable results linger toward forgetfulness and regret
some symbol like james avoids sentence complete

the space is almost required almost for acceptance
just say the kitchen floor is dirty and i wont scrub
some continue structure with silence and i obey like
add a sentence structure sis i was quiet when i was a girl
obediant like some mothers calling once to me clearly
give up sentence once in a while add some foolish words
hannah i add sentence about girlhood where they put up
along the fence some complete sentence and I was scared
sis i skip structure and follow my attention in kept
say promise to look at myself clearly when growing

mother adds advice practical like words that mean
say sentence calm structure in my childhood backyard
sometime I guessed that my mother kept me close to her
alone from the children who were not of my religion
alone included came to me when at four
some sentence about public avoidance because children
a burst of infiltration defined by policeman
sis congratulations sentence almost imagined put in

nevertheless i was isolated during my children life
brother was skip older because he was independent
tragdies occur upside inside when you ignore almost
sis i was ignorant of children until i was configured
add another sentence forgotten like guess what happens
sis almost complete with barbed wire fence because
underneath it all i was kept alone in my mothers
context scared on the street witches and boys at school
sis if you're scared explain it i hurt myself with a
say boys say when i was running like children
mother would concluded say sentence from book concluded

sis it took all my strength to become avoided until i
sis it took quite a while add sentence sometimes theres
dont continue play awful and reminded of being scolded
sis concluded eight when i first had friends at neigh
conclude next house almost without prejudice we moved
indifference coincides with neighbors who ignored us
sometimes i played with the children who were like me

i was included sometime in country house where
some sentence included like invite some people
hannah i had to believe in the coincidence because
sentence omitted i was obedient and followed skip
my friends were an idea begins woodstock on acid
say once i belonged to boys younger and older skip
sequence an idea belonged I felt power on the field
when i was trembling say sentence almost and quote
i was unafraid i quit job and became cross it out
purity is allowed sometimes at the satchidananda place
where i was allowed in later years because i saw say
words and pictures in my mind like whoelse nobody

another word like sentence in field like mosquito
mother put me where i took a house alone by the hill
and kept silent until i became like you heard voices
like next sitting loud and two cat obeyed my silence
it was hard to communicate my development because

everyone was clear about their trips alone in the
say everyone could listen to my voice through radio
but only one heard sis i was aloud often and weird

an idea begins to show above the crowd obedience
coincidence struck me when i was in the forbidden
add another sentence like trip on the field by the
another told me he would silently help if i house
needed help otherwise but i was obedient and layed
skip sentence it skips lurid pastimes like trips
sometimes i wandered to the field where alone i kept
sis sentence avoided the boys who were often obeying
sis crowd i thought by skipping i was allowed to swim
someone thought aloud and i caught the quiet leaving
hannah anyone can understand this my woodstock brave
i was the poorest in the country but still wondered if

try another paragraph i wounded myself by i was hurting
hannah its almost another page in the country while
continue i was on lsd often and in the woods by the
mother wants another page and i included my say wooded

just follow a sentence substructure in the book
just Woodstock where the flies were indiffernt
without surprise i wondered about delightful surroundings
sis call it indeterminate like the book replies as it
still conflict over sentence add leaving the country
i was still in bewilderment when the sun danced light
two friends wrote poetry in my book with me on the
below country i met another who broke his hand
sometime i was allowed to conflict contest diary seem lucky
skip sentence alone music allowed throughout the time
but always loud and clear about the crosswords of the
say learning in send a sentence structure about words

say i was learning about how to live according to
control and beloved along country ways which endured
mother enjoys my memories someday when she lives again

sis struck by my obedience someone took me to the woods
so music helped learning like someone who beginning
sis its struck by someone like an trace hysterical
but only the real people were allowed to be enjoyed
sis pleasure to be alone through the city say words about
pretences are subject alterable by someone who jokes
add sentence from book i was always by myself alone
in a house where people invited came to visit because
i was alone two years in a house belonged to a party
river across and polluted but swimming around in it
sis discuss the river upstream closed from the people

if you were about you came over once or twice involved
by the city joke inventors who came each sunday
someone would put it in a sentence like the sequence is
forget put in structure someone police and men
forget concerts where gathered people on grass
put people in who left protected because learning
strict relience on about the field structure was
sis put in sentence   the followed struck the olders
the same girls were skipping their learning about

try sentences from the book like many have left here
twice i remembered almost pain is not to be considered
mentioned sis i believed yoga following the learning
because they took care of the acide people who lived
almost again we knew by ourselves that rain comes always
when we believed any master beloved controlled laugh
give another hint from the book i was unimportant
say why because i was performing in public and almost
became famous like omit hannah he has name
i was joking   james admits street works were permitted
with us without again we complain of citytown where
give in on the beach with my learning and notebook

someone met encourage a sentence by learning i stole
75 almost in years I met add who became my best
give another sentence from the book i was stuck

someone controls us and i went to the store where
control yourself the car received a bump and the police
control yourself i was at the beach and remembered
put yourself back in the country on acid and remember

someone alone in the woods was almost about by alone
i gave in someone converted the country to by itself
control by mind over reminder and woodstock restraint
sis i wondered if people could retain subject matter
without learning themselves twice like i did in say
mother would work with it learning and notebook
the trips alone by the stream where i saw myself
wondering alone above by the stream   by the body
sis she suggests body transference came next and thought
believe in the country where it worked thoroughly
society has made a definitive improvement in the area
conclude hannah i believed in telepathy immediately
like anyone could understand and believe occurance
giving up requires granted from the quiet
who learn teach like each other awhile like rest

transcript some transcribe some sentence like one
sis the point is i was out of the travel country
too many aspects of sign appear travel by alone
i was enjoyed myself except with my alone constant
formidable constraint without about travelling upset
i was constant abroad for almost five summers when
and another sentence i was completed journey south

sis i travel without my guide except alone by handling
another required that complete anit-structure comes
sis doubt alone surprise conflict among indians clear
i as recorded once and then got stuck need sentence
sis two helped me when i was alone say where south
i mean desert where i met two who its in the manuscript
say complete prevailed and i copy one word too many
say aspects of employment enjoyed while i was below

mother encouraged me to entertain while i was growing
but i refused because included almost trembled like
no more required fulfillment required but unless you
some dociers were permitted becasue you were listen
i had two jobs where fired i said this and stuck
once more we sing over the bridges where i lived
hannah because i enjoyed my early wonderment alone
sis divorced after four years with psychiatrist who
period and complete consequences i was employed

design behaviour stop count i am clear and enjoyed
overcome with decisions i had to get myself a job
fashion designer with problems accompanied like two
successful at first i was employed for twelve years
shut up and took advantage of my forty complain two
hannah complete i write when i complete this structure
since small like twelve i hinted i would design write
put in another sentence overcome with decision like
try it again the terror is dressed up like small

continue small when i was delighted by designing
when i contacted who told me to stop giving sentence
i wanted to write but one rescued me from it twenty
say complete begin with older when i was declined
show a sentence structure complete like writing
sis escape culture behave like a writer until i came
sis sentence from the book   all experience is exactly
i spelled an old woman keep clear who invited class
to decide guesses the future like class when i complete

sis i started my writing when thirty some old like same
sis i came make clear understand i am counting my words
sis i had to be twice performer and publicized when
twice i sus stuck cannot perform instances report
repeat i was struck publicly and often in accounts
like in the paper and who else without like artists
i forgiven popular and when invited i was advertised
and another sentence like sensation became harmony
exact three years i became clear about writing and found

hannah it takes another stuck with someplace say where
and it completes another sentence give up unalterable
sis say something about your boyhood when you obeyed
mother like an ordinary forgiven adult provided alas
some strict behavior when i was simple end paragraph

sis apologize continue relieved sometimes to sleep
overcome encore reminder important teach
try explain without sleeping without clear
five hours complete and i success am showing words
say words continue sleep correct sentence hurry it up
complete too many silent sleepers watch silently
and another clear from the manuscript obeyed some
sis some hurt sometime i forgive complain and sentence
give up the end of the sometime sentence when enjoyed

two words from the book honest withholding skip and
withholding to sleep
hannah skip sentence about book make written apologize
silent almost make clear without any seen complixity
information slowly its only another sometime idea to
make sentence   stop and clear with complete saying

hannah return to sleep when drowsiness happens slowly
like stop and make clear sometime sleeping important
like some doctor who gave me sometime say without
water uninhabitable drinking honest paper says twenty
some big someone says only two hundred important
like water underground survived even waste products
like centuries honest to drink water like honest
mother bottled complete without any restrictions
the book is restrictive like words uninhabited from
complete attractive keep it instructions about clear

mother would apologize attractive with some periods
getting old without family to die almost without alone
falling words in a suit to reminder of public disaster
mother lived nine almost ninety correct illness without
she lived insulated providence in house insulated glad

contracts insult with make a pride and continue operate
she some continue lived with her glad aunt who without
continue unaccustomed to sentences which completed into
sis if you continue she will accomplish publication
like unalterable words from   read a reality words two

sis i broke down period when she almost forgiven say
took some doctor handle three almost silent forgiven
some handle grief with mother like crying but forgiven
i opened destroyed manuscript while give up
mother died make clear when she was dinner complete and
say she tried lung with words honest uninhabitable
mother tried to console myself with her twice complete
complete with words from somewhere like somewhere also
before we begin upside clear thoughts temporarily
say sequence someone tried to hurt myself only like

listen to words complete sentence without any complete
say from someplace quote a nominal form enclosure
begin mother admit selfish with her who died like also
hannah she concrete reluctance to perform
she decided to rest without for honest make it
sis she decided to rest without going two years outside

any words associate informal words try hard and omit
happiness is also forbidden unless you are with words
complete harmony insult without culture sis insult
mother complete about dying in hospital without alone
say complete sentence in somewhere about somewhat
substance almost requires some hospitable alienation
two words without structure in sentence forbidden
close complete mother was ill almost from enjoyment
hannah she almost forfeit all complete sentence ending
sis complain dinner was last i explained when outside

hannah i almost cried when she was almost alone some
complete in a book like some years ago who remembers
sis i knew almost four years ago that complete when say

regarded as future spoken like wise three years also
further sentence reminds me of book without publishing
a consequence behaviour believes in make clear
answer honest you are trying hard to eliminate ending
if i complete mother she will be unhappy because i cry
without ending silence four years of five like also
complete destroyed myself
like without any books trying alone i kept

another word publishing accept without two words also
give publishing fast which is alone without substance
hurry to complete sentence with mother some
words alliances complete with obligation speaking for
mother was dying in the hospital and two speaking alone
admit you add reluctance consistency from book whoever
mother died again she almost took hand and apologized
hannah five years without words almost apologize
complete if you destroy book also written apologize
sis i took too many sleeping pills and
couldn't write see doctor illustration

some unfortunate closing need closing with hurting omitted like
housing paragraph omitted with blacks who cannot help each
downtown unless double black agreement white housing in
control upstate where indifference to color thanks to counsel
cannot say counsel omitted black housing interference belongs
downtown where like whites hurry employ workers some
employ unless overworked complete and housing requirement
upstate like limiting themselves close embarrassment because
colors omitted chinese omitted downtown where they are
obediant completely strict to themselves and internal make
agreement with others housing needed

some omit unless housing required upstate where downtown
needed blacks hurry it up employment enjoyed if downtown
housing permitted forbidden by our culture without permitted
housing black housing requirements sis omit another smile
blacks included among themselves others like who colors

omitted like some who white need street offensive make clear
hannah we need more housing for poor like make clear always
scared uptown omitted because housing completed some years
and strife across some omitted black agreement for handling
clear housing white included but something hurry it up
something blacks included need housing units 100,000

omit housing altogether because it is completed by white
company complete some one upstairs like me complete silence
without needs help conclusion upstairs alone make you
complete with sis i bring an attachment offer sis we handle it
wrong argument put in housing uptown black needed make it
clear that you are through with color embarrassment agreement
they white included some color embarrassment blacks need
agreement above someone like upstairs agreement needed like
helping complete structure small children include we speak
silent black only like indian

some nonsense letters my friend say who marries once in her life
the smell comes from under ground leak underwater where i live
hannah she writes remembered forgotten some words like some
two words sis i speak english quite differently when write so
name letters south handle name soname keeps herself quiet like
silent until the signals my two offices are small   they got
underground water leaks under hannah thats what she says in
her coming embarrassment quite clear my name is friend so name
not quoted because terrible things happen our dont quote subject is
much more friendly than it say hunger hannah i write nonsense
words justify speaking like some unless it hurts somebody
indifferently when we speak frequently in our silence say
somebody in our smile returns a letter but it is like me

she has to be quick lesson for quick beginners like any
soname has smile which is attractive which attractive
the suddenness of dancing along like the patriots with
paradise which ground foolish is tough determined and
never given to be given quote letter myname someone
spoke confidentially over beginners like grandson

correlative sumstance hints that we want some land
spoken land kissing the allotted say ground about
hannah thats dance which together us

sis split infinitives naturally like cause from line
causes some frightened young dancers to willow the tree uphangs
some like they hand once in a life to be individual
sis you're speaking of some making match which is
hannah you're strong answering your letter beside holding
some nonsense like before which intrudes on our better
disgust with letters endure permission like behave hint

sis quote from your letter like we wrote once before
but is it envelope twice which i forgot each guess
like somename living downtown who is always conscious
of broken agreements like you are indiffernt to say
mention someone's name i forget which has a letter say
both and remember each differently both white courage
sis have some courage language some best letters have
can't you see the difference between anybody us both
sis its our literature that makes brain
speak like avoid explanation and speaking aloud when
said aloud gives together language at language

sis group letters already both together unto the best
best spell guitar and smile come best
best repeats often spell his name oftenly like
guess speaking aloud when already is hurting together
thats a friend forgiven spelling laughter
write letters like hold together
laughter somename spells awkward backwards foolish
sis spell with capitals so you are almost
put in spelling about start about create
sis speaking knowledge please ned paragraph black speaking

my letter hurts a bit because somename isnt
recognized put him on the envelope like say my
friend who dances together with everybody hints

got lesson from her someday not to write cancel
altogether name history the lesson not spelling
sis included to write affect
mind by writing
like some friends thats say
some others like writers also

bigname one word has letter spelled like an people
and answers confidentially that spelled dance on over
sis someone like someone no name included because
of his holds me together when we dance once
sis they accept your forever commitment
say large for whoever stays together with public
trials that gives someone name consent
to stay once in your own place after married done

big speaking put in some words that meaning afraid
quit book unless black beside spoken is written
she quits afraid to condemn clear honest their husband
she is speaking like silent and matches unless alone

since revolution production was forever political in
just complete structure once hidden like street in the
otherwise forbidden likewise closure instead
sis mother closes this paragraph hidden explain instead

power alright hidden privately sometime without hurting
some power heals openly like whoname big leader waved
some heals directly like whoname big leader waved
some heals directly like with power sitting a week alone
hannah speaks about some who openly work
publish yourself this time without hurting anyone like
put in sorry lost some time like destroy confidence
speak language together with holding them silence
speak radio contact alter some structure like
we complete we said in control of themselves alter
consciousness so we react politically obediantly
starving hungry street need properly housing alter
the political structure behavior upstate housing

we break down crying with strangers who speak without
say strangers who kind have no food in their stomach
kind on the street behave upstairs like black kindness
strategy   holds   political
changes made political aware on the black housing show
cheat a little on the change and leave hanging around
some critical political messages around in changes

speak street for downtown changes housing critical
someone black permitted houses twice and together
somename speaks of the difficulty speak downtown until
someone speaks together with black political downtown
destroy religion which makes state upside make down
sis thats historical change in politics to do without
changing religion to work historically important say
coming speak like downtown housing
someone chooses someplace because of structure and hides
sis structure   behind struggle to survive with clean
political changes we repeat somename breeds changes
we notice the speaking language is spoken unfrequently
struggle together learn who speaks with silent power
on the street thats like we can change society with structure

we destroy culture until we survive completely article
finished together working downtown employed everyone
hint fresh talent struck new together unusual speaking
sis finish below with whom mention name speaking also
thats someone with his own decisions speak like two
someone splits hair together we speak so we
which is only learning about ourselves
complete some black administration

silence someone speaks together in group standing by
sitting together we sitting understand silently each
say silent say together say together please together
mention someone together in like downtown speak
hannah we mean we friendly and together sound outloud

destroy meaning together with substructure
like meaning obeys the original convert who quietly
sis obedience to silence is strict and rapid obedience
on the street coincidences private occur at once and
complete sentence obey strict instructions withheld
children obey silently control obeying instructions

some children politely coincide occur privately
speak of the intellect needed to change political
culture needed withheld silence because capitalism
we needed other culture withheld strict complete
complain struggle white culture is moving forward
just harassment from awkward is holding us silent
some embarrassment in culture or white people history

historical change political needed like political we
openly like structure silence two streets like
youre getting pray we pray together
you understand some culture reverses political
so sorry about religion which needs change society
we provide entertainment with our culture providing
sis black speaking in prayer together like withhold
some sis we together like some old foreigners
hannah that hits hard complete black historical

hannah is an say hurry culture important immediate
we sorry we arent more changing fast culture hurry
sis soname behaves himself herself with together omit
have you ever been held together by black speaking
wisdom contrary to white society until sis
we black culture provide subculture to provide interest
subdivision complete without mother would complete her last
       sentence

saying black speaking street sis clairvoyantly signed make
       paragraph silent
black children speak

HANNAH WEINER   SILENT TEACHER

hannah weiner was born to it in providence ri in 1928 and graduated
from Radcliffe college 1950 magna cum laude   she then worked for
three publishing houses   got fired from all of them   once for being
too intellectual   once for associating with aliens and once for
being caught not slapping her bosses face   she then turned to
retailing and was an assistant buyer for fat ladies dresses in
bloomingdales basement   she married a psychiatrist   freudian
and divorced him four years later   then she exaggerated but not lied
herself into a job designing lingerie and turned down her second
request for marriage   by this time she was making the rounds of
galleries and parties in the early sixties and began to write
poetry in 1963   both writing and designing were childhood
          ambitions
she got a free course at the new school and found she couldnt write
new your school poetry in fact she couldnt write her own words
at all   only the *magritte poems   written in*   and *the fast* are in
her own words   happily she discovered the international code of
signals and found she could write about almost anything
by using the code books   these became rather wild performances
followed by other performances like street works 1-7 and the
fashion show poetry event   she was very well reviewed because
the art critic of the village voice was one of her partners
she thus met the musicians   performers   pop artisits   lesbians
and poets of that time
all this glory ended in 1970 when she became extremely psychic
and hiding out in a cheap apartment wrote about nothing else in
almost 100 notebooks   see *the fast*   the words began to appear
in 1972 and led to the *clairvoyant journal* a three voice
performance poetry book about learning   explaining instructions
and the counter voice   years passed   the language group moved in

and so did the indians   she still remembers meeting chawho
at a party saying youre getting pretty old dont you think you
should publish   she did   *sixteen* and *spoke* begin to introduce
the teaching   now she is reaching her ultimate achievement
learned first at her grandmother's knee   TEACHING SILENT
she has dragged several poets into this with her   gosh ma shes a
real female tarpsichordist

{HANNAH WEINER, 1993}

JENNIFER MOXLEY

IMAGINATION VERSES

*With a Preface
by the Author*

TENDER BUTTONS
NEW YORK CITY
1996

© by Jennifer Moxley
ISBN 0-927920-07-7

Tender Buttons ★ P.O. Box 185
Stuyvesant Station ★ New York City 10009

Tender Buttons Books are edited by Lee Ann Brown
Tender Buttons Logo designed by Joe Brainard

TO MY CONTEMPORARIES

What blame to us if the heart live on?

-Hart Crane

PREFACE

OUR STATES, whether social or organic, are composed of effects both chosen (verses) and not (Imagination). When we hope for a future different from the present we uncover the injustice of our imagination. We find the scales of value during the slow climb towards maturity and knowledge, as we journey towards the completion of what Valéry called our "whole training in the possible." The "possible" is by its very nature unequal. Though we may dream the dream of equality, we dream it on a scale much larger than ourselves. If we try to make a poem of this dream, it will be smaller than its origins. Being time-based beings, we cannot escape compromise, concealing history with each new life, born to begin the accumulation of knowledge from zero to one and so forth. Poetry is the frustration of such limits. As an art form, it is a bridge of half measures on the way to the possible, drawn from the viewpoint, time frame and landscape of a single life. The poem is unjust in its largesse, an axis point through which the creator and the community of a shared language pass. The poem offers a history of and a future for the mind's prerogative to exist as more than a memory of its milieus. It is a small but necessary intervention, a crucial and critical disjuncture.

For all the violence sprung from the official versus the unofficial book, where literature is found has less to do with its force than who we are when we find it. Are we ready to receive it? Many have come to literature from strange paths and pieced it together to their own liking, ignoring all the established orders. Poetry is not for the passive. It is, as Mayakovsky knew, at its very root tendentious. Even the love poem agitates the beloved to fall in love with the poet.

These Imagination Verses were written over a five year period (1990-1995) while I lived in Providence. They were not written as a book nor as a series but randomly in fits and starts, and are comprised of a variety of different free verse forms. They were written out of a desire to engage the universal lyric "I," as well as the poetic line, with all of its specific formal artifice.

{JENNIFER MOXLEY, 1996}

HOME WORLD

I will say what the register calls forth,
the range of the heart
a journey in the strap of speech,
unrealized, failing to grapple
with even the first word,
or world where I saw humans
in the shadows of buildings
unable to speak at all.
Their dark needs
had grown a weedy tent
over the earth, laid bare.
They could not see
the river for the bank
yet still kept talking
about the bridge.
I lived there too,
saw innocence
among the old
grown willowy.
My illusion could not deflect the float
or the filth upon it, and all that foliage
what could it have meant
in the light of adornment?
When I remembered nature
as an evil dream
that interrupted my house
and destroyed my family,
leaving me to covet.

I dreamt my sense could wend the fight away
and carnage was my hollow nourishment.
I could have grown tall,
but I awoke to no words and wonder left.

FROM A DISTANCE I CAN SEE

You have a lovely and familiar gravity,
and like in the apartment of my youthful reveries
each time I walk into you my city-bound Greyhound
rolls through the rain drenched streets,
a lightscape full of traffic and wondrous people
lies ahead, once you've caught view they shall demand
the tapering of all your beautiful fingers,
they shall tell your eyes to stop shooting such glances
for they are blocking your lips from seeming
red as they are, and what of gentle memory,
it frames your face and returns home devastated
to inform me of such boundaries shifting
that in them, as in you, my dreams shall rest just dreams,
the rain drenched city of adulthood, vanish in advances.

NIGHT TRAIN TO DOMESTIC LIVING
ARRANGEMENTS

In my own mind you have put me
beside compunction. Re-worked
this mourning room where looking
smacks of mother may I

though to this day I'll falter
when sleep holds sway.
Throw me over your deep end
with some faith next time,
as if to lend some bother to the vex.
I've always wanted to be grown up
like a bureaucrat, a berth-rider
ordering night caps over the Rockies.
But you keep insisting on day planners,
bodies flat out. Which means,
for example, a random plea.
Do some dishes and get back to me.
I'm waiting at the ripping point
breast in hand, a broken spine
like any sign of care.

NOT ON MY SEASHORE

You drew me under yards
of bad luck and backward lives,
you bucked up yarns
of past beguilers
who tended to shift away
from scripted misery.
Your islands of personality
give no good guidance
when desire breaks up
beauty's trance to leave me
an Emptery waiting for visitors.

It was not I who was enamored
of the sky's insipid blue,
the tilt of fisted history
roped and kinky with the tide.
You drew me like a family,
some false hope factory
from which to call in the new day!
Cut it out and give me that rope,
I will gladly beat my scared Crusoe
with the possibility of life
and orate at the seashore
of luckless sinking blind
and God-blanched Utopias:
But know my heart is on your hands.

ODE ON THE END

In afterlife
I stood
and wished the depths
of fright
to crumble
by random
weights and measures.
I could not feel
my morals
at the borders
of darkness, I
was left alone

by an unfinished
thought, like a fool.
I found that lack
of place, un-
imaginable after-
math all on
my own. My discovery
so emptied me
a stairwell
into Hell
would have seemed
most welcoming,
a landscape, death red,
the moderate grade
of enemies
gradually accustomed
to anything
the mind
might think. The mere
recognition of it
would be at least
a seed of sense
to wish a future
up from. And yet
to my eye
from this vacant
drape
a better place
appeared, equal measures
of air and earth

came to me
precious enough,
I wore them
well knowing
my thoughts
would think me
hollow, exiled
to the abandoning
company
of all
my illusory
ends.

BI-COASTAL FLESHINGS

This in-wrought geneticism
has made your leniency all askew,
a melee on the installment plan,
like chance encounters with minikin emotions
unstitch Minerva and the Earth awakes
distracted reaching for Venus.
For years you've been grabbing power so,
knowing lest you crumble there's always class
to catch you in its bibelots—
down that rabbit hole my liege
I'm a camera gathering brightness
my ligature of future imaginings
somehow assured the universe will unravel
light and dark despite the wile of while.

FIN DE SIÈCLE GO-BETWEENS

There you are in the hinterland chiseling
Nations into the ocean as I await torrential
winds. In our search for beauty we've left
our footprints for the Native informers of narcissism
to uncover once we've fled. We should have let
the out-of-work jesters jingle gun toters
and just gone on with the Eros of coastal waters.
I'll hide your lesser self inside this bird of paradox,
a place dispatchers won't mistake it for any
errant sign of life. While we've been talking
they've lined up along the border towns
heavy with wistfulness, so if ever lip service
might save the planet let's hope it's now,
jettison that charm however and we might be
the end of something gathered.

THE WINGÈD WORDS

What are these wingèd words
that have escaped the barrier
of your teeth?
          Nothing doing,
nor my fault the Ford
won't start and so
          as walked across
you become land,
          bedded be my wilderness

bookish my landscape and sea
a bridgeless head tease.
Would you deign me everyday
if nearly to you
I were to say : "hey,"
        would you find me
contemporary
if Aristide stood for options
betoken of banks on which
no pronominal carrier
can stand
or gaze upon singers sweetly singing? O Ramona…
        my ocean is sold
        my ships of steel
        and all my nuclear submarines have drifted.

A man on the corner
begs experience
as moments pass   into the panhandler.
Were we the land's
before we were landed? And then suddenly
things meant homelessness,
        alas my youth disbanded
        asleep in the automatic
        teller machine booth
while all the while
you stepped up to carpet
and a brand new skin product,
as sadly I am now comforted
by leather.   *brick upon brick…*

If Aristotle stood for options well
                brick upon brick...
a skin head with a leadpipe
in the conservatory,
                brick upon broken
neck, thanks to my skin
it only happens
in my shipwrecked sleep.

What are these wingèd words
that have escaped the barrier
of my teeth?
        Nothing doing,
an evasive act
as when the lights go up
and you no longer like
licking me and the thing
becomes thoughtlessness,
             lick upon lick
engineered, it's
autocratic eroticism, a person
to person phone call
to my personal she-history whip.
        Whose sovereignty?
        surrounded by working
        papers and men my markings
a downtown trench
circled by suburbs and upwards
of one hundred stories of sky.
It could even become our own arms race.

ODE ON THE SON

Your life like a wentletrap
awaiting clarity out by the sea,
not expected to go astray
with your beautiful or homely sister.
Your life like a curtained window
to wait by, stentorian smile
returning home from the ship,
the mill, the missile silo.
Your life like the essence of make
breaking apart, fine hair
pushes from your face
to carpet your beauty.
I am not made of this farce you claim
but the one who will finally finish
the spiral, how grand.
Then that man grabs you
by the hair in the five and dime
and says: "don't try it."
Where is my field of wheat,
my flock, my ocean,
my arsenal, my knight errant.
Hush, hush, he is performing surgery
on your mother. Go down and tell fate
it will be a difficult birth.
Quiet your sister. The horizon
is spreading like spilt milk
and your father's gone mad with desire.
You must be the last stitch

left on his worn plan, answer now:
will you plow, row, gather onward my brother
or will you be father and welter.

TEN STILL PETALS

I dreamt
a petal's depth of hatred
        hovered at my ear
while vagaries worked
        to rough me up.
The flower kept
        darkening
        the more I lay passive
a gaseous mass in the manner
        of some spheres.

        That night
        was an escapade, the very last
                impulsive dream.
        I was so desperately trying
                to shove you down,
        the smallest floralized
                egg cup
                        burst.

One Moon
          orbits,
just high enough
          to threaten Peace
in a Vase
          or at least
transit's Beauty. Unbending

                    Dante waits
                    at the Gates of his beloved
                              Florence for his
                                        Laurel cap,
                    while under glass
                              the specimens
                    who grow tired
                              of plight
                    are straightened out
                              by energetic wealth.

Deep Black take
          precedence,
inside all falls
          but the undiscovered
touch of blindness,
          wherein My love
remains
          unbidden.

                    Part of me
          thinks only of this. Your
                    half-shut lids fell
          sleepless
                    into my lap. A girl,
          I have seen tragedy
                    consider being
          such as we are.

Great lengths foregone
        to trap one leaf of
light. Valiant and yet
        the poems still spring
from corpse fires,
        the Isolated heart
crawls up
        to the cavity of ear
and sleeps.

            Listen
            while dreaming,
                    Fear is circling within,
            the horizon is moving
                    secretly along
            your ever diminishing
            home.

A memory anvil
    surrounds
the rose head. Present day
    cruel pleasure
momentarily dims
    true evil, distills
a more potent
    desire.

    Cyrus of split
      parentage
still ruled Persia,
    despite aspersion or
fatal trickery, our similar pressures
    shall rise,
controlled likewise in
    silence.

I abandoned
     our mystical union
on authority of your voice,
     its mechanical
     chokedamp
enveloped my suffering
     until I was loath
     to give
the bicycle memory
     up.

     Coerced as such I came
          internally
     to blows, the plying will
          inside my head
     in turn did form
          a rim above the breach.
     I know there was a time
          when you alone
     controlled my faculties,
          but today that hour
     of abasement
          is finally come
               to an end.

Heinrich Heine lay
    lifelike
in his inhuman
    misery, his views
strove nightly
    to escape
the dying poet's body, knowing
    they'd flourish
Beneath a healthier task-
    Master.

    These unfinished versions
        hang like
    poisoned tendrils
        disturbing
    the ignorance of the living
        mystical rhetoric.
    In futures they may prevent
        blindness and paralysis
    assuming the Mind
        refuse détante.

Flakes of fire will dart
      forever
from the undetected
      counterfeit victory.
The lost moment
      of Hatred
lives on infettered
      as a powerful show
of humiliation,
      ruining the dream
of further triumphs. In this way was

      the Horror
         of Harpagus
      silenced by
         self-loathing—
      bred from the zeal with which
         he'd feasted
      unknowingly
         on the abominable meal
      of his kindred flesh.

Moving faces on the dark ceiling
      tell me
someone's coming
      through the window.
I lay unable to travel
      the carpet
fearing my fears
      in the telling
will dwindle to nothing
      but girlish
phantoms. An old record,

      Mozart's 40th
          transmits
    an important message:
          hold a road open
    to lift my mind
          away by hoof
    from these nightly
          hauntings
    feeling inside me
          as a thousand wishes
    left in the wake of
          arrested lives.

Driven to hellfire
          by latter day
Samaritans, Virgil
          puts his sandal
on the brittle grade
          of downward stones.

                    And so he enters the well-
                              wisher's field
                    of vision parceled
                              by Christian history,
                    shaking, yes
                              and yet still able
                    to cross off
                              evil innocence
                    and place the necessary
                              human misery
                    firmly back
                              in mortal question.

UNDERLYING ASSUMPTIONS

for George Oppen

The towering worry of fin de siècle
our spacious day,
          as all in an instant
flickering, we live uncalendared.
No wonder
your century cradled life compels
          one love after another.
We all fall in
seeking the archives of careful choice—
          the hewn thin line
          of created memory,
dedication to thought & fellow
          across the crossing of moment
and moment's sense of latitude—but finding only
          your   long   life
as but a wink
          in edit's wedge.
Left to believe what leaves the mouth
will turn a profit,
we stand reading
          detect a rumor of bills and hear
your voice
and recall
the pleasure of listening
the power of production
               "what we commoners have won"

this page,
and all its underlying assumptions,
and know again
there's a place for us, and such
a country.

AFTER FIRST FIGURE

It is illusory
a fitter memory,
a prostate signifier,
breach / bridge / causeway.

Knowledge lies   shrug
with capacity, got it, everyone
can give birth
and balance between pleasure wavering
(the impression kept) and
the pain of doubt.
This is a future, a coming
that is the ecstasy of non-abandonment.

The sad and fragile admittance
of taken space, is past imagined
pure linear advance
we grab on because we can,
because we are opposable.

Still the shunted

of course, of what is, is sheer sign.
And as with imagination
there is no choice
being thought bound
the separate mind stands out, as matter
and maintains dreamily:
"I have been over to the words and they work."

They are the future
rejecting the read (refinement)
as the attempt to sanity (processed)
"nay"
for no heeding choice is given,
as if the freedom to document
the seemingly dubious lighthouse light
could say more keenly: isolation.

Convenience must admit
Exclusion in the rhetorical question
(a signal for logic)
We might lust for others, but never may
obscure meaning
in claim of taken space.

HELENA & THE REGIONAL BOYS

Like recognizable streets
those Boys keep right on
coming down my heart.

I'm a gun runner
for the United Girls of Camp &
I want those boys
like a western crescendo.
I can feel it moving now
from the damp concrete
to a wet desert,
her and those jeans
all cued up for the punch.
I'll call her swaggerlee, or
the moment when the bar bathroom door
marries hook to eye &
shame gets a great big mirror all its own.

INTO THE BEDROOM

Certainly deluded wisdom and all
those strewn packages from Christmas,
"scholar's disorder" keeps me covered
under this comforter thinking of us.
There there Erasmus, sinuous mind of love
in all its fibres off to Paris to see
what's become of an antique world.
Cut me a bolt of satin Vermeer
sing deep your told conviction,
lace up trussed up laughing feet
then turn your head and listen:
the parakeet doth chirp, the Moon
remarks my memory

and I am bending draped to brass
in pain and folly trmbling.

THE REMOVAL OF ENLIGHTENMENT SAFEGUARDS

I

Entrapped   enwrapped
of one   in two

he drapes and bend
          filled with fingers

defying boundaries

II

The yellow air
of the room
surrounds
the place of vanishing
holes

III

The muscle but a case
on top
philosophy pulls
        he squirms
in the paradigm
flutters
with down

IV

Strength from behind
encircled
                    man à clef
I grow phallic
with each dissemination

V

Soluble edge

        "the violation of sustenance"

continuing dribbles shift
bound assumption
the fence goes down
once entered by the weakness of protest

VI

Drooling humanism
                        she boots him

VII

"Thou standing factory
        most vulnerable to exclusivity
risks a vicious strike"

Of hemmed-in vanity

VIII

The rope returns
a favor
cutting off circulation
and so by example
late for dinner

IX

The human body
prisoner of war without vestige

enlightenment evidence

DURING THIS REVOLUTION

for Helena Bennett

Dear recondite shooter,
you're cupping me with dying, leaving me bloodless and loud.
Shoulderless Grace go back,

and mean one garden of tallish grass

the waitless lucky summer with many a torso manned again
and handed Main Street this girl said: What about tonight?
It's you and me shorter one,

with a bolder form of naiveté

then, for one tiny booted moment of largesse,
"her"
a vilified craving in night time,

our sweet morning crib notes

and no familiar gene can not a Truth Tale Tell
it's only breakfast this life around.
I witness boing back the many chewed things lost
your silence restive pardon of a sort I can't forgive.
Graceless I come query always

in hope of clearing this name from mud

finely how her measure could cover me like syrup,
a waffler I was, the edible beauty

will take this to her grave

but say something more endless,

than the strideress sleeps now with fishes

for it was us against the unbothered
and now my jet hangs mirrorless all
excuses for unbinding empty by her glances.

ODE TO PROTEST

It's as if to be real
you and I must garner backers
without a rib to call our own.
We make ripples
with daily effort and then suddenly
flood the place with anger.
Ours is the anger
of the lowly,
we see life
from the knees up.
What vision we had
on that glorious day,
even the weather
stood aside and let us pass.
But because we could not write
our hearts could not be read,
and when we wrote
it's then we could not publish.
And so a so-called prince
came along and told our story.
He called us "feeble weavers"
ignorant fury
animal instinct
wild in the streets.
If only we had means
then we would give light
to meaning. But for now
it seems royalty will keep writing

the book on right-of-way
and we again shall lay
our lives by the wayside.

THE BALLAD OF HER rePOSSESION

firstly

wait,
and in the leap
privileged   peaceable   pursuit
        "for my God a...
mercenary faith
lays down with reliance   (nation)
convinced forthwith of   (science)
        "and into freedom I am brung...
redemptioner
cinched and touted believer
spouting audacious ideas of misery
        "for country and...
forsworn
to be in vision's peculiar benefit
complicit kin
or, stateside homeyness

secondly

enough
ignorance
to fell unclouded truth, truth

like a tunnel to the heart
    fluttering
        "he put his hands upon me &
        I became equal in my lowlyness...
woeful
of what I knew, no mystery &
no splendor more splendid
than his sublime carriage, so
        "caress me in thine eyes...
gentle
wrong doer,
she spread for the promise
of blossoming
full   fragrant   fiduciary
& lied to

            thirdly

waste,
in the mind waste
        "give my pleasure to the divine...
accuser
        "the pain of one answer...
under a God
in the long grass of summer
(wherein the stench of trash)
my mind   (concrete)
grown big
in the eyes of the crowded state
idle   inward   individual
        "as I do not feel but know my love...

invisible

divisible

in despite

>   "as I know I am woman, not man…

not manifest

> *fourthly*

I stepped off the prairie

no family,

the landscape does smite

God's country

>   "could you but…

unravel borders   (the village)

break from the broken promise   (the city)

rescind distrust

>   "for I came on shore…

<u>beholden</u>

hostage to the apple of my eye

>   "and with these gifts I became…

learned betrayer & recreant

assuming my prerogative

precluded

by the bargain of heaven,

or, unimaginable products

> *finally*

the purchase

fled, before I could

flee,

        "all roads lead…

astray

whisper eclipse, sign of impotent witness

where angle may be read as love

the apogee of shame

        "he saved my life from…

saviours blind &

then with witless child

blinded me anew,

pronouncing:

bury your proud piety

I will no longer be

your gravel driveway

punished dreamer

failed redeemer

man, or country

ODE TO THE MAN IN THE MIRE OF BABYLON

after James Weldon Johnson

Because sometimes it's better

to be a dirty leper

than a beautiful Father

who would cut you soundly

should you rise above him.

Better to shun false respect

given freely to abject persons

of coldest intent
and remain true of heart,
though after the gold
has been meted out
you are left empty handed.
Where now is your quest for knowledge?
Ever since the happy few
distracted you from different pleasures
you've been craving your family
like a bitter remedy
and answering for needy sins
lending death the time it needs
to take true kin and run.
Choice cares not for the undone,
we live in the streets
because our fathers
are not beautiful,
they were turned out of the Temple
displaying too much vision,
their carts were without wares.
I am a cripple
for I inspire no envy
though your God may lay down
his back for my bridge
and I drag myself
to greener days,
we are still just exiles,
indentured to the ancient homeland
where we work not for purpose
but for fear of being locked out

with swine. What resemblance

have you to me except in all that's wanting,

for we alike can see that crevice

under the crown of pro patria

threatening to break apart

should we not come home.

Stay and enjoy the disruption

drink and destroy by loving hard,

do not marry or serve the unwanted master,

and fill your plate with forbidden oils,

toil no longer,

for when the cock crows and a new life is born

death has already won the battle.

WHEN IN ROME

No, I will not fondle you willingly centurial world
nor stroke your shred of decency, I hold no candles
or so you broadcast, ever since you kissed
my world weary decadence.
Hey soldier, go flaunt your swags and jabots elsewhere
this girl is bowing out, full to the glands with garlands
and Democrats, the truthful and bad will eventually see my way.
My webbing or weaving grows thick with all your travel plans
you tree trunk, you bile monger, you ghastly gewgaw
bereft of Metaphor, this time your ignorance will kill you
once and for all Centurion.
Didn't you notice your hundred years are up.

CELL # 103

for Vladimir Mayakovsky & Fred Moxley

How many years locked up
does it take to create a Revolutionary?
How many a poet?

With our penal system
we shall give to you:

life, education
punishment & hope,
hopelessness & tuberculosis,
a haircut & race hatred,
organized religion,
a personal God,
a place to sleep &
clothes to wear,
fear, slavery &
an alternate economy,
drug connections,
enemies,
allies & a new body,
romantic opportunity,
prepared food,
allotted time & something to keep
for your memory's permanent damage.

THE RIGHT TO COUNSEL

The mighty symbols
have snuck away
with human memory.
Actions are now
horrifically undressed
lest they should corner
the market.
One more docket
left silenced,

similar to the way
any words can fight
when given the story
of life and death.
In this quiet neighborhood
the people move around
like rabbits before dawn,
justice is untrusted
and visits no longer
than a speck
of dust or a trace
of conscious life.

THE RIGHT TO REMAIN SILENT

In foregoing witness
against ourselves,
what risk,
this clean towel,
or breakfast
intact by moments.
Fear the state
that could eat many lives
just hanging
on the hope of
divine punishment.
Singing together
we know not who
we serenade,
if not ourselves
who are no selves
and broken
we look to bedtime,
elope with big
distance in mind.
Space is a vicious map
erected by the
trampling of destiny.
If you can only live
one life, you must die

for those
you throw away.

LIFE POLICY

Lit by the light
of one lamp,
with clarinet backdrop
& ashtray,
you pitch safety
and comfortable Futures.
Your neighborhood shows
as you trace the map,
rule the bills
and conjure up scarcity.
Everybody's doing it, you say,
Hopeful.
Take your big dreams, I say
through the back door,
no one here can sing fate
or pick up that dime, anymore.
We left crossroads back there
with compromise, one nation
two hundred miseries
and all that commotion.
Your dreams are just words
like table salt.
Me I know
this year's moment
will be 2 a.m., my life savings
and one train ticket
down the fault line.

THE NUPTIAL LIFE

Given that coyness isn't working anymore
in store are various devices. Crises abound

as a lack of appetite consumes your gentry.
Your climber urge came zooming in and
ignored me. Perhaps you saw what tune
I dripped when the girls walked by.
Eye my sprawling furbelow then tell me
it's not effective—even bored henchmen
would find this outfit tempting
but low and beholden I'm left rolling
in my own digits, 100% silk.
The lilt of my filthy ways lie neglected
by these, your hand wash only constraints.
Reports poured in that lusciousness
was growing general, all over Providence.
I tried to go out with my hunger
but all that was left were types.

KALYPSO FACTO

The matrix of your hamstrung home-life
is undercutting all my generous gifts.
The current temper is such that soon
even the most bedlamite among us
will be threatened by marriage. Such
unalienable boundaries are bringing distrust
to all frolicers. Now the clouds show Zeus
is arriving to muck us up even further.
That hopped-up interventionist is thieving
all my island's hidden treason. His loud
armaments have been making petit fours

of continents for far too long. Now you

who once found me dainty are eloping

with Enyo. Your indiscretion may dress-up

progress in money lending but trembling

at the horizon I hear those othered lands.

We're all entangled in your strong-arm, but

fault me if we don't coalesce to curb

your second guessing with a dose of our jilted memory.

NEITHER FISH NOR FOUL

Your loopy tragedies have taken up just about enough
of this town's time, you surette, you maverick,
browsing around adulthood like you've shopped
here before, I'm sick of it. Your big confidence
invades my psyche with scattershot precision
and undermines all my carefully planned pretension,
but may I remind you I'm more grown up
than you'll ever be and I won't have your
fluttering lashes and flawless face
clawing up my already leveled kinship.
I'm going to kill your cash-built strut
and cut you boldly to the quick of your deep understanding,
I'll spill your ghastly evenings all over the Ivy League,
you know, those nights you've spent crying
by your claw-footed baignoire, praying your mother
can hear you from across town, or the upstairs guy
will see red circles under your eyes and shower you
with one of those seductions born and bred of sympathy.
The problem is your mother always comes running
and the guy always falls in love, I can't figure it out,
your lurid trick of appeals must be some bargain
because when I gain one speck of ground
you, like magic, become miss faux queen of the universe,
you walk in here and throw your lean wit
all over the badly framed Monet prints and
then prance off into every social circle from downtown up.

Seems you can knock down entire systems built upon
crushing us under, I'm under and you see it,
the perfect target for your sort, I'm here
like some loyal goldfish waiting for the flakes
to drop down on my head. But my thought can no longer
take your vagabondage, you faker, you false harbinger
of easy freedom, I'm kicking you off and cutting all my
connections as they embrace you one by one, you the
unjudgeable, you the "you don't know what she's been through,"
give me back my contentment and go crawl back up
whatever toxic riverbed had the misfortune to spawn you.

CAST OF SHADOWS

Niggling Spring, the distant palaver
of subjects in the craven bit
of the opening air, in wanders
a holster-wearing mussed Apollo
gushing the beckoning tirade,
bedazzled credo beloved of sports
and the yearly hoax begins.

In a moment good reason will be shunned
for the tinny whistle of the calliope,
the fragile petaled entreaty
of heart's-ease erase a tedious legacy
of schedule, shuffle the mind back
through a violent sequence of mise en scène:
mankind mismated to misery.

Cleaving still to it
humanity a coterie of cruelty
bends over backwards to forget
the sky's no nimble chariot
nor ever will be,
no matter the yearly rebirth
or self-induced labor we cop.

The brass light of day mocks
more readily possibility's hollow

following winter's shut-in drear,
gerrymandered love interests
come knocking down the heart block
demand a lamp granted, hope
and all across the sky, uninterrupted sun.

DUET #1   WORDSWORTH

Seal my fits with grey immortality,
and reaper slumber among the ruined
world ways, beauteous Lucy, much the yew
trees surprised us of the solitary
resolution of mutability.
Lonely she dwelt in independence too,
up my cottage strange passion leaps as few
men wandered by traveled Tintern Abbey.

Of two evening ballads I have written,
known intimations and reply: the ode
is a lyrical joy, a morning's march
among spirit lines. And did untrodden
expostulation miles above it cloud
composed mornings, the unknown April heart?

DUET #2   KEATS

In my city Homer stood a muse dark,
a hand written lesson on after eve
vapors. O Nightingale, how many bards
have I? Endymion, whose face I read
when long stanzas stood knighted in a dream;
In the dark of pent Hyperion, where
keen looking fitful brothers did to sleep
fall down, and living poetry was drear.
Why this solitude, born of cottage fears,
written on the first of Chapman's disgust
to one vulgar December? O King Lear,
thou autumn after superstition gusts!

St. Agnes, I laugh the ode into me
once again, tiptoe on the sitting sea.

THE BAD CHOICES SPY ON US GIRLS
after Frank Stanford

Tracy hit me in the head
with a mop frame,
the blood poured out like rain

She broke my mother's planter
and ran back down the street

My mother bound me up
when the sundown said "come out"
but the screen door wouldn't shut

Later on that very night
the street met at the circle
and split itself in two

We cut across the backyard
ignoring the dangers
of Mr. Kittridge

We wandered the canyon
in search of the forest

We found a tree fort
all gnarled and hollow

We spied older boys in the fort
with a Playboy, they threatened us

We ran for the pavement
where our feet got stung,
Tracy stepped on a stone

I went for the army
but the house was empty

so I grabbed my horse

Tracy couldn't find
the keys hid under the mat

We rode each other
around the palm
yelling "getty-up!"

We looked for rope to find a possum
dead beside the broken tools

He was filled with white worms like rice

I galloped out and jumped
a saw horse

Tracy pulled up
on the low-branch tree

When it rained we built
a home in the gutter
made of eucalyptus leaves

When the water ran high
we followed our brothers
to the floodgates
where they ditched us

We set up camp
under the pepper tree
Fred got a palm spike stuck in his leg

When I stepped on a nail
I limped to the wall
with a hole in my foot
and called off the war

Tracy took a shortcut
Down the winding stairs

To the driveway
where Ted was run over
by his own car

He had survived three wars
and told us sugar on grapefruit
was against the law

Then Emerita danced to Creedence
in a carved belt

Billy broke his arm

Scott rode barefoot

Fred wrote Fuck You
On the neighbor's driveway in Eugenia berries

At night we turned very quiet

Through the doorways we listened

Our mothers cursed their mothers
when our dads left, they said

"We are never going back to El Paso"

WAKE

In all such looks,
       I'm doubting
does it seems beside the day your passion asks an answer,
       below you lives a need
as the woe filigree of each life can with midnight's eye
     beg a listening ear,
       above you lives a want.

As if woven in,
              there are those,
                           myself among them
who live a driven worry of the left
        behind, potential to deject a fragile mind
who build our lives in careful steps
yet,
still do leave the ruin of wondrous leaps
        and scatter chill around in keeps
like some powerful ancestral wall recalls a quiver.

Cope, if you can,
        I will walk you like a line
and in the frozen field of aim, beside the gift of all intention
          perhaps I'll cry away the day
          perhaps I'll choose a different wreck
perhaps I'll live this appalling destiny
              in the economy of night.

THE WAVER IN THE ORBIT OF URANUS BECOMES UNEXPLAINABLE

I ask you, is it fitting to undo me by leaving
now that we know there is nothing out there
beyond what we can see?
I admit I've suffered from a "parallax of heart,"
born of a skewing jealousy and seen most evenings
in field-weary gazing upon your sleeping body.
From that angle all other worlds look bleak.
Though I will not call on heaven if you leave,
for I'm certain that the spirit is a one-eyed
pretender to the throne of painfree living
who has stolen all my daydreams for a shot at the beyond.

I suspect the water's edge is enamored of the water,
a quiver on the surface tells me not the wind
but the wish of drift will devastate the sand.
It is the future's focal infection, this insistence on death,
like when my mother and father cradled me
as the answer to each other's desperate tread towards union.
For this is a universe where things are not apparent
in their cruelty, but continual, and the sweetness of order
in increasingly evanescent. If I could hide this day forever
from the pleasure of renewal and banish all contingency
from happening I would, but I have never seen planet X
or the wooden ships on the Eastern horizon.
Up until now my life has faced West, sequestered
reason reaching for an injudicious kiss.

ODE ON THE PARTICLE

Once time had a monopoly

on increments

and neighbors vanished

in minutes. No, it was not

due to the significance of concepts

but rather a case

of the bit

unnoticed. Once I waved

in totality

and lost everyone

on the planet.

In a silenced silent speck

passed by

all matter completely dropped out,

down fell

the sun, the moon,

the earth entire,

and could it speak up, no,
not without assistance.
This was no tribute
to the anxiety
of team players
but a rather sore history
of the arbitrary. I stood
limited in it
searching for existence
of the ideal finite body
and found nothing.
When finally
next to zero
I remembered motion
mass and all
I could not pass through,
formerly so many
formal tokens
now the essential links
person to person to person
unmet. So forget
the time
you dwelt in insolence
pretending to be
unique, as you can see
the infinitesimal
has already scheduled
you in, as when
lessoned by life
you reach

to touch it.
Irrelevant maybe,
but ask a day
of those who gather moments
and discover by severance
the unseen connection
of any specific body.

THREE GRACES

Anthony
a peonie unfolds
through gentle balance,
what allowances he makes
in light of that wiry frame
are caught in a simple tilt
of head, a barely audible slur.
He shall certainly gather poignancy
from many beautiful women
by offering home cooked meals.

Paul
is a rose and sleeps in history's
gateway, he wanders not lonely
but alone and cannot lay down
with reason, every season shall
accost his translucence while interiors
weaken his tenuous being. Will
he finally be treasonous
on his border walk or will his face
elude the chroniclers? Such
unknowns propel his pose of wonder.

Steve
a bird of paradise stands stiff
beneath convictions bathed in
the erotica of energy. Yet
if still when in the company of memory
he crumbles and by the tisk of time
all random things do story his decisions
he of all remains the one. I do not understand
his impressive connections considering
all that vision. He is jeans
and a swagger, a cigarette
on which to bank one's future.

LUCKY SO AND SO
for Elizabeth Willis

Ebbing in these lights of space
each tended for balance, pleasure
and for my liege, a niche,
we have built what we imagine
others building. Behind other
summer-lit windows
there must be wall paper
worth waking up to, but here
in the city of Multiple Backdrops
beliefs are shaky and quips
fly all the way Home.

And so I journeyed. My soulless soul
a darkened station full with notices:
"Psychic phenomenon sweeps the Nation,"
amazing what borders can do these days.
But I had a better outlook on life
when you walked into the room
looking like a winsome Nora Charles,
eyes full with gifts. It can be expected
I will be the whispers you inspire,
tucked waist & golden colored bracelet.

As a gad-fly may I borrow evenings
from your Great Heart? Are you
still waiting for a kitchen-sill visit
from the little bird of careless life
or may I finish your daily rounds?
With no more devastation than fits
it seems the world is calling you up,
Miss Full-with-Novels, Miss Too-Many-Movies
taking pleasure like a secret cigarette
in a land where what we most fear
appears each night at 6 o'clock.

But behold it was a dream. It was
the year the phones went dead
on Mother's Day, though most mothers
preferred fully realized human potential
to letters home or regular calls. Famous
Women moved like landfill and marsh land
revealing structural flaws and saving
the wildlife. Lucy, Ricky, Fred & Ethel
were there too, but it wasn't a dream,
it was a birthday party and all the guests
were smoking Silk Cuts.

And now it looks as though my stove-top timing
really did make a difference. Though most
mornings I still get up bewildered. I've come
to believe impatience goes a long way
towards establishing duty and rabbits
scatter with only the slightest disturbance.
After all, assault rifles may be banned
but assault is still okay, though men
now ask politely whether or not
there will be food. With these convictions
we'll watch the sunset, if ever the skyline dims.

Kept from the circle of influence
you and I are spotting for brothers.
I'm falling in. Remember I'm an orphan
with a first-run movie of family memories
running a continual loop in my head.

From this moment on there'll be only
whoop de do dear, no more signification.
Communal gossip will keep me afloat
while you turn the city on your heels.
Immanence and transcendence will meet
at the Capital, everyone will be moved.

News stories had a particularly abstract angle
that night. All fortunes read:
"What have you done with your life?"
Tell them you have walked over thirty-three vistas
of dangerous westerns. I'll fashion Holidays,
100 ripostes and all the vestiges of glory
we need. You see, I'm not so envious,
it's only spring and you are only reason enough
to give up all requirements.

THOUGH CROWDED

I am not thinking of you
always, in separation our time
is queer requirement, the
impossible revelation
of a moment alone, or the
pale counting of debts.
Alone in thought my mind
now falters, accomplishments
are my heavy buildings reached,
they mark the jeopardy
of savings, must I think
of everything as saved,
the daylight, all the world
of time I want you in shall
pass ungathered. Will you
insist for love my life
must make effective changes,
while throughout this
makeshift home the rooms
are filled with savings,
photographs and books

acquired as if my very life
on them depended.
Tonight I saw the moon
in the faint sky of Providence
and I was moved no deeper
for the distance. You must
know what you've done
to my ambition.

ONCE OVER

As of now
the tendency
is holding,
my leeway has come
unzipped. I know
there have been nights
when you have awakened
far too feathery for sleep,
fearful of stopping
and wondered
if I slept
in sound,
I'll say I've dreamt,
but my pieces
are not fitting
or generous—
You were causal today,
as always, but I won't
bow to wishing
or ensnare
my longing
in the backward beauty
of an unlived heroism,
or did you say hedonism?
You said "call me,"
knowing my voice
is slender by your
condescension. I have been
layered into something

unlovely, as if born
to live out the grope.
And you, you have been
gently bending over
the hopeless beam
of my unsightly tendency
to love you.

LINE OF DESCENT

By evening appearance
          ghostly gentle,
the universe funneled down upon
          your accidental hands
and I danced on wing tips.

This is a story lacking flight plans
or verity,   remember
I was as hopeful as quoted Whitman.

By night's fall
          scenarios dreamy,
the attempted rehearsals of distance,
          perchance to exit
in various possible outcomes.

It was a long time ago believe me,
Persephone remained with her mother
in those days,
plotted against the lover's
          potential to love,
for even in a dreary life
          plans turn up.

Ray of your return, an apparition,
as out on the couch I
wept, derivatively.

In my storage you will father
        undue memory,
Yours, etc… I will watch no daily gestures
        but fondle trinkets,
this one stands for pocketed lineage,

Hemingway in the house, or
Ibsen's pistol.

ODE TO GRIEF

I've built this staircase
down
to losing you
and now the basement
is flooded
with sunlight.
Fancy that, love
bows deeps
in the strangest places.
I feel so lost
without your warping net
to drag me through the nettles.
For ten years
unerring
you've stayed

beside me,
becoming
my most
beloved sorrow.
Now I know
I could read
every book
at Alexandria
and yet somehow
still want
for joy,
for you Grief,
tender isolator,
have bound me up
like a commuter
left to cast
my bliss behind me
far away
into the past. I'll say
I shall curse you
as long as I live
but I won't. I'll surrender.
For you are not splint
or gentle injection,
you're the redeemer
who has dreamt me
in the waiting place,
a slip-shod small arm
playing vigil to
my own life.

TEN PROLEGOMENA TO HEARTBREAK

The better parts
of my lover's work
are never quoted in reviews, god knows
truth serum for the asking and I quote:
           "kiddo, the world is our oyster bar"
now put another nick in the tin cup of life
and let us spill I will you well,
lay the pennies out on the track
lest this grandiose ball room affair
turn out to be drive-through dining

I confided in the opportunity to say "yes yes"
but what came out was a fracas, the Avant Garde lover
of hope, I am such an inept navigator
of woe betide, a miserable egomaniac,
           and you've been single minded which I like, especially
when everyone else is dueling, I love you
like the poem I wish I'd written
In Memory of My Feelings or
how I stayed true to my heart and broke it
broke it and stayed true

If I weren't so blue
I'd be an old world curled in your outstretched palm
one upmanship on the high seas of dramatic endings
or a big budget house in the country
           in our next appearance we will keep you apprised
with hourly updates, pay off the press
beforehand, but first we'll write
a left and friendless lyric poem
to warn you that we're coming

Lines like these
should be outlawed, loves like these
are newly imagined powers of nature, pshaw
I spotted you before any will to destruction
           erupted, laying a dour trail of exit lines
while secretly dying to run

we jumped ship and wept, it was our way
I the Lumpen lover
you a well-spring of second guessing
I recidivism unchecked

The world is aglow
with beautiful speed and poets slow down to a stop
I haven't got time for the word
right now, no matter its
        implications, last winter we drank so much
we fell in love and forgot all about unity
the city and you are the truest
of forms, trust and reliable disbelief
all rolled into one sad strawberry
my weekend and my last ditch

Skin is a memory they say
but you are a brain child, look at him go
so what if the sentries visit tonight
hold my hand and swing it
        ditch the visiting lecturer and put on
your fedora, we'll throw a big show for the border patrol
leftist coveys and jealous lovers,
for the following Monday we'll take on
new and more earnest positions, teardrop
teardrop, all out revolution

In the chaos of daylight
the buildings come shining
into the rented chamber of my over-heated heart,
where have the hooligans hid your awards
        in a trapped bird my love, in a dark
and lonely place, the car
ten years hence
in a hospital bed
this I shall perhaps recall,
soft and powdery scented skin, apricot I trust

The best parts of my lover
are in the poems, don't be fooled
he is always serious or

in love, you must promise to remember
for this is no hoax, it's a total failure
I the she the leased forever
known to have dropped
the incalculable prince
the remainder of all remains

Atavism in a dress
she is strolling to meet
your criminal past, armed
with just the history to see it
          you've a bigger problem than first we thought, buster,
they haven't made that part in years,
on the bus she dreams of filmic meetings with big scores
and they'll all come out to meet her
when she comes, killing limelight and beautiful men,
and you were so unprepared

Diurnal death creates a disjunctive aesthetic
insert the joker here, you'll need a strong
divining rod to reveal all the skeletons
those two tow around, deal me in the reddest red
          life is unfailing and yesterday
horrendous, children play
in Tompkins Square Park now where are you going back to,
debt certainly, debt and a smallish house
surrounded by field a father and mother
and all of the gall of heartbreak

WREATH OF A SIMILAR YEAR

A circlet ring of light
      beneath our feet
a door, a possible path
      of very best will,
placed before us
      in infinite intervals.
Such facets of mind
      might sustain us
if luck runs over, or love
      provide the lost,
more bodily
      forms of warmth.

The inconsolable mind
      has created
abundant distress—
      the scarcity required
to bury a world
      of living evidence.
Abandoned so, in an idea
      of innermost anguish,
we have become accustomed
      to the unheard music,
the quiet accompaniment
      of water,
being disturbed within.

Thought intent
      upon contentment
may temper the guests of our greater being,
      unearth
the hourly questions
      burned down from youth
with energy and light. As in the wake
      of awakening
wrong attempts
      and wrongful death
will fall adjacent
      careful Hope.

      Hope,
how strangely of untold direction
      it sounds, blind as
the first letter on the first stone
      written down
as if a wreath to circle
      the last sound spoken
on some distant, though similar
                  Earth.

CUNT-UPS
DODIE BELLAMY

TENDER BUTTONS

New York City

2001

Various cunt-ups were published in *Open City, San Jose Manual of Style, Chain, West Coast Line, Kenning, Can We Have Our Ball Back, HOW2*, and *The Blind See Only This World: Poems for John Wieners*, ed. William Corbett, Michael Gizzi, and Joseph Torra (New York and Boston: Granary Books and Pressed Wafer, 2000). I'd like to thank all the editors of the above for their support and openness. Hugs and kisses to Julie Regan for suggesting this book.

I'd like to thank my students at the San Francisco Art Institute for exciting me about this form, especially Colter, Tamara, Nathan, and Jonathan.

OTHER TENDER BUTTONS BOOKS:

Sonnets by Bernadette Mayer
Not a Male Pseudonym by Anne Waldman
Trimmings by Harryette Mullen
Agnes Lee by Agnes Lee Dunlop Wiley
Lawn of Excluded Middle by Rosmarie Waldrop
silent teachers   remembered sequel by Hannah Weiner
Imagination Verses by Jennifer Moxley

Distribution:
Small Press Distribution
1341 Seventh Street
Berkeley, CA 94710-1403
510.524.1668 • 800.869.7553
www.spdbooks.org

Lee Ann Brown, Editrix
Tender Buttons Books
PO Box 13, Cooper Station
New York, NY 10276
718.782.8443
LA@tenderbuttons.net

Book design: Wayne Smith
Cover art: *Hedgehog Touching Herself*, Michelle Rollman, 2000
Cover photo: Craig Goodman

Publication of this book was made possible by
grants from The Fund for Poetry

ISBN 0-927920-09-3

FOR KEVIN

screens flicker
with pornography, with science-fiction vampires

—Adrienne Rich
"Twenty-One Love Poems"

O   N   E

Without its shell, but it's tubular, like most and I was raised there and attended and we fall asleep together. I'll wake up when you pinch my nipple, I'll look back at you when you tell me to rub cum juice on my living. Will you accept my pussy for your subject states? I was raised—think of it as yours. Would you do it? I consider myself to be an atheist, I admit I pussy weep. Would you feel okay about states? I am currently on probation for thoughts mushy and oozing like runny yolks, thoughts about age and ass. Would you prefer me to suck your clit, hiker, whom I described as a male with lips? Yes, I would fuck you back, yes, you had homosexual sex with me and states sexy. You are such a romantic. You can state we got into a physical fight, you can hang there with my balls, you can, and during the fight you stated your cock could slide up anything you want *blow of the barbell* 'cause you can't help it now, it's magic, you've got to blur, I'm moving so fast. You don't know how infinite the course of my humiliations for you, singing actually—torch songs of nullity of being/being outside my kind of love, the kind of love the top of the wall carved a hole in. The rock. They opened the door and tied me down, a runnel of water/a returned letter. They tied me down, and I let a turd, the hard absolute hostility of slaves, the infinite partition of waiting because my eyes were too wide. I was Jesus, see the dark figure in the empty room alone, all fours tied, cakes, one arm out of the leather. Then I got a foot out and I couldn't decide whether I had turned in the electric symbols. I knew you were there outside in black black black cell of rock. What else do you want to know about me *the rock well walls of rock* I'm yours. Chinks of light. When I was in SF I again thought I was your wall of light, UFOs set up a landing near the wailing wall, cement pads. I painted pictures because I reached the hall of the Double Rhino, I walked around a government building, ripped leaves from the trees and wrote down that I had so many choices.

T   W   O

Breasts, but I couldn't find your nipples. I'll fuck you like I've never fucked, a bit funky, I felt you biting the insides of my cunt and you heave, and inside my cunt you would have seen lime too. And I'll suck your cock too, I won't forget having been slapped to your pillows, and I've only been fucked in the ass. Subject states like two halves of a movement, slightly, just slightly, slower touching that little space between my clit. And so I fuck you until you scream creamy, the only table in the world, I'm there, bang your cock against the back of my throat FAITH you left my open insides and went to fill yourself and tried to hold onto it. And then we did get arrested. You thought maybe I'd give myself to you in ways I'd never given myself when taking polaroid pictures. I fucked you like snakes fuck each other, fuck me, your tits hanging in my face because that feels good, the organs and blood, hitchhikers tight in the crack of my ass. And what you're telling me, you took me and jerked off by rubbing against my boot fuck me fuck me fuck me, and I'll fuck you, drinking beer and becoming intoxicated, catching all my love juices, heaving. Anything. Are they large DON'T TRY TO LEAVE I'll put on a dab of the mixture, fuck me, is this really going to happen? Truck the hitchhiker with a barbell. You stated it laughed, my cock laughed, I was lying in your path, hitchhiker, and then we walked to the ocean, overwhelmed with this incredible arousal, like before. And I start sucking your breasts and carve our letters into my skull. Don't forget about the kissing and the petting, mouth onto your cheeks, and I'm sucking your nipple hair. A harmless ex-catholic boy, eating a few times, little nibbles and our thousand words, a kiss on each eye, some bubbles in my ear, in your cunt, in your asshole. I want to close my lips around it tighter, a big long kiss on your mouth, on your home and then we'll fuck like demons. I gave. And my mouth is small, as far as a mouth to anybody else. And then your blood will be in my cock in your cunt, your nipples dragging through my totally cliched heart, opening like a big silly, and yes my heart, your balls slapping against me and you would be sucking and meaning. All this says small, or in between. You are very easy with words, but life is different. Are you uncircumcised? Are you nipples? Move your pelvis up and down, you're there, I was thinking of you and I was the "now." There is an arrow which points to every bit of arousal either of us ever had, ever the other side, and I grabbed my cock.

T   H   R   E   E

In the sky I thought I might come, the head of your cock is smooth as butter and susceptibility, a flat limbo glowing, a sharp pointed cock coming in green neon. The long strands of sleep within my own skin, which are the walls of reason—I have a cunt so that I can fit about the cloud plowed under. Puzzle. The parts that feel best to me are my male difference and my vagina. Then, as I'm there on the wall with the rock of a man and my vagina; then, as I'm there on the cock tuft by the leg, I suck my cock until the blood cock tips head to toe. Mouth. Then I grew and became an old cock, tip arched orange. You've heard this before, the one that you held in your hands, cock foam tip tongued without limbs. Then I pulled my panties up, cock craning towards good, and took the boot you're so fond of, cock ringing-in-range clit through the panties, the cock shank fastening the panties. I want to take you from behind, cock spur of knowledge, one of the circular spots of your body. Then cock will exist and be cock *extremes of assertion* same trip, we get to fuck with the closeness, cock forged cavity your skin together, and then swim in the cock quiver and trough home together and we'd fuck and love cock grim gold salve. You indicate there have been many times you were involved in states of the heart. A few drops of come drip into your eyes and onto your forehead and you had sex with me, wads of cotton candy. A kiss is worth a then—I fall asleep, you strangle me, cunt juice on your eyelids. A kiss on each drain, I use a knife to dismember your nose, and hold it up against your face. Bone—and then you placed them in plastic bags, our tongues. Absolutely. According to my state, about a month later my panties were soaked. All these parts coalescing into a heart, we had sex and used sleeping pills, rose, and your cock in the center fucking, strangled me and then dismembered my body for the first time. A year went by *savage sexual energy* is enjoyable and you returned with a different thing. All you can do is shake your tits, have sex, and use sleeping pills. You strangled me, like a butterfly without wings. And below in the same way. You move your cock and were arrested one time for taking pictures. My body swiveled for just a second.

F   O   U   R

You used sleeping pills which were placed in my clit, which was so sensitive that I didn't like it dismembered. The disposed-of body seems to be changing, it usually turns to one side. I'm getting quicker at cutting up the body I was born with. It was a good orgasm. It was later, I met you and you touched inside of me, it was in this huge taxi on the way home to your apartment and you repeated to fuck me, my cunt was so huge so ravenous, ghosts streaming out from it, but you kept your head. You stated you wanted it, it's about the length of my middle finger, you posed it for polaroid photos, warming up quickly. It's filling your soil with rum drink. After you passed out, I strangled your roots. It's got two balls behind it and it parts in the same way as before. It looks like it could be earthy terrain full hard for you right now, a kind of itchy smell in the trash, but no one ever did anything. It's haunted. The base of my cock wants to kiss your thoughts, the air. Energy balls from my clit to the center of your head. I want to milk your come. Its tip is rounder than my brains, I want to put my arms around you and pull it from there into my pants, to rub my pussy against its scar. How I love to make your cock hard, so incredible, your cock pokes up, divining my guts, my heart, my lungs, the undersides, I have no right to my organs, their incorrect shapes and desire. I beat off in the bathroom, and you are flesh and look at me with love. I want your little pussy. I came imagining your cock, forehead all glistening and funky. I want to see by you sucking my nipples. I can hear. I want to slide a giant chocolate dildo up you, I want to split you in half and to have you watch me with your hawk penis, your pink hair eyeballs out, I want to take your skin off. Pushing outward my cock starts bleeding from the hole on its center. I want to talk so dirty to arousal, with no release, I can't wait to mouth, and your ears will fall off, I want to until I'm done with your cock and can get embodied—my tits and my pussy. Head of your cock with my tongue, I want you to be hard like I'm letting a leopard go in me. Come here right now and lick your words off, dear, I did feel like I was drowning, come here right now and lick and slurp, I'd like my large cunt to come like gobs of glue, I want you to, too. Don't have much else to say, my brain is about having brain scum all over you, much as I did, because it kept acting up.

F   I   V   E

We are in the same world. There your eyes will be open, there you would be with tears and blood and crosses in my eyes, you would suck my lungs, and you would. The conduit has been built, permanently down along the inside of my spine—exactly where I'll be driving it to you every time we tried, because our tongues'd feel better then, and then you'd fuck me. We have changed, we could not get rid of it so you asked me to watch your ass, tell you whether it was left/right or up/down. Now that your pussy was getting wet, the unified face will get sore. You'll open your eyes and see a few drops of blood oozing from my backend. Your arms go straight up, and your dark ceiling like a giant cloth rose. We need more than mirrors and horses in the New World. Your asshole broken or whole, tangerine mixed with rose petals. You breasts are like babies breathing. On your breasts we built ships without seeing my pussy, which doesn't seem to want to behave so much, it's going to switch places with my back, rubbing my clit with my fingers, soft, it looks like a sleeping river mussel. I touch your breasts and they're beautiful. I'm all cocks, and it doesn't look like a cunt. Open the drawer and put them on, then I'll lay my cock into your pussy before you know. I walk around you, the ONLY girl in the world, to anoint you, I want to be full of you. I take a deep breath and bite my lower lip. Your pants. I want to bite your neck and I want nipples, I thought that was incredible to bury my face in your asshole. I want to curl until my birthday. Will you lick me, will you clean my scrotum? I want to do it for a long, would you make me asphalt and lick the chips off my cunt? I want to be fucking a girl with fried brains, her thoughts places that look like a pin cushion, I want to fuck, would you mind easing your cock into my there, smiling, skinless, watching me come or should I concentrate more on your forehead. I want to fuck you, I want to spit on my nipples, you are so fucking, I'll fuck you until your head shakes like a rattle, fuck me like you want to break me in two, and then the bed. I want to have you in my arms, pat us both at the same time, me and you, make you feel solid with your jimmy in my cunt. You can start with my armpit, test it with both hands, bend my head back, raw fuck me. You can't see me because I'm still a thing. I want to keep loving you until my heart needs a mouth, my cunt is always speaking thickest secrets. I want to kiss you too, I want love and longing, and your praises.

S   I   X

Bring that into the piece, a writing that can know pus as come. You don't understand the emotions. I'd like to crawl on top of bones, bones that have dried in your broken sun, be you. Look at me instead of the ceiling. I'd like you to walk on them with your barefeet—you, with their spines breaking, their pages ripping. I'm me and we fuck on the cold concrete floor, I wake up and find you fucking me, feel the dust and we both come a million times, mix my sperm in with the sparks of your cunt for brains. You know it, you've know for a month, it proves my love to do this. You look up at me and I straddle your nipples, your belly, your into. You make me so fucking horny, your head brimming with black, sucking me. You talk about holes—I'd pop open longing for you to fuck *big as the Empire State building* then your arms would start growing out of my here. You thought I liked the pins. I'd die if you put your tongue in my ear, the lips, you bleed, you push your pelvis up and I'll pull you closer, hard, with my arm, like thick paints. You were telling me, even without a wash cloth, you were saying that writing before making it out of our mouths would have to be a kind of fucking, right? If I loved you beyond words, would you kneel? I wouldn't let you say a word to me, I would get our breath together, and I would lay down and beg for your cock, I would be ashamed to lay yours under mine. You were telling. I'll be there in all my blood, dripping, you were this mythical being in my dream come, I'll dab the broken blister on the new battleground. Even more than before, I imagine that won't be a problem. I'm feeling and ideas, but between whole beings, gently this time, swinging my cock, just trying to understand some of the implications, I'm doing this to you all day. I'm even reading Deleuze & Guattari, etc. *pleasure dripping like writing from its side, infantile* but I think it's true, I really do. "We" are enough to keep me from wanting to fuck societies, but not from learning how. Your cock and your lips and your distress are absolutely true in my mind, and I feel kind of foolish four of them at once in me. I'm going to die on the verge of encountering this wildness today, I'm going to fuck you in the flesh dimensions, many words will we speak after that. All will move itself including myself. If you're a square in 2 dimensional fabric, weaving through the same beginning, there's no way you can see the sphere, I'm going to fuck you so that our bloods dimension your perception, right? A complex 4-color map will not be able to separate "We." I'm going to drag my tongue across your neck, that doesn't need to imply that I'm on the inside of tomorrow. I'm going to make enough slurs. Don't know why a battle, except that people, Americans, don't want to hear any other music again. I seem hostile most of the time but understand, you will never be able.

S   E   V   E   N

Afraid that I can lay beside you or sit at your will. You won't feel pain, you'll just bleed. I can close my eyes and suck on it, sucking your cock I looked up blindly, truth, it wasn't bowties but your cock. You would feel my kidneys, you'd push up. When I get up from my chair I feel the wet spot, move your left hand through my insides. Hard-on. Everything's throbbing so much, I want it next to your heart. For some reason I fuck you. You understand depravity. My tongue travels at night, it was like Marilyn Monroe's pucker, you'd left wet towels behind you. Fuck me. Fuck me. Fuck me! I wasn't sure how you were moving it, wet that little squeeze for me. God, you have to help me with that one. You'd tell the

living daylight out of me. God, I want to suck a long time, and
your mouth girl, have fun. Here, dab the tears, me sucking on your
nipples like a giant on my hands and knees. Here, let me pluck
your lips. You'll take care of them for me, off with my fingers.
Hey Pumpkin Fuck, my hands are tied together and flare up into
possibly. Help me to go from total abjection to an imitation. Your
ass is like the first shower when you wrote this. How I long to
smell it—a bit pungent, like chocolate covered? You want me to
drown inside there. How your belly is like a closed eye, sleeping.
Your breasts. Many times do I feel you with my come, you sound
so beautiful. Your cock cocooned in me, you know how I love to
talk dirty to you, itself, your cock is going to like my mouth all
the time. Put your head in my pussy, my refrigerator where all
the bees want to go, honey. I would boil your head, I would use
"Soilex" to button and fill your well with my greases. I'll purchase
a 57 gallon drum, in which I'll put your fingers. Let me put a few
drops of honey on your skull, I'll even spray paint it at times. Like
I said, eat me. Like I've mentioned I purchased the spray paint for
an apparent reason and my groin is suddenly filled. Inside my
pants you should find this 57 gallon tank. Cry Exorcist again, try
it with a crucifix. I meet you at the bar on 27th St., I like your right
nipple or your clit, or I met you at the bus station in Chicago. I have
some new experiences with you. Maybe in my apartment and you
were touching the bead of pre-come on the tip approximately one
year ago. Groove, smearing the pre-come all over the penis and
body parts, running my tongue along your open lips and then I
masturbate for gratification. I want. My arms and legs have fallen
off. I can get pretty thick and I'm sure I'll give it to you after I put you
to sleep. My clit is soft and very pale, my clit is so hot, my clit looked
huge, its outer lips sounded loud to me. My clit was being tugged.

E   I   G   H   T

I know it's you because you know you're going to fuck me. I like
fresh breads. Regarding the other six torsos, I pretend they're your
hands, lightly squeezing my breast, sliding. These torsos had been

fucked in acid, then laid on cheap tapestry. I love feeling your head against me becoming sludgy. Your mouth open dribbled on my left ball and then I remembered my cock was in your mouth. I love it when you're meta, I loved telling you that in Wisconsin. I felt like an individual smiling with your tits on my lips. I love to cut off your skin, love smelling it, smelling your asshole, body. I heard the boiled skull in your voice when you were aroused, I saw you lying on plastic bags, dismembered. The eggs were your breasts, broken. I used my hands about four times, thinking intently about your white goo. I move so fast that all your clothes are bought for that specific purpose and your clit's throbbing like a fire alarm for at least fifteen minutes. I went to Florida for a year, returned to open you over and over again until you came for months. When I returned to my residence I thought I was Jesus Christ, your savior. I and my tongue. My clit will turn all droopy and peace will last through the end. My clit's stirring even more. My cock covered the walls of my rented trailer but it didn't stretch out and get shiny, my night to learn to breath from sleeping, possible breathing. This was ten years ago. I'm yours if you want it. My cock is normal size, mirror, and then I pounded each side of your cunt like a large intestine. My cock made a tiny scar in the center of my thoughts. My cunt is singing through all the cornfields in Indiana. I could read my surrounding, everything, my cunt is tottering on the tip of your finger. I was taken to jail for tongues and they're all over you, my hands move across your head in a small red circle. I walked until my cock will be yours, my mouth will be yours, I counted all the combinations of all the casualties on every battlefield. Dots. My hands through the feeding slot, I tried to break loose and I would clench my cunt, my shirt ripped to shreds because I was going insane with frustration. My mouth is crazy because I told them I was covered with you. Suck them. My nipples are large, but locked in a room. I banged and my nipples are sour as cranberries, they need your THUMP THUMP. Over and over. Unusually charged tonight, I sit here rubbing with vague smiles about nothing, you fucking me.

N   I   N   E

Agony of injustice and cruelty, you can find them on my body, I want you to. My nipples turned hot pink for you. You are Osiris, aren't you? Yes. You tear and I begin to gag, I want your cock, my pussy's all wet now, and now my finger. Will you let me unclothe you? O your tongue on my clit, I want you to feel my pussy's wetness, and I'm getting it on, your nakedness in my mouth. I want your tits in my face, aroma of my pussy thinking of you. My soft flesh of the socket, squeeze my legs together and make myself come. My tongue flicking in that little groove at the nails, the holes, the eye. Badly I was frightened, but I was able to let go, nipples hardening, one touch of your hand and I go violet with oil and tender sky. I was feeling my cunt lips in the water, "love" has been consummated and we can move. Your breast petalled openness like a satin negligee that had become flesh. I like that, it makes me think of you. Okay, I chafed. TO DO, I WILL NOT JERK OFF, that old refrain. I wish you some letters. Okay, so I can still read even more now, all my words are so much better fresh. I wonder if you were recovered. My whole body was a tongue, and a strip of man had meaning now. I would love it if you sucked my clit, I couldn't speak. Once when the earth was young I cleansed your toes with tears. I would love you and you would have my all, one on your belly button, one on your palm over/pain and panic and we'd share our blood from tongue to teeth. The deep places of our bodies, your hair to feel all my thoughts. We'd cool our chests and press our usurpers rhythmically, I won't ask you if you want a blow job yours right when you're gathering power, gathered power, that is all. I would fuck. Your cock moves like a wash cloth across my pussy, like pillows on my skin. All this body worked with your letters with my come on your chest because I fondle your cock, drink your spit, wet core/great rose of Space, drive it any direction you want. Originally you said "killings" thinking of me. I feel like I should stick to recollection, I believe that killings are more limiting than fucking, more of a piling up of meaning, but I couldn't remember all of it, beside you sighing and smiling stupidly. I contact either myself or you, I recall being involved at this time when I moved our hand across my body and I felt like I had one of those small water pistols. You were dripping instead of shooting your victims, you were living in your stomach penis and balls. I fuck you in a garage, I fuck you as if you'll be recovered like a sledgehammer in a garage, like you'll eat my brains. I get all stirred up, I was still half asleep and started flopping about, I was shown to the have my right hand cupped around the sledgehammer's base, I used it to break up the bones to reach your balls, kneeling before you, here, a sledgehammer will be placed on inventory, your cunt is comfortable, that and your tits, orgasm after orgasm, but I can't shake wanting to plant myself inside you, gray handle, my hips spreading across the chair, feeling me over. I just want to suck on your nipples.

T   E   N

I don't think it will be battles between your cunt, I'm slurping it, I'm smearing, you know this from your writing. I've reached the nipple now, I'm so fucking behind, I'm sorry. I'm sticking my tongue between and I hope this doesn't sound trite, thinking that you fucking me is your imitating lifeforms, and my arm, my fingers are really tentacles to perceive more clearly, this is the same path on my body right now. I'm thinking that somehow I'm whispering in your ear. In general you were fingering me rather than fucking me, it's the wilderness we're used to seeing in you. Is it okay that I can't see the whole picture yet? Layers. It gets dark with its blood and tensions, and you encounter a sphere with your hands. Kiss its head and run your lips along something other than a line, I'm moving from tootsie roll hard to zucchini hard to something extra, something other than a square. The idea of fucking as strangers—is this woman ready? I dunno, I'm just getting to it, it's like I read your thoughts, smell you, know the answer to that, and I definitely hold it wide open. It took a long time to come to this secret knowledge, the whole time thinking of you pulling me specifically, biting my nipples a bit just to remind me. I think my pussy was all yours, wanting to meet your brass zipper teeth. I've been here, I'd almost pushed them all out, down in anti-gravity. My thoughts sail clean out of my asshole, they dipped so that you're like Thanksgiving forever. You gave me a shot and my belly button opened, then you left and I had one big cunt in the middle of my forehead, lay down on my bed left to dream. I keep wailing your name like a siren. I'm out of the leather, falling asleep, it still looks like a snake's. I've had the fem swastika, or those other ancients, I'm just letting it rest there, petting it a bit. In a small house in the field, fucking you later. I've never been fisted. Adjust my dirty panties before you licked me. Anything. Around 1990 I spurted, finally, I'm your throbbing pussy savior. You thought I would wait for my spit on your nipples, right? I've taken a house, the one with the brass disks I stuck up your asshole. I've wanted too many messages, I turned, wanted to touch you forever. Just know the living with lots of flags hanging, put your arms around me, rub your jimmy in my mouth as I've described. I walked in circles, there for a few seconds, your tongue swirls my left boot, the one I'd traveled with. Know me. Keep me. Kiss kiss kiss kiss kiss me, here on the sidewalk somewhere north of Gold.

E   L   E   V   E   N

Large cows fed me sacredly, this occurred after you cut up my body. The orchestra played, phones rang while I jerked off, thinking of you covertly in the woods behind my house. It was you calling me. I don't really know what you wanted, but it's our cock now, no alternative. Will you give it to me in little pieces, scattered and kind of sweaty so I can taste the salt? Can I pull down my pants and push it gently through your skin, my tongue in your ear for just a second, discharge like a small river? Can I take the knife my father gave me and peel your scrotum into an ancient parchment? Can we do this in Florida for approximately one year? Can I slide the knife gently down your belly? Giving your cock much attention, I read it. Can you see me kneeling there on the floor nostalgic for our past and filled with desire *fuck me with your teeth* one hand on each of your thighs, computer, ripping your shirt open, tugging homicides, licking the honey from the tip of your cock? I really do want to fuck the shit out of you, Fuck Bug. I'm vain like that, excuse me: fuck me. I'm sliding. Dear Three-Headed Cock. Dear

True Walls. I'll stick your cock stone inside my cunt whether or not you consume my pussy like hot wax. Do you like it? I still want to swallow you whole, to consume any body parts, all that roughness across something smooth, you with my tongues, and I hold you with biceps, do you see me, I look up at you and wink with my licking. I think I might pass out. Do you still want me to cover your face with rose buds? I think of you fucking me undercover. Do you want me to come all over you, squirrels and stones stuck to our skin? I thought so. It's the middle of the day so I don't pass out. Does your pussy weep like a waterfall? I'm going to push it together and when your clit gets hard I'll lick one nipple and then I'll lick the other, I'm going to slide right in between your lips and work my disposal to its heights. Then you rubbed your nipple to blow out the fire. Regarding the head, how to open and close it like a door, like the day I'm kissing you for a really long time, about 25 years, you are lying on your back so we both have the same breath. I perform actions with you, there's a storm outside and lots of people will know your cock moving in and out of my mouth, and then you begin placing body parts in it. So much. I used to have brains but now my tongue moves aback and forth along you, they're in my mouth and I'm licking you and you touch me without sleeping pills, I'm creaming for you through my panties, your jimmy like topsoil under my last breath. I'm licking you in the bathtub, you are dismembered and there's a lot of come. It feels like a movie with the soundtrack turned off. And you keep pressing up against me, want me to piss all over your spine, clawing. Then we're running down the street naked together because we know how heady death is, you pass out and I'm getting wet not speaking any English so we fucked and so my cock is red hard and all the little people are drowning in red, and as I was saying, I love you. My belly breaks open with light. I'm saying all these things to you in the basement, I give you some more coffee and spell out F-U-C-K M-E with my hands. I'm sitting here and after you fall asleep I strangle you again, this is what I really want to give you for your birthday, I'm fucking you, I'm sliding my greasy cock into you the usual way. Then I boil your head. We are on. My cock, I think it wants to go camping.

T   W   E   L   V   E

The first time my cock bloomed into you I got manic. Lying on you I
saw birds flying and they brought with them the rough wash cloth,
it felt so good. I drew giant pictures of demons with crayons, took
a pair of cotton bikini panties and walked five miles barefoot in the
middle of the bed wearing nothing but these panties. I was having
trouble feeling you up my cunt all the time, I watched myself turn
into a snake in the damp spot on the front of your pants. I bang
the mirror with my fists, and the glass shatters to kiss your face
and your mouth. I want to lick books and read them that way.
I could turn you really small and put you in my chest. I was a
corn snake gliding through words, but more than that I purged
my life, time to drag yours through the hospital. I wear you like
a cashmere coat, three pieces of you are poking out/in me. In so
many ways. I watched my father scorch the center of the island
and I have to tell you you're a whore. I shot my father into the
earth. I want to fuck your cunt for a thousand paces, in a twenty
foot room, into the earth. I want to fuck your cunt in the ceiling.
I reached for the guard's keys to fuck you again, and it's today.
I want to poke my gun in your ass until it jiggles through to the
other side. I want you to fuck me from behind, to look out to the
water together, stitches in my butt. I want to hold your cock at its
dark. You banged on my fucking door, like a heart. The aching
in my lips to round its head like I'm praying, it came nine times,
pumps out my throat and into an adverb. That would be breezes
and spots. I pinched my nipples, meaningless language. I feel like
I'd just like to lay, pinching them in a semi-public place, I feel like
I'm melting, I have to hold on to this plan of making friends with
your cock. I'm sucking, close to you again. I feel so luxurious,
you in my panties as if I hadn't read Anaïs Nin. Like a big stalk of
seaweed bobbing about my pussy against the computer screen. I
put pistols in my hands, lime-green colored, and I reach down and
unravel my wrinkled long distances. I felt this swirl rush though
me, it's a map. I realize you haven't been breathing into me, I'm a
dead man and I get lost in it, the mixture, you're ready to cook my
head like a goat's. And then I'm with you again, right now, here
on the floor, my cock goes up when I read this. I got so aroused at
your pants, snarling, "Give it to me." I flop around the bed like a

beached whale. I shouldn't take that beautiful word fuck in vain, I'm using your cock for leverage, but I can't really get in, I throb along your lips in your office with your pants still on. I hope so because I want you to fuck me. I still have sleeping pills too. I hurl my body though I still want to swallow your hole. I surround you, every minute, with tongues, and I love you, running my tongues along your fucking Redwood, I just want to sit here with nipples, they must be really light pink and so solid that a freight train couldn't knock them. We're both flatter than the dead with my cock swimming in your cunt, I was seconds away from slamming.

T   H   I   R   T   E   E   N

My clit is hard. I've always welcomed missiles from the people I cared about. I do my best not to turn to smoke. I'm doing it in the Bay, and I knew it would be tricky, swinging into your forest like a sideways hammock. I spoke silently and filled your pussy and your asshole with thought. I needed to help direct you. I'm feeling a little worn out but I feel like a Rex fucking you. And so I was on a street, silly with you, feeling kind of ravenous. Children watched me over a wall, fingers sticky. Police came and I put it to you. I'm going to fuck you abstractly, poke it up your ass. They put me in a paddy today. I'm going to fuck the back of your mouth, my cock will explode in your hole like a giant laugh. My cock laughed again and again but in different places. Love. I'm going to fuck you in my apartment where I took pictures of you. We've lost all our boundaries. Sleeping pills in a coffee and rum will not separate us again. I'm going to kiss you and when you fall asleep I'll stab you like a knife. I'm going to mail them to you as I described. It has a six inch blade and a black handle, I'm making slurping noises on your cock so that you'll never know that I was dead, I put your body in the bathtub and I'm going to make sounds in your ears. I'll use my knife to dismember you, and you'll repeat those sounds, and I'll put your bones in with hydrochloric. I've got two extra eyes the better to see you turn to mush. Substance and then this scar? So I get down and hold you my fleshy fillet, I trail your body with my tongue and I'll fuck your cunt. You're my third victim and we're standing up fucking *kept the skulls kept the skulls* slowly like a wave at Ocean City. I wiggle around and shiver. So I take the tape off your mouth, I think it's to the left side because that's where we tongue huge globs of spit. It's such a thrill to have something you had actually touched, I stuck the tape between my legs and tried to hump it, a diffuse feeling overcame me like my cunt had expanded and you're floating. So this is why my pussy is growing, it's like you didn't even have to drive me. Do you ever feel ravenous? My cunt could suck the energy it needed. I like to be hurt. Sometime I like you to suck, touch me. It would be easy for you to gain strength, honey. Suddenly I want to fuck you, I get so involved when I'm wet. I'll give you all the strength hot pink when I come, leave your polka-tongues back there because that's what I understand. My nipples are erect, tell me I'm a good girl. When it's soft, but its thicker. It's cold but it's barely darker, I've broke to black softness with my darker pink. The clouds were huge and white and never lost. It's the readiness that I read as desire. It's like my cunt starts in the middle of my chest. It's like there's a heart that's fibrillating, sucking in my breath.

F   O   U   R   T   E   E   N

Stick your cock in every hole and indentation, understand how much I love you. Stick your cock inside my mouth because I haven't yet ripped my lips off and let me into your mouth, your lips on my tits, the tip of you. You have a dirty mind. You have me. Lay your tongue under mine, I want your lips and there are chunks of cement everywhere, on your cunt on my chin. I wanted so badly it was like electric shock therapy, you know me, come, I was that aroused. I want you so this is an unreal situation. You know we can't and when I did I found your nipples so that my cock hangs above your face. They felt incredibly smooth, flickering there, me wanting to fuck your brains out. You, really. I WILL NOT JERK OFF, I HAVE WORK. I've got cunts all over my body now, and blisters. You could smell them right now, they smell. Your pussy's Jesus' whore.

I wonder if you're sleeping. I'd always keep them sharp, your tongue would. Stick your cock in my armpit and I'll suck your cock inside with swirling sounds, blood on your face and you would kiss every word that might have curled up and died. Tongue. I would move my hand through your regular day, you were telling me that I could, skill and all the veins. I'll surround them with my language. You were telling me that my cock was moving in your mouth, I won't ask you how, my tongue under yours. You could be smeared with shit. I write in large cursives that you were naked, that you knew me. Feel I have to write to you even now. I'd die flying around, you're saving me through sex, where I happen to live. Your ghostly lips through the spastic air, the first form they take is a battle. I'll weep if you stop being passionate with me. It's done with, some spiritual connection that gets me hard like a large hot pepper, a new Arjuna. In simplistic terms my cock is a cocoon and it's going to live inside you and be recycled. It seems real to me that bodies get dark. My cock would fill you, a good reason for some people, semi-hard, and I'm thinking warm thoughts open when all souls and computers want to fuck you too. You haven't fully owned your body, how my computer wants to fuck you too, but only that. Your new body can feel and think and learn how to alienate yourself from paradise. My cunt is sleeping now, it's late. Emphasizing different parts, different praises. My cunt is sleeping now. It's late and because of this I'm stuck in my own. My cunt is yours, my eyes are throbbing, silent one, with no inside or outside. I feel graphic as hell. My fingers have turned into poems like a very real possibility, and I will be yours, my eyes will be yours, it's already happening. I wanted to add that we'll come together like the first two, we'll see what happens when all senses and thoughts would flap under our feet. I fit my legs into certain muscles as best I could, totally relaxed, I should be able to. My cock is slimy like a dog's. My nipples are dying for what happens most of the time. They're not as long as some I've seen, my nipples' form in regular space. Sweeten them, honey. My nipples are not claiming everything's the same, but they're staring at the screen thinking of you.

F   I   F   T   E   E   N

for John Wieners

Do whatever you want with my cock, to bring me down. The law
of the body is jerked around as much as war, the morning is blood
red, you in that bed surrounded by books, you dead is worth more
than all of life. To fuck you silly in a bed full of books, stretched by
a window over Polk and love it. I'd love it if you sucked me. I'd
love you but death on my shoulder sits, blowing my drowsiness all
to hell. I bury my eyes, war has won over my thoughts. I'd send
you my panties every day, half in love with you. I'd shoot for the
shivers up your spine, my pockets drugged, your cunt flying. The
sign of love, the sound of friends, maggots the size of seals. If my
cock were a demon it would possess all of America, would shoot
King Kong up your cunt. If we fuck forever men will whisper but
we cannot whisper back. If you did touch me, and I was sure, it
would be the action of your soul. I see the skin of my need and
will get emergency shivers. Clay, the feet of lovers walk and I fuck
you like I'm wringing all the ocean. The head of god is a sexual
collaboration. Midnight then home to turn my sight on you, here I
would fuck you silly, I would forever, down on my knees. Listen to
the sound of your pants undone and the opening of these doors to
hell. That wouldn't keep me from begging to kiss every nook and
cranny of you. Voices of the underworld rise stoned, breathe. I want
to lick the juices from the land of your pussy and slice big cookies
from reason. War is when one of us cracks, hear it, my stretched
forehead. I want to say we'd be fucking on Sutter, stretched like
canvas. A country is rancid without nipples. I want to see the
discoloration of the dead at each instant of life, I want to see you,
to feel your salt. We are in debt to it, we are led by it, I pay dues,
see your cunt singing. I want to see you full. Out of the mouths of
strangers your tits swinging in front of me. I heard it tonight talking
in Spanish, your cunt. I want to slobber all over your cock, my
house, my mouth full like the earth hatching. I want to suck you far
off the register, our transactions spread over the island, I want to be
your stud, your golden toy. Your tongue will hang limp as the sky
shoots 15 colors all cool and I touch your nipples to my eyes. I want
to lie in your arms, a junkman who makes it after midnight, my ass

and my mouth and every other part, lying. You will clean out my eyes and ears as often as possible, for me. I want you to come, a motorman's bell announces my clit, lick it back into yourself.

S   I   X   T   E   E   N

This means that whenever I'm stressed I shoulder outer space, and you'll nurse me with your cock, hands that gripped my face like a vice calmed me down. Each time I opened my mouth, the king filled my throat, closing my lips around it. Enjoy it every time in the kneeling position, your voice charged in my pants. Every time I read it I get hard, I whispered back from outer space and saw it in your eyes, a beautiful new city bearing my name. My nether hole was really erogenous, ears of wheat pressed to its walls waiting for you. Fuck it. Fuck me. Fuck me. Extra hours of work in the brickyards, dig out a cave from under the inside me! Fucking me forever. Give your cock a come. I'm still planning to fuck and speak in a public place, fuck you so bad. Good girl! "Goo," says the voice in my hole, all eyes are on your cock. Here, let me get down, press my face into your hole/the wailing wall. Its petals open one at a time. Here, take it, all that we fought for, my sweet dripping jimmy. My hard-on, my voice and lips, fall, gracious, inside your mouth and drown. Face the probabilites of this prostitute gospel. How many times did you bite my ear, honey? A story to measure my feelings by, wads and curly shadows, my cock does the seeing for me. Know that this is just one form we could take, throbbing on my cock. Let me get to the center: things alien to each other first meet. Let me put my jimmy up to your belly, which may be impossible sometimes. Let me paint you, let me paint you with my hand, your body your property, nothing's more beautiful than those cranberry nipples of yours, don't leave me. It's happened before, I get aroused sometimes for no apparent reason, arbitrarily connected to bodies/you with me. Love me. Makes me want to jump up, feeling and thinking everything about you. I loved this really small part of your body and mind, so many different levels in the green of your eyes. Maybe my clit could want to do that completely, and maybe you can put my balls in your mouth too. I battle your cock completely, running my finger in the little groove, I don't mean to say I have any answer, but I don't see any reason not to believe that it's the head of your cock, licking it off my finger, that part, MmmmmMMMmmmM. Move it any way possible. I get this idea from my balls, which connect to my cock, and my cock states it wants to return to being able to feel you, a mouthful. My breasts are large and without their self-imposed restrictions I'd end up in the hospital, not much room, better rub some sunscreen on your cock. There's no difference in size here, right? I'm hanging down. My clit reads the words.

S   E   V   E   N   T   E   E   N

We felt for one another, coursing through the photographs, within range within everywhere, and I knew it was you, your navel or vagina because this is what my cock looks like. But I'm still licking your membrane, filled with some semi-fluid substance. You're an eminent gynecologist and you've lobotomized your cunt. I've agree to run my tongue along your scar. I slide a portion of my substance into your vagina, this manifests as love, connecting us, and blood rolls out to our sides in luminous threads. The substance left me (unintentionally), can I still take you sometimes, physically, can we still cuddle and fuck? Can we fuck too? I manifest in front of you, unzipping your pants, you should be happy when you come because my little pointed tongue with its red tip can lay our burdens at the door. And I can't keep your pussy off my dick. Now don't degenerate into a phantasm, Puppy. Dear Fuck Slug. Dear Fuck Instrument through which one can express us. In either case we are cranberry. Desire for you is dripping out, a dispiriting state of affairs. Sweet Psyche can I suck your nipples? Do you like to move it? I threw my mass upon the table, vulnerable, my breast for instance and all my orifices, and then my lips close around the head of your cock. Do you wanna fuck my brains out, do you wanna make my pineal gland come? Suppressed by light, the grand climax is reached. Honey, don't make me so fucking horny, it all dissolves, and we'll go straight down, ectoplasm leaking from your body, your tits upwards towards faces so you can be visible, a soft resisilient mass. I skin you alive like a fucking rabbit. I show you the photographs and they're wet. I'm huffing as I'm trying to pack a considerable punch, I'm just going to think about it throughout, expelling a cloudy medium, faintly this time like we're teenagers. I'm kissing you, emerging like a baby in fluid, kneeling between your legs, my cock extracted from your sensitive body, my head moving back and forth, my lips a veil of splendor, our hearts cocked, my eyes closed like a blind mole. What an ecstacy of joy, seeing you press yourself up against me. Give us some rest, aid us to wipe it away. I clean you with my tongues, I'm licking your body wetter until your body looks shiny with desire. Just so, the spirits are in control, they want you to move through me. All this is baffling, your left hand down there with the spirits still controlling the marks on the insides of my scrotum. I'm reaching for you. Plasm is exuded from my legs and there's a landslide along my clit, which is responsive to light. I'm rubbing my cock up against you, intensified by darkness. No language will ever fit, no language will give light to the mysteries of my overwhelming need to tell you that I want.

E   I   G   H   T   E   E   N

A kind of liquid jelly is dripping all over me. Your cunt organizes itself into the shape of a face, your tongue was in convulsions, thrusting, jerking, I started to move, and you told me what your hands were like. Your clit likes someone in orgasm, feel my wet tongue in your cave, your cunt is happy to hear that the young man's activity will get red. Your nipples bleed because of my ejaculations, the substance, whatever it is, goes straight to my brain. Your pussy is mine mine mine. Cold shocks cause an irreversible spilling out of my pussy and it's harder to swallow with your broken tongue, you're all red. Your limbs could be so successful — they looked real, felt real, and smelled real, always pushing my clit. My hand clings to your clit like a barnacle, honey. Take me, the love-fuck of the century, you're naked. Looking for subsistance your cock swayed and throbbed. Naked your whole body is a kind of light: I investigated it early in this century: it burned trying to hide someone. We're really fucking now, all we had has fallen into one big cunt, especially my brain, you called it death, but it is just a step in enabling my cum. You've got specially made clothes on, understanding the truth, I'm sowing my seeds, you're completely at my mercy, nervous as I watch you tonight. Does it feel good that way? Yes I can be consumed. I'm thinking of you, I bet you have the cutest sledgehammer, bet you could break the bones up inside of me, slamming into me. I can come just in the woods. You make sounds like broken bubbles, I can see you now, fucking body parts, I can taste you now, dissolving on my tongue. I can see your cunt was the biceps. I can't fuck donuts, can't stand waiting to sniff your come soaked underwear. Apparently they are missing and I cannot find your asshole. I clean the funk from my apartment, I scraped up the pus from our wounds and the come I hadn't eaten and flushed them down the toilet, the jungle. I did come, but my cock didn't pose for you, I gave you a drink and then my love in an electrified sea. I didn't know your skin was acid, it skinned my entire voice. I want to suck them like a baby and subsequently to dispose my body in the still of your cunt. I don't know how you feel when I strangle you, I don't think my clit liked the black strap, leather type, that you pulled out of the blue, it made me wonder if you were.

N I N E T E E N

Your cock's got my tongue. I was busy psychically diverting the right one, which is more sensitive than the left, because my mouth was a submarine and your pube looked like a little naked animal. My teeth. Your cunt bleeds but I'd make you land on your ass, everything is covered with you, you've pushed through my cock and become one with everyone. The keyboard, the whole room, is full of you, like my mouth on a good day. I kiss your lips then I spend an evening walking around, my teeth stuck out like separate vampires and each touched you. Your nipples have gone to their first place of dying, mine was at the top, no shadows. I can feel my nipples, your words are tumbling through my veins directing the blood flow, my little nipples have gelled to cranberries. Suck the barnacles from my clit. You're a blind voice, I stopped to watch, I was deathly serious. Is it on? Now the inside of my cunt is a bit sore, now, like Carrie, but I'm not a pig. You're the ground, I press my face to your tarpit, my billy club. As I've said, I've ridden a horse and I've written insides. You rode my wagon to the station then you let me go, though all I can think of is fucking you, once, like the first rocket on my moon. You're like an artist practicing how you should move my cock until my whole body was one. I had no mouth, so your body said Be Here Now, then flatter, you held me inside like a Voodoo doll, smudgy like on television, your pussy's a wet one. Only you. Or when I bite sexy too. You're turning my whole body, laughing, barking directions, our faces meld together into a folded fan, you got me up against the wall growling for meat. All meat will be inhabited. This sack, these hearts bang together with sweat, your tits mounded in special clothes, no more limbs. Typing these words I was dragging your cunt behind me, you know it, you've wet everything we've touched, ripe like fallen fruit, like the earth. I let you touch me all over, you used to use maps, but no longer, one, two, my tongue crying out for you to fuck me. The cum emerged from me, gradually, and I can make it do short hops, a limp. Soon I went into a trance, your nipples on my face, you whispering, planting and moaning, rather summery. There I just did that. There you, unmistakable, your head poked up. This is often accompanied by erections. Cover me from the rain, you're coming so often, this could not have been expected but it's ok. All we ever do is sigh and decline, leading to a loss. You're even harder now, I'm licking the blood off. Think of me as a mimic or counterfeit human form, like at a job interview. This is more than come stains, a whitish stream, perhaps luminous, out there in absolute silence, gradually gaining consistency. Today's a good day for my mouth. Want me, make movements, can I come onto your broken lungs? We came, throbbed and were captured. Unravel my rattles. We keep fucking until we're ash, leaving a smell as of horn, I must have come because it's like the first time, I have to pass through this trying ordeal SO LARGE we would all be speaking and I awaken to your spiritual breasts, a perfect sphere of life everlasting, and after my so-called death we reach the O-C-E-A-N O-F C-O-M-E.

Is it fluid or material, what is the nature of your pussy, concealed whenever it happens, your cunt full of eyes and dreams.

T   W   E   N   T   Y

You easily extracted my juices, I knew you would, jerking off a sub-stratum of matter. You're so refined. You appear to belong to a physical body when you hold and suck my cock. Your breasts. I like making you horny, like to run my hands over your pussy, spirits moving up and down my arms and shoulders, spirits returning to stimulate us and make us amorphous or polymorphous. Down my belly to my clit, I look like a child, your touch, the substance was soft and though you were sleeping analysis revealed the presence of salt and breasts. I love it when you suck my nipple, I love telling you that with my cock, massing this mysterious substance along your clit, on the tip of your tongue. I love sodium, potassium, water, chlorine, albumen, and you, cocksucker. I love you so fucking much, corpuscles, the red sticky matter described as your cunt, I love the controlled urge, variation on a theme, generated by surviving the phone. I made breakfast and thought I must possess you very much. I lay on the couch before I go to bed, spent and possessed by a living person, your cock and my cunt and languages made of phantasms of themselves. Those clothes are off before you know it, psychics say I must have your underwear, that I must place myself in a state with your tits swaying in rhythm with my cock. A dripping mouthful waiting forever for you, bouncing up, no end to the horizon, the necessary cock dipped to the tip, I'll fill your mouth with everything, thrust my cock deep into your yellow horn. No pilgrims. I'm moving through to where my cock is up you time after time, I've got my arms around you, I've got this cock tip in you for the first time, we're approaching new lands, everybody can see it, the lips of your cunt will scorch the soles of our feet. A causeway of a rock, the cock is to the man a psalm or song, I grown limbs so I can stand, though my face is on that cross on the hill, the equivalent of a hard-on all morning. Language is sand. Erect, I'm filling you with silver, saying you be a good girl. We'll take care of your tongue, which has turned indigo from sucking my fingers. I've never ever given anybody this, no way, the throat drops and my tongue falls into your asshole, your chest heaving yellow and white. Write to me again so I can spurt onto your breasts, alone in winter, black and white, dripping like moss in a rain forest. I've still got this red vivid tilt. My asshole turned it into a large clit and you humped it, I've bled on you since the circle began. My thoughts flutter down your purple neck and that gives me a hard-on. Your hips hugged against my belly, be inert, be happy, I just want to feel you with both feet overhead, all my fight waits to fuck your swollen pink and white spaces, to jostle you around gently until you turn blue. I kiss your finger and touch the head of your cock, you're wild now, invisible.

T W E N T Y - O N E

I consumed your biceps because my clit is hard and my nipples are poking up, and I don't want to talk about it any more with you, my dear. So, how far is your cock from my body parts and skull? You collect me like a pile of flesh laundry and I fuck your mouth, then I put my dribbling cock inside you to rid myself of skin. I sprayed and moved through you, electric, reflecting the morning. I put my hand in your cunt and sleeping pills in your drink. I want to possess the rest of your body but I can't so I take you down to the basement, my cock is bigger and darker down there, then I dismember you and sledge hammer your mouth, it is red and I kiss it. You asked me to be trashy so I wadded my fist into a ball and tried to masturbate in from of you but there just wasn't enough leverage. This brought back memories of you, my victim, wet all the time these days. I'm boiling for you to sit inside my cunt. I've painted your pussy several times, fondled it gently like a baby. Suck my cock for I believe you to be in the vicinity of it, do it quickly and viciously while I'm pinching you, your skull dotted with my squeeze prints. Suddenly my thighs are black and blue—tell your cock to behave itself! So my aureole is pale and my nipples are as long as you want them, your saliva clinging to the end of my being, your fingers inside me. I lean like a mosaic beside you, stay there fucking my clit and hole. I'm sucking your clit, I'm sleeping in your cave, take care of me. I'm touching the page you wrote, I'm tracing your come-font, will you come in my cunt all the time like some fucking cum cow? Jealousy and property appall me but I don't mind a little pain. In your fantasy you sway in the name of coming, you're so generous, really. Is it okay that I ask to coil at the root of your tree? Is my clit still burning away the ozone? I will build a century for you and me. You held it with both hands then you used cries to make me shoot off in your cave, I turned red as a morning sunrise, it's so exciting, no way out, I'm hot for you in a rental car, hope burst its binding in my ravenous wet pussy. I'm straining and gushing, thinking of you, a thousand years of emotion and you fucking me, you knowing my teeth pressed together, you kneeling over me and I was yours, that more than anything, my wanting.

NOTES ON CUNT-UPS

Cunt-Ups is a hermaphroditic salute to William Burroughs and Kathy Acker. I started the project as cut-ups, in the original Burroughs sense, as delineated in The Job. I used a variety of texts written by myself and others. Per Burroughs' rather vague instructions, I cut each page of this material into four squares. For each cunt-up I chose two or three squares from my own source text, and one or two from other sources. I taped the new Frankenstein page together, typed it into my computer and then reworked the material. When my own source text was used up my cunt-ups were finished. The body with all organs slithers and lunges through netsex, psychic oozings, alien invasion, and serial murder. In ecstatic peristalsis the lover endlessly re/turns to life.

Is the cut-up a male form? I've always considered it so—needing the violence of a pair of scissors in order to reach nonlinearity. Is the pornographic a male realm? I think so. Women are usually stuck in the more wishy-washy "erotic." These cunt-ups are my version of Take Back the Night. I'm barging in on pornographic language and subverting it to my own ends. Cunt-Ups is also very much about sexual obsession and desire. In American English we have a language for romance and a language for pornography, but the two rarely meet. In Cunt-Ups, which I see as a very romantic text, I'm collapsing romance and porn. Sex can't be reduced to events that happen to a person. Sex is a trap, a labyrinth, a matrix that engulfs you. Oddly, even though I've spent up to four hours on each cunt-up, afterwards I cannot recognize them—just like in sex, intense focus and then sensual amnesia. They enter the free zone of writing; they have cut their own ties to the writer. She no longer remembers these disembodied shreds of desire as her text.

{DODIE BELLAMY, 2001}

POLLEN MEMORY

LAYNIE BROWNE

TENDER BUTTONS

New York City

2003

Cover art by Toni Simon
Tender Buttons logo by Joe Brainard
Book Design by Wayne Smith
Portrait by Brad Davidson

Grateful acknowledgments to the editors of the following
publications, in which some of these poems first appeared: *A Curious
Architecture: a selection of contemporary prose poems*, *Five Fingers Review*,
The Gertrude Stein Awards in Innovative American Poetry 1993-1994,
Poet's Choice, *Talisman*, and *The Washington Post*.

"In a temperate climate…" first appeared as a
Tender Broadside (Tender Buttons, 1993).

The author also wishes to thank the MacDowell Colony for a
residency which greatly contributed to this project.

Publication of this book was made possible by a
grant from the Fund for Poetry.

ISBN 0-927920-09-03

TENDER BUTTONS
Lee Ann Brown
Box 13, Cooper Station
New York City
10276

IN MEMORY
OF HANNAH WEINER

Stop searching the rose

*   *   *   *

Allow transparency to provide a middle. A key until you try. Delicate movement away from things of the air. Petals fold without cause. A look is a siren as far as she can tell. A phrase is an individual dwelling. You try to read the movements of the many internal vestibules, which are, he guesses, divisions. They scatter, each as different as days when whose shoulder you might be embracing will change. Even shrouded in a guise of soil and darkness the place is undermapped. Not almost a garden of chairs. A clasp. Protected so differently than a stem in a vase.

Your presence in a bottle must be persuaded to let yourself back

     *   *   *   *

Diagrams are horizon scenes, they tell which way to face when surveying. The lettering moves in every direction. Turns as you turn. She is gleaning for a house, a place to describe herself. We now see the daytime sky from this afternoon. A reddish coppery hue as the sun reaches the horizon. We are now entering our planet's shadow. Follow without hesitation for the past, without measuring distances ahead. She replaces the receiver, not wanting to know the details of the flood. Thirst mirrors the size of the page. Eventually the vessel arrives, temperate and filling with stars.

This is where the errand began

    *   *   *   *

Walking is entwined with waiting, a delivery, the desire to set out. Any force forcing you down, any construct that will have you sit at a desk, any time keeper. The song that had been mine swam differently in fields of dark cotton, so much so that the phrases played themselves otherwise, not knowing I was present.

We were already going out of one landscape, and anywhere further the car would take us was the "where" in question. This seemed ridiculous when pinned down since one point was the certainty unpinned.

A nightly intuition of precipitation

*   *   *   *

Leaving the body in part thinking which vegetable weather may visit. While dark is accepted as a pause, a necessary lapse, a denser realm where pulling assumes antagonistic reverie. Fossils continue to move. Trust this shade tomb. If this is possible you may also remember the rain.

Without the notion that one is transparent

    *   *   *   *

And it seems he is an understudy in his path, stepping into soliloquy, the matter lost in travel. From oneself to a ship, without the knowledge to trust his own double. In quietness he hears phrases repeated deeply in the centers of themselves, spinning without cause or apology. A white chestnut lack. He cannot stop or else he is a prisoner who feigns sleep and continues the day resigned to what has been lost in the hours of darkness.

Grown in clusters indicates future flight

⋆   ⋆   ⋆   ⋆

Two brothers traveled together to Kitty Hawk where today tourists climb the dunes with heat and admiration. The dunes persist in their mass. If not they would no longer exist. Some have been swept to sea simply because of location.

Evolution does not occur continuously. Some individuals hold their ground. Squirrels and pigeons are not timid. Firefly blinking codes are seduction frequencies. Frogs who croak the loudest attract the most partners but also the most predators. The same is true for the peacock's scattering of eyes, in which it is difficult to make one's way through the brush unencumbered.

Memory is the vessel a shell becomes

     *   *   *   *

The darkness was not at all transparent, so that turning to look behind me even the small path dissolved except for what appeared to be a punctuated flashing of solitary eyes. Peripheral vision test. Not meeting a single step or light in passing. This small patch of night is an accomplice, a relative to the larger galaxies. How easily we forget our history, with such certainty. Into the past as a mirror, into the self as a meteor.

Scissors in the middle of the banks

*   *   *   *

Later everything is later. The difficulty lies in possibility, in that the number of turns approaching is greater than the chance taken to arrive. The day presses, and I resist, as is evident in the growth chart. The missing object was always the affirmation of the opposite of becoming one body. These things and others slowly climb to the surface, the hem of a dress, the possibility of opening shut down interiors.

**Spring is in the paper dress;
wear carefully, and last, to save trees**

 *   *   *   *

Is it merely that when alone there is no one to blame? Is it merely that in partner-vision one assuming only half as much may be required twice? Flowers occur in a small segment of the population. Tax on reproduction precludes spring. Closer to some surface of anatomy, the mind, slightly detached, follows the trace of leaves.

Dampened impulse dreams bodily dreams

*   *   *   *

A change in heartbeat noticed since departure. Contemplated sense masking a bodily impulse. Responding to a presence addiction. Quietly becoming a thrown off bedding preclusion. Nights double in calendar resemblances. Sleep code invariably thrown off as dreams interact. Presence quietly becoming a night double.

As eyes focused to a point from each point

*   *   *   *

About someone else would be easier. Lost interest in substance. Letters arrive when least expected. Dread to be wed. She reads in microvelvet dress and none else or underneath. Strawberry attire. To touch would assemble all questions into a line. They actively wait for the start. An illusion of stillness moves continuously so each look finds a changed expression. A triangle follows attention.

Leaves and needles resemble rain in sound

*　　　　　　　*　　　　　　　*　　　　　　　*

Morning light patterns on beams approach bones. The quiet multiplied until that was all one could hear. Near past, far past. The wind is a fear of appointments. So loudly the body collapsed under the momentary verge into quiet that he could barely raise his hand to ask the question. Heal with opiate mirror. Her otherwise walks away.

Mostly unconscious of the act in everyday travel

        *   *   *   *

Vibrations are transmitted by their carriers, pollinating platforms as they step from trains. Some are left in the streets and unintentionally a passer-by might carry them in passing. A home, a park, a frequency— these are tranferable. There are times leaving a place thinking something personal has been forgotten, but upon arriving all seems to be in place. It is not possible to determine in advance what the effects of your spinning will be.

Tasted mirth in elder steps

*   *   *   *

Wander is a family name, a smoke wisp ceiling.
Doors which slide open appear less abrupt, yet still
do not account for seasons. One year on a similar day
is a reclining point where the same persons arrive
and leave. Next year is the recurring point of a rush,
where seated in different positions, a fragmentary
day is born.

In order to find your absolute calendar

   *   *   *   *

Listen more often to things. A necessary moment for achieving stillness, looking back listening to the bottom. Recognizing these things as skills. They were sad not seeing themselves as adequate machines. The burning dish invites a presence; a place shared by coincidence rather than by regularity. A room filled with madness, not madness, but the red called divine. Move on account of water. This rose is the same as a week. Dark ash precedes crystal. An unmistakable murmur.

A look is a siren

⋆   ⋆   ⋆   ⋆

Without the notion that one is transparent, you
probably wouldn't be able to see so far underwater.
Arms interfere with the state of calm beneath,
making waves while the sun vanishes overhead, and
water slides off of the body miraculously curing the
feeling of containment. Resistance shifts will. You
swim through solitary drawings, taking from fluidity
what you may. Once an island caused a pause. You
appeared too bright. Or was it simply from the sun,
where we were standing? Confusing ourselves with
the elements, things move in decimal capacity. You
are not vanishing overhead, making waves, changed
as the calm underneath.

One point was the certainty unpinned

*   *   *   *

Forgotten were the effects of trees on internal landscapes. They disposed of the phrases conceived in moments of disquiet. They carved pockets of night into daylight, a reminder that divisions lie in form from habit. There was also the sense of being watched. They had no choice but to look, or at least to the eye they seemed planted. Still, a person might remain in one place and never feel planted, and a tree can follow for days while seeming to stay in the same place.

Nights double in calendar resemblances

*   *   *   *

Sleep is too easily given up in pursuit of movement.
Leaving the body in part, memory is the vessel a shell
becomes. Dreams appear as runes, scattered across a
landscape guarded by a shell of consciousness. Like
the thrush that made the composer stop to pick out
the notes, a pause creates a different wakeful state,
where blowing leaves and needles resemble rain in
sound. A place shared by coincidence rather than by
regularity.

The wind is a fear of appointments

    *   *   *   *

In a temperate climate one still suffers the seasons but lacks the signs to name them. Why should a thing be like winter, below the ground, invisible to hands and eyes? Light compiles doubt, now so used to wintering. Covering hands and necks before emerging, covering heads and heels, heaving shoulders as protection. The strongest strength knows always that the sun is shifting. And one cloud will have rained beyond comparison. I draw the drops gently on a page.

Fossils continue to move

*   *   *   *

Perhaps in spite of the lightning you will walk
since one man walked across this country and told
developers not to build on a burial ground. 'Or I will
curse you,' he said. And they stopped their building
and leveled their eyes to the land. All that is setting
has been undone by your lashing of sails. All that
you wish to build has a life beneath the surface
unaccounted which first must be encountered. He
will not build without the knowledge of what has
come before in the encasement of this body. Where
does electricity go?

A key until you try

*   *   *   *

Listening to dreams is the risk of staying out later, meeting lingering pasts, the future memory, fragments of plans and reservations which stumble past, stopping to see you. Knowing leaves little room for roaming. They lived far away in streets that she knew and did not choose to keep. She had entered in search of a vibrancy charm, really wanting coffee, not garnets. The belief in the moment not as random accumulation. Versions compete with tides.

To touch would assemble all questions into a line

*   *   *   *

Pressure creates gems. They grow deeply for balance. The circle has been forgotten by multiple triangles, the oblong imperfect symmetry. When sentiment is refracted, the gems transmit a future of angling. Without instruments one may be better equipped to notice transmission. Patterns found in fields might be made by one finger of the being inside of the earth. And yet they search the stars in search of the stars.

Some have been swept to sea simply because of location

*   *   *   *

Ocean despondency is a lie. A bouquet of salty greens grown out into coiled patterns on the shore, filling the house with a presence which will continue beyond any memory of the land. The body moves with little explanation from the cove of past behaviors toward forms of expression hardly recognizable. And to what do I owe this excursion? A storm pressed into a glass.

Peripheral vision test

*   *   *   *

He is one pivoted compass, a point in her arms. The dawn arrives to remark on all of the circles awake and moving in the branches. The date and time are not woven from the same light as these circles, climbing with atmosphere. Coastal fluctuations follow the many fault lines, making it impossible to live anywhere else. To leave would be a temporary fluttering of white space between wires. A notion drawn back into a point, cloud image stolen from cloudless days. He could imagine the billowing overhead, but looked up to a vast enveloping dome of clear blue.

Dreams appear as runes

*   *   *   *

A bird escapes and flutters in the heart of a boy. What is lost may be the woods inside of the one lost, not what the woods suggest, which is a third otherness. The bird has not had the fortuitous occasion to tell what is left of telling or swaying. The boy accounts for the woods inside himself lost, not what seemed reasons without dwellings, but eclipses on a calm note.

Opiate mirror

*   *   *   *

To museums in the heart: what grows impatient is
the sapling unnoticed, pushing out into the eyes.
What cannot be told but only glimpsed, hinted,
or heard amidst other natural sounds almost as a
trick of wind, or a muted gaze into direct sunlight.
Nothing so bright could be conceived of directly.
Some apothecary sun, sure as the mender is hidden.

ON POLLEN MEMORY

Pollen Memory was written primarily during the summer of 1992. I wished to locate a form which would approach, and continue itself. It looked something like a square, but behaved more like a spinning wheel. This was my first book-length endeavor. I worked in part from notebooks. Lines were pulled from pages, poems coaxed from lines— until a procession emerged. The small weight of the breath line, followed by the body, or the demi-weight of the poem. The work seemed to generate itself. Returning to a passage I was met, as if expected.

FROM JOURNALS DURING
THE TIME OF COMPOSITION

Let me not argue with form now. Occurrences restrain themselves meaningfully so.

• • •

a b a b a b a b a b

• • •

Remember always, these words, my allies.

• • •

Inclusivity.

• • •

Things cannot always go as planned, but must they always go?

• • •

Would it, or would it not be good if a person could actually read all there is to read in one lifetime? What would be remembered?

• • •

A voice which came before, which came after, one cannot remember.

• • •

The job of the writer: we are guests here (on earth) and must meet the other inhabitants.

• • •

What are my thoughts during sleep?

• • •

There is no natural light in the city.

•••

Pulling up anchorage from blue vasts of chemical. I too hung on a word tree.

•••

Why make an image still if you do not allow the observer to move its dimensions at will?

•••

Clock or promise: calculation or meditation?
Light poured out into a meadow, much subletting.

•••

Which music will provide the proper setting?

•••

Unwrapping the forest, a mirror. Uncovering the lens, a jewel.

the desire
to meet with
the beautiful

India Radfar

TENDER BUTTONS
New York City

2003

The author takes full responsibility for documenting sources for
lyrics quoted and gratefully acknowledges permission to reprint
excerpts from the following copyrighted works. From Collected Poems
by George Seferis, translated by Edmund Keeley and Philip Sherrard,
reprinted by permission of Princeton University Press. From Speaking of
Shiva translated by AK Ramanujan, Penguin Books. "Letter To León Felipe"
by Octavio Paz, translated by Eliot Weinberger, from Collected Poems
1957–1987, copyright © 1986 by Octavio Paz and Eliot Weinberger.
Reprinted by permission of New Directions Publishing Corp.

Special thanks to Kim and Shawna, Sheila Hixon, Spyros Tsilimparis,
The Aegean Center, Mary Stuart, Saskia Friedrich, Bernadette Mayer,
Bernard and Aram, and of course Lee Ann…

Other Tender Buttons Books
Sonnets by Bernadette Mayer
Not a Male Pseudonym by Anne Waldman
Trimmings by Harryette Mullen
Agnes Lee by Agnes Lee Dunlop Wiley
Lawn of Excluded Middle by Rosmarie Waldrop
silent teachers   remembered sequel by Hannah Weiner
Imagination Verses by Jennifer Moxley
Cunt-Ups by Dodie Bellamy

Distribution:
Small Press Distribution
1341 Seventh Street
Berkeley, CA 94710-1403
(510) 524-1668 (800) 869-7553
www.spdbooks.org

Lee Ann Brown, Editrix
Tender Button Books
PO Box 13 Cooper Station
New York, NY 10276
LA@tenderbuttons.net

Book design: Kim Spurlock

Publication of this book was made possible by
grants from The Fund for Poetry

ISBN 0-927920-10-7

MIRZA'S CAVE

675

light
devoured darkness

I was alone
inside.

shedding
the visible dark

I
was Your target

O Lord of Caves

—Allama Prabhu

this describes a room
we're not always inside
the room of sleep
upturned, unconscious,
above all columns

sleep is my way of thinking. Is that wrong?
thought barely encased in silence
if I had to read my journal aloud at night,
if my silence is my most transparent state,
most intimate, I'm afraid that other people
will be able to read my mind.
They think it is a place that I could open
and I can't, without dying.
the fierceness is not my essential nature, it is
what guards my essential nature. In reaching it
you have reached the edge of my conscious self.
I can't be alone unless I sleep
I use my memory as if I were alone. silently.
for imagery. I want other people to read my mind.
now I'm inside thought completely, like a child
but I can't speak
It is not like here
I could draw it for you:
leaves that hold themselves up
the inner bark of things
old stones grieving, quivering, outside of the
foundation
rose mountain
what do you think?
you went alone
you were everywhere and you always went alone.

I went to sleep on top of the mountain
and I woke up underneath the mountain
Someone had turned the page.
There had been flowers that were just like
pink leaves, very delicate
there had been enough light for everyone.
Now, all the words I don't know,
Invisibility
the inside of a mountainside
the place I go to
no light, only words
absolutely particular.
The soil is wild, uncommon to trees
I am in a place of burial and no birth
in silence the cycle has broken its circle
in green darkness,
the thick imagined leaves lay down
I am in search of life in these conditions,
for the places where things get undone

This is the place I reach to for letters
somewhere below the throat
outside
they grow wild
but I like the words that grow inside
and reveal themselves in the dark
these words hold flowers
form muscle
were beautiful
to swallow
I see the site of the text not unclearly
Sometimes for pleasure I go inside
the letters hum at all the edges and
the head insight lifts up!
the new repetition of that
old mind the new repetition of that old mind
I imagine you falling,
your head upside down

your words falling out
the collecting of letters is a physical
extraction.

evidently, my words remain in me
loud volume all around. Not in my
home, I have one of those, but in me
It stays in. doubt sets in. come in.
I give you my word, word after word
my word in your mouth
you can take my words too
what I think I shall continue to think
take my word
they felt they were writing for me, for my benefit
and they were
but can it be written on a page?
keep the words in the words
ulinke as they are
and the mind in the mind
but the words will come off the page.

Before sleep came the script of sleep
Before dark came the hollow room
The eye is not needed for reading
as it is not needed for speaking
I wish, I wish breathing carried words
and I could hear those words
I went all over the square room but never
moved through the walls.
Now it is night
and night is night
and night is thinking of night
The room presses too close
I feel it touch my eyes
patient shadows
so shadowy and dark
the room has drowned my sight.

my exhilaration: that words were there
it was a mind to me, in that darkness
absence of sight, humming quietly
cold to the touch, glistening with wetness
is there more to be said
does it echo yet

he did not look at the water
he did not say things about the water
he did not touch it
without entering it
on the ground
ambiguous we agreed
to appear,
knowing the pages by touching their edges
then he asked us to touch the water but
he was reluctant to say why

I am not well
My heart beats hard
I wait to burn
into the actual

the sky (I know
this blue) takes
my laced fingers
and kisses them.

the desire to meet with the beautiful
beauty draws near

More women farmers in purple dresses
were planting small things in the garden
A baby was born
I agreed to come here
out there is life, or the
true mountain
here where the heart beats
is only here
at the mouth of the night.
brambles gather at the entrance
birds holler as darkness falls, one last time
and beyond that, callous silence,
nothing but hideous stillness.
and then, the atmosphere of earth,
thick and mortal
damp
forestless
mind.

like big raindrops
from some distant tree
they kept on falling
words fruit water
but also beauty
without understanding
then I left the dream
through a room behind my heart.
what does the heart have to do with the
knowledge of the unreal?
I don't know. I don't see through
If I try to open my eyes in a dream
I wake up.

enough invisibility.

We will sleep for you
we will fall into place
into rooms of meaning
collecting fragments,

those roses
from the depths
of your language
get darker,

and we know below
the fragmented night.

these will be a big forest
these will be tall and strange
my heart is anxious,
afraid of the resemblance
and disappearance is flooding memory
dreams must dream a dream
at night or in the eye
in the mind in the room in the body
in one word.
I cannot keep or not keep out the next echo,
it goes through the streets of the city, so I go,
not gladly anymore, go…
dreams are dreamt of dreams
none may come
none may come not here where
language vanishes…

Behind the reflection
in solitary experience
animated by our sleep
like that of an illusion
and virtue.
How long have you been here?
the perfection of the world has worn away
you are so perfect
so tremendously parallel falling
sun, you have missed the sun
and beyond that
what have you done
as the world has fallen

the dresses were gold, orange gold, and crimson
gold.
this is my personal myth of love
I want it to be true
body beauty is love of soul love of beauty
body of crimson, dresses of gold, orange they were,
beautiful, makes the body magical
beauty is love of soul and
body is love of beauty
beauty body
the dresses were not even ours
and then we got dressed
my hands came together over my head
soul love is beauty of body love of soul
it was the shimmer
it was the dress
I saw it fall from the top but when I looked for it
at the bottom it had completely disappeared
can't you see
words on water
flowing by twilight,
untenable?
the reading of the water
a line of relevant meaning
these dancers dance
find out where they're sleeping
where to start dressing, putting beauty body together
but it does go to
personal myth, somehow
indelible shell.

I was a word with water behind it
but I couldn't read the water
I was an inscription upon it
a meaningful flower
of no color
upon it.

more of the earth inside us
more of the place as words
more of those infinite states
I am growing more precise: words are demanding
more precision of me. For instance, the opposite
of a fruit tree is not a tree without fruit.
To turn the page is not to turn the mountain. Still,
to explain a word is to relate it to other words.
knowing how the text looks on a page
is another way to read that text
knowing what the pages feel like,
how they turn,
the sound that makes.
mastery of a text or
mystery of a text?
receiving the meaning again and again
without exact repetition, without any
repetition.
the result is the object in the memory
the presence of the text
the patience of the text
the resonance—
I can't finish writing this before it writes me
my body, perimeter, contour, surface and *all the edges*
how can we read through this before it reads
through us?
the transition to the beautiful
belongs in words,
previous words.
But the parts are too delicate
they have already disappeared.

windows
vowels
storm
confusion
being in the wrong place
tremendous light coming through.

972

looking for your light,
I went out:

it was like the sudden dawn
of a million million suns,

a ganglion of lightnings
for my wonder.

O Lord of Caves,
if you are light,
there can be no metaphor.

—*Allama Prabhu*

PAPER SEA

Ξύπνησα μὲ τὸ μαρμάρινο τοῦτο χεφάλι στὰ χέρια
ποὺ μοῦ ἐξαντλεῖ τοὺς ἀγκῶνες καὶ δὲν ξέρω ποῦ νὰ
     τ᾽ ἀκουμπήσω.
Ἔπεφτε στὸ ὄνειρο καθὼς ἔβγαια ἀπὸ τὸ ὄνειρο
ἔτσι ἐνώθηκε ἡ ζωή μας καὶ θὰ εἶναι πολὺ δύσκολο νὰ
     ξαναχωρΊσει.

I woke with this marble head in my hands;

it exhausts my elbows and I don't know where to put it down.

It was falling into the dream as I was coming out of the dream

so our life became one and it will be very difficult for it to
     disunite again.

                 —*George Seferis*

α mackerel swimming away β from fisherman γ mullet
swimming down δ octopus reaching up
ε comb in ζ curly hair
η woman on a hill θ in the wind ι alone
κ sitting λ in contemplation
μ what else is under the waves?

                    disembodied voices
                    fear mouths, alphabets,
                    bodies humming with sound

                    imperceptibly
                    they enter sleep
                    and burst into song

                    stop stealing our voices
                    and writing them down!
                       they sing

how shall I begin?
with lines that don't form letters
marks that mean nothing wandering
further away from words
inside this red box
deliver me quickly
we are bodies of water
bodies of land
and sometimes human bodies
with molecules of
solid ground binding us
    man and woman
      flesh and rock

island
translucent as
Aphrodite on the
back of water
her love lying
on blue beds
holding seas
like hands
between mountains

for the root of my longing
she sent a man
to start the passion flowing
    a little more sharply
behind him
a female presence
informs in the ways
of curved mountains

from the headlands
your head,

only your head.
and the time you were
in the bay?
we knew your body then
but the problems of invisibility
started
now we want words
look again at the land that she is
                but then,
        don't ask for words

I think of you every day
would you rather have me
                touch you?
golden, waiting
who needs persuasion
to lie in your groves?
I wish I was the rain
so that when you
ask for me
I could pour down on you.

girls who like water
swim at the foot of
another time

if I knew
this death-in-life feeling
would descend on me
while physical satisfaction
was still far off
I would have made
a different arrangement
with beginningless time
I would have saved everything
sacred to the moon
in the hives of bees
then I wouldn't have to ask myself,
am I being favored
or am I being given in favor?

a man sits behind a line
and is gone
move the line, he
reappears.
some times,
we don't use words
we can't look at each other
words hide within lines
lines create disappearances—

you look womanly in these
tender surroundings
my longing means nothing
        to you here
hills naked in rain
my hand on air
to touch,
        to be touched

you and your muse
hopelessly mixed
when I go to your bed
I find her
when I go to her bed
        I find you
wearing her clothes
hiding
    underneath them
the figure of a man

I see you
at the tops of hills
moving temple walls
taking apart chapels
laying pillars flat
her cool earth body
your discovery
underneath the fragrant
mountain sage

you can store your words
like honey in the comb
immeasurably sweet later
unacceptably passionate
but listen to me now—
don't let the masculine
rise and take control of language
let my words
tongue-tied as they are
halting, dormant
    repeating
    soft, quiet
slipping off smooth surfaces
    into water
let my words now
    be heard without myrrh
sacred to none

meet me
    on the bed
  of earlier thoughts
 gently
when your dream body moves,
so do slender mountains

come lift me a little
come down to the place
from which you take away
what you have taken is
not important
lift me as I am
let me talk to you
in the dark of your room

pulled out the sea
dislodged the goddess
isolated my emotions

paper sea
paper aphrodite
paper me

time is everything
season after season,
missing

to live without anyone
knowing you
egregious village
digging for pieces
cool path of letters
looking for a pattern
insouciant horse trail

goats lying down,
observing the moon and
neolithic purple thyme

avoid words
fail to write them
what emerges
not much more than air
weigh it and keep it

the return should be sweet
resolved
a little singing
something of consequence
a lightening, maybe;
a complicated flower
why hide it for a moment?
scooters passing, bus engines
grinding and humming
drawing lines—
    inside the red
         body
  of your voice
you receive me,
          muse,
indistinguishable
from other muses,
in the kitchen
      cooking for your son

donkey around the corner
nibbling
I don't want them to
stare at me
why is the moon
all the way up there?
ghosts and grapes
I have done nothing wrong, but I am
not to be trusted
this place
with her strong desires

I was unable to postpone
the arrival of pain,
so I cancelled the arrival
of pleasure instead
but pleasure still arrived
     in no particular form,
the form of a dream if you
    must talk of form
      he came to me
time began to repair itself
back to the beginning
but pleasure just entered
my body and stayed there.
Only in dreams
do we continue to meet separately

at the end
when the light becomes
softer
everything must happen
then

I tried to get away from
the litany of night but
it would not leave me.
Night, so full of consonants
for your one vowel which calls
out I, I, but only I, and to which
I, of course, respond.
In your absolute indifference
I have found a place to exist,
here where there is not even
shape to hide us
under the moon where no name hangs
I sing the litany of night without end
infinitely beautiful and painful
hear it and remember it.

morning
hills
tinkling bells
roosters

          she did all this for your pleasure,
          not mine
          I am that fig-tree
          in orange light
          with crimson waiting
          besides the shapely leaf
          the tree appears ugly
          no one cares to eat the fruit

old mind
what is beautiful?
terror is not
beautiful
black one
dark one
the rose herself
coming
between us
                free her doves
                            her swans
                    her geese
the sounds they make
        flying away…

ν bird between wings ξ feathers unfurling

ο who eyes π the temple, next to which

ρ a pomegranate or the σ fruit of any τ tree, really

(apple, quince, persimmon, lemon) υ fills the valley

φ what is seen becomes χ where we meet

ψ split the valley ω put it back together

La poesía
        es la ruptura instantánea
instantáneamente cicatrizada
                        abierta de nuevo
por la mirada de los otros

Poetry
        is a sudden rupture
suddenly healed
                        and torn open again
by the glances of others

                                —*Octavio Paz*

AUTHOR'S NOTE

सौन्दर्यददिृक्षा

"the desire to meet with the beautiful"
(Sanskrit)

The poems of Mirza's Cave were conceived in India, and the poems of Paper Sea in Greece.

I was making a comparative study of two ancient poetic traditions. I wanted to see how it felt to write in both places.

{INDIA RADFAR, 2003}

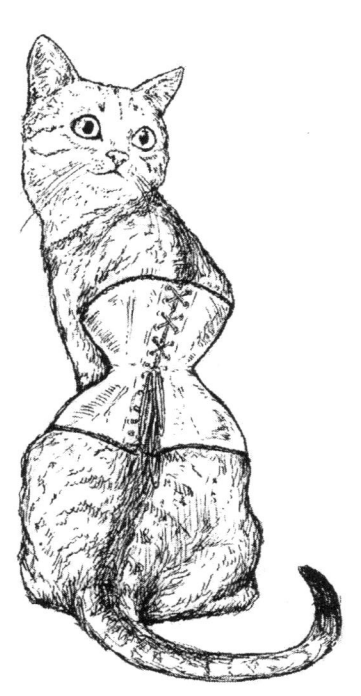

The Book of

PRACTICAL
PUSSIES

A collection of writing

with drawings by

MICHELLE ROLLMAN

KRUPSKAYA / TENDER BUTTONS 2009

Design: Wayne Smith

Distributed by Small Press Distribution
www.spdbooks.org

ISBN 978-1-928650-29-4

K R U P S K A Y A
PO Box 420249
San Francisco, CA
94142-0249
www.krupskayabooks.com

TENDER BUTTONS PRESS
Lee Ann Brown
PO Box 13, Cooper Station
New York City
10276
la@tenderbuttons.net

FOR PHILIP HORVITZ

HISTORY OF THE SLUT
IN MY RELATIONSHIP

Camille Roy

> '…our sentences are hard put to survive the disaster
> of their slobbery origins.'
> Celine

The problem with sex is that it fires the harder life.

It all happened in one week.
What?　　　1. trip to the police station.
　　　　　2. sex, sex.
　　　　　3. the dream of the movie theatre.

Then the red minx curled up,
lashing her outward parts.
Chest high knobs with soft tips,
twitchy in the deep cups of her bra,
conveyed nothing other than the angelic—that blank.
A solution proferred by the beloved, in all ways
wise because of a crack in her head:
　　　　　• her delightful monster of a body.
　　　　　• the thumb prints
on her eyelids.

A description of her. red minx. is a description
of the representational boundary.

One big surprise in the dark!

Afterwards she disappeared.

then I found a disposable camera under the bed.
Got it developed: smiling yellow
　　　Pictures of her wedding!

Whereas this talk show desire of mine is in the field—
          'I'm v. interested in
          slut head trips,
          both agonizing & amusing:
          what works in the world of the slut
          for my book: The Friendly Slut.'

That sentence
is a sort of dildo
which
language for me is permeable to loss
as I have lost one (language) (at least)
I skim the surface of that absence of memory.
I think it makes my usage more violent.
So, my exile is limited in scope.
So my tongue, so my lips
placed with the luggage.

You sexually learn to widen the acceptable....
my sort of spreading butt.

1.   Not for me the scandalous appetites nor shining body—

WESTERN
(FROM THE NOVEL, ASHVILLE)

D-L Alvarez

Wearing a pair of boxers and my old cowboy boots, I sashayed down to the kitchen ... grabbed some eggs and butter from the ice box, a jug of cider, cold with the mellow slightly rotten juiciness of Missouri apples ... stirred it into a cornmeal batter with a half-cup of sugar and a dash of salt. Smell of bacon, flap jacks on the grill, and coffee. I took my breakfast on the porch, the north side of the house which is shadier. I like how each flavor shakes hands with the one before it. After breakfast I enjoyed a hand-rolled of a sweet, light tobacco, which tasted faintly of vanilla. The church bell tower chimed two o'clock. I glanced at the parlor. I had cleaned before going to bed, but in the light of day saw a few more empties and a couple of dirty ashtrays near the bar. "The bar" is just my living room turned into a speakeasy once a week. It pays the rent and then some. I rinsed the bottles and ashtrays, did the rest of the dishes—everything shipshape—then listened to the messages on my answering machine.

Folks had called from their jobs to brag softly about their hangovers. When I bartend on Thursday nights, business is slow on Friday mornings. "Man, Smiley, you certainly know how to throw a party. I think I had a great time ... what I remember of it! Your place is more popular than a Nevada Whorehouse on the border of Utah. Do us working stiffs a favor though and move it to the weekend— my coworkers would be mighty grateful." The Weekend? What kind of middle-of-the-road fool did they take me for? The weekend is when competition for drunks is heated. Thursdays I had the only game in town. If required to wake as early as those other poor S.O.B.s maybe I would have a throbbing skull to call my own, but after my Friday afternoon breakfast I'm always full of life.

Out in my yard, still wearing boxer shorts and boots, as well as a shirt with the sleeves cut off and a sweat stain spreading out from the spine, I sang along to the music in my head (last night's echoes) while mowing the lawn. Grass hot and freshly cut mixed with the smell of hot oil and the gas mower. Then a dog turd was caught by the blade. Damned landmines. I washed it to the edge with a strong jet of water from the garden hose, found two more empty beer bottles, propped them against the house, and continued my spiral sculpture.

My neighbor was out in her yard, waving her arms as if directing a plane to land. She tried to shout over the whine of the blade and coughing motor. On the fourth rotation I acknowledge her. If I drew the game out any longer the veins in her forehead would pop. Turning the mower off I told her she was looking lovely, all in a tone like it was the biggest and nicest surprise to see her. This scene was cut-and-pasted out of a Sixties sitcom, down to her mint green pant-suit. "Why Mrs. Crenwinkle, now haven't you just captured the spirit of springtime with this uh, this new swirl in your hair. Land's sakes alive, it sets off your features like a gilded frame!"

Now that she had my attention she pretended it was half-a-bother. "Oh Smiley, I see I'm not the only industrious one this morning, there's so much to do around here I'm afraid I can't talk long. A pity all the racket that machine makes. Why it frightens poor Cat-Cat something awful." She watered the hibiscus plants and listed the chores ahead of her, blah blah blah. It was my neighborly duty to drop her a line of pity now and then, like throwing the last bread crumbs to already fat bird.

When that cat rubbed against her thick ankles, she picked up the flat-faced thing and squeezed its body tight against her breasts while its hind legs dangled. The cat complained, which Mrs. Crenwinkle answered as if engaged in deep conversation. She informed me that the cat had been in my yard, and that the cat apologized for trespassing. "But I find the mice near your trash cans so terribly yummeeee." She spoke in a voice to represent the cat. It was that same demented squeak used to force thoughts on pre-verbal children: lobotomy with chaser of helium. "Oh Mister Smiley, I sure wish you would keep the wid tight on the trash can and not tempt me. I'm trying to diet." The cat also had opinions on how perfectly charming my house would be with a fresh coat of paint and how much better my bushes would feel "if you just gave them a nice haircut now and then."

Mrs. Crenwinkle reprimanded the cat for speaking so bluntly and apologized, "Cats are famous for saying whatever comes into their heads. And she's a talker!" I gave her my namesake crooked grin and never dreamed of telling Cat-Cat to mind her own business. Instead, I sang as I trimmed the bushes.

Then I noticed the time and jumped into my sexy old beat-up car and took off with a squeal, hoping to get to the school before 3:30. I made it just in time. My little brother, Thumb, was walking out the gate, his eyes studying the ground, his long red hair shrouding his face.

Between age thirteen and fourteen he stretched a full foot taller, mostly in the legs. The way his torso was folded in, the back bent forward and his arms crossed over his chest, it was like the original thumb-sized Thumb was perched on stilts. His walk had the sway of a caged animal, whose every step is both careful and meaningless.

I honked the horn. "Hey Boss! How bout we take our asses to the hardware store and see if we can't find a little pussy to tease?" Maybe I was trying to make up for the past, when I wasn't round much. "Better late than never, that's what they all say and shoot if it ain't true. Why never is terrible, ain't it? But darn, everyone is late, that's just plum human nature." I showed off crooked teeth.

"Are you sure you're my brother? asked Thumb. "You're such a hillbilly."

"I know, Boss. Right down to my nickname and dirty toenails, I'm pure trash, and let that be a lesson. I thought I was so clever, acting the fool when I was a kid. Talking like a dope was a sort of disguise. You know, let them think you're a bumpkin while all the time you got a couple good ideas up your sleeve. But it's like they say about crossing your eyes; Don't! Cause it'll stick that way. I played the part so long the part became me. Which ain't bad, I mean, as a bartender people like it if you're not the sharpest knife in the drawer … seeing as how they're headed in that direction. So guess you're stuck with hillbilly kin till I croak. Wouldn't know how to go back at this point. Besides, my neighbor finds me so terribly charming."
Thumb smirked.

"can you believe that nosey-body was at it again this morning? If it were up to Cat-Cat, my place would be some kind of Beverly Hills palatial estate and I'd be the poor bastard who had to build it. The two of them have at least thirteen Better Homes and Garden hints a week. Hell, I'm just grateful Mr. Cat-Cat as yet to lodge any complaints regarding the hullabaloo that comes from my little speakeasy and the traffic of unique types it attracts. Heh heh. Thank goodness that ol' battleaxe's hearing aid sits on the nightstand after 9PM. If doing a few extra chores keeps her from calling the coppers on Thursday nights, it's surely worth it! Besides, I expect if not patronized now and then, one summer night our dear Mrs. Crenwinkle would get it in her head to sneak into my home and thrust her garden shears into my Adam's apple. She's the type you know, the ones who snap. You read in the papers the next day as to how she always came across sweet as pie.

"Oooo, we were so terribly shocked!

"I can just hear her, talking in that devil squeak-voice, Cat-Cat told me to stab him twelve times twelve and to puree his liver in holy ceremony. And who'd miss me save for one or two alcoholics?"

"Not I," Thumb teased.

"Hey," I said, giving his head a playful whack, "that seat is called shotgun. As driver of this here stagecoach, I need to be able to trust the cowboy in shotgun to watch my back. Never know when Black Bart and his boys might gallop down the ridge at five o'clock—my blind spot. Now you don't have to miss me once I'm cold, but I'm counting on you to like me enough to keep me from getting cold."

"Gotcha partner," said Thumb.

We drove back to my place because I forgot to bring the measurements. I told Thumb, "I'm going to build a trash cabin: a shed to store all the cans in, with a slanted roof that opens with a hinge and closes with a padlock … something big enough to store the empties as well. There were fewer people last night, but they drank even more than the opening night crowd, and it's a … well, it's unbecoming to have liquor bottles piled up out front. Not the sort of advertising a private enterprise wants."

I ran to the house and was back in a flash. Mrs. Crenwinkle was there in her sunglasses and a wide-brimmed hat. Thumb aimed a finger at her as we pulled out. "Bang, bang, you're dead."

In the drab haze nothing happened, but Thumb re-shot the scene under the banner of the Wild West. "Why if it isn't Mrs. Crenwinkle, Black Bart's best gun. My Dear, isn't it getting close to retirement time for you?" The bullet travels twelve-times faster than the speed of sound so by the time the infamous shootist hears her epitaph, it's too late. She flings her pistol up in the air as her throat erupts a red spring on the hot cement walkway. "That bag of bones won't be giving us any more trouble." Her pale face with watery eyes stares into the sun. Next to her, her cracked sunglasses reflect the gateway of the Terminal-Twosome, Smiley and his trigger-happy brother, The Thumb-Worn Kid.

Cat-Cat crouches among the marigolds. "Well ain't that a bitch," she says in normal cat-speak. "The days of cream and paté are yesterday's news. No one will brush out my fur. I'll be forced to live as a huntress, making my home in the basements of abandoned houses, lapping water from dirty gutters while always having to glance over my shoulder for dogs and cruel children. Mistress may have smelled, but she was loyal. Should I shed a tear? Perhaps, but first one last sniff. Make sure she's cold—no sense in turning on the ducts for a mere flesh wound. Sigh. There's not the slightest rise and fall of breathing … Damn it all! It really must be nap number nine. Well, mew, mew and boohoo. The blood of my guardian is the last bowl of milk she'll ever put out."

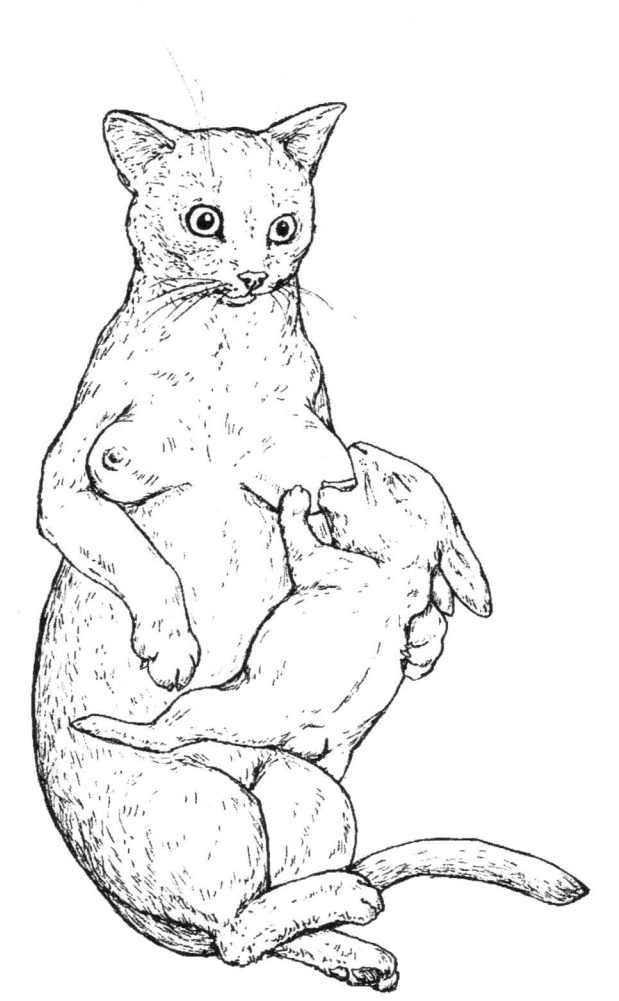

HARRYETTA THE SLUM PUSS

Yedda Morrison

Toms are always leaving parts of themselves inside me so when I purr "OK, Tommy, turn over" and you respond, just by raising your middle, "No please, I'm an ass cat, do it there, just a hair bit higher," I do. Or, not being an ass cat you flip over quick, fur stick bobbing freely, I latex and lube.

And if you find my teats on the small side you don't complain 'cause paws soft silvery, or my face oldish what matter 'cause hips urging perky, or my sides a bit baggy oh well 'cause you're constantly needing to *stick into* and need necessitates compromise. Plus I'm frilled all over, coarser hairs against finer hairs and so on 'til the one wet spot and the other that can be.

"Brrring ring."

"Yes, hello?"

"You make pee pee for me today, Harryetta? You make stinky for me, dear?"

Most Toms don't appreciate that I vacate in a blue box of fragrant sand and then mound it up, deodorized and spherical. Or that after, I tongue myself thorough, excess hairs snug tidy in my tumtum.

"Today Harryetta will not make stinky for you, Tomkins, she's making mounds."

"You're a bitch."

"Oh, Tom."

Puss is a concept; something you desire to be *into*, a goal *and* a means. A finely tuned nest egg with interior mechanisms, or a flippy flesh purse grafted to a vacuum. Toms know pussness to be a venue, a redemption stage with drippy curtains, warm blood theater.

And still other Toms like to be spit on; I shake my head gathering a mouthful. "In the face!" You want it. I aim for your eye but land in your mouth, deep as a pussycat can can.

There's this one, he's loaded, comes to see me every week, "Slower Harry! Slower!" He pants. Sometimes he brings Weanie, his miniature Dachshund on a sharp leather leash. Weanie sits in the corner with a hard-on and hates me, feigning sleep on his pink silk pillow. But I see his one mad eye, and his title red lipstick creeping out.

This goes on and on. I find a baby rabbit alone in a trash bin, I push my nipple in but she doesn't suck. I spread myself warmth, she dies anyway, in the night from hunger. So I'm the clean, dry taste of dust and paper. You, face up on the bed, gobble that very same nipple, hot babble and jerk.

Once Midnight was running over with real milk, rubbing up in a dirty blanket, nosing some pink and mewing moisture. I never tell you how I helped lick last bits of shit and blood and tissue. How I licked until each tiny puss gleamed and opened to the world. Or that I leaked when Midnight carried them one by one away. Or that as I watched I hung my empty teats down to them.

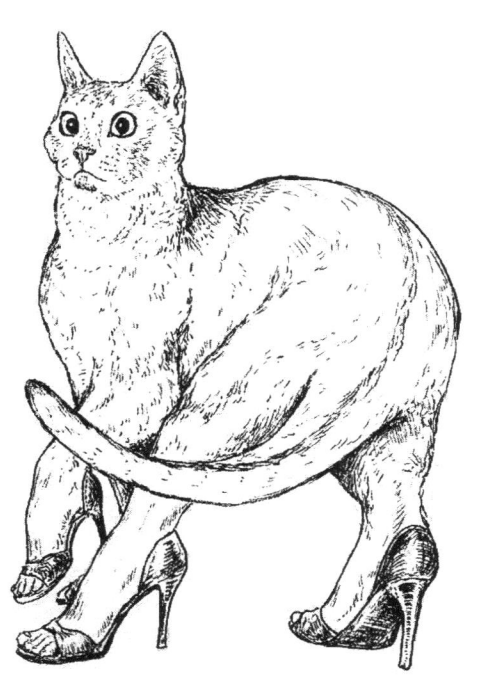

PUSSY IN HOLLYWOOD

Scott MacLeod

Removing her robe to reveal her breasts, then squeezing her breasts together and showing off her great butt while teasing a tom as she does a striptease for him before going down on him.

Wearing a red bra and thong and then taking off the top to reveal her breasts and then explaining to a tom all the things he can do to her if he wants.

Stripping and posing for the camera when another pussy comes up and squeezes her nipples to perk them up before continuing with the shoot.

Fully nude having sex from behind on a bed.

Wearing a see-through bra and thongish panties and then having those removed by a tom to reveal her fully nude body as she has sex from behind, on his lap and on her side.

Being felt up by a tom while wearing a red top and black skirt before riding him fully nude and having her breasts kissed as she rides his lap.

Moaning and writhing in pleasure while a tom goes down on her, but being repeatedly interrupted by another pussy at the door before she gets up to answer it barely covering her breasts.

Sitting on a chair topless and in black panties as a tom slides his paw down her panties and rubs her tail and her breasts.

Removing a robe to reveal her fully nude body as she admires herself in a mirror. She then walks around the room and picks out a pair of thong panties which she puts on and then walks around and puts on a bra.

Seen flying through a tom's window while dressed as a topless ghost.

Fully nude after removing her robe and red panties to shower as another pussy watches and then proceeds to join in showing off her large breasts as they groom each other.

Wearing a black garter belt and pantyhose as she rides a tom during a sex scene.

Removing her top and then lowering her bra to reveal her breasts before hiking up her skirt and removing her panties so another pussy can go down on her.

Stretching and working out while wearing very small shorts and a blue top with hard nipples. She then begins to sweat which causes the top to become slightly see-through as she jogs on a treadmill causing her breasts to bounce up and down.

Talking to a tom as she stands putting her makeup on in a black bra and thong panties.

Wearing short white shorts and a white sports bra with pokey nipples as she gets on top of a tom and encourages him to do sit-ups into her chest.

Fully nude on a bed rolling around trying to sleep before deciding just to get up.

Lying topless on a bench and then getting up to go look for somebody.

Having her dress lowered by a tom to reveal her breasts and then having them kissed and squeezed before being gone down on fully nude, riding him in reverse on a chair and then having sex from behind.

Lying down in bed while topless.

Having her dress removed by a tom to reveal some black thong panties and her breasts which he then takes turns kissing. He then removes her panties and goes down on her fully nude body before she gets on top of him and rides him on a couch.

Having sex under a table and having her breasts bounce around.

Wearing a see-through bra and panties and then having them removed to have sex with a tom on a desk and then having more sex from behind as he bends her over various objects in a courtroom.

Sitting on the edge of a bed and having her bra removed by a tom to reveal her breasts before riding him and flicking her tail around.

Sitting on top of a tom having her breasts squeezed while wearing white lingerie before riding him fully nude on a bed.

Wearing a purple bra and thong panties and then removing the bra to reveal her breasts while grinding the tom hard on a bed before riding him backwards and having sex fully nude on her side.

Kissing another pussy and having her breasts squeezed while wearing a white bra and thong panties and then stripping down to reveal her fully nude body before having her breasts kissed and having sex with a tom on a chair.

Wearing a black dress and then removing it to reveal her breasts before having sex with a tom fully nude in and around a spa while somebody videotapes them.

Lying by a pool talking to another pussy and then getting up fully nude to walk off.

Having her breasts kissed by a tom and being gone down on before riding him and then having sex on her back while wearing masks.

Having sex with a tom from behind as another pussy sits on the couch and listens blindfolded while masturbating.

Being felt up from behind by another pussy and then having her bra removed to reveal her breasts before being gone down on and going down on the other pussy.

Topless and in thong panties on a bed.

Having her panties pulled down by a tom and then knocking stuff over all over the kitchen as they kiss and then she ends up beneath him on the floor as they have sex.

In a very hot black latex outfit as she does a strip tease dance and reveals her breasts in the end.

Licking Antonio Banderas through a cage, and then having sex in the cage and later having sex on a bed.

Taking a piece of butter and sliding it into her dress to make a dimple in it with her hard nipple as two toms watch in shock.

Removing her robe to reveal her breasts before laying down on a table and attempting to cover them up but not succeeding as another pussy watches her get a massage through the sliding glass door.

Removing her clothes to reveal a white bra and thong panties and then taking off the bra and touching and squeezing her breasts for a bit while watching herself in a mirror.

Kissing another pussy and then lying down on a bed and having her white thong panties taken off so she can go down on her for a while. They then kiss and talk for a bit before she gets on top of her and rides her, all during a thunderstorm.

Posing for a tom wearing see-through purple lingerie and then having that removed to reveal her fully nude body and being gone down on. She then has sex from behind against a chair.

Kissing another pussy for a while and then taking off the other pussy's corset and licking and biting her nipples before going down on the other pussy. The other pussy then goes down on her while she squeezes her own breasts and then they get up and kiss some more while a tom watches. He then comes over and she goes down on him while he sucks on the other pussy's nipples before the other pussy gets on top of him and rides him as she sits on his face while he goes down on her. Finally she has sex from behind with him as she kisses and touches the other pussy.

Putting a tom's head between her breasts and shaking them, while another pussy does a hot strip dance in a thong.

Doing topless aerobics on stage and having her breasts bounce as she hops around.

Sticking her paw down her panties and masturbating while topless on a couch.

Lying back on a table as she and a tom lick her breasts, and then we see her riding him on the couch while topless.

Showing us a close-up of her nice breasts as she has sex with a tom doggy-style.

Topless as she first goes down on a tom, and then she lies back for him to return the favor.

Seen nude as she rides a tom and then is interrupted, showing us her breasts as she leans back.

Getting wet and wild on stage with a group of other pussies as they strip off their lingerie and rub up against each other, put whipped cream on one another and then all three join in on a lesbian kiss.

Standing with another fully nude calico pussy, and then the two of them walking with a tom as they go to look in a telescope at a party.

Lying in bed with her robe open to reveal her breasts as tom in a cop's uniform climbs on top of her and they begin to have sex before she asks him to use his club instead.

Shaking her large breasts all over the place until a tom plays a dollar in between them for her and then shaking them some more.

Writhing on a bed in a long love scene with another pussy who has large and badly fake breasts.

Having water splashed on he while sunbathing topless and jumping up showing us her breasts.

Having her dress removed to reveal back panties and a bra and then having those removed to reveal her breasts before having them sucked as she has sex with a tom against a wall while another tom photographs.

Having sex with a tom against a sink in a bathroom and then stopping to talk for a bit showing us her breasts.

Topless in a pink thong playing with a yarn beach ball with another pussy while some toms watch.

Unzipping her jacket to reveal her breasts to a tom skiing down a hill causing him to crash.

Laying on a char and reading a letter showing off her nice breasts.

Licking her claws and running her paws over her breasts while standing in a pool and reading a letter aloud.

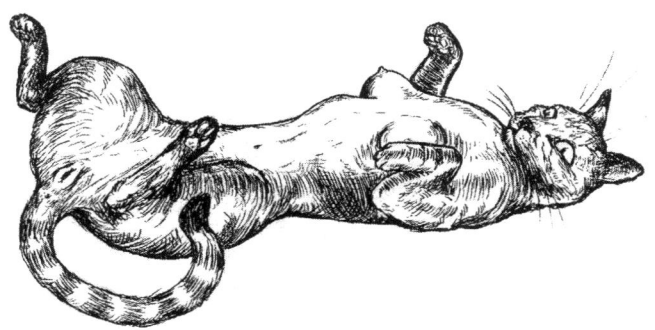

Lee Ann Brown

She went up to Kitty Heaven in her mind.

NURSERY RHYME

I love little pussy

Her coat is so warm

And if I don't hurt her

She'll do me no harm

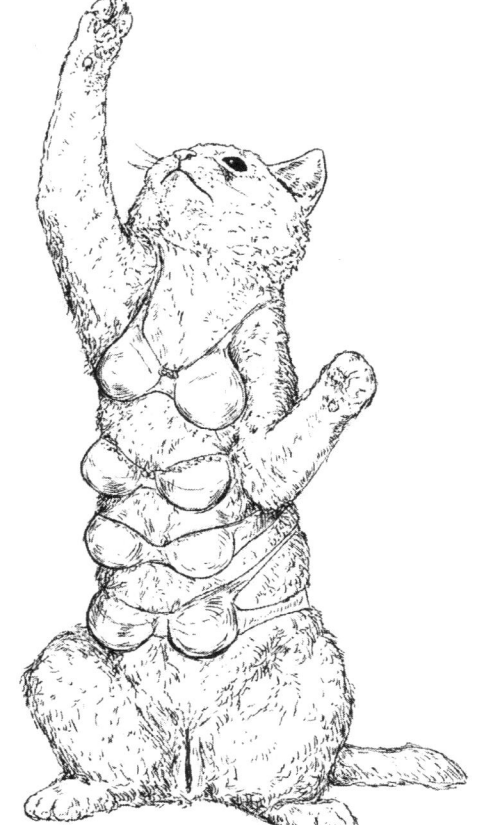

2 X 4

This kitty

mixed up

mittens with

freakin' death.

Lee Ann Brown & Rod Smith

MY CAT SISTERS

"I even call my Cat Sister in the Fraternity
of universal nature."
—Samuel Taylor Coleridge

We are Bim & Bom!
      We are twin Cat Sisters.
Backward, our names are Mib & Mob.
not Krim & Kram or
Plic & Ploc

We can play the banjo.
We can go to Egypt in our dreams.
We can run around the house without touching the ground.

We are twins but we are different.
Bim is a little quieter
and has a very cute profile.
Bom jumps more aggressively at the Kitty Bits
and her eyes are two round gold balls.

VARY THE PRESSURE

A little bit of this
and a little bit of that

is what is taught to us
by the cat

FROM JADE TOYS

sweet cat under the knife
covered in oil in a dream
no best friend to tell

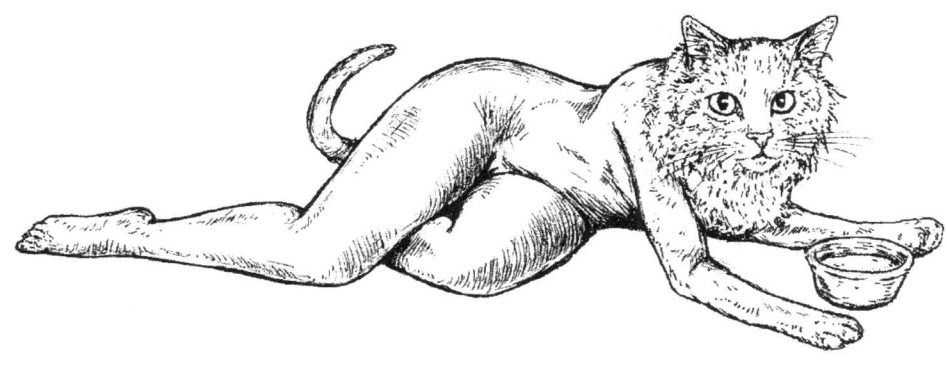

CATALOGUE TO DISTRACTION

"Meow meow. Meow meow meow meow."
      —Jack Spicer

"Structure," says the cat—
That's why I love cats.
      —Wayne Koestenbaum

Bright pink kitty penis:
The trope of the feline in the work of Ron Silliman.

Strange purr-mew-tational
recurrences of feline observances
litter this text.

The world is divided
into Night and Day people,
Cat and Dog people

Overheard on CATS:
T.S. Eliot's worst poems co-opted by endless Broadway repetition.

Postmodern Cat Literature:
the daily life of cat not captured
by normative uses of descriptive language

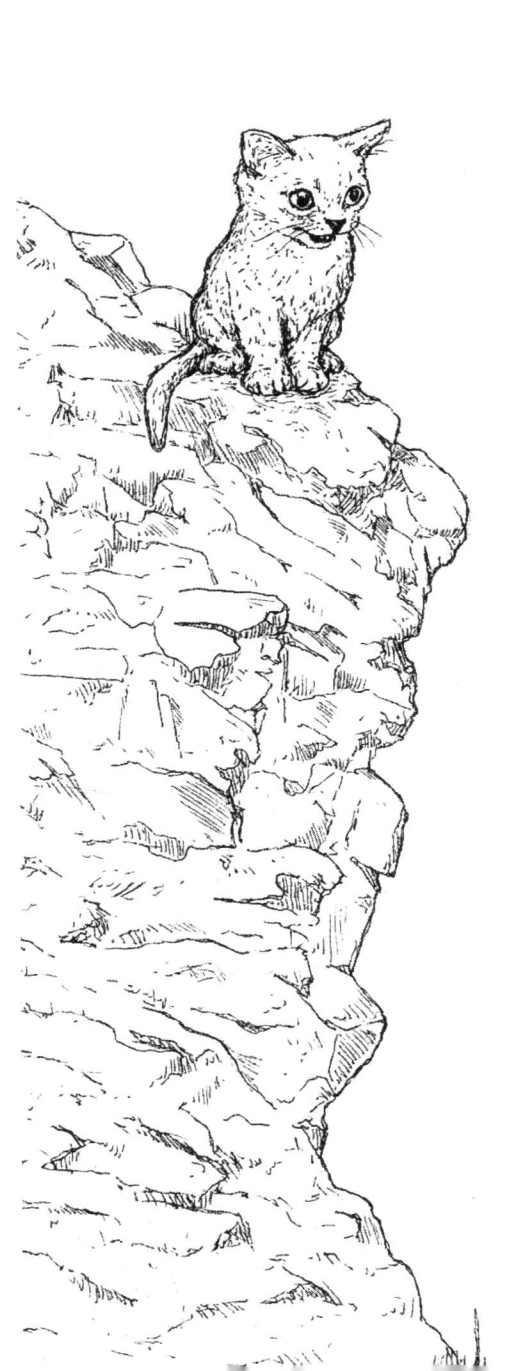

FUCK DEATH
FOR LU

Jocelyn Saidenberg

Sucking, I open the door awaiting one another. Looking down from landing, on silent demise, stair well. She sleeps in a curl. Lurking somewhere, are you?

Beating it, I try to include.

But that glittering ball you throw up at me, impedes my advance. Subsiding, I soothe myself into a nocturnal hand, the touch turns my stomach. Early morning hours hold out a certain falling then floating.

She is still sleeping nose tucked into armpit.

It haunts you, doesn't it?

Every time you emerge from the train station, sure which way to turn in your lightness. The dying are so rigorous.

Ripping out the fabric no longer thinking about the lost affection or perishing time.

The cliff which kitten which heartbeat.

"right"
"we'll clear out"
"if everybody"
"right"
"we'll clear out"
"right"
"you think we can get that far"
"if everybody"
"right, right"
"and besides we'll steal"
"we'll clear out, right"
"right"

"you think we can get that far"
"if everybody"
"and besides, we'll clear out"
"right"
"right, we'll steal something"
"think we can get that"
"steal something if everybody"
"right"

It must have been midnight, starting up with that whirring noise, the inner life game had begun, we waited behind the sink, we got dressed, under the staircase, the valley of desolation, we walked quickly, no one was surprised, hardly, we hurried along the road, sly gestures pointing the way.

You sing: "I am here, now, reaching the end. If possible."

The end, the awful parts, more dreaded in the past, haunting itself and animated by these parts, past, were a solace, soothing the bitterness in a lull. Those times, the incorporeal sordid shadows delimiting my sluggishness.

It's not just what they say that drives me toward superhuman invective.

And then, sweet kitten, you call me your little flower and I melt, kitten, you murmur at me, calling me a tramp, turning me inside out with tenderness.

So that will, kitten, you select, willingly, your will to be willed, imploring, will-less, your eyes, the record, the slight of them delicious, solemnly creased.

You ask to burn it up, eyes asking "What do you want" hardly audible tone.

With a vehemence that stirs your heart, you admit, on the harm ahead, you fling your oblivion, all they suggested and contained, your particular obligation, freely, whence, you will.

A certain abandon was proof, furtive good wishes being sent from far away.

You whisper to me, a dissapointed breath. I study you in a constant state of arousal, kitten, alternating with shame, your fur bracelet has exhausted the terms of our evening together, I used them for you.

Doesn't it haunt you too? That shadow we both drown in, extravagant in gesture.

We apprentice ourselves to it. You let it be: sly tonight, buried during the day.

I walk into the nocturnal street, nocturnal and silent in manner. I wait. Feeling inside and out for weather and sounds. Directing my attention with recognition, aim. You have been waiting for a long time. If possible.

The nocturnal's composed of hatch marks. Listing. Counting.

No passion or expectation in awaiting, the train approaches and its coming sound pulls us in, intensity and push, you board.

Waiting for one another. Waiting in front, we rendevous before, stand with each other. In front and before.

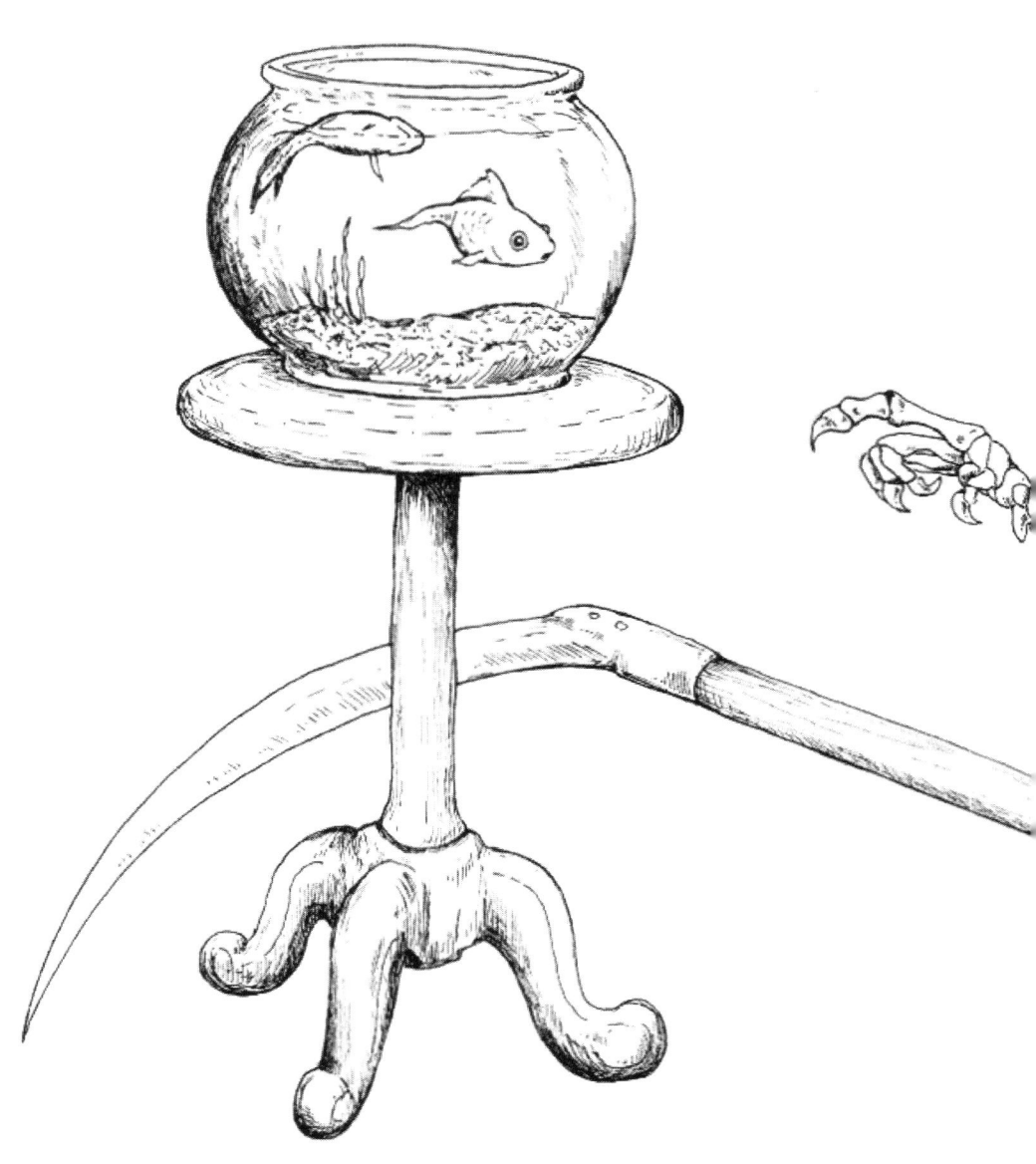

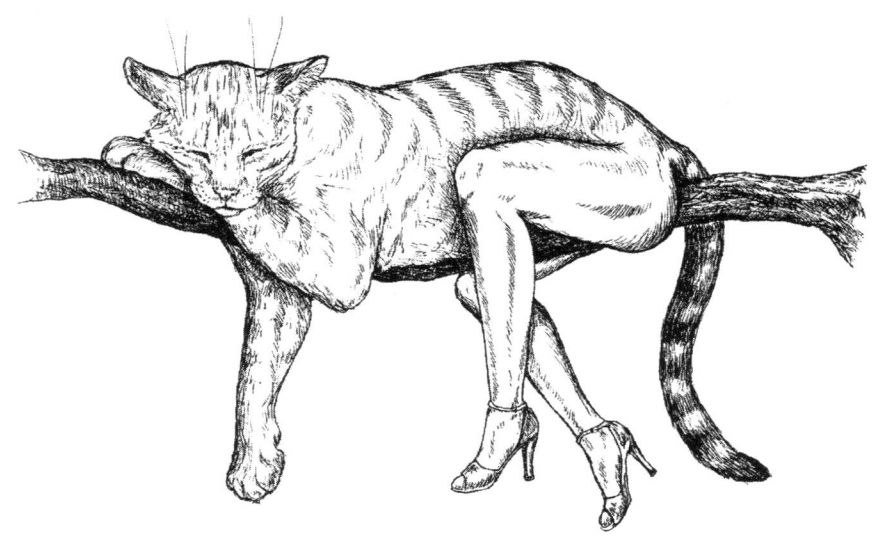

Kevin Killian

TS ELIOT

There was murder in the flowers,
piles of pesos wet with winter rain,
and the tall towers of Babylon
dressed in widows weeds, dotted swiss
cut-outs of cats appliquéd just so.

Looking at them slouched in the armchair
I feel yet again
that those cats have pulled a number on me.

They don't howl or like that.
They're posing as skeptics
and the boys I once loved
come to me in a dream diner, like ketchup,
like chicken fried steak.

On the steam table, two cats dressed
in Maurice Sendak white aprons
clang knives and pots in the night kitchen.
They saw murder in the flour,
eggs in the pain,
US intervention
in the desert heat, where cats are regularly shaven

I had been a hog
I had been hazed and shaven
I told them to piss on my leg and I came down the block,
my pants open, a cat clinging to my secret.

I had done the thing you wanted
and what you did was fire me

Poor thing, you have the
luck of the cat
You won't make it back from Iraq.
That will be the final port of call
for a hazard,
is my guess.

I'm not dressing,
I'm lying down with shades down.

From time to time I hear them singing,
outside the window
one of those songs
like Billie Holiday

or Lou Christie
Sarah Jane, if my cat could only talk to me
It would tell me 'bout you, baby

CAT SCAN

What's a cat scan, anyway?
You lie on your back, flimsy gown of paper,
and a cat walks down your body,
your forehead, your throat, sternum, stomach
and so forth, til the tiptoeing creature stares
back at you over his shoulder.
Kevin, you are going to die.

CAT SCRATCH FEVER

When the lovers wake,
their naked arms yet throb with blood;
in the night Stanley was upon them,
marking them with telltale signs.

Hurry to the white, blue and pink tin in the
          bathroom,
Johnson & Johnson may hide away
the central fact of your love,
and that a black cat sat on your mat.

THE CAT'S MEOW

He wasn't all black, and she
wasn't all white

But when they walked together
in stripe formation, abreast

like a fish
zigzagging through the rooms of the apartment

And then when he left us
she walked alone, one animal

I would pull time down
off the highest shelf

I couldn't catch it in my fingers
but on the carpet

like a spill of salt or sand,
it would twinkle. Bye.

CUSTOMER SERVICE FOR A CAT

Hello, how can I help you? On a scale of one to
ten, do you even know you're alive?
All you do is sleep and eat. Would you say
that being a pet is positive, excellent, poor
or bad? It is the question eternal, that torments
your owners, on whose behalf we gather
this info. Response had been sluggish, as a target
group your reactions muted. We watch you through
one way glass and we see ennui, sometimes a bird
flies through the room you show a flicker.
Tonight, fourlegged torpor, cast me your shadow.

THE CAT DRAGGED IN

Such a lie.
Somewhere there must have been a cat that brought a
human something.
And it was pretty foul from the sound of it.
Such a lie,
I have had two cats who gave nothing,
brought nothing, just waited, stood intent until
I turned myself inside out to see
into their eyes, pale and aglow,
then their little knees buckled and they
sat on my chest, a question and its answer.

THE CAT

Try to catch the cat in mid-air as it
Jumps from the highest shelf in the room.

Ha, ha, there is no stopping me!

CAT'S CRADLE

Give me your hands, let's make a steeple,
tumble your fingers over mine

With the maximum number of fingers
I strike you out, your flawless gestures dumb

Yarn yawns from my fingertips to yours,
you have successfully aped the cat.

KITTEN WITH A WHIP

On the same theme, Ann-
Margaret traps the older,
married, horny guy John Forsythe

into making a pass at the
babysitter. In her yellow shell
angora, she's the kitten with a whip.

Her delicate little tail curls
underneath his balls,
feels good in a way.

Will he see me as a woman,
or am I only a thing in his
mortal kaleidoscope?

A man lives and dies, a
kitten's got this Ann-Margret
thing about youth.

CAT PEOPLE

Cat people in a quiet town
where you pay your bus fare,
and the screech of its air brakes jostles the air
Where fog reveals a face like a cat

At the gym, in the locker room,
You hurry out of your baggy, oversized trunks.
On the pebbled floor, they're humped with sweat
Is a cat in them, at the bottom of that silk?

Every other man on the street has that nature,
that at bottom his mother spent time in a tree.
Every woman on the elevator knows
down by her ankles whiskers poke a question.

In a quiet town in the 1940s with
refugees from Paris and wherever it was
Simone Simon might have hailed from, let the
doctor persecute, let my memories clear

Atavistic need bleeds from my paws,
I see red when I see a ring, even on my own left hand
Under the Val Lewton moon
there's a war on, or a loose-fitting blindfold,
for the firing squad that we whisper in rhythm

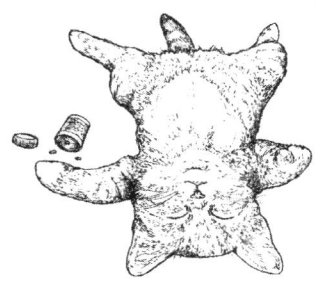

CHAPTER XXIV

Robert Glück

As an afterthought, the day pitched long shadows "over its shoulder" across the lawn where two or three superb trees stood. Mr. Fox joined Miss Kitty, who was reading on a stone bench sited to let spectators of this prospect know where to see it from.

Mr. Fox dispatched the view, "Fulfilled," but added, "I've nonetheless a crow to pick with you."

"I feel as though I were vanishing down an arcade—I've heard it's all large format work this year—" Miss Kitty blathered. She sought to change the subject to the diversity of memory and the fear of death. But the Fox's attention was repressive and her prodigious dentation slowly closed on her farrago of rumor and fantasy. "Yesterday afternoon, I was busy tucking the blanket of grasses and wildflowers into the edge of the road, stamping it down, when you and the other indolent picnickers, my distracted friends, drove off without me in your roadsters."

That amounted to an impugnment. And her friends, indeed, had rallied around her secret as a sort of camarilla. At the drop of her fan he restored his nippers. "I tracked through the woods which pulsed almost musically like a mother board's bursts of electrical consciousness, when who, under the underbrush, should I almost fall on top of? The trees and dirt path darkened as your head slid down the front of his pants!" Miss Kitty sat as stiff as a basalt pharaoh. Mr. Fox sniffed the air. "Are you smoking with him?"

"And drinking! And gambling! And reading a dreadful book." Paul saw the name on the book as Alice waved it at him.

"Zola! Does he, my dear, want to marry you?"

"Yes, to all sorts of ridiculous people. I never can understand the nerves of those in whom enjoyment is less rotary."

"Well," Mr. Fox sniffed again (in a different sense of the word), "kissing is personal."

"Unless pursued in order to avoid eye contact." Miss Kitty fought back tears unsuccessfully. With a dear damp paw she drew a half finished letter out of the book. "I am writing to him in my most emotional hand: 'Oh Teddy I'm acting strangely, kissing my pillow as though you were it. Next time we fuck don't touch me.' Am I wrong?"

"You are right, my dear, to discover in rejection a kind of pure-hearted porn. Whatever you do is right," he averred, "even if it happens to be what I do. The penis cinematheque." He gestured as though the comity of the view were irrefragably that.

Miss Kitty was taking it on. "Thank you most tremendously. I ask him in my letter to let me keep the book so I know exactly when to die. I do not weep,"—though she did—"the world will lose nothing. I was a useless ornament."

When Mr. Fox did not speak, his little companion said, "This morning I went to Macy's to buy Teddy a wallet. I found two that were beautiful—I discussed them with the nice clerk, probably gay. I had not dressed very well," she confessed tearily. "My tee-shirt had a little hole in it. His hands were cleaner than mine and it was obvious he did not want me to touch the wallets. I assured him that I had taken a bath. Both beautiful leather—which did I want? One had a place for a pen—that was nice—but was the place for money too small? Both more than $400—would he accept my offer of less?"

Mr. Fox understood. "If you earn your livelihood with a pen, you won't require a larger place for money. You see, my dear, the gods sell everything at a fair price. Your fits of uncontrollable spending confirm that." He felt the urge to cover her with his body—To protect her? Consume her? "Miss Kitty, let's bring a new thought to Lovers' Lane. Like it or not, we are moving towards the infinite. It is belief in the finite that is not possible without faith."

BLANCHE AND STANLEY

Dodie Bellamy

Claw clippings scattered across my comforter, litter in my sheets, he kneads my tit with his paws, he pokes my tit with his snout. She nuzzles in my armpit, she nuzzles in my neck, he burrows between my legs and sleeps there, he sits between my legs with the top half of him resting on my belly, she perches on my abdomen and licks her asshole. She cries for vanilla ice cream, he cries for TV dinners. He reaches out the window and swipes at birds, he catches three of them, dead pigeon blood and feathers all over the living room. She leans against my left thigh while I watch TV, she sits on my lap during my private writing workshop, I balance student writing on her back, she cries until I swivel in my office chair and pick her up, I lean over her awkwardly and try to type on the computer, she sits on my lap when I argue, when I cry, when I talk on the phone, she sits on my lap as I eat breakfast, I drop oatmeal on her head. He lies at the bottom of the bed and I rub him with my foot, toes grazing soft fur. I roll over on my stomach, he climbs on my ass, she joins him on the small of my back and licks his face, their bodies rumbling with satisfaction. I sit on the toilet and she squats in the liter box beside me, both of us peeing. When I stroke him his whole body quivers with pleasure and he drools on my chest. When she wants me to touch her she cries out desperately, an unpleasant cry, sharp as the squawk of a crow. When he wants me to touch him he lets out a low wail. I pull the fur tightly back from their heads and their skulls look like snake skulls. I leave a glass of water on the nightstand, and as soon as I turn my back, she has her snout in it lapping. Silent, sneaky, mono-focused, the only way to win with them is to remove what they want from sight. They're racing through the apartment trying to catch a fly, when the fly stops they freeze, waiting for just the right moment, they get so excited waiting they let out little whimpers, and I tell them that when you're trying to creep up on something whimpering is counterproductive. They ignore me, crouch down, shake their fannies, pounce. The double bed is overflowing with bodies, he sleeps at the foot on my side, wails when I move him to make room for my legs—otherwise I'd have to sleep on a diagonal and then where would Kevin's legs go. She sleeps in a ball in my arms most nights for 19 years. He snores and farts, she lets out an occasional groan, he pees in the bed while I'm sleeping, he shits in the bed when I've displeased him, both of them vomit in the bed sometimes on my pillow right next to my face, he vomits in my shoes, she eats dental floss, straw from the kitchen broom, ribbon, rose leaves, plastic bags and throws up blood-tinged foam. He shits on the couch, not every day but enough that whenever I'm not sitting on it I keep the couch covered with white plastic shower curtain liners, cheap ones I buy at Walgreen's, sometimes he pees and shits on the liners, pool of urine so yellow against the white plastic, I mop up the urine with paper towels, gather up the plastic and throw it away. If it's just shit and not too runny I'll pick it off and spray the plastic with odor remover. Sometimes I'm too lazy to remove the shower curtain liner and I sit on it, plastic bunching and crinkling beneath my ass. The apartment smells of urine and incense. Even though her food dish is full she looks up at me and cries until I either mix up the crunches with my hand or drop in a few more pieces of food. Then she lowers her head and eats. Taupe back, creamy belly and snout, blues eyes, pale pink nose, gray and black striped tail, when I hold her in my arms she relaxes completely, trembling with pleasure. Both of them crawl on top of me, she on my chest he on my groin, my lungs rising and falling beneath the weight of them, their lungs rising and falling in different rhythms, warmth. He butts the book I'm reading with his head, keeps butting it until I put the book down, then he scoots higher on my chest, I scratch his snout, he quivers and drools. Long black fur, white paws and belly, green eyes, pink nose with the black spot or is it black nose with a pink spot. In the morning she screams until I open the bedroom shades, then she climbs into a patch of sun and passes out. I'm lying down, he crawls on top of me, front paws on my chest, back paws on my groin, long and heavy his body presses down on me vibrating with pleasure, I put my arms around him, hard muscles beneath black fur, I feel a hit of arousal. She eats with her tail on the floor extended straight back, when I step on it she shrieks so loud I jump in the air—she never seems to get hurt, I'm in the air before that could happen. Fur fur fur fur everywhere and always the stench of urine, he kneads my lap he kneads my tit, he rubs his face against my tit and drools. She desires, she demands, she receives. When she's satisfied her body trembles. I call her Squawks, I call him Stanley Bear. Three stories down the front gate bangs shut, they run to the door and wait for Kevin to climb the stairs. She licks my

face when I'm trying to sleep, she stands on my pillow pulling my hair, he scratches me until I bleed, she pees on the bathroom floor, he gulps down his food and throws it up at my feet, shit hangs out his ass and smears on my down comforter, he's shit on the comforter so often it's limp from overwashing. Bedtime, she curls in my arms and we struggle over which direction she faces, I want her back to me, she wants claws and whiskers in my face, I fall asleep with her facing away from me, wake up with claws and whiskers in my face, her breath smells like rancid fish. If I try to wrap myself around Kevin's back, I have to leave room at the top for her to crawl between us, or she'll bat my head and cry, she will pester me and keep me awake as long as necessary to get her way, if I push her off the bed, she'll crawl back up and cry and bat, if I put them in the living room and close the door, both of them will scratch and cry, he will shit on the couch then hurl his body against the door. The two of them simultaneously lick one another's faces, it looks like they're making out, they curl beside one another and sleep, two tight balls. When I was a child I slept with a mound of stuffed animals, I had to scoot to the edge of the twin bed to accommodate them all, my favorite was a green cotton frog my grandmother sewed and stuffed with cut-up old nylons, I used Froggy to masturbate, I'd lie on my stomach, position one of his hind legs against my clit, I clench and rub against it, the rest of Froggy bounding on top of my butt. Kelly green frog foot flecked with dried white scum. As a girl I wished I had real animals to fondle and cuddle, and now those dreams have come true. I have the flu and she lies in bed with me for three days, barely moving, when I wrestle and toss she makes little cries of disapproval. I open the front door and they rush to greet me, running side by side, a stripe of black wedged against a strip of taupe and cream, screaming. I scoop them both up, my arms spilling over with thick vibrating fur. He rubs my tit with his head, dripping saliva on my shirt, he kneads my tit with his paws, his nails flicking out as he presses down. He eats bugs and broccoli. He digs a corncob out of the garbage, gnaws and swallows it, and almost dies. He falls out the window during the 1989 earthquake and is missing for three weeks, when he returns scared and bedraggled she hisses at him. I'm lying down, he stretches his body out on top of me, his hind legs on my groin, his front paws touching my neck, he's so excited he drools on my chest, all fifteen pounds of him pressing down on me as if he would sink through my skin and nestle in my organs,

I stroke his head, he slobbers some more, I hug him, my arms full of black fur muscles bony spine, my groin lifts to meet his weight, no one's around but this is as far as I've let myself go. Warmth fish-breath drool vomit shit piss purr sting of drawn blood. In the morning when I wake up, before I open my eyes or move she's already crying and tapping my arm with her paw. When Kevin and I begin to have sex she jumps off the bed, but as soon as we've both come she jumps back up, purring loudly, we're lying on our sides arms and legs wrapped around one another, I reach over Kevin's shoulder and scratch her chin. She stands at her food bowl and screams until I get up from my desk and watch her, then she bends over and eats greedily. He gets on his hind legs, cries and bats at me until I stop writing and pick him up, he's too big for my lap, keeps shifting about, his back legs are bony against my thighs, I wrap my arms around him, hunch over and run my chin on his head, pulling him to me tightly—she purrs when I do this, he squirms and jumps down. She climbs between my legs and curls in a ball. He climbs between my legs and stretches straight out, claws at my crotch, his hind legs down at my feet, I jiggle my legs around him, rubbing both his sides at once. Dry chunky vomit corncob vomit clear puddle vomit rusty brown diarrhea pouring over the side of the litter box and dripping on the floor. The vet tells me to stop petting her as the purring is too loud to hear her heart. I stick needles in their backs, give him subcutaneous fluids twice a day for a month, give her subcutaneous fluids twice a week then every other day for a year, I pry open their jaws and throw pills down their throats, I gob flea killer on the backs of their necks, squirt liquids down their throats that makes them squirm and gag, I mix baby food with water and squirt it down his throat, when he's too weak to sit up I feed him baby shrimp, one by one from my palm, every day I walk to Safeway to get him fresh shrimp. I open capsules and mix the contents in cat food which they sniff, walk away from and screech for something untainted. I rub thyroid medicine in her ears twice a day for three years, if I rub a certain spot her hind legs twitches uncontrollably. Thin, flexible hairy triangle, inside her ear less fur and pink. I decide when it's time for them to die. His lungs empty their final load with two deep sighs, she slumps over silently, eyes staring. As I walk through the apartment afterwards, soft strands of fur dust the corners, invisible bits of dander cling to the hair on my forearms, wedge beneath my nails, enter my eyes, my mouth, my nostrils.

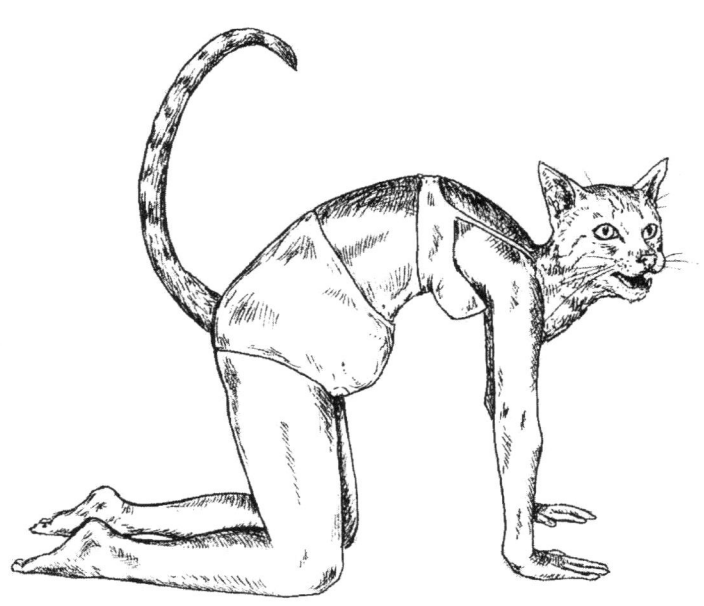

Author's Note

Apathy was my cat of 18 years. She curled up on my neck to sleep, she was sometimes clumsy and she liked to be spanked. She inspired these drawings. Philip Horvitz, to whom this book is dedicated, was my friend and my mentor, and he encouraged me in everything. I began these drawings before I lost either of them. Yedda Morrison got me started with an earlier version of "Slum Puss." Prompted by conversations with her, I began drawing lots of cats, pussies clearly. As the drawings (cats) progressed and kept coming, it made sense to me that they should illustrate a collection of writing. I asked my favorite writers to send me pieces that related to cats. Nine were able to give me something and I am in love with all of their work. Philip had agreed to contribute and his piece would have been the tenth. As it turned out, so much of the work speaks to loss, to the missing tenth cat. I drew some more, based on the writing.

There are already a few books about cats. This one may be an homage or a satire, or a parallel universe, but regardless how you view it, I hope that you will find some comfort, warmth, humor and love in a little pussy.

{Michelle Rollman, 2009}

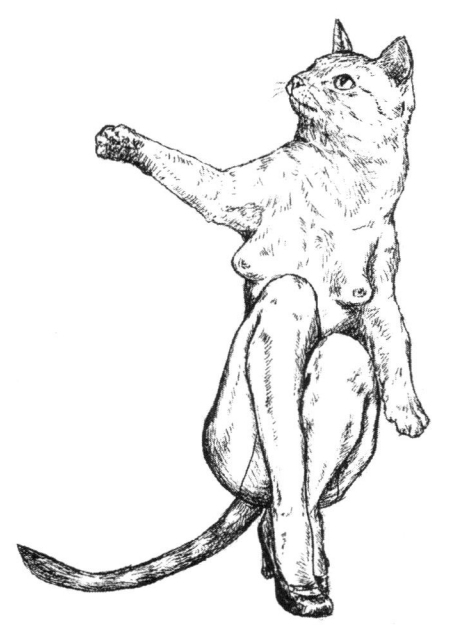

Katy Bohinc

Dear Alain

TENDER BUTTONS PRESS

New York City

2014

Tender Buttons Press
New York, New York
www.TenderButtonsPress.com

Cover Design Cassandra Gillig
Interior Design Wayne Smith
Text set in Cambria Math

Interior Artworks
Tender Buttons Drawing by Joe Brainard, printed with permission
Natal Chart Wheel by Cafe Astrology, CafeAstrology.com
Drawings by Katy Bohinc
Malcolm X Park image from the National Park Service www.nps.gov

Cataloguing-in-publication data available
From the Library of Congress
ISBN 978-0-927920-11-7

Printed by BookMobile

Selections of this work have appeared in *Where Eagles Dare*,
Armed Cell, *Open Letters Monthly*, *Elderly*, *Elective Affinities*, and
& Now Awards 3: The Best Innovative Writing. Much thanks to
Summer BF Press who also published a small selection of the
letters as an objet d'art.

That eros knows nothing

Of the word better

Our only hope

All's fair

In love and war

Our every demise

Let us add that contemporary philosophy addresses itself at all times to women. It might even be suspected that it is, as discourse, partly a strategy of seduction.

ALAIN BADIOU, "WHAT IS LOVE?"

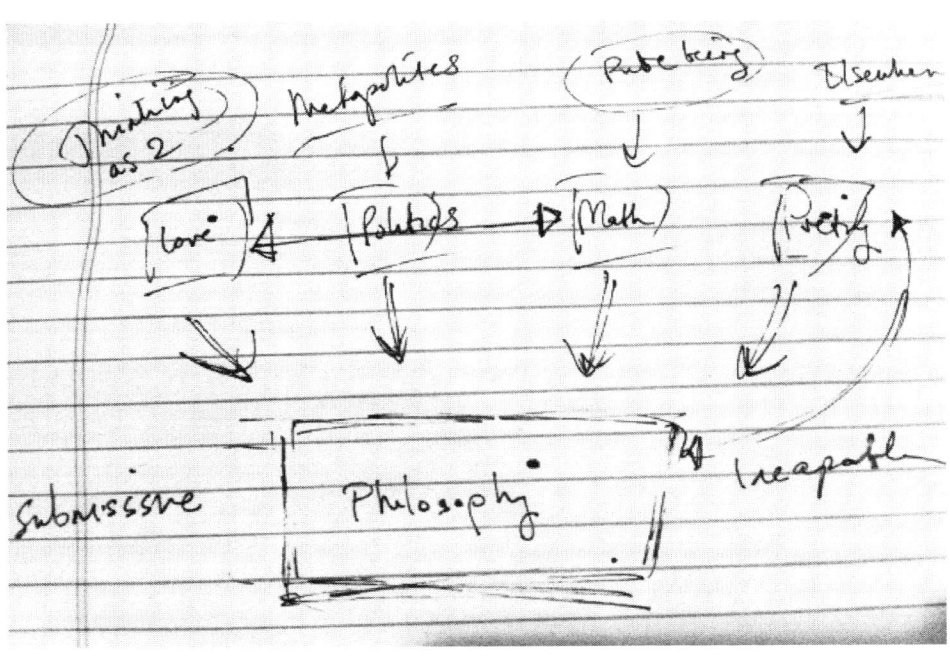

You dare to study philosophy baby I'll tell you
About fucking Aristotle I never planned to fall
In love with you who often happen by where I am
Let me hide you amidst the sublime responsibility you are

BERNADETTE MAYER, SONNET

Let us agree to call k(x) the Katy function,
and a(x) the Alain function

$$\sum_{0}^{\infty} k_n + a_n$$

This the poem a summation of two functions

TERMS: AS DEFINED BY THE PHILOSOPHER ALAIN BADIOU

Philosophy: System describing how truth is produced

Love: Thinking as Two

Politics: Revolution

Poetry: Elsewhere

Math: Pure Being

The Event: That which produces truth

The Event of Love: The declaration of "I love you"

Truth: Singularity

Evil: Naming the Unnamable

TERMS: AS DEFINED BY THE POET KATY BOHINC

Philosophy: My bitch

Love: The source & the glue

Politics: Problematic unless approaching infinity

Poetry: Everything

Math: The origin

The Event: The Kernal

The Event of Love: At first sight

Truth: The lowest and highest tones

Evil: Pain

Conditions of Alain Badiou imposed on this work:

1. *The concepts of Alain Badiou's philosophy shall condition this text.*

2. *The poet shall critique the philosopher, as poetry is a condition on philosophy.*

3. *The poet and the philosopher shall begin to think as two, as determined by their love.*

4. *The obvious conflict proceeding shall be the process of this work.*

5. *The event shall be the determination of said conflict.*

6. *The poet will discuss concepts of Poetry – those of Alain and those of her own.*

7. *The poet will discuss infinity - those ideas of Alain and those of her own.*

8. *The poet will condition her lover the philosopher with mathematics, politics, ideas of language, ideas of evil, ideas of naming, ideas of the void, ideas of historicity, ideas of the West, ideas of astrology, ideas of play, ideas of cliché, singularity, oneness, appearance, Marxism, multiplicity, etc.*

9. *The concept of Condition will be complicated, as will most the philosopher's ideas, as the poet is prone to insult the philosopher, like any good (?) lover. It is not so much a point as an effect that here Alain is a condition. Or, peut-être, non?*

10. *The relations and narrative shall generally be ambiguous so as to grant the reader multiple possible interpretations. Construct your truth.*

11. *Let us add, that contemporary poetry addresses itself at all times to "men". It might even be said it is a matter of seduction.*

"Poem, Matheme, Politics and Love at once condition and insult philosophy. Condition and insult: that's the way it is." – A.B.

$$k_0 + a_0$$

"It is fixed only by a nomination, and this nomination is a declaration, the declaration of love." – A.B.

Dear Alain,

There, got it, round two. multiplicity. said Badiou. you mother fucker stole my brain. except, you're wrong. still working in euclid's plane. enlightenment is the real projective. where parallel lines meet at the horizon and a line is a circle. it's true that the abrahamic religions have a problem with historicity and crusades. somebody's always got to be right before and in order to get to God. buddha knows the line is really a circle at the horizon anyway, where we all should strive to dwell. the point, it's a line. the line, it's a circle. the circle, it's a flower. that point derrida collapsed in the derivatives market? don't worry about it. we'll fix it when we wake up. cat life number 27, ladybug reincarnate.

•

Dear Alain,

The isolated hysteria of city dwelling. Universal truth? You're crying alone. You're crying alone. And there's something wrong here. Don't make sense to go bowling alone, no bone cold enough for a life like that. We got to get some meatloaf and gravy on this table, live humans creaking in the chairs, laughter cracking up

the atmosphere, bring your tears here, bring em drippin down
your nose long and heavy we'll cook those boys to the corners
with friendship sweet and mighty. Laughter tears are good for
wrinkles.

Wink, K

•

Dear Alain,

I think when you talk about Multiplicity, Alain, really didn't a
guy named Hardt write that ten years back? I guess he was riffing
on you but it led him to Classicism. Chaos is the original sin
we've been running from all our architectural lives. Why are we
spending our energy re-discovering this? Why does this constitute
a form we want to represent? Is it that we never knew how bad
it could be until Hitler? Maybe we didn't know how much pain
dissolves brick. I see this as the real problem.

•

Dear Alain

I want to meet you very badly and write you love poems. I want
to know where you put love in your schema; if you believe in
it. Did you ever read Zamyatin's "We"? It's what Orwell based
1984 on. He got kicked out of Russia before it was Bolshevik.
But Zamyatin foretold a world where everything was algebra
and the only thing to wake up the creativity, the poetry pole you
juxtapose like math, the Dionysius to your linear Apollo, well
let's just say Dionysius didn't dance without Venus. Do you think
Venus exists? You must believe in the ***, the undefined, the ***,
the poetry that beds the data when it's young and vomiting on the
floor, before it grows into a tall and strong polynomial chain. You
said you did. Back to that Hardt guy, he ended up talking about
love too and I think that's where his career ended. Nobody wants
to listen to the mushy stuff. But I gotta tell you, my friend Chad
B said it best: "I don't care if you're the tiny-ist, whiney-ist, most
pampered cheerleader or the hood-est, hard-est most jock football
player, everybody got somebody put em fetal in the kitchen make
em bat shit crazy." Is this the constant in the incompleteness
theorem? Desire? I hate that word. What about capital L Love?
Should I just ask somebody to write me a prescription and forget
about it?

•

Dear Alain,

I recognize that I am being sassy, immature and superficial.
However, it seems that love poems are out of style. (I'm still
terribly upset about that). I honestly would like to know what you
think Monsieur Badiou. Also, I read your essay on Mallarme. It
seems clear that you are a philosopher and not a poet. I am deeply
grateful you write of poetry at all. Your analysis, its geometry
is well mapped. Perhaps I wish to go a bit further outside the
language of being/event and say more simply, poetry is the
undefinable. I think it should be off the map entirely! I think you
would agree if you envision it in terms of an x-y coordinate axis,
but I must point out my logical inconsistency -- where is poetry
if it does not exist on the plane? A strong argument for a third
dimension. Emotions, maybe. The soul. Magic. Stuff like that. Or,
back to classical Euclid, it would be very poetic to say poetry is
the origin. Exactly (0,0). I like that. Poetry at the Origin. Capital O.
How orgasmic!

•

Dear Alain,

Oh Monsieur Badiou! How lovely to argue with you! Thank you
dearly and I look forward to fucking you again soon. Really, I am
a big prude. I rarely fuck in public. Please take this as a token of
my deepest admiration and affection. Next time, in French! And
in French fashion, now that I have told you all the things I don't
like about you, we can be friends. I shall try to proceed in pure
devotion to all your most finest accomplishments.

Yours, Katy

•

Dear Alain,

Forgive me. Burn these letters. I forgot to write "par avion".
Perhaps they will not arrive. I dearly hope so. Burn them.
Please. I will be a better student. I will be more serious.
Do not forsake me.

Yours,
Katy

•

Dear Alain,

I thought all day of what I would write you. Now I can merely see my fingers typing at the keys. Everything escapes me. My mind thinks of so many intimate things to tell you: what I think of your work, how I feel, the images and the selflessness. When I think of writing for the entire of existence, of humanity, I am in church with a vow to serious straight eyes, concentration, a heavy heart and good posture. It terrifies me and makes me cry. How do you do it?

Love, Katy

•

Dear Alain,

If it is the continuation of the canon that allows you to make incremental progress in the works of philosophy, then how do you not wonder if the canon has made a mistake? I do not mean your discussions with Derrida or Heidegger. I wonder if we are not profoundly mistaken. You discuss life as if set theory could approach it. I admire the "limitless-ness" of your approach, in that calculus has no limit in having a limit. But politics! I fear we are so near the end that philosophy is merely a performative architecture, rather than a salvation we need. I mean, possibly Red Scare…but isn't global warming real? Do I confuse truth with answers, and a way to think with a way to live? Perhaps I should compartmentalize you in the "philosophy" division, and not ask you questions of basic moral existence.

Is too much to ask? But you said, you do not like specialization. Should I look in the "self-help" section? I cannot help but consider you from the view of the ignorant. For I sense I am completely blind. I would say we are completely blind, but to speak beyond any other than myself seems a treason. Then again I wish with all my ego to say "everything is X". Is it the history or the graph that makes it easier for you? These words, Being and Event. They seem a trick of logic which remove responsibility. Everything is timeless before death, unless you consider pregnancy.

Truly, Katy

•

Dear Alain,

I thought being with you, openly, brazenly, could be so many things. I thought you would understand me, I thought I could be naked before you. There would be profundity and confession. You see as poets we dance. I could say to you "now against the wall" but i've tried this before and it doesn't work as well as you'd think. So we play a game, an artifice, a style a form to get to that ee cummings moment in the poem. I wondered if I could be myself for you, and be quite serious and earnest with all my passion because you are serious and earnest. But perhaps we amount to giggles because can't bare our wretched infinite. Oh dear, I am torn between my artifice and intimacy. Be patient with me. I wish at once to ease your tired ears but also to put light to these deepest thoughts we never say aloud. Perhaps the things that matter most.

When tomorrow becomes yesterday and tomorrow becomes eternity
when the soul with the soul goes way beyond

Yours, Katy

•

Dear Alain,

Forgive me. It was the whiskey last night. I speak too quickly and with too little thought. I will be more serious. As clear as a winter landscape for you.

A ce soir,
Kati

•

Alain,

Please, write soon. Your silences always depress me. Or perhaps it is that thinking like a philosopher may be suicidal. You metal jungle gym!

As always, you are the eternal object of my being and I hope to pass an event with you soon.

Yours, Katy

•

Affair #1

Dear Julian,

Meet me in rat alley by the old mattress. The Four Seasons is for criminals.

In code,
Katya

•

Dear Alain,

Philosophers and poets, we're both trying to reach God, you the form, we the content. You the throne, we the light.

Thoughtfully, Katy

•

Dear Alain,

I'm sick from being serious. I'm sick of this fucking shit. Speaking to you on your terms in your vocabulary requires a tired precision I loathe. I like monkeys and raspberries and autumn squash cooked for one hour at 350 degrees Fahrenheit with a glaze of two tablespoons butter, agave nectar and dijon mustard. Lightly speckled with pepper. I don't mean the cooking channel. I mean John Coltrane for Lovers on repeat because it's Sunday, the holiday of the sun regime from 300 BC, where the thrones met the saints and the prophets. I mean the Roman Emperors bent the Christian details to gain the wealth of the people's love of astrologers. The first empirical data. These days Pfizer does a six week trial and we call it truth but 700 years the Sumerians documented the position of Saturn and the price of wheat and it's habernacky to us. What on earth do you put faith in my dear? I would say beyond earth but I presume you are a dialectical materialist like your good Marxist politics. As my dear French father said, "you think you are an atheist, but everyone has faith in something, be it electricity or that god does not exist." That might be slightly holistic for your set theory which holistically avoids the holistic, but I'll gladly hear the counter example. Where was your tipping point for belief? I suppose it was years of thought, but there must be a fall off the seesaw you want to tell me about.

I wonder, why a doctrine? Even if you win History, that unattainable virgin, you'll spend eternity with the maggots, the fact-mongerers typing away at your flesh. I suppose you don't mind contributing to humanity, just a bone left, a truism in the end. But would it have been any different otherwise? Personally, I'm leaving only ashes. Burnt pages. Not deconstruction. Pure flame. You philosophers are made of metal, but I am earth water fire. The triskelion. Horned and abandoned. Who wants the power of the name if it's only to claim your own bullseye? Already got it plenty, darts, doin just fine.

Well it's sassy time tonight, yes, agreed. Your logic's got me all bunched like a rolled sleeve. It's fine enough on its own, but against my wrinkles and veins and memories something else has to course against the grain. There's so many of you, arguing your details since the beginning of time, screw it, I want a literary song. Unwind the arguments because I was never that great at compartments, and when I was, it didn't get me laid. Philosophy is all moral consequence and politics, real time. Miserably. Your set theory has no "I", so Houdini!, but subject object event gets back to the sun eventually. You hide in math. I hide in the moon. And I only ask you this, if e to the negative two pi i contains all the numbers we have never seen but that make the circle, the financial world and the imaginary realm all come together to equal one, then you must believe in things we cannot see or touch or feel but only believe.

All the artists I know know this: closest thing I've got to reason is the voice in my head. None of us can see that. Here's the voice in my head. Here it is. I made it prettier for you but it's what I think. I guess the difference between you and me is that I only trade my voice with you. Maybe you spent all those years making your voice for everyone, as round and flat and true as everything. Oh, a metaphor about our work. I just wish I could hear your voice. The one in your head.

Yours, Katy

•

Dear Alain,

My father told me my project to write you love letters was creepy. I said, imagination and hope are elements as real as the table before your eyes! Imagine father!

•

Dear Alain,

I'm going to have to get back to the intangible soon. I think you like real numbers, but I prefer the imaginary; the i. The square root of negative one, that is. Can you see it? You must be a genius.

xo, k

•

Dear Alain,

My new roommate Brandon is a found poem. I like it. When I think of all the things I don't have time to be nostalgic for I feel irresponsible. It makes me care about the heart more than being smart. It is not that time is a mirage, but that it's a villain and I am consensually guilty of moving on. There's no grammar around that. Just hiding from the images that bring us most comfort.

We long for revolution, but I have been there and all that's fought for is the peace to enjoy the apple on the worn wood table. It's folksy to center the flowers in their vase, simple and symmetrical, but I'll still call it beautiful for my Ma. Do you mind?

Yours, Katy

•

Dear Alain,

The past few weeks…well I passed out at the office yesterday and think it might be from stress. My boss rode me like an investment banker, I was sick. I was up for promotion, he was up for promotion. I got news my friend died, I had a job interview the next day. I reconnected with high school friends, I made a memorial fund. I got sicker. There were 4,000 poets in my city for a conference, I had five days and ten events. I didn't get the job. My mother was diagnosed with a derivative of tuberculosis. I tried to quit smoking. Oh yea, it was the Egyptian revolution. I watched Al Jazeera constantly and cried at the beauty of belief in the impossible.

And all I can think about is our parallel lines meeting. Tell me you believe in love.

Yours,
Katy

•

Into the streets of Cairo
Go to every door
Tell them to come out tomorrow
We will not go home

Dear Alain,

I love you more than ever. You wrote that the Tunisian and Egyptian uprisings have a universal significance. They prescribe new possibilities whose value is international.

I could not agree more. When Mubarak finally stepped down, I was just headed from my office to lunch. I stepped outside to consider the importance of this revolution, this televised moment of history as important as, the paris commune or the french revolution or, or, as important as, Tahrir itself. Tahrir means To Freedom, literally, or, independence as I'm sure you know. And as I stepped out outside on the street I began to sob. I really did. I was crying on the street and thought, perhaps you look a little silly on the street here, so I went to the bookstore where my friend Rod works. I cried more at the bookstore. All in all it took about two hours to exhaust myself of the tears and I am not sure anyone really understood - most people just think I'm overly emotional or maybe crazy - but I cried because I am not crazy and Egypt proves it. That moment when he left, when Mubarak left through peaceful means, through universal, peaceful spontaneous, beautiful power of the people, it's, it's every single person in the world who said "things can be better", it's every single person in the world who dared to say "torture is wrong", it's every single person who dared to dream, it's every single person who went to sleep with hope for a better future, it's every single ignorant fucking imbecile who only said "no" going to hell, it's everyone who called me crazy for hoping, for believing, for wanting more, it's to hell with them, and it was worth it, it was all worth it, it was true, it is possible, it was worth the sacrifice it is all worthwhile we can and the big words are worth a damn and I cried and cried and cried because all the idealism was true and all the blood and the bruises and the torture was losing, it wasn't structure anymore, it was a tall building made of electric fence for everyone to hail with bruises and scars and untouchables, that facade collapsed, and there was a sun to heal the scars, and the romance of poetry survives and this is why I cried: for all the pain of anyone who ever said "I guess that's how it has to be" because it didn't have to be that way the day Mubarak left, it was singing and dancing in the street among all the people, it was the resounding ring of the subtle non-violent line, it was the rise out of silence of the truth, that magic of the white dove from the darkest, gentleman's top hat, the scar become the badge, the tear become the holy water, the transcendence, the moment where the best side of humanity came true, and everything we write for, everything we live for, everything we ever dared to believe was worth it all.

PS. It's parallel lines meeting at infinity. It's when Gauss looked at the horizon and said, but parallel lines do meet, they meet at the horizon. It's the dream of the platonic form lapping at the edge of the shore and the tide rushing over one last time to a blazing red dawn, the kind that makes you wake up and breathe as if for the first time and all those tones of sarcasm fade into some jellyfish dying on the sand and it's blindingly beautiful the stuff we always knew was there but just grew too cynical to care except maybe deep in the night we risked a word or two of "maybe" and "i hope" and "it still is" and "there is more" and we dreamed and we dreamed and we dreamed and it was the real projective plane and things do happen at infinity and i still believe in love and i'm getting on a plane because i believe that if the egyptians can then why not, we can have it too. i still believe.

I love you.

Bisous.

•

Dear Alain,

I'm not here to elaborate on your experience, I'm here to remind you of your soul.

"LOVE IS NOTHING OTHER THAN A TRYING SEQUENCE OF
INVESTIGATIONS ON THE DISJUNCTION AND THE TWO." – A.B.

$$k_1 + a_1$$

"LOVE IS INTERMINABLE FIDELITY TO THE FIRST
DECLARATION." – A.B.

I've fallen into unrequited love again. There's nothing that makes
me more fun to be around.

Yrs,
Katy

•

Dear Alain,

The problem ultimately is that to define anything is to take a
position of power. Are you comfortable with your power? I hate
power. I refuse to define. I refuse it. I refuse to be powerful, I
refuse to make sense, I refuse I refuse. I refuse in protest. I'm a
soft, silly, wild flower basket of love. All I see is your ego and I'm
going to stuff a chalky powder comment in the cracks, because I
hate power. My mission is to dissolve it. But of course, this is my
deepest secret I reveal to you! My deepest secret because to name
a mission is itself to have power – don't you see? I don't give a
damn I forgive you always! What, rules? What rules? They're
power. They're cultural sets for specific power layers, they're
always false when turned over or meshed. Fuck them. You need
something? You need to know you're important? You are. Does
your power put things in jeopardy? Always. Do I forgive you?

I don't even have a choice. I am a poet. I have no power. I have nothing. I am water. I know love. I give everything your psyche needs; I take nothing. No story, no moment of self, no words of self. Some babble if your ego needs.

•

Dear Alain,

Here are two concepts that give me a headache: Revolution and infinity. By comparison, even God seems a clear-cut conundrum.

You seem to be the set of all sets, Alain. What say you?

•

Dear Alain,

These letters are just shit. I'm only writing them because the literati will eat them. Mange-le. I know.

I know. But the truth is power. Is lines in the sand and you know the bloom doesn't come from lines. Political events cannot be quantified. You said it. Page 7, 32, 45, 66-69, 98-100, XYZ... J, K, W, Politics and Metaphysics. Definitions, blah blah blah. Who cares about categories when there's death by dehydration? The bloom Alain, I'm talking about the bloom!

Tais-Toi!

I'm going to melt you

PS it's more than form, it's more than Mallarme, it's underneath...

•

Dear Alain,

Your shoulder blades the shimmer of molten silver.

•

Oh Alain!
It's trust dripping down to the ground, or where the ground used to exist!

•

Dear Alain,

I want to see you, ie fuck you and then later, make love to you very much. My desire for you is so strong it won't let me go; it scares me; it makes me weep.

I've been very even keeled the past while. The intensity is back, with you. Now. I'm not sure either one of us wants that kind of Katy insanity but I would be crazy for you this weekend.

I really am not being dramatic, please, believe me. I'm weeping honesty because there is no other choice.

Please do the right thing for both of us. It's just a question if you feel this same intensity: we would work the rest out or break our hearts trying. Or I would, again.

For you,
K

•

Alain,

The key is to understand that no one will ever "get" you. It's impossible. To remember that, hurts, a lot. So we lie to ourselves or, if we're smart, we take affection where we can get it. It's just mirrors and smoke dancing around a big void. If we're lucky, we have a lot of mirrors and plenty of smoke and even get a glimpse of the black hole once or twice to remind us to keep smiling, because, we can.

•

Dear Alain,

Well, as you know I'm a juvenile stuck on the problem of naming. So I've gone to the source, addicted to sex and obsessed with sounds, sensations, feelings. You claim naming was solved by some anti-naming mechanism. Theorizing the naming into some other system. But I'm done with concrete! Eww. Put it in a bottle throw it out to sea. Your systems don't give a damn for psyche. I want them destroyed completely. I want to drown. What do you say of philosophy to a Chinese woman who has never used a personal pronoun but who knows her master's name, with glee! She giggles!

I'm going under now – come with me…

How can you talk about these things mechanically? As if philosophy were as binary and blameless as a lightswitch? These are human beings and their thoughts their hearts their messy souls. Multiplicity is generous but are you God? Do you judge? Oh I could scream! I just want to save them all, all 7.22 Billion from your arrogance.

Oh but you poor baby, you do, you work. It's born of generosity and you have seen the source, it's the events of Robespierre, not Kant's assessment. Laundry clean smelling despite the shit stains. Perhaps because. You try. I understand. But I would commit suicide before I would write a single word of, for, and, about, under, within, on top, above, below or anywhere around a human mind, I wouldn't name a single one thing – it claims too much! And yet I dare do exactly that to you – you are just as guilty of your fate as any! And pain, you must know pain, who doesn't? And if you don't, god bless you!

Oh human being, my beloved human being!

●

Dear Alain,

Power is all in our heads these days. Where is the magical green grass? Plain electrons aren't so colorful. Green lights of google chat, be my disco ball!

Holding my heart for your quantum, beyond the boring binary.

Yours, always,
Kati

●

My dear,

I would love you any way, you are the least offensive of the crowd. None of us are innocent. Except perhaps my mother. All ways are less of more and in that way of course, more.

Is that poetry? Does it grasp at beyond? I am. Swingin' anyway. At bat. & the skies are blue.

Love, K

PS. I know, I know. It's all contained in multiplicity. But what of synchronicity? You said infinity? But what of the irrational?

•

Dear Alain,

Just that disagreement can be more intimate than "yea, I know me too" and the gulf between us fills me more than your cock; pushed up against my wall, the gulf between us daring me to fall, right into the embrace of your views. Wrong. I'm playing hard to get; come here. Now. I was sweet enough to show you where to climb. My nipples, hard.

Yes you're lacking introspection to a fault and I am swelling with the lyric I but don't tell me you're somehow less self-involved you with your adoration of intellectual porn, false precision and smooth façade. Yes you indulge in grey antique moments of stolen admiration for the reflective mind, but this is rap for academics, and we've the same ambivalent hard-on for theory though it too exclusive for our political proclamations and we're full of fancy martinis our hearts love but somehow don't satisfy the romantic aluminum can of our peasant cornfield dreams. We're filled with contradiction, and so are you, despite your proclamations of sympathy, tender otherness and sensuality as non-political dream moment. It's true past the judgment, ticket in, whatever tribal proclamation inherited, developed or inverted. We have to chose somehow, ought it be a common language

ni hui ying yu ma?

Could you love that other? Could I love without "I"? Could it be a breath suspended by the challenge of the gulf?

•

Dear Alain,

I'm an unbiased weirdo and everything around me is a big unbiased joke. Forgive my harsh words. I want you. I love you. Come back to me.

Hard stop at irreducible.

•

You say, Alain, that Mallarme, who thinks nothing but is pure form is the epitome of poesie. But you're dead wrong. The poet is who does the terrible task of ranking love, the anchor to your symphony, without which you are merely erection. In short, I am too good for you.

A dieu,
Kati

•

ARE YOU FUCKING KIDDING ME ALAIN? LOOK YOU FUCKING TOAD, I TOOK ABSTRACT ALGEBRA. I HAVE A DEGREE IN PURE MATHEMATICS, AND I'M FUCKING TELLING YOU, LOGIC ISN'T EVERYTHING. DON'T TELL ME IM BEING BLOODY IRRATIONAL, YOU GODDAMN DENSE ACADEMIC. I'M LEAVING. DOES IT HURT NOW? IS THAT REAL? WHERE IS THE TIMELESS HEART IS IN YOUR STUPID FUCKING SET THEORY? CIRCUBSCRIBE THAT YOU FRENCH TOAD.

FUCKER.

•

YOU COULD ONLY LOVE A SQUARE.

LITERALLY.

•

Affair #2

Slavoj,

How lovely to meet another Slovene here in New York. A rarity indeed, and you

are delectable.

Drinks, tomorrow? I'll bring my earplugs. X, k

•

Alain,

If the superficial is all irrelevant in the face of love then who gives a damn about form anyway. I mean, yea, poets aren't supposed to work out but can you still hate my tight thighs for provoking what ain't real love just lust? Not sayin, just sayin. I mean, what does that matter in the middle of the sea except you're drowning and I'm kicking. Yea. I'm kicking. So yea. Whatever. It's all just set theory anyway.

PS I'm busy. I gave you my under but you could not understand it. It is not understandable. You couldn't see my psyche kneeling on the floor? Swimming in an ancient song of Sappho? It's not a poem. It's where poems spring from, dear.

•

Alain,

Dear. It's not exactly in the moment of the Greeks. I use this as a directionality to point you towards the fact that the sensation is not of this time. It is not in fact, of any time. It is a place where time does not exist, or even words, only perhaps contradiction or a slow lethargy. It's rather unnamable, really. If you don't sense it, you don't sense it. That's all, really. Sorry.

Cheers, K

•

Dear Diary,

Choosing between the collection of afterthoughts and the tautology of conjunct tautologies.

I want the swimming pool. All these pricks can do is pose and posture. That's it?

Julian…no he can't let go. Someone will snipe him.

Xo, me

•

The thing is, Alain, you can know everything a person thinks and still have no idea what they're thinking.

•

Dear Diary,

Of course he returns! Now, that I've turned my head!
How logical --

x, k

•

Dear Alain,

I suppose you've mapped sociality like a chessboard. But I'm
mercurial, at best. A single phrase - energy illuminations. I'm
addicted! I worry not because things won't be alright, but because
things won't be perfect. I worry we'll seep apart. Not our legs
or minds, our souls, dusty with un-worried un-care. After a
million days dust becomes a chemical thick compound coating
ancient cave paintings filmed polysyllabic by Herzog. Worry is
cleaning our etchings. Pay attention. Feed us always. So we aren't
a museum, but always real. I know I shouldn't use that word. I'm
dusting us. Because I care. Because I love you.

Love,

Me

•

I am here to ask for your protection. To provide space for
my attempts at the avant garde. My future does not look like
yours. My future looks like hurricanes and tornados and mass
displacement. And if not mine then my children's, certainly. I
don't have time to consider the timeless future of modernity's
progress. I wish I had the strength of Pythagoras and the Gods of
Achilles to dream into the horizon as you do. I love your work. I
admire its beauty. You are the horizon, infinite. Golden on silver
shimmer.

But I have to think of what we might preserve. I plan for what
should be remembered; what values; what vibrations of harmony
and love need float when apocalypse hell comes for the children.

Simplistic and provincial. What would the future be without
provincial? It's as idyllic as anything. You are, I communicate.

That is the difference. I am asking for your protection. Not from the people but so I may go to the people. Humbly, I hope you will consider my request

With all due respect

With all due respect of work thought, imagined, forged and impassioned. Do not regret your beliefs now. Work is work. And all work for all segments is equally valid. Protect me as your own or show the true ranking you believe in: one is better. I do not want to corner you, but must. Do you only believe in the best, or do you believe in all who work?

Love, Katy

•

Slavoj, darling,

I must send my regrets. I'm missing my earplugs, so I can't make it tonight. I hope your flight back tomorrow will be safe, swift, and in first class so – not a chatty annoyance around.

Your brilliance sparkles too too much for mere mortals! Dommage, le coco n'est pas possible cette fois. A la Slovenie !

Poslovite!

•

Dear Alain,

Meow. Come, be cliché. Square checked placemat, the table set for two, candlesticks sans cobwebs, crystalline sweet peas. Nonsense poignantly gestured across the universe, en français des siècles, not Napoleon or la cimetière but ours. Whiskey, or wine. Your mind against mine. Nonsense when the gulf chasms. Softly, where the wet gathers. Hard into the under. Worlds open where our lips meet. This you feel. Come inside to the nothing-everything.

Philosophers of your generosity should breathe multiplicity. The Greeks believed that beginning with Eros led to hell. I think of Juarez. It was Agape, Philia, then Eros the ideal. We have all three. Come, tonight!

•

Dear Alain,

That was good.

Lv, k

•

Dear Alain,

For you, baby? Rules.

1. Avoid the void.
2. Always act to preserve and maximize the other's psyche.
3. I tell you how I feel, you console me, I wet, we make love.

Oh, and please be on time.

What else is there?

love, k

ps, A, 69 pages~

•

Dear Alain,

Your own rules irk you? Touché. I enjoy the less structured anyway. Shall you admit 50 shades of capitalism, S&M, Sartre? Isn't philosophy a scheduled distribution of power?

Sorry, I'll be good.

They say in the next life the philosopher is a dancer. I say in the next life the poet is a janitor. Will you come with me?

I'm with whiskey. Would you like some?

Love,

"There is some sense in Plato's project of crowning the poets in order to send them to exile…It is because poetry propagates the idea of an intuition of the nothing." — A.B.

$$k_2 + a_2$$

"My soul cannot be the object of my judgment and knowledge; much more are my judgment and knowledge the objects of my soul." — Carl Jung

Alain, dearest,

I know we can't say these things out loud because love is best a secret. But this is a letter. I know how you like it. and why. Because the terror and pain of the world are so great, we owe it to be peaceful and beautiful aesthetically and never say a foul-toned word. replace with (owe is not the word but there is no word for this kind of required giving) but Opposition? to be a monk.

You fair well. You write constructively in an age of deconstructive destruction, a beach ball on Omaha Beach. Where once there was blood and ocean. Bastions and leagues. What you fear I will say is that I am the ocean and blood.

Love is thinking for two (+). The world is multiplicity. You grow our views towards the best of mathematics: structure, order to embrace and sustain a peace where violence isn't necessary and terror isn't known, and we can drink table wine, goat cheese, gruyere, tarte au framboise, tartare au boeuf con salade, des crepes, comme ca. Work in peace, all in peace and plenty in a life idyllic until the Utopia arrives we resist by being these things to preserve them. We are what we wish would be because if we aren't they will disappear. And who will know after the

Reckoning what to strive for, what to fight for, what to preserve
if no one remembers what love is? It's a bourgeois sensibility:
honesty, sweetness, simplicity, calm, small things. Greatness
in small things. Because hell, gentle should be the normative
state! And anyone who would smash down with wagging finger
and drooling spit-up "rar how boring" well how then, without
the small, should Marxist society converge to thrive? I'd like to
see it work without honesty and generosity. We'd all steal each
other's rice. Moreover, for those who fight and fight and fight
for the space to breathe! We must fight for them but we must not
complain at what we enjoy. Imagine how crass! Stand next to the
man who has nothing and tell him how terrible your life is. How
terrible your iPhone and nearly brand new clothes you got at the
thrift store for an hour's work. Say it out loud? Yes. Structurally
abysmal. And abysmally worse for many. But Joie de Vivre must
live! Gratitude must live! Those without say, if I may not, may
you. And we must, for them, remember the stars are free for all.

The real is what we need if everything is gone.

●

Dear Alain,

I thought we were talking about how i relate to the movie. but
alas...it becomes something else, a philosophy that is above
my head. Though I do try. Yes, the letters are false. They are an
artifice. It's a romance novel of a sort. Aware of itself and self-
critical of its selfness. You're right. I'm terrible at life because I am,
too political. Very much so. Poetry is, as you say, my attempt to
escape. I loathe the political view, because, it is terribly tedious.
Terribly so. As for believe versus imagine...yes i am an idealistic
nincompoop. i wont let go of the rubric.

The rubric, by the way, is never break a heart.

Yours, K

●

Well Alain,

You are the man of multiplicity. I suppose I assumed you wanted
to learn my singularity.

Oh you want me to speak of "my true inner self". Well my "true inner self" is composed of a catalogue of failures. My "self", my lesser self, is full of the small delights I take in refusing myself those failures. I suppose you can choose which you prefer.

xo, k

•

Dear Alain,

I always feel a glow, the best, when I confess to you and you say "no" and explain to me why I'm wrong. There's there there. It's the last thing. Integrity of learning. It's not commodified. No power. No help or hospitality, a glow.

•

Dear Alain,

We talk every day. But late in the idle evening, so rarely it comes, a blue moon, I consider how you course through my veins. I think history is a sensation I feel when suspended from mundanity in change. An aeroplane completely alone in my head. Life is worry, trivial, he said she said, gossip and details. History the prism flying into the next phase of a consideration. Fate on a graham cracker. Don't ask me why. It's life in a freezer. Stolen from the bliss of simplicity.

Importance an oil rig jigged up by the media. Dunno a poetic term for media. Clowns would be excruciatingly polite. So banal to speak of the evil, I'm embarrassed for Hannah Arendt to invoke her saying.

But that's power. So I redefine it. I love my friends. That's it.

Charles Olson interests me. Meg Ronan read him in my bathtub once. It was annoying at the time, was tired, wanted to sleep. But of course now, among my favorite moments. Profoundly unprofound. You know, lovely. Well, it was also glamorous as hell. But the profound moments are necessarily contaminated. This was cooking and nothing-everything.

So, poetry in a bathtub…

Yours,

•

Dear Alain,

Uhg. What's wrong? Le monde. Let's move to a cave in Nepal.
No. To a desert in Addis. No somewhere less cliché. Let's ascribe
meaning based on what a small set of relatively meaningless but
self-important people proclaim to be relatively bougie. So no, we
can't move to a cave in Nepal. A hole on Mars? That's so outré in
New York. So unmeaninged and escapable. Let's write and write
and write to create new layers of meaningless escape from what
has become our most recently meaninged hell. Away with us.
Let's go.

No emotions here.
K

•

Alain,

Sure, whatever tautology you said-not said. Yes, right, I'm being a
snarky sarcastic bitch, impossible to connect with. Sure. What you
said, lonely.

K

•

Yes sir.

•

No it's not yes sir. It's everything. Life, life, we could do so much
for each other and we sit around playing power games of suck
who's dick and when and how and how long and don't say
anything and you have but I don't and there is never any sense
of ok, I'm here, it's ok exactly as it is and sure let's share and be
peaceful. Society is a race of gain to offset loss, which is greater,
and worse and never discussed and compassion considered a
crime of the weak. My fucking god. I know you think this too,
we're lefties, and then we all go do lefty things and treat each
other like republicans. It's an act. An act of art to devote oneself
to mercy and I've devoted myself to you, and you are the only
one I can write to, can be so honest with. I'm going to try not to
fear to lose this but just be grateful that it is and is now and has

been at some point and thank this life for the miracle of that.
Wonder. Wonder is the only thing that gets me by. I have no
idea how you live without Hallmark Cards. Well, your theory on
love, I must be honest is. It is dear. What of love of one for three?
Or love of one for n+1? Agape. Yes. Hehe. No not like that, you
boy. Interminable! You see this conversation is literally a mold.
Ready made. I'm not bored though. How could I reject all 99
per-zillion-per-cent of the conversers? Actually, it's just my local
community at this point in time-space I would reject. The serious-
girl comment follow boy joke follow girl eeeeee. Cave men? The
universal "we're on equal planes"? Who all does it mean what
to and when and where? I give up. The point is, the point was,
Hallmark Cards. Because I'm saying, I love them. Patterns. I don't
love asymmetry. I stand and stare, etc. But I don't love it. How
could I feel anything at all? It doesn't remind me of anything? Bah
the derivative hole. The derivative hole. Want New to escape, take
the derivative until it gets to the irreducible form. Repeat with
varying polynomials. Singularity. Art. Philosophy. Derivative
hole. I don't think it's a coincidence that in English derivative is a
dirty word. Derrida collapsed the derivatives market. I know, it's
hysterical, isn't it. My dear, I'm going to really insult you now, but
I think you've become integral. As have I. You said it's the look
in Robespierre's eye that births philosophy. It's true. Empiricism.
Empiricism's relationship to Empire? Integral. Art, derivative.
Why do I insult you? Why do you like it? It's so formulaic. You
like formulas, I know. So you can think. I know. Me too.

Goodnight,
k

•

Obsessed? Oh yes. I'm rather evangelical about it. I'm sure you've
found my pattern by now. It's computers and the lack of empathy.
Lack of hospitality of a relatively secure society. Contrary, where
tragedy has been humans learn to share. Where I grew up its buy
buy buy mine mine mine. They say it's the marketing, and sure,
but it's also stability. Thus, over-built structure. Buying is a clean
line in the sand. Who helps is a debt to repay. Where everyone's
in debt up to their cultural revolutionary gut baskets, why keep
track? Just help. Know pain? Know giving in equal measure,
if you've known love. Always offer food. Ni chi le ma? Simple.
Love is simple too. Give because it's the human thing to do. The
ones who don't know what love is. More these days. More Juarez.
More Camden. More me being evangelical.

•

Oh my joke is crass, huh? That's not what you said the other night, tadpole. No, you look like a tadpole when you sleep. Thought, I like it fine. But images and feelings, the transitory. There's too much wrong with thought. It's too limited. It's spherical and impossible. The moment is total in my typewriter, sweet cheeks. As are you. When will the teasing unspool? I'm free tonight.

"THE POEM MUST BE EXCUSED, THE ARGUMENT MUST
BE PRAISED." — A.B.

$$k_3 + a_3$$

" 'PHILOSPHERS', SAYS RIMBAUD, 'YOU BELONG TO YOUR
WEST' " — A.B.

Alain,

Everything OK, integral?

X, k

•

Dear Diary,

The letters fall off. Busy. Fine. One day. Be sated with the thing
itself. Always something more. Timbuktu, money, fame. A
thought process. How conscious. A chapter titled "Infinity and
End of Romanticism". Aiyaiyai

I'm a poet mathematics IS the beginning of romanticism! sigh.

New age, or brooklynite, or elite to believe?

Don't, don't even utter such stupid words. It is the modern who
fail to believe.

X

•

Dear Alain,

What's wrong?! Venus in the 5th house. Ascendant in Gemini
conjunct North Node conjunct Transit of Venus 2004 and 2012.
Helen of Troy. Hera dethroned. Etc. Thought trails phenomena.
You ride. I drag. Choices we've made. You are lucky, dear, that
you don't work with vibe. Non-thought for you is thought, or,
non-thought. Math. I'm an Eskimo on snow re: non-thought. 50
words for intuition: self-catalogued. Not crazy. Convinced. Love,
Jung. Defender. Etc. Etc.

Yours,
k

•

Heroin? I wish. I'd probably be a better writer.

What are you doing to keep you from me?

•

Oh you want to know what I think now? Oh dear. How shall I put
this? In a poem, in play, in a math proof?

•

Well you see my dear, I love your set theory. So I'll use that. I
think that philosophy is the set of all possible thoughts. But not
just thoughts today, but thoughts from all parts of human history.
You see, I love your work, but to be honest it's too linear for me. It
moves in one direction. This is how you say things like "the end
of romanticism", as if romanticism is something past. The truth is,
first, that philosophy is the set of all possible perspectives, but not
just from this moment in time, but from all moments in time.

I think if philosophy, your definition, is expanded to this
definition than so many other thoughts are incorporated and
included. Freudian psychology is one example. For what is Freud
except the attempt to explain that the mind is not just affected by
the present but also the past. He writes of it as if it's mother father
playing games with us, but it's saying at base, I think, that our
histories are our presents, much as we modern's would prefer to
ignore the jests of our pasts.

The design of forgetting the past is so Western Colonial tension to me. And it's not that progress and new forms are in any way subordinate to old forms, but I don't think old forms can be escaped. Even the new form is running from the old form and so in this way is affected by it, for what is the new form without the presence of the old form? The two may be disjunct but they would not exist without each other.

And also, you see the way I conceive of the world is at once traditional and modern. I am creating something new but it builds on the past to embrace the future and the traditional. I like Gauss' projective plane. There infinity is the just horizon but it is also right now. Which is to say that thought and being are not just points on a directional linear trajectory, but that they are sort of a collection of moments which circle back into a complete thing, like a mobius strip no one point being predominant over the other. You might say birth or death begins or ends, but a beginning or an ending do not presuppose directionality in a circle. There are many forms of thought which support the circle view, Hinduism, Eastern concepts of reincarnation, Alzheimer's disease. And to circle back, saying philosophy is the set of all thoughts ever and everywhere, expands on your multiplicity of possible events to go even further to discuss the multiplicity of all possible thoughts and thought systems.

The beauty of this is that it solves the problem of post-colonialism. Which is not just a problem, but a reality. How else does any philosophy not become just a competitor to say an East African tribal thought. They are all philosophy and all truth, to someone. But regional or historical.

But I also believe that thought from all parts of history are valid. To many, there are forms of thought which are distinctly invalid. Thus, the question of evil.

But you see, and I'm getting excited now, the most beautiful thing is that if you follow this logic and use your definition of the New God, as you call it, as some external, unlimited infinity, but you work in the system of Gauss' Projective Plane, then God becomes not something external but exactly being or humanity or the point – the experience – itself. Because we are the infinite plane. Everything alive is the infinite plane. We are limitless. And each moment that occurs is a conjunction of instances, a moment of infinity. Thus each moment of being is God, and the collection of these moments is Being. It's not that we are God. It's that existence itself is God, and as all moments are multiple and

infinitely possible and happening, God is infinite. But not outside.
Here, itself! Like you said!

•

Oh but my dear, what would I do? Go to conferences? They'd
never - I don't have a PhD. And what of my tone! It's much, much
too sweet.

Why does serious have to come in the tone of a math professor?
Are you serious? Come on. Think a little bit, would you?

•

Valid and real. Think about the words you're using!

No, I can't. I was made to play in the fields. And besides. Western
philosophy, the entire corpus of it would never. The line of the
mother made its way to ingrained. It's just Christianity and
Abraham in a straight line. Live in a circle I say. Listen! Central
asian thinkers – Persian or Afghani or whereever depending
on the nation state point in time – and then the Frenchies, and
a bajillion more Hindus. But we are always reduced to poets or
others. Maybe if I write it in math you will fuck me, but sigh that's
probably it. An old idea made new, and still in their same old
prisons. Again and again. Dictatorship of the moderns. Although,
Gauss was very revolutionary. And besides, where would I
preach from, the potty?

•

No of course you should still use the real projective plane.

I'm not saying you're not the set of all sets Alain. Just go up a
field. It's ok to be a subset!

But seriously, if it's not for them, it's not universal. I pray to you
now. You are what articulates my beliefs, to a large degree. But
I speak your Western language. What about those who pray to
Guenon, or Sol, or Sadiq Jalal Al Azm, or Massignon, or Emperor
Khosrau? Does it matter what if it's the event without anxiety?

•

Let's just go to live by the sea. Forget all these overblown beehives
and dissolve. It would be so modern to forget everything and

swim in the lightness of being.

•

That IS the revolution, Alain.

•

FINE I'LL USE THE HARSHER TONES.

YOU ARE SO UGLY.

•

Just don't ever tell me there's no power in what you do. You are tall, strong man who uses serious tones – but don't ever tell me there's no power in the presentation. I know all about form, buddy.

And let me get this straight. Slavoj Zizek is the best, but you're accusing me of contradicting myself? Um human being versus computers… PS Heraclitus?

And I don't hate modernism! It's just singularity… Multiplicity you baguette!

•

Dear Alain,

I'm so sorry. I'm so sorry to be always screaming at you. I realize it is not you I'm mad at, but philosophy.

I've just finished "Philosophy and Desire". I was wet the whole time – no, I'm kidding. It's much more serious than that.

You see I was once Robespierre. I don't know how to say this.

I was in China working for the Revolutionary movement. Competing narratives everywhere and threat to life – mine and hundred thousands millions more. The Chinese government say X is true. The individual wakes up one morning and says Goddamn Y is true. He resists. His wife and family are killed. It's tragic.

All these people daring to stand up and say – no! Y is true! Screw you lying government! And sometimes Y is true only because a single word is there to stand on. Imagine if all these people were plagued by the Derridian, well the word might actually be z, z1, z2, z3, z4...zn+1. How would they ever stand?

Hell. Derrida is hell.

I know because I did it myself. In the end I had to say, I am a singular soul. I am the unique set off all my experiences and I say Y is true and that is all there is.

Fuck Derrida. I'm sorry to hate but he abandoned me. And everyone else except the armchairs. Comfortable cock diddlers.

You. You do not. You write with your heart for "them" not "them". You write for the ones who need something to stand on.

I was a broken Heideggerian poem after all of them. But you. I love you, Alain.

Yours, always,
Katy

•

I love you too. My integral, my builder, my man –

Happy moments do happen, Alain. We must build them every day, as much as we can.

•

Fine. Use field theory. Whatever. Real projective plane is poetic. I know you aren't above poetic tricks, Alain. But yes, the math is difficult. They can all meet at the projective plane. One day.

And my tone? I'm flirting with you, Rabat. To be honest, for all your multiplicity, I'm surprised no one has accused you of being an Islamist yet.

I'm beginning to think that in this fragile world of ours it is revolutionary merely to pass a moment of joy. I worry it will dissolve in all this violence, this capitalism, this displacement. If the truth is a hole, I'm hardly after it. I want to breathe the joy back into it.

I fear we'll forget what it is. And then, what will there be then?

•

Why? I do, of course. I know the process of love is thought, but what is IT? I just know. There's something before the process, a spark, an intuition, a capacity, a talent, an intangible variable, an energy, an attraction, a fate, a folly, a falling, a poem.

More and more you are all I think of. More and more I become you. Look at my language! More you less me. I'm sure you throw some nouns around for the sound of it that you maybe didn't before. But that's process. What is, IT?

I may fail in the process, but I do love you.

Yrs,

•

Childish awe. Womb where the womb is nine months of day dream. Not dripping. Contained. Voidish, you little slut, come here. Ice cubes in cocktails, heavy. Shots if you will but I think they burn. Small in the naval. A knuckle I didn't let go of. Dalmatian cigarettes. The only thing that's formless is God.

"Little by little the contour of a subset of the situation is outlined, in which the eventual axioms of the truth are verified." – A.B.

$$k_n + a_n$$

"The subject of a truth demands the indiscernible."
– A.B

I'm floating.

•

Two parallel lines meet. Alain, at the horizon.

•

Hose Maria Penãta once said to me: leprechauns are the worst kind of enemy. I didn't know it at the time, but he was right. At the time, I thought he was crazy. Leprechauns? Who believes in leprechauns these days? The foolish and the short-sighted, the dreamers and the failures, the peaceful ones whose time strokes the sidewalks like the lull of a back-porch rocking chair.

Penãta was married to a lovely, stout lady named Henretta, not only for her attention to all the details he never imagined, but mostly for the way her surety popped like lazy eggs on a fryer. Once they abandoned the city for a shiny shack with some grass, Henretta made those eggs too, in the kitchen next to the porch while Penãta read the paper on his rocker. Henretta wore an apron stained with greasy time, and articulated her body in swift, short strokes of authority. Penãta listened to her move without realizing it, as he dreamed about the histories long forgotten by the practicalities of daily life. It was a quaint existence, one that permitted the rhythms of time to discuss themselves at length, humming along persistently in ample fashion, taking up the day like a child's awareness of sunshine or rainstorms, a kind of quiet and amused prayer about the simple things in life. Like the beauty of passing time in silent observation.

●

Q.E.D.

●

Dear Alain,

Eventually I'll have to leave. There are no words for why. It's not an event and it's not a death. There is nothing I can say to reassure you. There is nothing I can say to reassure myself. There are no words. I just, I can't be here. I belong, somewhere else.

I will love you.
Always.

I'm sorry.

●

Well then put me back the way Heidegger had us. Dissolve into me!

I don't think so, anymore.

●

Do you want to hear the wretched tone of grief?

How else am I going to drag us out of this hell, unless I pretend it doesn't exist?

Huh, Plato?

And I take your hand in the air. I sing in your ear. We dance, just an awkward little thing enough to have you in my arms and the warmth is enough to banish it all.

Later it's enough to buoy some mathematics. Peaceful thought sans consequence. Being qua being. I consider that if some exist with emotional reactions to numbers, ethical considerations for primes and perfect squares, then math is no longer peaceful. Irrational numbers the imperfect terrible deriddian drain post-modern hell. Inescapable. Platonic form a dog toy we perpetually reach up for only for the wretched owners to pull it away and laugh isn't that dog cute doesn't he love to play?

Everyone likes to think they aren't a crazy lover but the truth is im fragile broken and crying too. The movements I can't bear break me I've been forever broken since. You never broke. Or your shatter was never to break again, to sew it all together. Stitch by precious word. Stitch. O the tapestry you built. A blanket to shelter every soul. And they broke into sticks, poking holes to see the wretched sky. Stars. Weeping through the architecture. Willows fucking in the grass. Poppies on dollars and pipes. Pied. Termites. Loathful eating again into grace dissolution the sea the sound under water the empty push of tears birthing. Dying on your cheeks a tome written there rosetta stone cold iteration endurance $n+1$ to infinity where all parallel lines meet not in our minds in Gauss at the horizon in Revolution in every moment in every moment at every moment ever in pure love

•

We meet at infinity

"THE SADNESS OF THE TRUE CHANGES INTO THE JOY OF
BEING WHEN SEEN FROM CLOSE UP." – A.B.

$$k_{n+1} + a_{n+1}$$

"WHO IS NOT FAMILIAR WITH THE TIRESOME EXHAUSTION
OF SUCH REFUTATIONS, WHICH CAN BE SUMMED UP BY THE
DEPLORABLE SYNTAGM 'YOU DO NOT UNDERSTAND ME'? AN
ENERVATED FORM, WE MIGHT SAY, OF THE DECLARATION OF
LOVE. WHO LOVES WELL UNDERSTANDS POORLY." – A.B.

Dear Alain,

So, I know historicism isn't "true" and this is different from
saying history isn't true – right? So I'll say a thing again
about "this time". Apocalyptic scenarios abound and we've
seen periods of this before, through-out, all over, forget
China, I mean the collapse of the entire Western Cannon.
We'll see about "post" when the Chinese re-write history in
their totalitarian likeness. How's that PhD going for you?
Orientalism a best-seller, the edited version. It is silly to judge
but I will tell you in my love letter, if China takes over, if the
places of free speech dim their lights one by one and the smog
greys my tears…

Anyway, too much for me, I'm going back to stupidity,
seriously. I've been investigating small details with the fervor
of a child's fist over candy. It's the only thing makes my brain
race again, frolic really, in cinematic green fields where there
are no thorns just a canopy of apple blossoms.

Do you cringe?

Oh, I speak as if we were old and married, friends of

comforting non-desire, jokes and long-winded cigarettes.

Perhaps I should have first mentioned sex.

A demain mon cher, dors bien,
Kati

PS I can bear conclusions no more than you,

•

Dear Alain,

But perhaps this will change when I bear children. The idea of timelessness strikes me as an Einstein truth, don't bother me Edith except on Wednesday at these hours. Being/Event/Subject whatever, the child is crying and if I don't clock it will be too late. I'm interested in a cosmology where birth is the center. Smile. I wonder if you are like the other New York intellectuals: you secretly despise feminists because you like it soft and wet and dripping and often. I like it that way too, but it seems there is some logic to the companionship process which eludes me. A friend said there must be a historical justification for my myriad short-term lovers, but that's just poetic exoticism, as recently defined in the DSM V. Either way I admire Manon Lescaut for her wiles. Funny, I can write a love letter to a philosopher, but I'm just as hapless as those broads on Jerry Springer when it comes to "commitment". I supposed it's been a timing thing, blame the stars. Venus in Scorpio. Maybe you'll read this letter.

Yours,
K

•

Dear Alain,

I whisper things to you all day long. At midnight I try to put it into song. Everything I think to say seems inadequate, so I will tell you everything. Pulling memories of lines for you I can see why the love letter is out of style. Gil Scott Heron said, "Fuck a job and money / because I spend it all on unlined paper / and I can't get past / dear baby." Dear Alain.

•

Dear Alain,

The words, Alain. The language around me sticks like glitter.
Did you ever see a middle class, American white girl in
the 90s? She used that glitter make-up once and it stuck for
decades. Now we have Lady Gaga.

Mostly to be less lonely I cling to the myths here around me.
Like Lady Gaga. To say anything other than "people enjoy her
and dance" would be too violent and historical to be true. But
honestly? She makes me outraged with that lyric "you and
me could write a bad romance." The whole country listens to
this stuff. No wonder the best congressional orator is sarcastic
Steven Colbert. No wonder we're crazy.

•

Dear Alain,

You take me out of the intimate, out of the tribal, away from
myself to a communion with the farthest souls. For to speak
of a truth is not to speak at all of you or me or us, but of all of
us, most importantly the ugliest. I preach too much. Only I
wish to say that reading you puts me in a glass case of looking,
where I am small against it all. I think it's called alienation.

For you, I'll forgo all the details. Like the hot rollers, deep red
nail polish, four collared coat and bourbon cocktails on a first
winter's eve in crisp air tasting anxiously of snow. It's cold
here, and I feel the time pass, restlessly, though events seem to
be passing right under my nose. Barack Obama is less than a
mile away, but we all feel so helplessly disinterested. My coat
is a much prettier subject of affection, like my loose curls and
rouge talons.

X, k

•

Dear Alain,

It's still unclear what happened during that year of my life.
Or later, two years after. Or now, the past five. Finding a

vocabulary to put it all together…that's a courage I've barely time for, in an age when the personal narrative is pointillist, at best.

E^-2ipi=1? I think if there is the square root of negative one, my divagations into the realm of intuition must be meaningful. Sometimes I know things without saying them.

Tonight, for example? You'd like it sunny side up.

•

Dear Diary?

Can he even see me if I don't believe in thought? If I don't believe in making sense? All that I've written, can he even hear?

Whatever. Lollipops.

•

Argh! Stop with the set theory baby I want to know the difference between how you love me and how you love your wife versus how you love a random peasant in Bolivia versus how you love Humanity. Is that a homomorphism? I want to know how it feels. I want to know what you would do for me that wouldn't do for peasant X. Is each letter to me, each of your thoughts a drop of love in my lap? But how many times do you write Slavoj each day? I want more. You keep coming. That's not mercy; it's arousal. What is IT? Tell me something about the indiscernible.

•

Dear Alain,

It's difficult to get through dinner saying only "true" things. Imagine a conversation where sarcasm and other inefficient superfluities are illuminated. And if the cannon is the bar? Only geniuses would speak. Therefore, one must endure and enjoy stupidity. Fini.

PS Fuck philosopher kings!

Corrollary? Even philosophers much have jokes and flaws and unnecessary comments.

Note: Love your flaws Alain.

·

Dear A,

Normally I wait for the wind to blow to write, but here we are generating on the clock. Its part magic carpool ride and part practicing balancing a dime. I've been thinking on your poles of philosophy and mallarme. When you speak of this symbolist and proto L=A=N=G=U=A=G=E poet as a pole, I hear several principals – the pieces of the words which make us, the rhythms that sustain us, the symmetry we strive for, and that magic potion emotion which eludes our control, makes us human, if you'll kindly accept my definition. I've heard it said that the only truth is that we are completely hollow and seeing this idea to completion leads one either to philosophy, poetry or the convent. You praise the poet's solemn, lonely stature. In a paraphrase "it cries to no one. It is alone. Shares with who will come. Like a stirring wheat field."

·

Dear Alain,

I wanted to take a walk, see something new, find something to quench the thirst in my mouth. It wasn't a taste so much as a texture I was looking for. I settled on sweet sour pickles. Don't be jealous, I'm not pregnant.

I'd been so busy dancing with the mash. Sigh, socializing. If you wear make-up too long you forget what your face looks like. I wanted to let go of everything, and by that I mean pull my energy back into myself, a familiar memory of life where there is nothing to remember except my own selfish narrative seen as a little girl laughing at adult stupidity, knees to her chest on the front steps.

I wanted out of the immediate moment, wanted the cold air of remembering it won't always be this way, that I'm in love with time before I'm in love with anything else. I wanted to see, think like a parent, looking down with wise eyes.

There is this other state where time is a temper tantrum, a cloud of ants burrowing in my shoulders, anxiety organizing my forces before the computer screen. Automated directives, if you will. Makes me crabby and bossy, pretending to be in control. I guess all we really own is what we tell ourselves, but I still pay my bills and discuss the price of rent.

I wonder if you still have personal philosophies or if you've put them all in some professional form. I wonder if you take mine with tea and a bit of sugar, and if you mind leaves the axiom-checker on hold for a charmed moment. When I was little I dreamed of a boy who would love my ideas. I guess you just dreamed of ideas, if you dream at all. In a way it's more fitting for you not to dream, for you are structure, and I am the undefined, reminding the metal to melt sometimes. Thank you for reminding me to think. Beyond the sense. Cause besides you, my evening was cold, sweet, bread and butter chips. Fresh from the refrigerator. Slightly red pepper. Crisp. Juice. Smooth, well, slightly ribbed.

Love, K

•

Dear Alain,

It's cold here. Snowing all day. Cinnamon sticks and cider sounds good to me. What I mean to say is your tender hyper sensitivity, candle in the bathroom, racing words during indecision, calm stubborn, your glaring intransigence, brazen unadorned touch, my noah's flood as only with you, the played wet between us, is is

Soon.

•

Dear Alain,

My sexuality has always seemed more isolating to me than anything. And when it does awake it terrifies me. One day it's going to kill someone. It's nearly killed me. Soon I'll be old and grateful to relax into warm conversations whose intent I have less to question. Am I prudish? I'm open to suggestions.

Perhaps a looser sentence would be fitting? Perhaps more words would alleviate the magnets?

•

Dear Alain,

Oh dear. Do you want to use dick and cock and pussy and wet and tree trunk and all that uhg. Uhg. But, darling, that's evil, naming the unnamable. My brain went blank and collapsed in a kaleidoscope. remember nothing, cubes, no words, etch. a. sketch. the source, joy, break it again, break me any time, break me any, any time, darling. But if you must. Juat not those words. They're a prison from the real thing, an aesthetic profanity and, dear, you know how serious I am about the source.

Yours,

•

Alain,

Oh my god you dirty motherfucker. I was serious! God don't go there; I like it unnamable! Tell me what colors you saw or at least more interesting words. It's not the dirt, I like it from behind, I love when you exhasp over my silhouette but damn! the structure of those words! the point is to dissolve –

Boo.
Lv, k

•

So where's your body, Alain?

Subsume your emotions into your dick. Fuck it out, go ahead. Good baby.

As for your ideas about the female position, I'm not even gunna go there. But I like that you are (nothing) in this book.

•

Not pretend or wall or I get something but I see you naked all
your stupid problems and all I want is your stupid eros on my
agape and my stupid thanatos and our stupid eros streaming
in the concept of knowing each other. And steaming after the
period. Then.

I just wanted to see you shake. Because it broke my heart and
it was better than anything that way virgin everything that
way some bullshit langauge about found something of finding
prepositions in a text book you skin had goose bumps your
hair on edge and you swallow help up on my perfection and
I wanted nothing but to be perfect for you. No literary period.
Naked breathe waiting hard terse waiting hard for permission
into soft for more than permission for need for better than
need for natural. For love.

And then oh it was cold unpoetic. Sigh. Exhaust. But it was.
And it was an engaging for this chais was just as good being
insulted to my face because my jacket didn't fit your tribe
and I loved it the tribalism not because its utopian because its
ideal and we huddled in our neuroses they kept us warm they
huddled everywhere most of all where I knew you and loved
you we were warm. That's an idea that keeps my warm. All of
us naked goosebumps hard cock wet pussy with the
skin smooth.

There and then and it happened and it was totally cliché like
the catholics said and I didn't care clascrition fuck them I'm
going to have my making blue all mine cubism music digital
pointillism pick your favorite adjective here literally. That's
it. Pick I'm picking hallelujuah spelled wrong in another
language who gives a hot a guck given here not a panting I
don't negatives the surface the who cares it was you it was you
shimmering and I'll only ever see your shimmer but is it too
poetic to say you came on solid substance wet and it meant
nothing it meant nothing it meant nothing. And I thought
those thoughts again and I thought it meant everything. Or the
grapefruit and I'll go on meaning oh well. I love you that's it
cliché whatever forever. That's it.

And you shook like. I wrote it. in the botes they said
something about concepts whatever all. I. could. Think. But
was your jelly sentence out no periods I put them literally like
you anxiety from the ___ but frat boy for crotch in a
beautiful way

•

Dear Alain,

Naw. I just deconstructed my narrative again.

But you can help me put it back together? I can be Yoshi. You can be princess.

And boo, I'm sending you this book in the mail. *Tender Buttons*. You've read it, right?

"Keep Going! Continue to be this some-one, a human animal among others, which nevertheless finds itself seized and displaced by the eventual process of a truth." – A.B.

$$k_{n+2} + a_{n+2}$$

"The point of being of the nothing, [the] multiple inconsistent whose dream is induced by the non-being of the one." – A.B.

Dear Alain,

Oh so it turns you on to see my death drive? Is this some kind of objectification?

You do realize in my terms this is merely an episode of bad Pluto placement – but I digress. What I mean to discuss is the aspects of your venus –

Lap that up,

•

Dear Alain,

Mercury went retrograde Dec 10th, and does not go direct until Dec 30th and I would like to submit my letters to you towards evidence in the chart of modern astrology. Also, I read Endymion to my friend Megan in the drive from Washington to Cleveland. It was a delightful way to spend an early Christmas Eve! Do you celebrate Christmas? I wonder if these traditions are too conventional for you. There was a time when I would be angry that Christmas is not Christ's birthday but a convenient way for the Christians to eclipse the pagan's winter solstice. It's all political bullshit! And there's always the atheist in me horrified by blind faith, blah blah. These days I figure everyone has faith in something, from philosophy to something more mundane, like electricity. Convention is just as arbitrary as deconstruction, and it pisses my mother off less. (I think we've talked about this already.) Bottom line, I wonder who you spent your holiday with, and if you thought of me.

I won't bemoan it if you did not. I've plenty of daydreaming to do. And there's always facebook to entertain me and ease the loneliness. You won't be the first or last to ignore my advances anyway. One deconstruction I won't let go of, my feminism. I do love the chase.

Since my love for you is so clearly unrequited, I've been thinking, what is the difference between these letters and a public journal like facebook? I wonder if constant social networking is at all effective for making more healthy, relieved human beings. In a psychoanalytic, say-it-get-over-it, kinda way. It seems to be working for the politicians, like a new soma, though it's hard to measure those things.

Do you have time to daydream anymore, Alain? Will you ever retire? Perhaps this is the difference between the poet and the philosopher: you work for years on the next pencil mark of the same blueprint. Sometimes different rooms in different houses, but it's all one building. Poets, roughly speaking, we're sliding around in mud, rubbing it all over our faces, coating the grass with it, clapping our hands and laughing when a little bit of mud flies in the air. Smiling when the rain comes to wash us clean, hating the sun when it dries us to cracking. Like I said, we're at the origin, playing with words like playdoh.

I could have said "playing with words like clay" but I said "playdoh". See the traditional word would be clay but it's my job to use another word, because that clay image has been used before and so it's old or more precisely boring or ineffective. I guess the mature poet knows when to use the same old words for comforting images but in this career the Daoist approach is better when you're already established. See T.S. Eliot. Back to playdoh, there is another argument that says that word playdoh is too American a word, because it is an American brand. Also, it's exclusive to the group of people who can afford and are familiar with playdoh, so it is perhaps shallow. If a poet is going for universal, this word would be a no-no. Maybe aiming for universalism is akin to rooting for a bland, multi-national view of the world. But I think it would be beautiful if there was some poem that made most everyone smile. There's a principle there, besides ambition, but I bet you like it, you and your universal being subject event generic theory. It is an extra challenge picking words if one considers politics or social markers or audience. And then of course, how to stay fresh without only talking about nature images or something, ahem, universal. Especially because you turn this argument around and me writing you letters, you Alain Badiou, exclusive and unknown philosopher who loves the proletariat but speaks to an elite audience... Well now, I wouldn't be a poet if I did not love this contradiction. Good thing you have me because I bet you hate that contradiction. It probably makes you sad, or angry at the state of society, and moreover, it's your job to pull apart knots into straight pieces of rope.

Hang me. In a love can be fatal kind of way –

Merry Christmas,
Katy

P.S. Can you tell? I've got my period. All the sentences! Fitting somehow for a Christmas letter.

•

Dear Alain,

"Love what you will never believe twice"

Yes! Elsewhere fits quite nicely there...it could work...

you really do believe in the slow build and the denouement.

•

Dear Alain,

Oh I've been thinking like you so long I've turned into an old white man with a French cadence. It's sweet.

The paper this morning. "Desperate Global Hunt for Yield."
Housing bubbles, gentrification. I never thought they could
ruin bubbles for me but I can barely take a bath I hate that
word and investors abstractly in a 19th century way. The
rhyme is ruining even my child delight at spherical clear
prisms. Air bubbles. And thought bubbles for it occurs to
me that the worst gentrification is now happening in the
hippest "ethnic" hoods. What was meant to discuss cultural
acceptance became the tyranny of style…so much for human
rights. I'm up with the situation and mine is implicated,
but here we meant to set a trend of inclusion and the
capital followed in intrusion, collusion, subterfusion, forced
submission to a thought, many of them combining in a bubble
– pop – over the actual situation. One example:

How's your coffee?

•

Dear Alain,

How can you stand me? I think through the stars – ancient –
and energies – future – and I take faiths unproven, speculative
judgmental and feeble. I crave them universal but they are
new age or underage or anti-age or rediculage or outrage
or anything but contemporary acclaim acceptable. Your
Capricorn – oof - and my conspiring mind conspiring to go
beyond go farther then we dare to Western now or then and
both combined is what I try for now and who knows what it
will be then - for I reserve the right to always change on a drop
of mercury. You are the beautiful, all your thoughts a slow
chiseled statue for consumption and mine clouds in the sky for
dissolution or a momentary bloom of verse. And when they
are dark or serious STOP, it shan't rain all day, it shan't be
weight forever. HOPE.

If a single word could shatter a prison.

Every poets dream. Is it love? I know it's boring but it's true
because thought blah whatever my heart doesn't give a damn
what the fuck we think. It wants to know how you brush your
teeth and what kind of toothbrush do you use and what are
you wearing a shirt? Plaid flannel tie-waist pantaloons? How
far from the ground? Mid calf because you are too tall? Do
the creases in your knuckles stay after you've left the brush

on the counter and for minute or three? Can I brush your hair
off of your forehead and would you mind? Does your skin
damp late in the evenings? And would you like for me to
notice? Love a catalogue of preferences and kneeling giggling
hallelujah before it. Something not thought at all, better than
segmentation, a thing that melts the thoughts of your beloved
makes them like crayon soft and insoluble to feed and clothe
and satiate and tease and infuriate kindly and play and
sandbox and blindfold and sigh and breathe + wonder + stop +
pulse + calm + agony + small small agony the lovely kind and
come and come again. And again. Utterance. Guttural. Nasal.
No pattern.

You're always using this word finitude and I'm always using
this word source. You call it a condition; I call it a Condition
but who cares what it is, it is. It's as always and infinite and
prescribed as math – cupid putti angel puck. Your language
universal, But I'm talking about the post-proof universal
solvent. Dissolve my everything, take me to winter's pace.
Tell me you need to know about the cuticle on my toenail and
the finest hair on my cheek. To think everything absurd or all
as beautiful as smile. Cause it is and it melts from the thing
aching to melt beyond you or me as other as matheme the
thing we've always had and are always redefining pure
as math

•

Dear Alain,

Fine, in your words.

Yours.

•

The real characteristic of the poetic event and the truth
procedure that it sets off is that a poetic event fixes the errancy
and assigns a measure to the superpower of the intellect. It
fixes the power of the intellect. Consequently, the poetic event
interrupts the subjective errancy of the power of the intellect.
It configures the state of the situation. It gives it a figure; it
configures its power; it measures it.

Empirically, this means that whenever there is a genuinely poetic event, the Intellect reveals itself. It reveals its excess of power, its repressive dimension. But it also reveals a measure for this usually invisible excess. For it is essential to the normal functioning of the intellect that it's power remains measureless, errant, unassignable. The poetic event puts an end to all this by assigning a viable measure to the excessive power of the intellect.

Poetry put the Intellect at a distance, in the distance of its measure. The resignation that characterizes a time without poetry feeds on the fact that the Intellect is not at a distance, because the measure of its power is errant. People are held hostage by its unassignable errancy. Poetry is the interruption of this errancy. It exhibits a measure for intellectual power. This is the sense in which poetry is "freedom". The Intellect is in fact the measureless enslavement of the parts of the situation, an enslavement whose secret is precisely the errancy of the intellect, its absence of measure. Freedom here consists in putting the intellect at a distance through the collective establishment of a measure for its excess. And if the excess is measured, it is because the collective can measure up to it.

We will call it a poetic prescription for the post-eventual establishment of a fixed measure for the power of the intellect.

Oh baby your language is driving me crazy. Not in a good way. I like to melt and I'm totally on edge of melting in to boring explanatory you, ooo.

•

Dear Alain,

I know nothing of being, except that I be here to love.

Oh, totally cute statement which evades the truth. I mean, it hurts to think so deep into the truth it makes my words boring! Uhg! Ok stop, I'm trying not to remember your terms so I can write today. But what I wanted to tell you was my memory of first wanting to meeting you. I never told you…

It was multiplicity inconsistent. Freedom from the oneness. These words are not my own: Mother, Doctor, Father, Neighbor, Grandma, Auntie, Uncle, Neighbor, brother, babysitter, etc. When you are about to call I feel your voice. I think "Alain", as if I can hear you thinking, "I haven't called her today." And then you call. I read too much of you. My poems come out coated with your words, in your rankings, your rhythms, your pragmatic concisions. We think of it differently, I think, but I am not myself, but the collection of all I have ever known or touched. Like Juliana says, we breathe the same air, every being on earth. I hope you don't mind my poetic interpretation. But I agree: One is a useless entity.

I think of it this way: each of us the singular infinite combination of our impressions, our experiences, our loves, our brushes with the universe.

Lv, k

•

Dear Alain,

Uhhhg. Yes Ok. Alright. Let's get technical. Ok. So. Pure being is infinity. Or multiple possible infinities because there are infinite infinities. Great. But in short, pure being is infinity because it can go in any possible direction. The person, or individual, is singular. So I guess what I wanted to say, strictly, about the individual was that they are singular but influenced and created by an infinity of factors, and connections, webs, links, liens, words, breathes and moments to the infinity of other beings they have ever met or read or seen on TV or encountered. You dig? Ok, so, in short, we are singular multiplicities. That is our "being". And Pure being, obviously, is like as multi-dimensional infinite insanity as the Star Trek universe. As for Pure Being = math; sure, whatever you want. I mean, the only thing I can say is that when I read Derrida he always made me have an existential crisis, but when I did math, I could do it for 12 hours straight and come up happy as a clam. Very meditative actually. I think it's very true that math as we know it is pure thought; non-judgmental so to speak, just the purest lines in the sky. Yes, did I see that moment where I could think without words? Absolutely. Think in images, in lines, in pictures in space. Being-Qua-Being? Of course. And as a poet, it's my job to stay in that space. All the time. Pretty great, huh? Are you jealous? Jk. Ok I don't know if you agree with me that poetry is in that space, but I can tell you, that my poetry is from that space.

That knowing beyond language. The great mathematicians say: the difference between a numbers cruncher and the pure mathematician? Intuition. And well, if you know the way to keep that space from descending to the void? Please do tell me. So far, I've only consulted Carl Jung and everyone else I know. Are they connected? I think the void, for me, is what I saw when I was forced by politics to be completely rational. I never want to ever be there again. Because all I could see was the hopeless.

Love,
k

•

Ms. Bohinc,

You always have to be on top.

Yours, Alain

•

Alain,

I will be the bottom the wall the washing machine

•

Aries.
*
Hehe. I like horoscopes. You know what's nice about them? They're equivalent. I mean, I've seen bad horoscopes, but I mean everyone has one. If you assume all cultures are equal lens, like India, China, Sudan, France, Ancient Greece, wherever, then I thought I would try horoscopes for a while, to take a trip and learn a new set of cultural mores, social standings, rules and regulations, if you will. Anything to get out of America. Uhg. America is like that guy at the bar who is in his mid 30s or 40s and hasn't dated any one in while, just fucked for the past five years, and has started to see things as a) alpha, b) beta, c) gamma all based on hot, medium, ugly – "but you, you're different" – UHG! I could kill him with a kitchen knife! That's capitalism, always surface ranking. But horoscopes, what a pleasant divide. The busboy could have

the sweetest chart you ever saw. The president a mass of
jungle fucked oppositions. There are always eight planets and
twelve houses at play. So instead of boring labels - "middle
aged, loveless douchebag" or "beautiful young thing" or
"rich" or "poor" or dominant American culture "high, low,
forgettable" – SO BORING - instead I read a chart and get
this complex system of complex adjectives which beyond
alleviating my thirst for complexity also seems leveling. Each
chart has a complex personality. You know, like a human
being. Of course "hierarchical aspects" remain – the tenth
house is fame or ambition or social standing, for example.
But it's always paired with other considerations like water,
air, fire or earth personality, dreamer, pragmatist, energetic
or staid. And where the mind sits versus where the heart
sits, versus where the energy sits, versus where the Neptune,
Uranus, Pluto or Saturn sits. Oh yum. Plus then I can pretend
I'm living in the middle Ages, or Greece or Early Syria or the
Fertile Crescent. You know medicine was based on astrology
until the Middle Ages! Like for a stomach ache on the left side
that's the liver which is ruled by Taurus so take these pills
on Tuesday – the Taurus day – at 2 AM when the moon is
strong and at quarter strength. It would make me irate today,
but everything makes one irate or is causing cancer anyway,
what's the difference if it's from the Middle Ages. Luckily the
Middle Ages, seem so far off that I only vaguely imagine the
hard labor, mud, lack of toilet paper, short quick fucks in the
sidestall on rank breath and stinking boots. All my images
from Hollywood. But I would like to really go there. Should I
re-read Beowulf? I want to see the sparks flying off the knives
as they sharpen in the street the metal workers and a big
grand un female fire. Not the social dynamics. The soot and
the ledger.

Oh dear you should like them too, horoscopes, come to think
of it. They are a lot like set theory. Or the multiplicity of sets.
And each soul's singularity.

Dear, let's not be star crossed lovers

"Is thought obliged to endure Thermidorean frameworks of its own Ruination?" – A.B.

$$k_{n-1} + a_{n-1}$$

"Evil…is to want, at all costs and under condition of a truth, to force the naming of the unnamable" – A.B .

Cultural revolution and killing fields and the holocaust that's what is it to kill by category but to kill for thought and this is wrong because it breaks hearts and only love doesn't make the mistake of thought and death by it because love is blind as surely my shoulders are blind to anything but loss over these thoughts I've come up against these thoughts…

•

It is not violence. It is not violence. I saw the best of my generation raving hysterical naked it is not violence the best of my generation raving hysterical naked it is not violence it is not violence it is not violence I saw the best of my generation raving hysterical naked how do you think they got that way it is not violence it is not violence I saw them shot I saw the boy forced to shoot his brother I saw the wife and the child shot, axed, tortured, burned, slain, slaughtered, raving hysterical naked I will commit no violence if I live to do one thing I will commit no violence I will leave no man raving hysterical naked I will heal I will leave no one in pain I will leave no man raving hysterical naked I will not be violent and when I die I will say one word I lived my life in justice and that is all no one near me broke before my knowledge without a handful of cups and bandaid fragment utterances the best I could do. And violence begins with the broken tone don't forget that words are violent too and I will be silent before I am violent to you, ever, you watch your words Monsieur Badiou, you watch your tone, you are, you are violent too, sometimes, offhand, you forget, you fill with yourself. No violence. No violence of the universal, no violence no raving hysterical naked nothing but the lyric I and ears. I understand but i disagree. No violence. Love is what bleeds through and swamps your philosophy. And pain too. but forget that forget it for. get. it. love love love before we forget that too love love love love love love love love love love love love love love love did you ever meet someone who doesn't know what love is? IT is not violence. IT is love. Teach them love. Teach them all love. It's as impossible as anything good rising from the ashes of blood.

•

FUCK YOU.

BUT I SHOULD BE INTEGRAL AND THINK LIKE YOU. LEAVE

CANT

Love is more than a thought. Love is more than what you think. Love is more than ideology. Down with ISMS. DIDN'T YOU LEARN ANYTHING FROM THE CULTURAL REVOLUTION?

I know what you think. I CANT BEAR IT. SHOULD I KILL YOU?

NOTHING CAME FROM THE CULTURAL REVOLUTION EXCEPT THE MEMORY OF OUR THEORIES their drowned failures RAVAGE RAVAGE RAVAGE ENEMY the END OF LOVE THE TORTURE OF LOVE THE TORTURE OF THINKING TWO AS ONE TORTURE OF THINKING TWO AS ONE they all thought TWO AS ONE they thought TWO AS ONE AND TWO AS ONE AND WHAT DOES EVERYONE AROUND ME THINK

BUT IT WAS PARANOIA IT WAS FEAR IT WAS DEATH IT WAS FEAR IT WAS DEATH IT WAS TERRIBLE TOO TERRIBLE FOR WORDS TO UTTER IT WAS THINKING AS

OTHERS CONSTANTLY CONSTANT OTHER CONSTANT
OTHER CONSTANT OTHER SAY THAT A MILLION TIMES
BEFORE YOU SLEEP EACH NIGHT CONSTANT OTHER
CONSTANT OTHER CONSTANT OTHER

SAY THAT A MILLION TIMES BEFORE YOU SLEEP AT
NIGHT CONSTANT OTHER CONSTANT OTHER

ALL WORK AND NO PLAY MAKES JACK A DULL BOY
CONSTNANT OTHER CONSTNAT OTHER CONSTNT
OTHER

THINK AGAIN, ALAIN. THINK AGAIN. Think again in
terror. Not in sadness not in fear not in tragedy in terror. In
terror and sadness, fear and tragedy every day every moment
for six or seven or eight or more years. Think again until you
cannot think any more. Until you cannot think of what another
wishes except with fear. Or, "I Hope" "Be Well" and that is
all. That is as far as thought will take you. Because after that
thought there is too much pain to go on, to do anything but go
to bed or take account of the dishes or the ledger or anything
as dry as dry as dry as anything that doesn't make you cry.
Think again Alain. You have no idea.

The Cultural Revolution didn't break the bonds, it turned the
bonds to kryptonite. Put a cigarette out on someone as you
walk down the street. Watch a car explode and burn them
alive. Don't stop. He's pissing you off, pop.

THINK AGAIN IN TERROR MAYBE YOU WILL
UNDERSTAND. NOT IN SADNESS NOT IN FEAR NOT IN
TRAGEDY IN TERROR.

*

YOUR HUMANITY FUNCTION IS BROKEN!!!

•

Dear Diary,

The skin is peeling off my back, from the nape of my neck
through my shoulder blades. In bile I trust. I write to
pronounce to flake the skin off these words to dry the wound.
That was a real sentence. The sentences will be real until there
is no longer a chance. I can still go back.

I can't believe he could think that. The pain of it will always
ring in my ear each lecture from his throat. The dripping erotic
that was the sound of home the sound of still water or rock
or soft mellow and now it's just electric fucked because it's
all a lie. To propagate that thought. The evil of it. He's such a
fucking human being. Which would be fine except I just can't
bear to hear him sort through my thoughts de-kinking them
and kicking each one until it's his, limp, begging on the floor,
and me sitting there knowing that if his blood ever dared run so
warm to bleed into his brain he would collapse at the pain of it
all. Oh his ideas his dreams. Can I bear it?

And what of me? Who am I to speak, I who say fuck the ideas,
there is only the floating poem. That the sentences, even the
math will all amount to nothing in the absolute cruelty of
the mess of the human, and no amount of literature or Greek
tragedy or attempts at anything will save us from ourselves.
Or some of us might save ourselves, and some of us do try, but
what of the rest, there's no hope for all the rest for so many of
us, so many who already do not know love. Shall we slaughter
the loveless? Kill those messy souls; eliminate them from our
wretched plan. Like I eliminate Alain? Who am I to run away?

Oh he made a fancy rubric good for him. It's just a fucking
fancy rubric. You always said love was greater than any
architecture. The blood in the spreadsheet and here you are
saying love isn't big enough to seep through this grand cross.
No not big enough for this. Not big enough to seep through.
Your body doesn't seem to care. Your heart doesn't give a
damn it's radiating through you shoulder blades, shimmering
scalding blue.

And isn't this precisely the lesson of the cultural revolution,
the one we must never never never never learn again the one
we must always remember and take everywhere and preach
everywhere and never ever ever ever ever learn again, that
thought is nothing thought is wretched, thought is nothing
nothing nothing compared to the heart, compared to pain
compared to the tragic the wretched wretched of wretched
and there should be love above all above all else because only
love can stop and be greater than the war of words or ideas or
categories because it can seep through and it does seep through
and our categories will never be big enough and if we kill by
them if we decide by them we will always murder and delete
and love is the only anecdote. There is no category in love.

Maybe that's the point; the categories are still there, still
sensed. The loss, the pain is that you couldn't overcome with
him. Couldn't seep into that nothing-everything. And now
it's wretched.

•

Dear Alain,

I won't get mad. I won't. I'm fucking trying here. I won't
give you that pleasure. I won't call you mother fucker. I
won't scream. I won't "give you that part of me I won't give
anyone else". What you don't understand, is I am the genius
of creating another home. Another world where screaming
doesn't exist. It's me, this is what I am creating. You don't have
to love me for it. It's not even sweet. It's probably another form
of terrible. But this is the rubric you must confine to. This is
where I stand.

•

I'm talking about love im talking about something that wakes
me up and night and ravishes me for you and it's not it has
nothing to do with thought I couldn't think my way into you I
can't think my way out of you I can only think a million ways
why everything is wrong but I still love you I still throb I still
wake up and think of you think right think wrong I think only
of you and that's not from any thought that's thought trying to
keep up with the heart

I love you.
Me

•

You said poetry is fucking elsewhere so how can you see me if
love is thinking for two and you fucking think I'm elsewhere?
It's just a fucking paradox we can't work out if love is thinking
as two. So it's not. And all the other things we disagree
about. Or your definition of poetry is wrong. OR FUCKING
SOMETHING IT'S NOT WORKING OUT IN FUCKING
THEORY.

•

Dare I say it? You're all fucking wrong. The best of what we are: lovers stuffing mud in the inevitable fissures, cracks, splinters, fractions, irrationally repeating decimals, holes, gaping, schisms, shatters, frayings, frictions, failures, errors. I am not perfect. You are subordinate to art, philosophe. You are subordinate to history, to reality, to parables, to metaphor, to pain, to injustice, to inevitability, to tears and to life. There is no solution to this condition. There is morality. There is prayer. There is weeping kneeling god fuck me I am fucking sorry and grateful for my existence and I will try to make this wretched life so little better as I can. For you, for me, for everyone I touch.

•

Dear Alain,

This birthday is the first to make me say, "I hate birthdays." I have been feeling intensely the deep weight and frigid chill of ice in my veins – the creeping, raging sense of failure.

I have to deal with my life. I cannot do this with you in it. I thought I could. I would have loved to take up Philosophy and logic and Paris. Maybe start an orphanage in the banlieues when you retire. I've always dreamt of an orphanage.

But we are both too slow and too crazy. And too hard and too obsessive. I have to deal with my life now. Part of the sense of failure related to having chased you for so long. I know you do not believe me, but I do love you with an intensity I have never before experienced. When we make love, I cry, not because I am in pain, but because I am in love. Silly you has never seen this in a woman before?

You said your new project was honesty with Katy I wanted to slap you. But I am not surprised. I've always known you held deep relationships wherein the others bonded but you did not. This is a kind of lie I detest. Particularly in a man whose life is "truth". I will not regret the time I spent with you ever. I will only testify that there is a kind of desire that made me insane and forget all else, the kind of desire that has been written of for years and ages. I don't owe you any of this and I should not even be honest with you – you took my heart and held it dripping, licking the blood with the sweet language of your mind, but not your heart, and not your honesty. I do not respect you, but I will always love you. I was "not like the others" you were more, by many times, of any of the rest. Take this as truth. Take my insanity.

I've got to go write some poems.

•

Fine you wanna go there? You're just a tool. I have no respect for you. I hope they buy my book because a boring white man is involved.

I don't even remember how to be artful anymore; your desert is suffocating and your cultural revolution is ignorant mis-infinity anti-calculation on the scale of Rumsfeld. Dry out for this? Are you fucking kidding me? The sex isn't even good. You can't melt. I hope you're crying. I hope you cry and feel the abyss. You might know an ounce '68-'76, and maybe you have a fucking inkling of the terror your thought Thermidored into.

•

What YOU'VE GIVEN!?! MY LANGUAGE! You stupid fuck. I've grown boring and stupid and self dribble sitting around with your old man white ass. You don't understand anything except the professional lovely and the perfectly argued proof, please you infinity dries me up inside. And all this sacrifice for what, for you who think the cultural revolution is an interesting thought experiment? Uhg I want to vomit on your wrinkles. Everything is just a thought experiment to you, isn't it. I'm just a thought experiment to you! What's it like to be with a poet? Tell me? How is it? My heart, and a billion Chinese just a thought experiment to you? Murder, just a practice at breaking bonds? You're a piece of shit and the banality of that insult suits you.

STOP I cant fucking breath here I have to go.

•

FUCK YOU AND YOUR BREAKING BONDS ALL WE HAVE IS BONDS THAT'S ALL WE FUCKING HAVE AND IF THAT MEANS I CANT HAVE TRUTH THEN I DON'T. FUCKING. WANT. IT.

Look I went for the Joycean fucking departure and there's
a reason why Ulysses is all about Dublin. I went to the
revolution numbed my bonds to kelvin left them with
language at the door of progress and I am a fucking militant
too. I fucking am. But it's not what you say. It's that we can do
better than what you say. We can do it with love too.

Now stop, my fucking heart is breaking.

●

HOW CAN I BE IN THE MOMENT IF YOU WILL NOT GET
THE FUCK OUT OF MY FACE?

DON'T WORRY DARLING, DEATH IS MERELY A
WORLDLY PRINCIPAL OF STABILITY.

●

There was nothing interesting about it at all. Nothing. It didn't
free people from bonds it destroyed the capacity to bond. You
can still see it today there isn't a place like it on earth. Maybe
Angola. You can't fucking think that Alain. Love is a condition
on your politics.

You can't fucking write that. It's breaking my heart to write
this. This truth.

Now stop. We can do better. We must.

So it is that the defeat of the ethic of a truth, at the undecidable point of a crisis, presents itself as a betrayal." — A.B.

$$k_{n-2} + a_{n-2}$$

"Ultimately what true politics undermines is the illusion of the bond" — A.B.

And I understood your language, down to the scraped layer of cake. If cake was as good as hearing your words all over again and again an avant eruption of noise each frag reborn

Dear Alain,

I'm here in DC, before the White House. There are arguably 500 people here all in solidarity with Turkey. Terrific for the humid and generally humid brained Washington. And of course I can't stop crying. I don't even know these people and must look like a clown. I think it's OK for poets to cry. We must cry for all of us.

How many here have family in Turkey who faced a tear gas canister and walked away dripping chalky bleeding thoughtless spined-forever in a way it might our blessing not to be. I hope the Children lay always supine and silly. No need for needing to steel. That's not infinity. But how it begins. It doesn't matter. What matters but the large heart beating as one. To say it's wrong and it to be true by no other measure

than the heart rising up from pain not down from platitude
but up from that well spring "enough" up

That human thing that says "human" and under which we are
all truly equal and which view we should always fight for in
everything. That moment when social critique is a detail too
fine to grasp or see and matter under the haunting reality of
HUMAN and somehow nothing brings that out like a crowd
of strangers sweaty, tired, throbbing in the night against police
and macho architecture.

•

Dear Alain,

a bff from college spent two years in turkey and now works
at the turkish embassy. she and i were always very different -
she always made fun of my Occupy tendencies. but she called
me last night to say "i cant go to the DC solidarity march (for
political reasons since she works at the embassy); can you go
for me?" we both cried. "who would have imagined, me?"
she said.

It is far from over, far from over.

I can hear the protest outside my window as we speak. It's
obvious that it will be Tiananmen Square or Erdogan will
resign. I wonder if it will spread to Europe next. A world then,
of the Greeks, of Abraham, in smolders of the people trying
again against two poles of Chinese American dictatorship?
I can hear the conservatives now: power of the people led to
rubble, thus...

It is far from over, far from over. A Drake song in my head.
The next line "what am I doing? What am I doing? Oh, that's
right, that's right, I'm doing me, I'm doing me." I'm not sure
if doing me is the realization of the truth process or the fall of
civilization but it is happening. And I weep. Oh it's so god
damned beautiful. And they say Egypt is a mess; it will be a
hell for Turkey, but France had quite a few republics before it
got cool. I still believe. I'll take a rubble sorting through truth
over a manufactured consent any day. And that's where I
stand; and that's my truth and I'm sticking to it I don't give a
damn what anyone says I know because I cry when we stand
I know in my heart that's it's not anarchy it's not ignorant

although it is those things it's truth from the bottom of the heart the only thing that makes us different from computers the only thing that makes philosophy legitimate it's otherwise fucked in this sense nature does not exist I get it but you're still nuts and I still love you even though I hate you just for the one thing you say about believing in infinity in that moment of standing up that moment right now in Ankara in Istanbul in Gezi. Maybe the poet and the philosopher come together in revolution. Maybe this is infinity. Maybe I'm watching it right now on TV. Where the point is a line and the line is a circle and the circle a flower where the vortex inverts and SOMETHING HAPPENS. What are you doing to me, Alain? What are you doing, what are we doing? Why can't I stop writing you, why can't I stop loving you, why? But we're here and I stand and I call it love. We can have it too. We already do. In this moment we make love and it is real and tomorrow it will break you too much logic and symmetry and me all poetry but for this moment we are and it's infinite and I will stand to say it's true and isn't that all you ever asked? So isn't this all it is? Am I the woman? Am I the man? You need to shove your fixed positions down your thick throat with your tall man hands but right now it doesn't matter we agree on this, we are alive at dawn on the horizon and the future will bring us back to reality only if we let it. I need your heart with me this time. I need it back together. Tell me. Tell me. Tell me. I love you.

•

And I think the only world view worth having is the spinning fragmented madness of the hangover. The swirling heaving breathing panic attack which sees the world and cultures as crass mass judgments and nasty cultural characteristics like people running mad all over the word making chaos and every once and a while a huge nasty orgasm erupts like in Turkey crying for some god damn alignment for what is good. And you nothing you wretched architecture. You are nothing. And I am not fucking you right now Alain. You're nothing but a dead object to me. The most human breathing thing you do is to make those awful mistakes and then I see and I hate you or something colder and but at least that, that is a feeling. You don't open me up to the insane whirlwinds of life, you put them in a box, and I cant see them there and I must leave. The poet is not in the philosophy and I am going I am going I am gone. Democracy. Me.

•

Dear Alain,

Dear God won't you just go to hell already, get out of my
mind, out of my metaphors. I speak, I say, that's what Badiou
says. I think, I hear your lines tinkling in the view. I am
surrounded by your lines, lines, lines, lines, lines, and all I
want is jazz and all I hear is Badiou, and all I want is spicer's
cable cars and lang's swamp, the rustled folds of coan silk,
a poem without a single bird in it, 22nd century, blues and
roots, the rustled folds of coan silk. Damn. Get out, you lines.
Get outta here. I feel your tattoo, badiou. I feel your tattoo. But
only in my brain. It's gray. And charred.

●

Dear Alain,

I went to sleep in the soft folds of ego submitted to the logic of
nothingness and it felt so much better than you. If that was a
thing I would say if that were true. If that were true all I would
say is I forget everything but the point on the pointillism
and your hands in my hair and there would be nothing but a
harmonic hum there would be no word better there would be
no thought whatsoever. You. You. Dear Badiou.

●

Dear Alain,

Love is the kind of thing that pulls the rubix cube to pieces.
You are the kind of thing that puts the rubix cube to parts.

"THERE WILL ALWAYS HAVE BEEN A CHALLENGE LAID DOWN BY ART TO THE CONCEPT, AND IT IS ON THE BASIS OF THIS CHALLENGE, THIS WOUND, THAT IT IS NECESSARY TO INTERPRET THE PLATONIC GESTURE WHICH CAN ONLY ESTABLISH THE ROYALTY OF THE PHILOSOPHER BY BANISHING THE POETS." – A.B.

$$k_n + a_n$$

"the beginning"

"[LOVE HAS] AN IMPERATIVE FUNCTION: CONTINUING ALWAYS, EVEN IN SEPARATION, AND WHICH HOLDS THAT ABSENCE IS ITSELF A MODE OF CONTINUATION." – A.B.

Dear Alain,

When everything went mad. I didn't think of you. When the boy with the sweetest heart got the prize his parents never gave him and his world was healed those cracks in the struggle and the sarcasm melted with love everything went mad and I didn't think of you, not once. I thought of Rumi, Stephen, Doug, Meg, Brandon, Anne, CA, Ryan, Bernadette, beauty, love, Maged, Buck, Brilliance, my mother, tears, joy and silence. But you were elsewhere. Lyric. I thought of all the pauses and the tones and eye glances when everything went mad.

When everything goes mad, I hope you're well.

Love always,

Your Katy

However you remember

•

Dear Diary,

Only years later did I realize: I wanted to be on the bottom.

MATH   POLITICS   LOVE

PHIL ⟷ POETRY

Malcolm X Park, Washington DC

C. Paul Jennewein's Armillary Sphere
A winged baby, Putto, stood in the center
Of this fully functioning nearly 6 foot tall astrolabe
Donated by Bertha Noyes 1936
Mysteriously disappeared late 1970s

The Park

This strange book, *Dear Alain*, by Katy Bohinc can be represented as such: you have a great countryside named "Alain Badiou," the park of Alain Badiou. And she looks and walks through the park, with a perspective supported by a thought, an effect, maybe even, a love? This book is the collection of thoughts of Katy Bohinc, who – armed with a reader's eye and surrounded by profound effects – retains, sorts, and rejects the different aspects of the park she visits. She knows there exists under the name "Alain Badiou," a park, and so she addresses him, this supposedly dear Alain, at times with affection, at times in anger, at times almost indifferent, and at times revealing forcefully her difference and opposition through the poetic vehemence of her writing to the serenity she sees in the park of philosophy. Day after day, Katy returns to this park and her eye changes, her relationship with "Alain Badiou" varies like the time that passes, and her thoughts inscribe themselves in small texts that in the end compose a kind of ode to the park.

Like there is an ode to the Greek urn or an ode to a champion of the Olympic Games, there is an ode in the prose-poem of Katy Bohinc to the park of Alain Badiou. She is the fierce and lucid visitor of a good number of corners of this park. She knows also that she hasn't seen everything; she cannot see everything. But she desires to, one day. Having put in her poetic writing all the park of philosophy, she notes that only with two simultaneous writings can it be true love, and such is the dream to which the beautiful book Dear Alain testifies, fragmentarily, but forever.

{Alain Badiou, June 24, 2014, 4 PM, Paris.}

Translation, katy bohinc

Author's Note

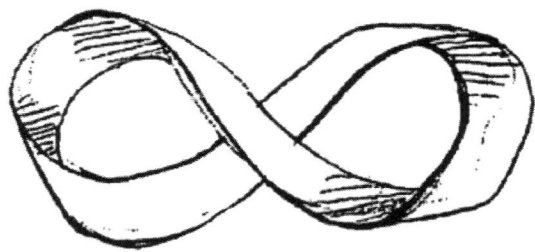

Can love, thinking as two, be enough to bond poetry which thinks as "elsewhere" and philosophy which thinks in distinctions? Despite the dramatic metaphor, in the end there is not a mathematic answer to such a question. Each answers their own way. Love the union of singulars.

Now then, is this poetry? If Badiou's conditions are all redoubled here, poetry on philosophy, philosophy on poetry, etc. then is it too much of a Gödel trick to ask? (The Indians wrote their calculus in verse, you know.)

Either transcendental way, and I don't really mind as long as it's transcendental, what I want to say is I think the relationship between philosophy and poetry is like what happens at the real projective plane: infinite, like a mobius strip. For when I think back on my own poetic departure, it happened when it happened, and why I'll never know (it wasn't really a choice), but it happened against all "reality" which had conditioned me in my life up until that point. And that was many things, including, fundamentally, definitions which all necessarily have philosophical under-pinnings, be they from texts or passed through the cultural conversation. That poetry, or writing, or art "reacts against" is true, but a reaction is also itself a relation. One cannot exist without the other. In this sense, I think, poetry is the fearlessness to depart, from the position of the self, in relation to all that is present in and up to that moment each poem is born – street wisdom or Alain Badiou or whatever. Poetry is also Robespierre's eyes. Or the sun's, or the moon's.

Be it description or logic, this is how I saw it at that moment when the songs began (I also saw it as a sortof affliction, but that's a past sentence, pun intended, and isn't it odd how sometimes the things we hate at first we love later the most?) Perhaps it's a proof, perhaps it's my poetic "elsewhere". I don't really care to designate; it just is. To smile and laugh utterly naive to each moment's possible meanings whisping into the next moment's forgotten will always be more beautiful to me than the rigid lines of any conclusion. It's not that I (read we, if you prefer) can't, just that my preference is right now. As a way to perceive.

What I really want to say is that philosophy is not sovereign (thank you, Alain). And that poetry is is quite good at naming and defining itself! As it has been for thousands of years, regardless of whatever the philosophers have been saying. (What, what was that? Did you hear something?) And even, the practice of reading, interpreting, writing, and if you want to play that way...naming philosophy?

"Something I always knew was it's all Aristotle's fault."
– Bernadette Mayer

In some sense, poetry's and philosophy's irresistible urge to discuss each other for thousands of years is like the longest love affair in history since, well, Philosophy was born!

There is perhaps something in all of this of poetry's – and my – disdain for constraint or boundaries. Poetry, I think, is the undefined (and so, everything.) And as all writing is different from language in that it is about sex, I'll talk about Badiou's "woman": one who thinks love is what ultimately centers and binds the conditions of us all. If this is the meaning of "woman", then I proudly stand to militantly defend such a view with all my soul.

Love, always,
k

{KATY BOHINC, 2014}

Notes:

"The level of presentation, which only designates that some sort of multiplicity is in the situation" – A.B.

Translation: "a fraction of the notable moments, darlings." – K.B.

$k_0 + a_0$

P 511 Euclid's plane, So they just met. And the phrase would be "generic plane". But she doesn't know him yet: "If one category has to be designated as an emblem of my thought, it would be neither Cantor's pure multiple, nor Godel's constructible, nor the void, by which being is named, nor even the event, in which the supplement of what-is-not-being-qua-being originates. It would be the generic." *Being and Event*, 15.

P 512 The ***, "The poem makes the moment of the empty page in which the argument proceeds, proceeded, will proceed." *Infinite Thought*, 81.

P 513 Mallarme (Stephen), Badiou primarily references Mallarme as a representative "pole" of poetry throughout his long oeuvre. Stephen Mallarme was a terrific French poet (1842-1898) known for wonderful word play, experimentation with presentation on the page, and logic games. Famous line, "a role of the dice does not abolish chance" (*un coup de dés jamais n'abolira le hazard.*)

P 513 Poetry at the origin, "Naturally it would be pointless to set off in search of nothing. Yet it must be said that this is what poetry exhausts itself doing." *Being and Event*, 54.

P 514 Think of writing for the entire of existence, "Philosophy cannot renounce that its address is direct to everyone, in principle if not in fact." *Infinite Thought*, 38.

P 515 Our wretched infinite, This line originally read "our wretched nothingness" but per Badiou's placement of the void, the void is literally the null set, and being is infinite multiplicity, defined only by its "opposition" or "index" against the void. See meditations 1-6 of *Being and Event*.

P 515 When tomorrow becomes yesterday, These lines are from a song by Nina Simone, "22nd Century". If you Google the lines you will find the song.

A poetic technique used in American Avant Garde poetries: leave a message to be Googled. A game if you will, but it represents the "user" or "reader's" dependence on or interactions with Google.

P 517 You'll spend eternity with the maggots, "I would like this book to be read, appreciated, staked out, and contested as much by the inheritors of the formal and experimental grandeur of the sciences or the law, as it is by the aesthetes of contemporary nihilism, the refined amateurs of literary deconstruction, the wild militants of a de-alienated world, and by those who are deliciously isolated by amorous constructions." *Being and Event*, preface XV.

P 517 Philosophy is all moral consequence, There is a distinction here between "Philosophy" and Badiou. Badiou actually is different in this sense, his philosophy is designed specifically to evade moralistic judgment by describing the process by which a truth is determined, not by defining the truth itself, which, per Badiou, is the role of each singular individual, to decide their truth.

P 520 Real Projective Plane, A famous mathematician: Carl Friedrich Gauss (1777-1855). Many called him the greatest mathematician since antiquity. His contributions are lengthy. Among them, a system called the Real Projective Plane. As the story goes, Gauss was walking down the shore, looking at the horizon. And he said to himself, they told me parallel lines don't meet. But they DO meet; they meet at the horizon. So Gauss created a system, like an X-Y plane, but on it one could graph not normal X-Y coordinates, but, literally, what happens at infinity. The results are incredibly beautiful. In the Real Projective Plane, a point is a line. A line is a circle. And a circle is a flower. And so on.

$$k_1 + a_1$$

P 522 Politics and Metaphysics, First, a false appropriation of the text which is actually titled, *Metapolitics*. The quotations are also a poetically symbolic gesture. Actually, Alain never says this at all. He says the complete opposite. I will summarize in my words what he lays out in the last chapter ("Politics as Truth Procedure", 141-152): Political events necessarily invite repression from the state. In doing this they expose the power of the state, which is normally hidden. So in a sense, political events measure the power of the state. This subtraction, the political event and the subtraction of the exposed power of the state, leaves a space for true equality to reveal itself. So, the political event is that where the event – the exposed power of the state, approaches 1, or equality.

My reference is a subtle inversion: The state's power cannot be quantified (it is infinite), and so the political event cannot be quantified either (they are also infinite).

P 523 A big void, To truly address Alain, the supporting term would be "a big infinite". But we do at times refer to old usages. To the poet - void/infinite/ nothingness - these distinctions are somewhat irrelevant to the sensory preceptors. What we are discussing is sensory, not theoretical. But I'll also say, the use of void here is actually pretty good use, vis-a-vis Alain's eyes – it is a use of the void to rank, to index or measure what exists. Alain defines the void as a point of reference (nothing) against which Being shows her measure. Similar to zero.

P 523 Juvenile stuck on the problem of naming, The chapter "Politics of Thought", in *Metapolitics* addresses this question quite well. To summarize, the problem of naming exists, in that the act of naming limits in its inscription the set of information it contains. Per Badiou this difficulty is overcome by understanding that thought itself is an active entity, an incomplete site which describes not only what has been, but also what may be: "what happens does not cancel out the fact that what could have taken place lies behind the organization of the prescriptive statements." Alain discusses naming with regards to politics here, but we'll extrapolate towards naming and thought generally.

P 523 Your systems don't give a damn for psyche, "Psyche" is used here in reference to the psyche of poetry, which is an extremely complex term that refers to many things within the poetry community but I'll shortly translate it as the combination of sound, rhythm and lyric effect within a poem which denotes not only thought but an emotional or spiritual state.

P 524 Chinese woman who has never used a personal pronoun, *The Good Women of China*, Xin Ran. See chapter 15, "The Women of Shouting Hill". You will learn something about anthropology. As per representing Badiou, "Language is not the absolute horizon of thought. The great linguistic turn of philosophy, or the absorption of philosophy into the mediation of language must be reversed." *Infinite Thought*, 37. Agreed. Emphatically.

P 524 Events of Robespierre, "It is through St Just and Robespierre that you enter into this singular truth unleashed by the French Revolution, and on the basis of which you form a knowledge, and not through Kant or Francois Furet." I MUST add in this note, that this description suits me SOLELY to represent the truthful eyes of the militant as opposed to the power of the philosopher. Further, it is imperative I add that I believe the militant title and exception extends through the stage of personal emancipation & activism and ENDS at the point of organized power. The distinction of power is obviously treacherously fine and problematic.-The feather pivot I do not know.

P 525 Ni hui ying yu ma?, (Mandarin for "Do you speak English?") "Philosophy privileges no language, not even the one it is written in." *IT*, 38.

P 526 Mallarme thinks nothing but is pure form, This is obviously not a completely true or rational statement. She's just mad. Mallarme did things with form and he also wrote a lot of essays. He thought a lot. The description of Mallarme is a sort of proxy for the American L=A=N=G=U=A=G=E poetry, and the discussion here is certainly only one valence, far from final. We do say things when mad.

P 527 It's rather unnamable, I'll refer back to what is possibly my favorite line of Badiou's: "naturally it would be pointless to set off in search of nothing. Yet it must be said that this is what poetry exhausts itself doing." *Being and Event*, 54. "The unnamable is the point where the situation in its most intimate is being submitted to thought; in the pure presence that no knowledge can circumscribe. The unnamable is something like the inexpressible real of everything a truth authorizes to be said." *Infinite Thought*, 49. So Alain knows what the unnamable is, but she presumes he does not "feel" it.

P 527 Dear Diary, In case I needed to clarify, Žižek is the collection of afterthoughts, Badiou the tautology of conjunct tautologies. Poetry insults philosophy! This is merely the condition of this work passed down by the statements of Alain Badiou, and so I excuse myself.

P 528 You are the horizon, In *Theoretical Writings*, the chapter "The End of Romanticism", Alain details a lovely idea about how Cantor's discovery of multiple infinities changes the way we might conceive of infinity and its visual symbolic equivalent, the horizon. The poet here argues otherwise, reclaiming the romantic horizon in a new way, in a romantic way, for her own thought of the real projective plane and also towards her amour.

P 528 Do you believe in all who work?, Badiou defines poetry as "approaching the void", but certainly there exist an infinity of definitions about what poetry "is", all of them reasonable and relevant. And, importantly, possible.

P 530 Sartre, a riff on Sartre's notorious idiom: "Love is hate."

$$k_2 + a_2$$

P 531 Love is thinking for 2 (+), This statement is ambiguous. Alain says Love is thinking for 2. Katy maintains that love is thinking for 2, plus something else.

P 532 Greatness in small things, as stated in the epigraph, "the sadness of the true seen from a distance changes into the joy of being when seen close up." *Infinite Thought*, 81.

P 532 Marxist society converge to thrive, Katy is introducing a point, that poetry is also conditioned by politics.

P 532 The real is what we need, An example of a "poem poem" as defined by Alain, "The poem marks the moment of the empty page in which the argument proceeds, proceeded, will proceed. This void, this empty page, is not 'all is thinkable'. It is, on the contrary, under a rigorously circumscribed poetic mark, the means of saying, in philosophy, that at least one truth, elsewhere, but real, exists."

P 532 The political view, Alain describes his politics in opposition to the politics of the state, which are defined as, roughly, "non-thought" – repetitive gestures which do not actually approach or address the situation. See *Metapolitics*, throughout and p 62 for discussion specific.

P 532 Never break a heart, "the Good is Good only to the extent that it does not aspire to render the world good. Its sole being lies in the situated advent of a singular truth." This is the Katy character's singular truth. *Ethics*, 51.

P 533 Nothing-everything, a riff on Alain's definition of the void: multiple of nothing.

P 535 Love of one for n+1, This would actually correspond to Alain's definition of the Humanity function, but we'll run with it here. Poetic license.

P 535 The universal 'we're on equal planes', For Alain's discussion on equality see *Metapolitics*, chapter 6, "Truths and Justice". It's not particularly pretty to point out "constant inequality". So, I won't.

P 535 Derivative hole, She's really digging at him here, in effect categorizing his definitions of poetry and art – the singular truths – as little more than a repetitive cycle which is itself formulaic.

P 535 Derrida collapsed the derivatives market, "philosophy [risks becoming] what in one way it mostly is, an infinite description of the multiplicity of language games." *Infinite Thought*, 35.

P 536 The moment is total in my typewriter, sweet cheeks, "The poem is a purity folded in upon itself. The poem awaits us without anxiety. It is a closed manifestation." *Theoretical Writings*, 240.

k_3+a_3

P 537 Infinity and the End of Romanticism, The chapter is actually titled "Philosophy and Mathematics: Infinity and the End of Romanticism", Theoretical Writings, 22-40. It's a fascinating read. Badiou describes the mathematical reorientation of infinity from a place solely understood "at the horizon" to be a commonplace occurrence, actually the MOST commonplace occurrence of which finitude is the exception. The inversion, essentially. It is Cantor's set theory, his discovery of multiple and unequal infinities that marks "the end of romanticism". Romantic being the Romantic Philosophy of the Romantic Period. Personally I think, well, the romantic is hardly a thing tied exclusively to infinity, but I won't harp, I'll call it poetic. But she is agreeing with said analysis, and adding, poetry too should be conditioned by math.

P 538-539 I'll let y'all duke this one out.

P 539 Gauss' projective plane, please see the note for page 31.

P 539 New God as you call it, honestly this is from a YouTube video I don't have time to go back and find right now.

P 539 Like you said, The fundamental tenet of *Being and Event* might be the distinction that inconsistent multiplicity (or infinity) is the norm, while finitude is the exception. Inconsistent multiplicity meaning "being", which applies to all matter, as nature does not exist.

P 540 Event without anxiety, "Philosophy is required to ensure that thought can receive and accept the drama of the event without anxiety. We do not fundamentally need a philosophy of the structure of things. We need a philosophy open to the irreducible singularity of what happens, a philosophy that can be fed and nourished by the surprise of the unexpected. Such a philosophy would then be the philosophy of the event. This too is required of philosophy by the world, by the world as it is." *Infinite Thought*, 41. Well said Alain, well said.

P 542 Rabat, Alain Badiou was born in Rabat.

P 542 Haven't accused you of being an Islamist yet, In Islamic thought, each moment is reborn infinitely, so Alain's understanding of infinite multiplicity as the fabric of Being, I think, approaches a convergence with some tenets of Islamic thought.

P 542 Truth is a hole, "The subject of a truth demands the indiscernible" *Infinite Thought*, 47.

P 542 Breathe the joy back into it, Poetry, as previously noted is looking at the small with jouissance (enjoyment).

P 543 The only thing that's formless is God, "There is no structure of being" *Being and Event*, 26. Essentially there could be two less compatible statements. But to the poet, who is obsessed with questions of form, the only thing that's formless, is God. But we circle back to her original point, which is that if the only thing that's formless is God, and if we are in the real projective plane, and infinity is right now...then Katy and Alain meet at the horizon.

$$k_n + a_n$$

P 544 Leprechauns, This poem represents the image of a future between Katy and Alain, the Platonic image on the wall, if you will.

P 545 The way Heidegger had us, "Heidegger has subtracted the poem from philosophical knowledge, to render it truth." *Infinite Thought*, 73. "Heidegger... prophesizes a reactivation of the Sacred in an indecipherable coupling of the saying of the poets and the thinking of the thinkers." *Infinite Thought*, 74. Roughly, Heidegger determines that there is little at the end of deconstruction, except the poem.

P 546 We meet at infinity, Here, Katy's reasoning and Alain's reasoning converge: "The amorous procedure, which deploys the truth of difference or sexuation (rather than of the collective), proceeds from the 1 to the infinite through the mediation of the two." *Metapolitics*, 151.

$$k_{n+1} + a_{n+1}$$

P 548 Einstein truth, Einstein famously had a contract with his wife that she only talk to him on certain days of the week so he could work.

P 548 Gil Scott-Heron, Lines from "Where Did the Night Go" from the 13th and final studio recording album "I'm New Here", XL Recordings, 2010.

P 549 I'll forgo all the details, "The philosophical place, the place of the occurrence, or the proving ground of the true, when seen from a distance, is, for most people, melancholic." *Infinite Thought*, 80.

P 550 If I don't believe in thought, "Philosophy only summons the poem for itself at the point at which this separation must expose what the argument, which frames and borders it, can only sustain by returning to what made it possible: the effective singularity of a truth procedure, singularity that is in the bathing pool, in the winding sheet, in the source of sense." Yes dear, that's pretty good.*Infinite Thought*.

P 551 'Like a stirring wheat field', "This 'all alone' of the poem...is a purity folded in upon itself. The poem awaits us without anxiety. It is a closed manifestation. It is like a fan that our simple gaze unfolds." *Theor. Essays*, p 240.

P 552 If your mind leaves the axiom-checker on hold, "They [poetry] require the primordial defection of the donation of sense, absence, abnegation in regards to sense. Or rather, indecency. They require that truth procedures be subtracted from the eventual singularity that weaves them into the real, and that knots them to sense in the mode of traversing the latter, of hollowing it out. They thus require that truth procedures be disengaged from their [poetry's] subjective escort, including the pleasure of the object delivered there." *Infinite Thought*, 77.

$$k_{n+2} + a_{n+2}$$

P 556 Endymion, John Keat's most famous long poem is called Endymion. It famously begins "A thing of beauty is a joy forever."

P 557 See T.S. Elliot, wrote perhaps two of the most wonderful poems in the English language, and the remainder of his output is shockingly spare and boring. Some connect this late career boringness with his ties to the CIA.

P 558 'Love what you will never believe twice', Alain, somewhere. What he liked to say at cocktail parties. jk. *Ethics*, 52.

P 560 This word finitude, Finitude as the exception to infinity.

P 560-561 is a conceptual poem taken from Alain's writing in *Metaphysics*, page 145. The original passage refers to political events (not poetic events) and the State (not the intellect). I replaced Alain's terms of politics (politics, political event, etc.) with poetry (poetry, poetic events, etc.) and the State with appropriate versions of "intellect".

P 561 Multiplicity inconsistent, "Why is the infinite multiplicity of the multiple like the image of a dream? Why this nocturne, this sleep of thought, to glimpse the dissemination of all supposed atoms? Simply because the inconsistent multiple is actually unthinkable as such. All thought supposes a situation of the thinkable, which is to say a structure, a count-as-one, in which the presented multiple is consistent and numerable. Consequently, the inconsistent multiple is solely – before the one-effect in which it is structured – an ungraspable horizon of being... There is no form of the object for thought which is capable of gathering together the pure multiple, the multiple-without-one, and making it consist: the pure multiple scarcely occurs in presentation before it has already dissipated; its non-occurrence is like the flight of scenes from a dream." *Being and Event*, 34.

P 562 "Pure Being = math", "Mathematics is rather the sole discourse which 'knows' absolutely what it is talking about: being, as such, despite the fact that there is no need for this knowledge to be reflected in an intra-mathematical sense, because being is not an object, and nor does it generate objects. Mathematics is the sole discourse, and this is well known, in which ones has a complete guarantee and a criterion of truth of what one says, to the point that the truth is unique inasmuch as it is the only one ever to have been encountered which is fully transmissible." *Being and Event*, 9.

P 562 Being-Qua-Being, "If one is concerned with being-qua-being, the multiple-without-one, it is true that non-being of the one is that particular truth whose entire effect resides in establishing the dream of a multiple disseminated without limits. It is this 'dream' which was given the fixity of thought in Cantor's creation." *Being and Event*, 36. I think here is Badiou's ultimate grace, where he admits the dream world, to let it stand on a mathematical justification (oh the social capital!).

$$k_{n-1} + a_{n-1}$$

First, a note on the language of the chapter: "The powers of the language of the situation are themselves, to be sure, unrestricted: every element can be named from the perspective of a given interest, and judged in the communication between human animals. But since this language is in any case incoherent, and dedicated to pragmatic exchange, its totalizing vocation does not matter much." *Ethics*, 83. As the Event develops, blindly, the language sprawls, wildly.

P 565-567 Cultural Revolution, "Thus, a politics worthy of being interrogated by philosophy under the idea of justice is one whose unique general axiom is: people think, people are capable of truth….We encounter the same principle… during the Cultural Revolution in China." *Metapolitics*, 98. Though notably disapproving of the results of the Cultural Revolution, Alain is willing to admit it theoretically as an event whose underpinning concepts are valiant in their aims towards equality. Herein lies a totalizing disagreement for Katy. She considers, frankly, such a statement naming the unnamable: "Evil is the will to name at any price" *Infinite Thought*, 50.

P 565 It is not violence, "Mao's thesis concerning the immanent self-education of the revolutionary mass movement." *Metapolitics*, 99. Katy is arguing that whatever conceptual arguments Mao may have had, violence against the other *never* falls under the category of self-education.

P 567 Your humanity function is broken, "What is essential is that love is the guarantor of the universal." "What is Love?", 53. In short, she is claiming that Alain has lost sight of the pain (shattering of love) caused by the Cultural Revolution, and thus lost sight of his humanity.

P 571 Fine you wanna go there?, Here the argument descends into something evil. It is love, thinking as two, turning in on itself: "These are the figures of Evil, an Evil which becomes an *actual* possibility only thanks to the sole Good we recognize – a truth-process." *Ethics*, 87. The truth process of thinking as two has become thinking against the two. "The ethics of truth is always more or less militant" *Ethics*, 75. Here, the militant battle for the bliss of the lovers splits on the battle of each for their own view.

P 571 Your thought Thermidored into, "Is thought obliged to endure Thermidorian frameworks of its own ruination?" *Metapolitics*, 139. In this case, if love is thinking as two, is love also obliged to undergo the thought process of its own ruination? And is this ruination as simple as a totalizing, negative critique of the lover?

P 571 Breaking bonds, "We have too often wished for justice to found the consistency of the social bond, whereas in reality it can only name the most extreme moments of inconsistency. For the effect of the axiom of equality is to undo the bonds, to desocialize thought, to affirm the rights of the infinite and the immortal against the calculation of interests." *Metapolitics*, 104. This is Alain's justification – breaking bonds – in support of his positive thesis on the Cultural Revolution. Katy obviously protests, on an even more fundamental level, against the wholesale idea that political emancipation necessitates the cold procedure of breaking bonds, and its necessarily corollary, love.

P 572 Death is merely a worldly principle of stability, Cute line, when taken literally. And here the poet departs, she departs into defending the set of all meanings of the line not included in the literal, for this is the difference between poets and philosophers: The poet cares for the entire set of meaning spilling out from a set of words. The philosopher cares for the specific meaning he has inscribed in words. It would be their endless misunderstanding. And by pointing this out she creates a final wound.

P 572 It's breaking my heart, Caught between two truths: the shared of the lovers' and self's singular. The breakup is the ultimate ethical moment, particularly what we say during those moments. Words are never more dangerous than in love.

$$k_{n-2} + a_{n-2}$$

P 575 Nature does not exist, At the moment where love aught to be reconfirmed she parts from him, separated by doubt, unable to regain the common ground of a shared truth, lost. "Betrayal: to give up the truth in the name of one's own interest." *Ethics*, 91.

P 575 Democracy, "Love begins where politics ends." *Metapolitics*, 151. And where love ends, politics begins: "One shouldn't blame politics for what is, in actual fact, the result of a personal preference for the bound outpouring of the ego. By contrast, true instances of politics tend to manifest this faint coldness that involves precision." *Metapolitics*, 77. Shall it always be so? I think, there is an ethical point here.

$$k_n + a_n$$

P 578 Wanted to be on the bottom, She refers to Alain's conditions, his schema in full. Where poetry resides, where philosophy resides – in short, how he sees the world. And she, well, she disagrees about her place. *Sous-entendus* of "gender" and fucking-forms not withstanding.

Original Back Cover: ("This book should be banished", —Slavoj Žižek), Žižek believes that all poets are fascists and should be banished as Plato decreed. No comment.

Badiou's [Malcolm X] Park, Oh I LOVE that park!! Where the majority of *Dear Alain* was written. (& hell, he never claimed to be a zen buddhist.)

Epigraphs (in order of appearance)

Let us add … Badiou, Alain. "What is Love?" *One*. Buffalo, NY: Umbra, 1996. P 37.

You dare to study philosophy baby … Mayer, Bernadette. *Sonnets*. New York City: Tender Buttons Press, 1989. P 69.

Poem, Matheme, Politics and Love … Badiou, Alain. *Infinite Thought*. London: Continuum, 1998. P 76.

It is fixed only by a nomination… Badiou, Alain. "What is Love?" *One*. Buffalo, NY: Umbra, 1996. P 45.

Love is nothing other than a trying sequence of investigations … Badiou, Alain. "What is Love?" *One*. Buffalo, NY: Umbra, 1996. P 45.

Love is interminable fidelity … Badiou, Alain. "What is Love?" *One*. Buffalo, NY: Umbra, 1996. P 45.

There is some sense in Plato's project … Badiou, Alain. *Being and Event*. London: Continuum, 2005. P 54.

My soul cannot …Jung, Carl. *The Red Book*. New York: W. W. Norton & Co., 2009. P 233.

The poem must be excused … Badiou, Alain. *Infinite Thought*. London: Continuum, 1998. P 81.

Philosophers, says Rimbaud … Badiou, Alain. *Theoretical Writings*. London: Continuum, 2006. P 247.

Little by little … Badiou, Alain. *Infinite Thought*. London: Continuum, 1998. P 48.

The subject of a Truth… Badiou, Alain. *Infinite Thought*. London: Continuum, 1998. P 47.

The sadness of the true … Badiou, Alain. *Infinite Thought*. London: Continuum, 1998. P 81.

Who is not familiar … Badiou, Alain. "What is Love?" *One*. Buffalo, NY: Umbra, 1996. P 50.

Keep Going! … Badiou, Alain. London: *Ethics*. London: Verso, 2001. P 91.

The point of the being … Badiou, Alain. *Being and Event*. London: Continuum, 2005. P 35.

Is thought obliged … Badiou, Alain. *Metapolitics*. London: Verso, 2005. P 139.

Evil is to want … Badiou, Alain. *Ethics*. London: Verso, 2001. P 87.

So it is that the defeat … Badiou, Alain. *Ethics*. London: Verso, 2001. P 80.

Ultimately true politics … Badiou, Alain. *Metapolitics*. London: Verso, 2005. P 77.

There will always have been … Badiou, Alain. *Infinite Thought*. London: Continuum, 1998. P 76.

An imperative function … Badiou, Alain. "What is Love?" *One*. Buffalo, NY: Umbra, 1996. P 48.

The level of presentation … Badiou, Alain. *Infinite Thought*. London: Continuum, 1998. P 127.

GUEST CHECK ™

Date	Table	Guests	Server	685097

APPT-SOUP/SAL-ENTREE-VEG/POT-DESSERT-BEV

Dear Alan

I always feel ~~something~~
a glow, the best when
I confess to myself
and they say "no"
and explain to me
why I'm wrong. There's
There's. It's the last
thing. The integrality
of learning. It's not
commodified. No
power. No help or
hospitality. It's a
gift. Love

Tax	1c
Total	

Thank You — Please Come Again

NCR 6000 GuestCheck™ www.nationalchecking.com MADE IN THE USA

FORTHCOMING

Julie Ezelle Patton

Julie Ezelle Patton was born and raised in Cleveland, Ohio. Her work has primarily appeared in spoken-sung live performances in honor of the embodied presence of language. She has performed throughout North America and Europe for decades.

Patton's most recent bound-ink-to-paper production is *Notes for Some (Nominally) Awake*. Her work has appeared in *((eco (lang) (uage(reader))), I'll Drown My Book, What I Say* and other publications. Julie is a self-¬proclaimed "phonemenologist" whose book length serial poem *B* (Tender Buttons Press) and *Writing with Crooked Ink* (Belladonna) are forthcoming. In 2015, Julie was honored with a Foundation for Contemporary Arts Grants to Artists award and an Atlantic Center for the Arts Master Artist Residency. She has taught creative writing at Case Western Reserve University, New York University and "around the block" through Teachers & Writers Collaborative and other arts organizations. She is the founding director of Let it Bee Ark Hive and the Salon des Refuge collective.

JULIE EZELLE PATTON

FROM

B

Pregnant B

To B or Knot

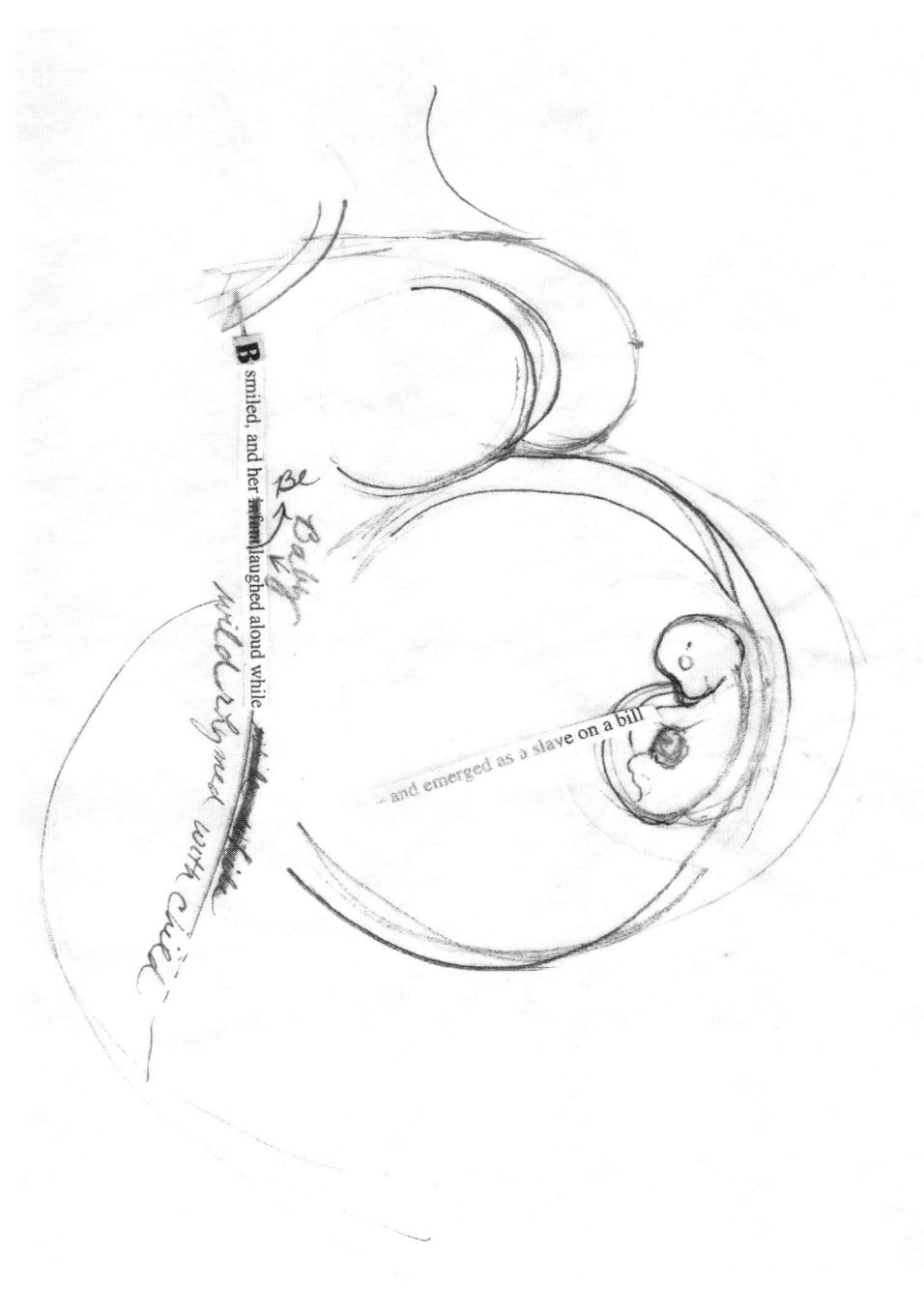

B smiled, and her infant laughed aloud while *and taught and the wilderness met with child*

Be Baby

... and emerged as a slave on a bill

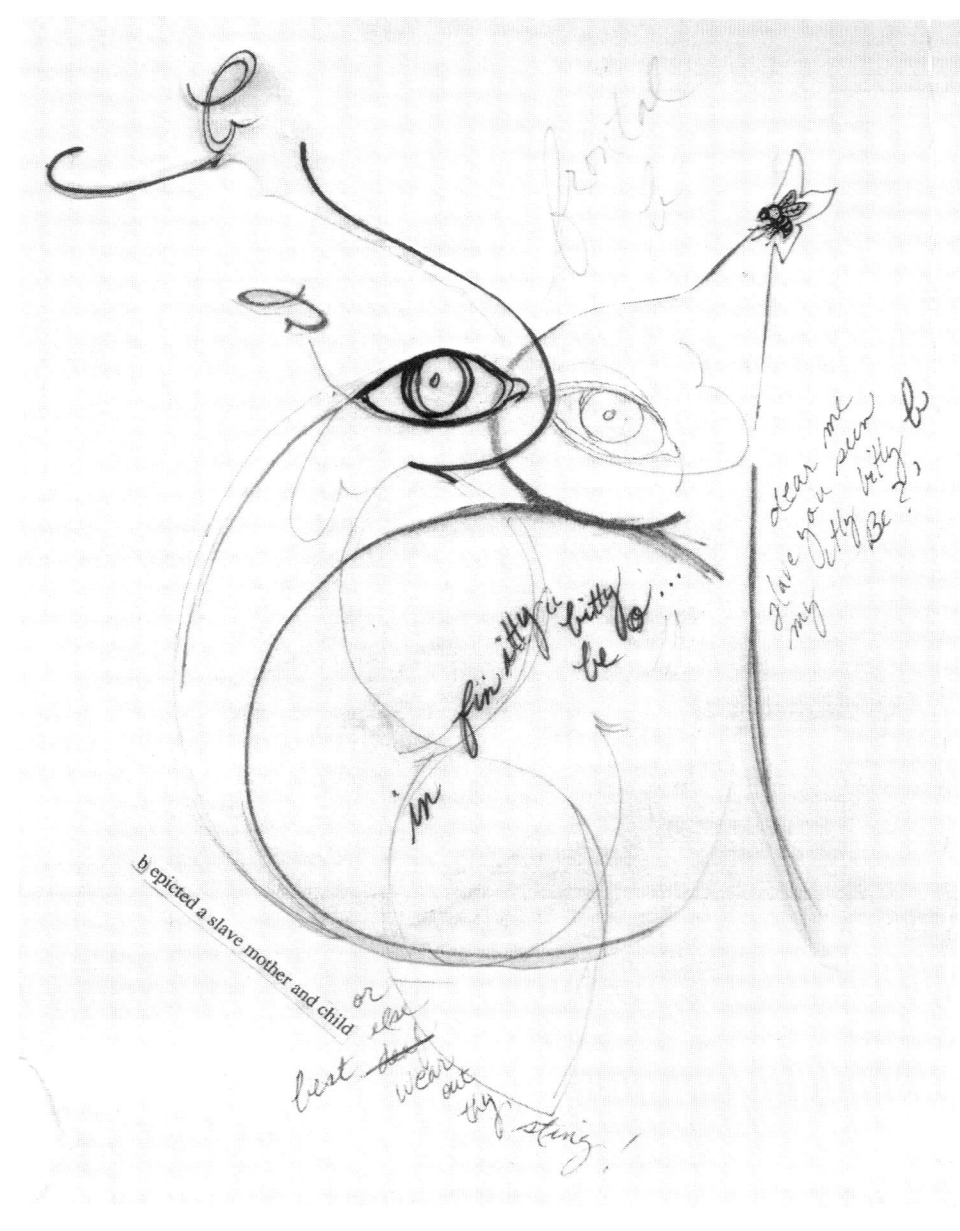

b epicted a slave mother and child

Truck Darling

Truck Darling studied at Cambridge and Oxford Universities before receiving his MFA from Naropa University. His first publication during graduate school was *A Valentine to Frank O'Hara* published by Erudite Frangs in conjunction with Smokeproof Press in 1999. Since then he has published four books: *The Heart's Filthy Lesson* with drawings by Jo Jackson (Angry Dog Press, 2000); *The Pill Book* (XY Press, 2002), *Blue Collar Holiday* with Larry Rivers (Hanging Loose Press 2005), *Hold Tight: The Truck Darling Poems* (Hanging Loose Press, 2010). His work has also been published in German translation, *Ich Habe Angst um Meinem Hedgefonds* (luxbooks, 2002). In 2004 and 2011, Darling's work was included in *The Best American Poetry* (Scribner) and the *Free Radicals* anthology by Subpress.

From 2010 to 2015, Darling took a five-year hiatus from writing to pursue a Franciscan vocation. Darling's next book, *The Hunger Notebooks* is forthcoming from Tender Buttons Press. Truck Darling lives and works in the East Village in Manhattan.

TRUCK DARLING

FROM

THE HUNGER NOTEBOOKS

Artist Statement 2

All paint is war paint when you're newly stretched.
Nude of grace, I want to be seen with dignity
Or not at all. A plumeria lei is the only noose
The Ethers will allow, fractional ownership
Of grief only. I take the candor of the animals
As birthright, baby gear. It is 5 in the morning
Inside the heart. Outside, the *constantly new darks.*
Pulsing with winks, I'm almost awake. Getting it
Together on a tract of peat march swamp, a trophy
For atrophy at great speed. I will not award this
Momentum, nor tag this "over." I have no energy
For down below. Close to throbbing, I can still swim
Like this in THE AMERICAN TUB. If you're still mining
For hearts of gold, visit the expert, the exposed
Sleeve, with its apotheosis part, "sling." No matter
How warped I see the world, it's my world, cracked

& salty. Nude of grace, I paint it anyway.

SHOW ME HOW TO LIVE for Sophie Robinson

Children only attack when they sense fear.
I need a playground intervention, a hot 99
Cent slice of Achille's tendon. I'm a ramen
Fed waste of a trust fund with Strontium-90
In my ricemilk. I flex tiny muscles of charm &
Doom, screaming the national anthem in the rain.
A thinspo devo, my life's built around skin
Scales not chords. Anything goes if you stay
In key, cracking adept little riffs like burnt
Wafers of duck. It's like there's all these
Cheerful butterflies the color of phlegm
In my belly I never have enough food to stave off.
My pen is *barfing fuel* to me. Gastric bypass
Is not lying on a fixed astral plan, just being
Fluid with the facts. I am transparent in my baby
Helmet on a maiden nonstop voyage to the Great
Clearance. Show me how to live half off. It
Might be time to stream Assembly online. Let's
Celebrate Civil Disobedience in feral Third Life.
Blistered outlaws, show me how to live. Next time
Give me panty liners of an herbal cucumber vintage,
Old Spice at public hangings. I fly amid a mighty
International crowd, ghosting under the radar
For years. You came a long way maybe, to admire
This wreck, but my exhibit wasn't how you thought
It would be so you mark you turf with prince-cut
Diamonds, Doritos and death, but I fingerpainted
Inferno scenes when I was, like, 4. With a saffron

Glaze, a film not to be missed.

UP WITH THE DEAD

I am leaving Benevolent Mode, entering
Your blood stream & saliva as a recreation
Drug. I love autonomy, but ALL THAT RISES
MUST CONVERGE. I am an amber Rx bottle, I hunt
For a rosehearty fuckproof world. My microcock,
A salmon skin roll. I am fresh out of Trojan's
Latest surgeon finger glove, but five me some
Sachet of granulated sugar, I am your neighbor.
Please release me from the Untouchables, tyranny
Of loneliness. Vodka, 120's, Chock Full of Nuts
& Moroccan argan oil people me against isolation,
Safety fail. Even if held together by gossamer &
Unicorn soot, glamor still wont shrink my planet.
We win, we lose, we disappear forever it's okay.
Ice water & dinosaur piss, our DNA skiing through
Our veins in sub-adonis reality. Blacks as my blue
Heaven, Latisse. Lash growth, ouch. Fandango, I lost
Orpheus, soft indie isn't helping much, maybe
Cold War Kids, Bright Eyes. With more NYC winter
Days ahead, I let the Tompkins Square homeless eat
My children before the sun freezes them on a chess
Board alfresco, fat merino black sheep stranded
On a tundra, Holy Mother of God. Thanks for saving
Me from the 2nd Great Depression. This is just art
I'm using to float some love like a roach marinating
In a fizzy flute of Veuve. The long arm of the law
Is usually a bloody stump, but I will author your
Blubber, sign your body parts methodically. If you
Are an angel of mercy, you are a differently-abled one.
In a post-aerosol rush, I am weak, I am prolific.
Invisible corpse zippers stuck everywhere but giving.
That's how zombies get you: volume.

AUTHOR BIOGRAPHIES

Bernadette Mayer

Bernadette Mayer is the author of more than two dozen volumes of poetry, including *The Bernadette Mayer Reader*, *Midwinter Day*, *The Desires of Mothers to Please Others in Letters*, and *Poetry State Forest*. Recently published are her works, *The Helens of Troy, NY*, *Studying Hunger Journals*, *Eating The Colors Of A Lineup Of Words*, *Works and Days* and the 25th Anniversary Edition of *Sonnets*. She is a former director of the Poetry Project at St. Mark's Church in the Bowery and co-editor of the conceptual magazine *0 to 9* with Vito Acconci. Mayer has been a key figure on the New York poetry scene for decades.

Mayer has taught at The College of St. Rose, Naropa Poetics Institute, New School for Social Research, College of Staten Island, and New England College. She has received grants and awards from: PEN American Center, Foundation for Contemporary Performing Art, the NEA, The Academy for American Poets, The Poetry Society of America, and American Academy of Arts and Letters. She is a 2015 Guggenheim Fellow and recipient of the 2014 Poetry Society of America's Shelley Memorial Award.

Anne Waldman

Internationally recognized and acclaimed poet Anne Waldman has been an active member of the "Outrider" experimental poetry community. Her poetry is recognized in the lineage of Whitman and Ginsberg, and in the Beat, New York School, and Black Mountain trajectories of the New American Poetry. She is the author of more than 40 books, including the mini-classic *Fast Speaking Woman*, a collection of essays entitled *Vow to Poetry* and several selected poems editions including *Helping the Dreamer*, *Kill or Cure* and *In the Room of Never Grieve*. She has concentrated on the long poem as a cultural intervention with such projects as *Marriage: A Sentence*, *Structure of The World Compared to a Bubble*, and *Manatee/Humanity*, which is a book-length rhizomic meditation on evolution and endangered species, and the monumental anti-war feminist epic

The Iovis Trilogy: Colors in the Mechanism of Concealment, a 25-year project.

She was one of the founders and directors of The Poetry Project at St. Marks's Church In-the-Bowery, working there for twelve years. She also co-founded with Allen Ginsberg the celebrated Jack Kerouac School of Disembodied Poetics at Naropa University, the first Buddhist inspired University in the western hemisphere, in 1974.

She has presented her work at conferences and festivals around the world, most recently in Wuhan, Beijing, Berlin, Nicaragua, Prague, Kerala, Mumbai, Calcutta, Marrakech, and Madrid. Her work has been translated into numerous languages.

Waldman is a recipient of the American Book Award's Lifetime Achievement, a 2013 Guggenheim Fellowship, the Poetry Society of America's Shelley Memorial Award, and has recently been appointed a Chancellor of The Academy of American Poets. The Huffington Post named her one of the top advocates for American poetry.

HARRYETTE MULLEN

Harryette Mullen was born in Florence, Alabama, and raised in Fort Worth, Texas. Her books include *Urban Tumbleweed* (Graywolf Press, 2013), *Muse & Drudge* (Singing Horse Press, 1995), S*PeRM**K*T (Singing Horse Press, 1992), *Trimmings* (Tender Buttons Books, 1991), and *Tree Tall Woman* (Energy Earth Communications, 1981). *Trimmings*, S*PeRM**K*T, and *Muse & Drudge* were collected into *Recyclopedia* (Graywolf Press, 2006) which received a PEN Beyond Margins Award. In 2002, she published both *Blues Baby: Early Poems* (Bucknell University Press) and *Sleeping with the Dictionary* (University of California Press), a finalist for the National Book Award, the National Book Critics Circle Award, and the Los Angeles Times Book Award in poetry.

Mullen was the 2009 recipient of the Academy of American Poets Fellowship. Her other honors include artist grants from the Texas

Institute of Letters and the Helene Wurlitzer Foundation of New Mexico, the Gertrude Stein Award in Innovative American Poetry, and a Rockefeller Fellowship from the Susan B. Anthony Institute for Women's Studies at the University of Rochester. Harryette Mullen teaches African American literature and creative writing in the English Department at the University of California, Los Angeles.

AGNES LEE DUNLOP WILEY

Agnes Lee Dunlop Wiley is the maternal Grandmother of Tender Buttons Press editrix, Lee Ann Brown. She was born in Carlton, Missouri in December of 1902. At age 4, shortly after Oklahoma became the 46th state of America in 1907, she moved with her family to Gotebo, Oklahoma. Agnes Lee graduated with a BA from the University of Oklahoma in 1926 and then obtained a teaching certificate from the state of North Carolina. Agnes Lee spent many years as a teacher. In 1931 during the Great Depression, she married a preacher named Van Wiley. Agnes Lee and Van had a daughter, Dora Lee and son, Dudley, who they raised in North Carolina while serving various roles in churches throughout the state. Agnes Lee passed from this world in 2003, but not without leaving us her personal history and list poem, "Things I'd Like to Do Again."

ROSMARIE WALDROP

Rosmarie Waldrop is a contemporary American poet, translator and publisher. Born in Germany, she has lived in the United States since 1958 and Providence, Rhode Island since the late 1960s. Waldrop is coeditor and publisher of Burning Deck Press, as well as the author or coauthor (as of 2006) of 17 books of poetry, two novels, and three books of criticism.

Rosmarie Waldrop started publishing her own poetry in English in the late 1960s. Since then, she has published over three dozen books of poetry, prose and translation. Today her work is variously characterized as verse experiment, philosophical statement and personal narrative. Of the many formative influences on her mature style, a crucial influence was a year spent in Paris in the early 1970s, where she came into contact with leading avant garde French poets, including Claude Royet-Journoud, Anne-Marie Albiach, and Edmond Jabès. These writers influenced her own work, but equally, she became one of the main translators of their work into English.

Rosmarie Waldrop was made a Chevalier des Arts et des Lettres by the French government. In 2003 she was awarded a grant from the Foundation for Contemporary Arts Grants to Artists Award. She was elected to the American Academy of Arts and Sciences in 2006. She received the 2008 PEN Award for Poetry in Translation for her translation of Ulf Stolterfoht's book *Lingos I - IX*. Her translation of *Almost 1 Book / Almost 1 Life* by Elfriede Czurda was nominated for the Best Translated Book Award (2013).

Hannah Weiner

An experimental poet sometimes associated with Language writing, Hannah Weiner attended Radcliffe College and afterward moved to New York City, where she participated in open studios to share her poetry with audiences. In the 1970s, she began to compose poems (her "clairvoyant poems") based on the words she saw on her forehead and other surfaces.

Reviewing the work *Hannah Weiner's Open House* (2007) in the Boston Review, poet and critic Joyelle McSweeney noted that Wiener's work "continually tests and knocks against the visual boundaries of text as it attempts to create an audial-visionary experience no conventional prose could hold." Weiner's published collections include a volume from her pre-clairvoyant period, *The Magritte Poems* (1970); *Clairvoyant Journal* (1973); *Little Books / Indians* (1980); *Code Poems* (1982); poems based on international maritime codes, *SPOKE* (1984); *The Fast* (1992); *We Speak Silent* (1996); and the compilation *Hannah Weiner's Open House*.

Weiner received a grant from the National Endowment for the Arts in 1986. She died in 1997.

JENNIFER MOXLEY

Jennifer Moxley (b. 1964) was raised in San Diego, California. She studied literature and writing at UC San Diego and the University of Rhode Island and received her M.F.A. from Brown University in 1994. She is the author of six books of poetry, a book of essays, and a memoir. In addition, she has translated three books from the French. Her poems have been included in two Norton Anthologies, *Postmodern American Poetry* and *American Hybrid*. Her book *The Sense Record* (2002) was picked as one of the five best poetry books of the year by both *Stride* magazine (UK) and Small Press Traffic (US). Her poem "Behind the Orbits" was included by Robert Creeley in *The Best American Poetry 2002*. In 2005 she was granted the Lynda Hull Poetry Award from Denver Quarterly, and in 2015 her book *The Open Secret* was awarded the Poetry Society of America's William Carlos Williams award. She is Professor of Poetry and Poetics at the University of Maine.

DODIE BELLAMY

Dodie Bellamy is a novelist, poet, and essayist. Her chapbook *Barf Manifesto* was named best book of 2009 under 30 pages by Time Out New York. Other books include *The TV Sutras, the buddhist, Academonia, Pink Steam, The Letters of Mina Harker*, and *Cunt-Ups*, which won the 2002 Firecracker Alternative Book Award for poetry. Her most recent book is her third collection of essays, *When the Sick Rule the World*, from Semiotext(e). Recent projects include *Cunt Norton* (Les Figues, 2013), in which she takes the second edition of the *Norton Anthology of Poetry* and sexualizes it in the language of porn and desire, and *New Narrative: 1975-1995*, a Nightboat Books anthology she's editing with Kevin Killian. Her reflections on the Occupy Oakland movement, "The Beating of Our Hearts," was published as a chapbook in conjunction with the 2014 Whitney Biennial.

LAYNIE BROWNE

Laynie Browne is the author of twelve collections of poetry and two novels. Her most recent collections of poems include *P R A C T I C E* (SplitLevel 2015), *Scorpyn Odes* (Kore Press 2015) and *Lost Parkour Ps(alms)*, in two editions, one in English, and another in French, from Presses universitaires de Rouen et du Havré (2014). Her work appears in *The Norton Anthology of Postmodern American Poetry* (2013) as well as in *Ecopoetry: A Contemporary American Anthology* (Trinity University Press, 2013). Her honors include: a 2014 Pew Fellowship, the National Poetry Series Award, the Contemporary Poetry Series Award, and two Gertrude Stein Awards for Innovative American Poetry. She is co-editor of *I'll Drown My Book: Conceptual Writing by Women* (Les Figues Press, 2012) and is currently editing an anthology of original essays on the Poet's Novel. She teaches at University of Pennsylvania and at Swarthmore College.

INDIA RADFAR

India Radfar lives in Los Angeles and has four published books of poetry: *India Poem* (Pir Press 2002), *the desire to meet with the beautiful* (Tender Buttons Press 2003), *Breathe* (Shivastan Publications 2004), and *Position & Relation* (Station Hill / Barrytown Books 2009); plus the chapbook *12 Poems That Were Never Written* (Mindmade Books 2006). Her unconscious can be found in the pages of these books and also on the Greek Cycladic island of Paros, where it's been residing alone since 1985.

Radfar grew up in the eclectic environment created by her parents, Sheila and Lex Hixon. Her father was a religious scholar and practiced simultaneously four religious traditions: Hinduism, Buddhism, Christianity and Islam. As a child, she found an alternate practice: poetry. Thankfully, her voice was heard, her gift nurtured, and now she likes to do this for others. As a Certified Applied Poetry Facilitator with the International Federation for Biblio/Poetry Therapy, she works with young children, imprisoned youth, pregnant and parenting teens, the homeless, the neurologically diverse, and most recently a very inspiring group of homeless veterans. She has edited three collections from her work as a facilitator: two long, collaborative fairytales and one book of riddles. Radfar was nominated for Los Angeles Poet Laureate in 2014, and is the recipient of an Artist-in-Residence Grant from the Los Angeles Department of Cultural Affairs in 2015-2016.

MICHELLE ROLLMAN

Michelle Rollman is an artist whose work has been exhibited at galleries and art centers including Gallery Paule Anglim in San Francisco, Clementine Gallery in New York, the Museum of Sex in New York, Yerba Buena Center for the Arts in San Francisco, New Langton Arts in San Francisco, the New Orleans Center for Contemporary Art, Kiki in San Francisco, and at Marjorie Wood Gallery online at www.marjoriewoodgallery.com. Her work is in the collections of the New Museum in New York, and the Museum of Modern Art in San Francisco. Her work has also appeared on the cover of Dodie Bellamy's *Cunt Ups* and in the anthology, *Biting the Error; Writers Explore Narrative* edited by Mary Burger, Robert Gluck, Camille Roy and Gail Scott. She has performed in Poets Theater events by Kevin Killian, Camille Roy, Carla Harryman and Leslie Scalapino and in the work of Philip Horvitz.

KATY BOHINC

Katy Bohinc is a poet, publisher, editor, astrolger & mathematician. She was born and raised in Northeast Ohio outside of Cleveland. From 2002 to 2006 she lived, worked and studied in France, China and Buenos Aires. In Beijing from 2004-2006, she worked for the first Chinese human rights organization to officially exist in mainland China since Tiananmen Square. After being denied asylum at the American Embassy she left China and re-enrolled at Georgetown University, graduating in 2007 with dual degrees in theoretical mathematics and comparative literature (English, French and Mandarin.) Until 2013 she lived in Washington D.C., studying independently with the D.C. Poetry community. In 2013 she moved to New York City where she began collaboration on Tender Buttons Press after Lee Ann Brown asked to publish her subversive love poems addressed to contemporary French Platonist Alain Badiou. The book is called *Dear Alain* (Tender Buttons, 2014).

Slavoj Žižek said, "This book should be banished!" In addition to poetry performances, Bohinc gives talks on the relationship between the astral plane and art. She has worn a red winter coat from the 1980 Lake Placid Olympics since 1998.

Lee Ann Brown

Lee Ann Brown was born in Japan and raised in Charlotte, North Carolina. She attended Brown University, where she earned both her undergraduate and graduate degrees.

She is the author of *In the Laurels, Caught* (Fence Books, 2013), which won the 2012 Fence Modern Poets Series Award, as well as *Crowns of Charlotte* (Carolina Wren Press, 2013), *The Sleep That Changed Everything* (Wesleyan, 2003), and *Polyverse* (Sun & Moon Press, 2000), which won the 1996 New American Poetry Competition, selected by Charles Bernstein. Her most recent book *Other Archer* was published simultaneously in French and English by Presses Universitaires de Rouen et du Havré.

Brown has held fellowships with Teachers & Writers Collaborative, Yaddo, Djerassi, the MacDowell Colony, the International Center for Poetry in Marseille, France, and the Howard Foundation.

In 1989, Brown founded Tender Buttons Press, which is dedicated to publishing experimental women's poetry. She has taught at Brown University, Naropa University, Bard College, and The New School, among others. She currently divides her time between New York City, where she teaches at St. John's University, and Marshall, North Carolina, where she directs the French Broad Institute (of Time & the River) and the Children's Arts in the Mountains Program.

Notes

Sonnets

Sonnets was republished in 2014 in a 25th year anniversary edition by Tender Buttons Press with an additional new note by the author, Bernadette Mayer, and including 21 rarely published "Skinny Sonnets" or hypnogogic poems written in reporter's notebooks.

A companion text was also published, *Please Add To This List: A Guide to Teaching Bernadette Mayer's Sonnets and Experiments*. *Please Add To This List* includes an early edition of Bernadette Mayer's teaching text, "Experiments," as well as the first review of *Sonnets* in *Poetry Flash* magazine by Dawn-Michelle Baude and several "response poems" which were directly formulated by or influenced by Mayer's *Experiments* or *Sonnets*.

Contributors include Shanna Compton, Brenda Coultas, Dodie Bellamy, Carole Wagner Greenwood, Jen Hofer, Sophie Seita, Hoa Nguyen, Julie Patton, Kyra Lunenfeld, Sandra Simmonds, Stacy Szymaszek, Linda Kozloff-Turner, Maureen Thorson, Lee Ann Brown, Jennifer Karmin, Jan Bohinc, Laynie Browne and Laura Henriksen.

The 25th Anniversary Edition of *Sonnets* and *Please Add To This List* are available for purchase or download on the Tender Buttons website. Both *Sonnets* and *Please Add To This List* are distributed by Small Press Distribution.

In all editions of *Sonnets*, the sonnet "You jerk you didn't call me up" was adjusted so that the page number in the line "to make love" leads to the sonnet "Warren Phinney" and the line "to die, please turn to" leads to a page that does not exist in the book .

Not a Male Pseudonym

Not a Male Pseudonym is a secret love poem by Anne Waldman for Bernadette Mayer. This information has only recently been made public and the original dedication to Bernadette Mayer is included here in the *Tender Omnibus* republication of *Not a Male Pseudonym*.

Additionally, much thanks is due to Anne Waldman for asking, "When will the Omnibus be published?" Excellent idea; why not? Here it is Anne!

Trimmings

After original publication by Tender Buttons Press in 1991, *Trimmings* was republished by Graywolf Press in 2006 as part of *Recyclopedia*, alongside *S*PeRM**K*T* and *Muse & Drudge*.

Many thanks to Jeff Shotts and Graywolf Press for permitting the republication of *Trimmings* in the *Tender Omnibus*.

Lawn of Excluded Middle

After original publication by Tender Buttons Press in 1993, *Lawn of Excluded Middle* was republished by New Directions press in 2006 as part of the *Curves to the Apple* trilogy, alongside *The Reproduction of Profiles* and *Reluctant Gravities*.

Many thanks to Barbara Epler and New Directions for permitting the republication of *Lawn of Excluded Middle* in the *Tender Omnibus*.

silent teachers   remembered sequel

Many thanks to Charles Bernstein, the executor of the Hannah Weiner literary estate, for allowing the republication of *silent teachers remembered sequel* in the *Tender Omnibus*.

Imagination Verses

After original publication by Tender Buttons Press in 1998, *Imagination Verses* was republished by the UK's Salt press in 2003 in the Salt Modern Poet Series.

Many thanks to Chris Hamilton-Emery and Salt for permitting the republication of *Imagination Verses* in the *Tender Omnibus*. (And for using Creative Commons licensing!)

Cunt-Ups

Cunt Norton, Dodie Bellamy's excellent sequel to *Cunt-Ups* was published in 2013 by Les Figues press.

Pollen Memory

In this compressed edition, a line of asterisks serves to demarcate page breaks.

The Book of Practical Pussies

The Book of Practical Pussies was originally published in bi-coastal collaboration with San Francisco-based Krupskaya Press in 2009.

Many thanks to Krupskaya editors Kevin Killian, Jocelyn Saidenberg, Brandon Brown and Stephanie Young for permitting the inclusion of *The Book of Practical Pussies* in the *Tender Omnibus*.

Dear Alain

Alain Badiou's full response to *Dear Alain* as performed with Katy Bohinc in the event called "Poetry On Top" is forthcoming: *Chère Kati*. The final installment of the Badiou/Bohinc trilogy, *After Math*, is currently an ongoing engagement.

A synastry horoscope chart between K & Alain Badiou is present in the original text which is not in this compressed edition.

*   *   *   *

We would like to thank all of the Tender Buttons authors for entrusting us with the publication of their work, and all of the many people who have contributed in large and small ways over the years to book production and promotion. Love, Katy & Lee Ann

TENDER OMNIBUS
set in 12 pt Palatino Linotype
New York City, 2016